AFRICAN AMERICAN, CREOLE, AND OTHER VERNACULAR ENGLISHES IN EDUCATION

More than fifty years of scholarly attention to the intersection of language and education have resulted in a rich body of literature on the role of vernacular language varieties in the classroom. This field of work can be bewildering in its size and variety, drawing as it does on the diverse methods, theories, and research paradigms of fields such as sociolinguistics, applied linguistics, psychology, and education.

Compiling most of the publications from the past half century that deal with this critical topic, this volume includes more than 1,600 references (books, articles in journals or books, and web-accessible dissertations and other works) on education in relation to African American Vernacular English [AAVE], English-based pidgins and creoles, Latina/o English, Native American English, and other English vernaculars such as Appalachian English in the US and Aboriginal English in Australia), with accompanying abstracts for approximately a third of them.

This comprehensive annotated and topic-coded bibliography provides an invaluable resource for researchers, teachers, and all those interested in the complex issue of how knowledge about language variation can be used to help schools better appreciate and augment the intellect and creativity of students who speak a non-standard language variety.

John R. Rickford is the J.E. Wallace Sterling Professor of Linguistics and the Humanities and Pritzker University Fellow in Undergraduate Education at Stanford University, USA.

Julie Sweetland is Director of Learning at the FrameWorks Institute and an Adjunct Lecturer in Linguistics at Georgetown University, USA.

Angela E. Rickford is Professor of Education at San Jose State University, USA.

Thomas Grano is a Postdoctoral Research Associate in Linguistics at the University of Maryland, USA.

NCTE-Routledge Research Series

Series Editors: Valerie Kinloch and Susi Long

Alsup
Teacher Identity Discourses: Negotiating Personal and Professional Spaces

Banks
Race, Rhetoric, and Technology: Searching for Higher Ground

Daniell/Mortensen
Women and Literacy: Local and Global Inquiries for a New Century

Rickford/Sweetland/Rickford/Grano
African American, Creole, and Other Vernacular Englishes in Education: A Bibliographic Resource

The NCTE-Routledge Research Series, copublished by the National Council of Teachers of English and Routledge, focuses on literacy studies in P-12 classroom and related contexts. Volumes in this series are invited publications or publications submitted in response to a call for manuscripts. They are primarily authored or co-authored works which are theoretically significant and broadly relevant to the P-12 literacy community. The series may also include occasional landmark compendiums of research.

The scope of the series includes qualitative and quantitative methodologies; a range of perspectives and approaches (e.g., sociocultural, cognitive, feminist, linguistic, pedagogical, critical, historical, anthropological); and research on diverse populations, contexts (e.g., classrooms, school systems, families, communities), and forms of literacy (e.g., print, electronic, popular media).

AFRICAN AMERICAN, CREOLE, AND OTHER VERNACULAR ENGLISHES IN EDUCATION

A Bibliographic Resource

John R. Rickford, Julie Sweetland,
Angela E. Rickford, and Thomas Grano

Routledge
Taylor & Francis Group
NEW YORK AND LONDON

National Council of Teachers of English
1111 W. Kenyon Road, Urbana, Illinois 61801-1096

A co-publication of Routledge and NCTE

First published 2013
by Routledge
711 Third Avenue, New York, NY 10017

Simultaneously published in the UK
by Routledge
2 Park Square, Milton Park, Abingdon, Oxon OX14 4RN

Routledge is an imprint of the Taylor & Francis Group, an informa business

© 2013 Taylor & Francis

Library of Congress Cataloging in Publication Data
Rickford, John R., 1949–
    African American, Creole, and other vernacular Englishes in education : a bibliographic resource / John R. Rickford ... [et al.].
    p. cm. — (NCTE-Routledge research series; 4)
    Includes bibliographical references and index.
    1. African Americans—Languages—Bibliography. 2. Creole dialects, English—United States—Bibliography. 3. English language—Spoken English—United States—Bibliography. 4. African Americans—Education—Language arts—Bibliography. 5. Language and education—United States—Bibliography. 6. African American students—Language—Bibliography. 7. Black English—Bibliography. I. National Council of Teachers of English. II. Title.
    Z1234.D5R53 2012
    016.427—dc23
    2012008697

ISBN: 978-0-8058-6050-4 (hbk)
ISBN: 978-0-415-88867-7 (pbk)
ISBN: 978-0-203-83168-7 (ebk)
NCTE Stock number: 88677

Typeset in Bembo and Stone Sans
by EvS Communication Networx, Inc.

Printed and bound in the United States of America on sustainably sourced paper by IBT Global.

CONTENTS

FOREWORD

Walt Wolfram

WILLIAM C. FRIDAY DISTINGUISHED UNIVERSITY PROFESSOR
NORTH CAROLINA STATE UNIVERSITY

Landmarks in the study of regional and social varieties of English have often been marked by the compilation of annotated bibliographies. For example, *A Comprehensive Annotated Bibliography of American Black English* (Brasch & Brasch 1974) followed the first wave of research on African American English and *An Annotated Bibliography of Southern American English* (McMillan & Montgomery 1989) followed a steady growth of research on Southern American English. This compilation is based on several different periods of strategic advances in the study of vernacular varieties and education (Harris, Anderson, Bloom & Champion 1995) that had not been documented bibliographically in a comprehensive way until the valuable precursor to this work by these authors (Rickford, Sweetland & Rickford 2004). This significantly elaborated reference collection, with more than two times as many entries as the earlier work and the addition of annotations, is especially welcome to those of us who have become reference-challenged by our myopic research and/or simply overwhelmed by the proliferation of studies in vernacular varieties of English. Even the most obsessive readers and sociolinguistic workaholics just can't keep up with all of the essential studies and the critical publications in our focused research specialization, to say nothing of the subfields that we track in a more cursory way. But the value of compilations such as *African American, Creole, and Other Vernaculars English in Education* is not limited to a professional audience of engaged sociolinguists; it is absolutely indispensable to allied professionals in a wide range of descriptive and applied fields who have a need for an accessible reference guide to extend their understanding of vernacular varieties in an informed, representative, and inclusive way. The broadly based field of vernacular language studies is deeply indebted to the authors for collecting the references, topic coding, annotating, indexing, and writing the introductory essays to each topic. They have significantly enabled the work of their professional sociolinguistic colleagues as well as that of allied professionals in allied fields that include education, speech and language pathology, literacy, psychology, and many other fields. It is clearly not just another annotated bibliography that encourages a cursory examination to amplify literature references in our studies; it is a purposeful, topically organized, cross-indexed compilation enriched by discursive introductions for each topic that reads like a textbook on essential research about vernacular dialects and education. In today's digital world where we can readily search references and access online many of the articles we need for our research and edification, we might, at first glance, question whether we need a print copy of references. The most cursory examination of this compilation should provide an answer before completing that question. To begin with, these compilers are among the most active, respected researchers who are well-known for their exhaustive knowledge of the literature in the field. Further, they are at the forefront of research in a number of the topics included in this compilation, and are as thoroughly grounded in engaged research and scholarship as anyone in the field. The wisdom of seasoned, highly esteemed professionals is transparent in every dimension of their work, from the comprehensive inclusion of references to the meticulous cross-referencing of the bibliographic entries that makes this work invaluable to both the career sociolinguist and to the curious, entry-level student and the allied professional who is interested in the research literature in a particular strand of study on language diversity and education.

The elaborate topic-coding and cross-referencing allow users to narrow their search to relevant lists of entries, circumventing the unwieldy and sometimes-numbing task of searching through endless pages of references for possible items of interest. The reader can focus on a topic, check out references, and follow the cross-references in a systematic way that enables efficiency and comprehensiveness. To heighten efficiency, the user can read abstracts of selected articles and books written by professionals well-integrated into the field, thus assuring the reader of a faithful, informative account of primary research for those who need to understand the content before retrieving the actual article or book. To ensure inclusiveness in the references, the compilers contacted major authors in the field personally to check out the references and to ensure that primary works were not overlooked. As a long-term, engaged researcher in varieties of American English, I was amazed at how many references I needed to know—and unfortunately, wasn't aware of before examining this compilation. I can only imagine how a student or an early-career professional might profit from ready access to this tightly organized collection.

One of the most useful dimensions of this compilation is the discursive introduction to each topical area, ranging from assessment to writing, and the labeling of entries to represent the language varieties represented by each. The introductions strategically frame and synthesize the major issues and strands of research, including the naming of prominent figures who have made significant contributions to the specialized domain of language and education. These readable, informative overviews are highly beneficial to readers regardless of their level of expertise or involvement in the topic.

In many respects, this work establishes a new standard for an effective reference compilation. This template includes an exhaustive, comprehensive tracking of references that relies on the social network of cooperative professionals as well as conventional reference sources from the literature; a rational, coherent segmentation of subject areas for organizing entries; a meticulous, exhaustive cross-indexing of entries by topic for more extensive reference connections; and an introductory essay for each topic and language variety that frames the issues and guides the reader to the prominent studies and the leading researchers. But this formula also has a human element. When these organizational and presentation procedures are adopted by the most distinguished, credentialed professionals who have led the field in engaged research, the result is a *tour de force* in bibliographic compilation that is unparalleled in the field. Regardless of status and experience, all of us are incredibly indebted to the authors for making our work more inclusive, representative, and efficient.

ACKNOWLEDGMENTS

This bibliography is the culmination of many years of work, and many people have helped to make it a reality. For encouraging us in the first place, we must thank Alicia Beckford Wassink and Anne Curzan, the co-editors of the special issue of the *Journal of English Linguistics* in which the precursor to this bibliography (Rickford et al 2004) appeared. Once we decided to expand that project and annotate it, we were helped by several brilliant undergraduate interns and research assistants, supported in large part by grants from the office of the Vice Provost for Undergraduate Education at Stanford, which we acknowledge with thanks. Marissa Ann McGee, Mima Mohammed, Jessica Kuang-Chuan Stanley, and Oluwatomi Onatunde were in the initial intern group in 2006, and Sasha Arijanto, Amanda McFarlane, and Cybelle Smith contributed substantially in subsequent years. Ellie Ash played a huge role in the home stretch, working tirelessly to secure permissions for journal and ERIC abstracts, writing scripts to convert our keywords to numerals and codes, and uploading our Endnote entries from web to desktop to *Word*. Linguistics graduate students Jessica Spencer and Rebecca Greene were also helpful with abstract writing and other phases of the project.

Faculty colleagues from universities across the United States and around the world (Australia, Scotland) also volunteered their time and expertise to help us identify relevant work: Anne H. Charity Hudley and Geneva Smitherman helped with references on AAVE; Karen Carpenter, Velma Pollard and Jeff Siegel with references on Anglophone pidgins and creoles; Elaine Chun, Yuri Lea Kuwahara, Lauren Hall-Lew, Adrienne Lo and Angela Reyes with references on Asian and Asian American English; Beverly Flanigan with references on Native American English; Bob Bayley, Otto Santa Ana and Ana Celia Zentella with references on Latina/o English; and Jeff Siegel and Walt Wolfram with references on Other Vernacular Englishes. To Walt Wolfram we are also indebted for writing the

Foreword, and for supplying the answers to many other questions that arose as we were preparing this work.

To the many authors who willingly obliged when we asked them to write abstracts for us when necessary (for instance, when we could not get reprint permissions from journals in which their articles had appeared), we are very grateful. And to the many journals and the staff at ERIC (especially Brian Smith) that gave us permission to reprint abstracts, we are grateful too. They are all acknowledged after the relevant bibliography entries and abstracts. Finally, we thank editors Naomi Silverman of Routledge/Taylor and Francis, and Zarina Hock and Kurt Austin of the National Council of Teachers of English for agreeing to co-publish this resource in the first place, and for their patience, encouragement, and advice over the years. Without them, indeed, this project would not have come to fruition. We are also grateful to Emma Håkonsen at Routledge and Lynn Goeller at EvS Communications for steering this volume through all the stages of production, and responding graciously to our requests for changes and additions.

While acknowledging the assistance of everyone named above, and anyone else whom we may have forgotten to mention, we also retain full responsibility for this work and any shortcomings it may contain. As noted elsewhere (in our introduction), we would deeply appreciate learning about omissions or errors, so that they can be corrected in future editions, increasing the continuing usefulness of this bibliographic resource.

INTRODUCTION

John R. Rickford and Julie Sweetland

More than fifty years of scholarly interest in the intersection of language and education have resulted in a rich body of literature on the role of vernacular language varieties in school contexts. At times, this field of work can be bewildering in its size and variety. In this annotated bibliography, intended for teachers as well as researchers, we have attempted to compile many, if not most, of the publications from the past half century that deal with this critical topic. Our compilation includes 1624 references on education in relation to African American Vernacular English (AAVE), English-based pidgins and creoles, Latina/o English, Native American English, and other English vernaculars such as Appalachian English in the United States and Aboriginal English in Australia. We will say more about the features of this book and other pertinent matters below. But to illustrate the kinds of relations between education and vernacular English that have been considered, and to explain why we considered it important to create a bibliographical resource like this in the first place, it is helpful to begin with some historical perspective.

Modern Creole studies and the study of African American Vernacular English and other social dialects both date back to the 1960s. Although these subfields grew out of research traditions in regional dialectology, contact linguistics and historical linguistics, the emergence of the educational-linguistic line of inquiry in a decade known for social change is not a coincidence. One impetus for its development in that decade—during which the Civil Rights and Voting Rights Acts were passed in the United States, and numerous Creole-speaking countries in the Caribbean and West Africa gained their independence[1]—was an interest in contributing to social equity and political development through education, where language plays a key role.

That this was so is clear from two scholarly works published exactly forty-five years ago—one a study of the "Non-standard English of Negro and Puerto Rican Speakers in New York City" (Labov et al. 1968), the other a discussion of "Problems to be faced in the Use of English as Medium of Education in Four West Indian Territories" (Le Page 1968). The Labov et al. study, like Shuy, Wolfram and Riley's (1967) community study of Detroit, and Wolfram's related (1969) description of Detroit AAVE, was funded by the US Office of Education. The problem that motivated it was "the low educational achievement" (p. 1) of the non-White population in urban ghettos like Harlem and elsewhere in the United States. The report identifies "reading failure" as the root of the problem, and divides the linguistic aspect of reading failure and school success into two elements (p. 2):

> (1) There are differences in the grammatical and phonological rules of standard English and the non-standard English of Negro speakers; in various ways these differences lead to interference in learning to read (and speak) standard English. (2) The vernacular culture of the street differs from the schoolroom culture in its patterns of language use … We will refer to these areas of interference as *structural differences* and *functional differences*.

The focus of Le Page (1968) was "language problems that beset the educational systems of the former West Indian territories of Jamaica, British Honduras [later Belize], Guyana … and Trinidad and Tobago" (p. 431). As Le Page noted, "the political expectations aroused by independence have not all been fulfilled," and "the expectation of greatly increased social mobility through education has been frustrated …" Failure rates were high (70-90%) in all four countries in English language examinations set by universities in England; Le Page attributed this in part to interference from the students' Creole English (pp. 434–35):[2]

> … as a spoken language it [Creole speech] has its own phonological, grammatical, lexical and semantic structures, which differ, often quite sharply, from those of the spoken dialects that underlie the standard usage of the textbooks and of the examiners. But neither the teachers nor the children are equipped to recognize the differences.

---

1   Countries with robust creole or vernacular varieties that became independent in the 1960s include: Barbados (1966), Cameroon (1960), Guyana (1966), Jamaica (1962), Nigeria (1960), Sierra Leone (1961), and Trinidad and Tobago (1962), among others.

2   Le Page's 1968 paper was a major influence in John Rickford's decision to switch his undergraduate major from Literature to Sociolinguistics (independently designed). See Rickford 1999:162.

A few comments might be made about these early studies. First of all, they were not the *earliest* nor the *only* contemporaneous studies to combine interests in language and education; for the Anglophone Caribbean, see Cassidy 1970, Craig 1966, 1969, and Jones 1965; and for vernacular varieties in the United States, see Aarons et al. 1969;[3] Bailey 1965; Baratz 1969; Davis et al. 1968; and Stewart 1964. Second, a number of these early works (Bailey 1966; Labov 1972; Labov et al. 1968; Shuy et al. 1967; Wolfram 1969) provided detailed description of the features of AAVE and English-based Creoles on the theory that teachers could neither understand nor help to solve the schooling problems of their students until they adequately understood their language. This in turn means that the voluminous descriptive, theoretical, and even creole origins literature on AAVE (see Stewart 1969b) and other vernacular Englishes that developed from the 1960s on is indebted to those early interests in social dialects and education. Third, concerns about the relative "lag" of vernacular speakers, or, more properly, about schools not teaching vernacular speakers of English as successfully as they do speakers of standard or mainstream English, are as real today as they were forty and fifty years ago (see Carpenter and Devonish 2012; Craig 1999; Labov 2001; Rickford 2002). Hence the continuing *relevance* of research on English vernaculars and education, and the *need* for a bibliographic resource like this one. Finally, while some of the themes represented in those early works have continued to be of interest to researchers, our methods and knowledge have also shifted, evolved, and expanded, as a perusal of the citations in our lists on any subtopic from the 1960s to now should show.

Scope of the Bibliography

We use the term *vernacular* in this book in the sense of Le Page (1997:6): "the everyday spoken language or languages of a community, as contrasted with a standard or official language—generally a 'Low' as opposed to a 'High' variety in Ferguson's (1959) terms." This is similar in spirit to the definition of *vernacular* in the *Oxford English Dictionary*:

> 2. Of a language or dialect: That is naturally spoken by the people of a particular country or district; native, indigenous. Usu. applied to the native speech of a populace, in contrast to another or others acquired for commercial, social or educative purposes; now freq. employed with reference to that of the working classes or the peasantry.

---

3 Aarons et al. (1969) is an anthology of 43 articles spanning ethnic varieties in as broad a range as our book does: AAVE, American Indian English, Appalachian English, Mexican American English, Chinese immigrant English, and Creole English.

Our usage is similar too to the *standard/vernacular* contrast in Eckert (1998:64–65):

> Standard pronunciations are part of the *standard* language—the variety of language that is associated with education, central government, and other institutions of national or global power. In opposition to the standard is what is commonly called the *vernacular*, the language of locally based communities—most people's everyday language. The vernacular has local and regional features—features that are muted in the standard. [Italics added]

Although it's increasingly popular to refer to "African American English" or "African American Language" without the "vernacular" qualification that Labov (1972, p.xiii) coined, we think it's useful for distinguishing it from the standard or mainstream varieties also employed, at least some of the time, by many African Americans.[4] The *vernacular* label also links AAVE with pidgins and creoles, and with the other English varieties included in this volume. Precisely because these are everyday, non-standard spoken varieties, as used by the descendants of slaves, ethnic minorities, immigrants and subjugated populations, they usually do not have social prestige, and are not used for educative purposes. But the fact that they tend to be either ignored or disparaged in formal education, is, we believe, one reason that schools often fail to help speakers of these varieties reach their full potential.

AAVE is the primary language variety represented in this bibliography—about half of our entries refer in one way or the other to this variety. Anglophone (English-based) pidgins and creoles, resulting from contact, mixture, simplification and/or restructuring among speakers of English and African/Pacific indigenous languages in West Africa, the Caribbean and the Pacific, are second, with nearly 20% of all our entries relating to varieties such as Hawaiian Creole, Jamaican Creole, and Nigerian Pidgin English. These twin foci reflect not only the research interests of the co-authors, but also the relative depth and breadth of the literature on the intersection of vernaculars and education. We recently expanded the scope of the project to include Asian and Asian American English (4% of all entries), Latina/o English (about 7% of all entries); Native American or American Indian English (about 8% of all entries); and other English Vernaculars, including Appalachian English, Aboriginal English in Australia, and White Vernacular Englishes in various parts of the world (about 12% of all entries). The varieties

---

4   The fact that *vernacular* comes from Latin *verna*, meaning "a home-born slave, a native" makes the term infelicitous or objectionable to some (e.g., Noma Le Moine, personal communication). But our use of this term, despite its roots, is an attempt to invert its negative associations (cf. Holt 1972). For AAVE and many Creole English speakers, their vernacular IS the language of former slave ancestors (cf. Baugh 1999); but it allowed those ancestors to communicate with each other and survive despite their linguistic difference and sociopolitical oppression, and it unites them with the descendants of other subjugated peoples. This is also one reason we've continued to use it, despite Phillipson's 1992:40 opinion that the term vernacular "stigmatizes certain languages and holds others up to the norm."

in this most recently added group together account for about 30% of all of our entries, but even though we were advised and assisted by linguists with more expertise on them than we have, we also expect that our coverage of the "linguistics and education" literature on them may be less complete than for the AAVE and pidgin/creole varieties. Nevertheless, the speakers of these vernaculars often face challenges in schools similar to those of AAVE and pidgin/creole speaking students, and researchers working on the former might benefit from reading what researchers working on the latter have written, often in similar but sometimes very different linguistic, cultural and socio-political milieux.

In view of our focus on "vernacular Englishes and education," we did not include references that were otherwise interesting to us but did not cover all three of these elements. Thus, we have excluded work on vernaculars that is not relevant to education (such as discussions of their genesis or historical development); works related to education, but not on English (such as work on French creoles or bilingual education); and work on language in educational context, but not specifically on vernacular language varieties (e.g., many studies of the Language Awareness approach in the UK).

A list of ERIC thesaurus descriptors that we searched and re-searched periodically includes: American Indian Education; American Indian Languages; Asian American Students; Asian Americans; Black dialects; Blacks; Creoles; Dialect Studies; Dialects; Language Attitudes; Language Usage; Language variation; Pidgins; Sociolinguistics; Standard Spoken Usage; and Urban Language. In addition, in ERIC and other search engines, we frequently used keywords such as AAVE, African American English, and Ebonics. When necessary, searches were narrowed using education-related keywords or descriptors such as "teachers" or "instructional methods."

Using the Bibliography

In the course of compiling these references, we annotated each entry, by means of single-character codes, to indicate the main topic(s) of the piece. About a third of the entries have also been annotated by the inclusion of an abstract.

Following this introduction, we provide Topic Overviews of each of twenty-two topic categories of our own devising, each of which reflects a significant theme or body of literature within the field. Each overview is followed by an abbreviated list of the bibliography entries relevant to that category, providing, for reasons of space, only the author's last name and year of publication,. The topic coding feature, an innovation that we introduced in Rickford et al. (2004), is designed to assist college instructors, researchers, or classroom teachers looking for all the relevant references on a given topic (e.g., the *assessment* of vernacular English speakers).

The Topic Overviews are followed by the full bibliography, presented alphabetically by author, with full citation details. To illustrate—the entry for Pollard 1998 is as follows:

Pollard, Velma. 1998. Code Switching and Code Mixing: Language in the Jamaican Classroom. *Caribbean Journal of Education* 20.9-20, 2 B S U

The numeric code "2" at the end indicates that it deals with a pidgin or creole
variety (in this case Jamaican Creole), while the alphabetical codes "B," "S" and
"U" indicate that it is relevant to the *Bidialectal Approach (B)*, to *Strategies and Suggestions for Instruction (S)* and to *Code Choice (U)*. (See the Table of Contents and the
Topic Overviews for the full list.)

Where an entry has more than one code, they are listed in alphabetical order
rather than by order of importance. Numerical codes refer to the language variety:[5]

> AAVE (African American Vernacular English): 1
> Anglophone Pidgins and Creoles: 2
> Asian and Asian American English: 3
> Latina/o Englishes: 4
> Native American English: 5
> Other vernacular Englishes: 6

Alphabetic codes refer to the topic(s) of the piece, and are usually mnemonic
in nature—for instance, M stands for *Materials for Instruction*. When an abstract is
included, it appears directly following the bibliographic entry.

Background on the Bibliography

An explanation of the methods used to identify, collect, and compile the references included in this bibliographic resource is in order. This project evolved over
time, expanding in scope from a few AAVE-related topical lists of a dozen or so
references each, to its present form, encompassing 1,626 entries and including
several vernacular varieties of English. Beginning in the mid-1990s, John and
Angela Rickford endeavored to compile, for their own research and publication
projects, a list of items relevant to AAVE and education, labeled for their relevance
to reading, writing, and a handful of other topics. At that time, the compilation
of references reflected the authors' personal knowledge of the field, and represented primarily works that they had encountered in the normal course of scholarship and teaching—for example, in preparing Rickford and Rickford 1995 or
A. Rickford 1999. Shortly after the Ebonics controversy in December 1996, John
Rickford developed a new course at Stanford University, "Ebonics and Other
Vernaculars in Education," for which Julie Sweetland, then a Linguistics graduate
student, was a teaching assistant. In preparation for the course, Julie conducted
purposeful searches of multiple databases to broaden and deepen the representation of the relevant literature, with the goal of expanding and updating John

---

5   For lists of entries for each language variety in this book, visit www.johnrickford.com

and Angela's pre-existing lists. The Educational Resources Information Center electronic resource (ERIC) was the primary database for our searches; we also made extensive use of Academic Search Premier/EBSCO; Multicultural Education Abstracts; Social Science Research Network; and Wilson Web, in addition to searches of the Stanford Library catalogue.

After several more updates, John Rickford, Julie Sweetland and Angela Rickford published a list of over 650 references, topic-coded for 18 different categories from "Assessment" to "Writing," in a special issue of the *Journal of English Linguistics* edited by Alicia Beckford Wassink and Anne Curzan (Rickford et al. 2004).

The current book represents a considerable expansion and updating of that 90-page article, in several respects. The total number of entries has been expanded from 650 to 1624—through the inclusion of about 430 references published since 2004; through including vernaculars beyond AAVE and pidgins and creoles; and through more systematic and diligent search methods. Unlike the case with the earlier work, only works that are published or accessible through a website/URL are included, so unpublished dissertations are generally excluded. Most significantly, abstracts have been added for nearly a third of the entries. Most of these abstracts were written by the co-authors of this book, primarily Tom Grano, who started out as a Stanford linguistics undergraduate research assistant to this project in 2004, and was invited to become an author on the basis of his sterling contributions to the project. We also benefited from abstracts written by other Stanford undergraduate research assistants over the years (see Acknowledgments), and incorporated abstracts from journals and the ERIC database when we could secure permissions. Finally, when other options were unavailable, we sometimes asked authors to write new abstracts of their own, which we then edited. In general, decisions about which articles or books to abstract were made on the basis of the importance of the piece to teachers or scholars, either in terms of historical significance or continuing relevance. Where we used pre-existing journal abstracts, the preceding criterion was also relevant, but sometimes we decided that we needed to reprint the abstract because the title by itself didn't sufficiently convey what the work was about. We did not always get permission to reprint abstracts that we wanted to use, however, and because we weren't always able to write new abstracts ourselves, some important titles regrettably remain unabstracted.

Our ability to expand and revise the 2004 bibliographsy into a book was facilitated by the emergence of *Google Scholar* and *Google Books*, and by extensive use of *Endnote Web*, allowing us to work on a common database from different parts of the United States. Innovations in search engines such as Google's "related articles" suggestions brought other texts to our attention. Throughout the process, when identifying a new reference, we typically scanned the new entry's bibliography, and added relevant references to our compilation as well. At periodic intervals in the course of preparing this manuscript, we sent excerpts of it to other scholars and asked them to review it with an eye toward completeness; we received many valuable suggestions for additions in this way.

Despite our attempt to include *most* educationally relevant linguistic references, we cannot claim to have included *all*. This is so partly because of space limitations, and partly because, given the organic growth of this project over two decades, we did not start from the beginning with the sort of strict parameters that might be expected in a formal review of educational research. In the end we know that omissions and errors are inevitable, and even as we take responsibility for these, we ask that those who discover them draw them to our attention so that they might be rectified if and when we do a revised edition. Until that time, we hope that researchers and teachers find some theoretical and/or practical value in this work, and that students who speak vernacular and creole varieties turn out to be the ultimate beneficiaries. We are as vibrantly interested in contributing to social equity and political development through linguistics and education as our predecessors were half a century ago.

References Not in the General Bibliography

Eckert, Penelope. 1998. Gender and Sociolinguistic Variation. In *Language and Gender: A Reader*, ed. by Jennifer Coates, 64–75. Malden, MA, and Oxford: Blackwell.

Ferguson, Charles A. 1959. Diglossia. *Word* 15:325–340.

Holt, Grace Sims. 1971. "Inversion" in Black communication. *Florida FL Reporter* 9:1–2, 41–43, 55. Reprinted in Kochman 1972, *Rappin' and Stylin' Out*.

Le Page, Robert. 1997. Introduction. In *Vernacular Literacy: A Re-Evaluation,* ed. by Andree Tabouret-Keller, Robert B. Le Page, Penelope Gardner-Chloros, and Gabrielle Varro, 1–19. Oxford: Clarendon Press.

Phillipson, Robert. 1992. *Linguistic Imperialism*. Oxford: Oxford University Press.

TOPIC OVERVIEWS

Assessment and Achievement (A)

Students who speak vernacular varieties of English often perform more poorly on achievement and intelligence tests than students who speak standard or mainstream varieties, and in informal assessments by teachers and potential employers they are often considered less capable, confident, or prepared. But to what extent is such negative performance by students due to the fact that the tests themselves are biased on standard English norms, for example, explicitly requiring the respondent to provide plural forms like *two boys* which would be *two boy* in a student's vernacular (see Vaughn-Cooke 1983; Washington and Craig 1992; Wolfram 1986)? And to what extent do negative evaluations by teachers and others reflect inherited prejudices and unvalidated expectations that standard English speakers will invariably be smarter, more logical and more creative (see Labov 1969; Lippi-Green 2012; Seligman et al. 1972; Shepherd 2011)? Moreover, if our assessment instruments and methods are faulty, are we perhaps failing to recognize and develop the potential of talented vernacular speakers, and simultaneously over-rewarding what Le Page (1968, p. 438) called "mimics [of the standard] who lack real creative and critical ability"? Misdiagnosis and misevaluation may also route dialect speakers inappropriately into classes for students with language disorders (Seymour et al. 2003, 2005; Velleman and Pearson 2010) and negative perceptions may lead to lower teacher expectations and diminished student performance (Rosenthal and Jacobson 1968; Tauber 1997).

These and related issues have come up repeatedly in linguistic research on vernaculars in schools since the 1960s and 1970s, and they remain vibrant up to today, as evidenced by the fact that nearly half of our references in this category date from 2000 to 2012. For various reasons (testing is especially frequent and varied in the US, and research traditions on testing are more developed there too), the references in this category come primarily from the United States. And they relate especially to African American students, given perennial concerns about the Black-White achievement gap in American schools. Indeed, much of the sociolinguistic research on AAVE in the 1960s was funded by grants from the Department of Education, intended to address and redress this issue.

Nevertheless, there is a small but significant literature on assessment and achievement issues in Anglophone pidgins and creoles, represented by D. Craig (1999), and most recently by Carpenter and Devonish (2012) on the experimental introduction of bilingual education in Jamaican Creole and English. (The use of Jamaican in schools apparently had the effect of boosting achievement scores for boys but not girls.) The influx of Caribbean immigrants to the United States and Canada has added creole issues to existing concerns about assessment and achievement of students of color there too (cf. Coelho 1988, 1991; Irish and Clay 1995).

Our coverage of language-related assessment and achievement issues for speakers of Latina/o, Native American, Asian American and other vernacular Englishes is limited, but the references by Buly (2005), J. Ball and B.M. Bernhardt (2008), Cheng (1987), Fish and Pinkerman (2002), Garcia and Menken (2006), Kuhlman and Kalecteca (1982), Santa Ana (2004) and Valdes (2001), among others, provide some treatment of this area.

Finally, it should be noted that language is at the heart of many assessment tests and achievement measures, not only in the obvious cases of reading and writing (H. Craig et al. 2003, 2004; Kynard 2008; Piche et al. 1977; A. Rickford 1999, Rosa 1994), but also in math and other subjects, and in general tests of intelligence and aptitude.

Short Citations for Assessment and Achievement (A)

Adger et al. 1992
Adger 1993
Agnew and McLaughlin 1999
Ball 1999
Ball et al. 1997
Ball and Bernhardt 2008
Bartel et al. 1973
Baugh 1988
Baugh 1999
Becker and Luthar 2002
Bereiter and Engelmann 1966
Bliss and Allen 1981
Bogatz et al. 1986
Bond 1981
Brice and Montgomery 1996
Buly 2005
Burke et al. 1982
Carpenter and Devonish 2010
Carpenter and Devonish 2012
Carter 2007
Carter 2011
Cazden 1970
Cecil 1988
Chambers 1983
Champion et al. 2003
Champion et al. 2010
Chaplin 1990
Chapman 1994
Charity et al. 2004
Charity Hudley 2008
Charity Hudley 2010
Charity Hudley and Mallinson 2011
Cheatham et al. 2009
Cheng 1987
Cole and Taylor 1990
Cook-Gumperz 1993
Cosden et al. 1994
Council 2010

Coup 2008
Craig 1999
Craig 1996
Craig et al. 2003
Craig et al. 2004
Craig and Washington 1994
Craig and Washington 2000
Craig and Washington 2002
Craig and Washington 2006
Craig et al. 2005
Craig et al. 1998
Craig et al. 1998
Craig et al. 2009
Crotteau 2007
Cummins 1986
de Kleine 2006
Delpit 1986
Delpit and Dowdy 2002
Fagundes, et al. 1998
Farr et al. 2010
Farr et al. 2010
Farrell 1983
Farrell 1995
Feldman et al. 1990
Fish and Pinkerman 2002
Fordham 1993
Fordham 1999
Fordham and Ogbu 1986
Foster 1999
Fry and Johnson 1973
Fryburg 1974
Gadsen and Wagner 1995
Garcia 2011
Garcia and Menken 2006
Gay and Tweney 1976
Gee 2007
Genshaft and Hirt 1974
Gilmore 1987

Gopaul-McNicol et al. 1998
Grant et al. 2009
Greenberg et al. 1984
Gutierrez-Clellen and Simon-Cereijido 2007
Harber 1977
Harber 1982
Harper et al. 1998
Hart and Risley 1995
Hart and Risley 2003
Hilliard 1983
Hilliard 1997
Hilliard 1999
Hockman 1973
Hoover et al. 1996
Hoover et al. 1996
Hoover et al. 1995
Hoover et al. 1996
Horvat and Lewis 2003
Hunt 1974
Hwa-Froelich et al. 2007
Irish and Clay 1995
Irvine 1990
Irvine 2002
Irvine 2003
Irvine 2003
Isaacs 1996
Jencks and Phillips 1998
Johnson et al. 1998
Kachuck 1978
Kamhi et al. 1996
Kuhlman and Kalecteca 1982
Kynard 2008
Labov 1967
Labov 1969
Labov 1976
Labov 2003
Labov and Baker 2010
Labov and Charity Hudley 2009
Labov and Robins 1969
Le Moine 2001
Le Page 1968
Lippi-Green 2012
Long and Christensen 1998
Maddahian and Sandamela 2000
Mocombe 2006
Moll 1988
Moore 1999
Nelson and McRoskey 1978
Nero 2006
Nichols 1977
O'Neil 1990
Ogbu 1991
Ogbu 2003
Orr 1987
Paige et al. 2010
Pandey 2000
Patterson 1994

Pearson et al. 2009
Pena and Gillam 2000
Perry and Delpit 1997
Perry et al. 2003
Piche et al. 1977
Politzer et al. 1974
Pruitt et al. 2010
Reaser 2010
Reaser and Adger 2008
Reveron 1984
Reynolds 1999
Rickford 1999
Rickford 2002
Rickford 1999
Rickford 1999
Rickford 2002
Rivers et al. 2004
Roberts 2007
Robinson-Zanartu 1996
Rodekohr and Haynes 2001
Rosa 1994
Rosenthal and Jacobson 1968
Rubinstein-Avila 2006
Sandoval et al. 1998
Santa Ana 2004
Scott 1993
Seitz 1975
Seligman et al. 1972
Severson and Guest 1970
Seymour et al. 1999
Seymour and Bland 1991
Seymour et al. 1998
Seymour et al. 1995
Seymour and Jones 1981
Seymour et al. 2003
Seymour et al. 2003
Seymour et al. 2005
Sharma 2005
Shepherd 2011
Shin and Milroy 1999
Shuy 1973
Simmons-McDonald and Robertson 2006
Simpkins and Simpkins 2009
Singham 1998
Singham 2005
Sligh and Conners 2003
Smith et al. 2001
Smitherman 1973
Smitherman 1977
Smitherman 1992
Smitherman 1994
Smitherman and Villanueva 2003
Spencer et al. 2001
Steele 1992
Steele 2010
Stockman 2000
Stockman 2010

Stoller 1975
Strickland and Alvermann 2004
Tauber 1997
Taylor 1986
Terry et al. 2010
Terry 2008
Tett and Crowther 1998
Thomas-Tate et al. 2006
Thomson 1977
Torrey 1970
Valdes 2001
Van Keulen et al. 1998
Vaughn-Cooke 1983
Vaughn-Cooke 1999
Velleman and Pearson 2010
Washington 1996
Washington 2001
Washington 2003
Washington and Craig 1992
Washington and Craig 1992
Washington and Craig 1999
Washington and Craig 2004

Weddington 2010
Wheeler et al. 2012
Williams 1970
Williams 1973
Williams 1975
Williams and Rivers 1975
Wolfram 1976
Wolfram 1983
Wolfram 1986
Wolfram 1998
Wolfram 2001
Wolfram et al. 2007
Wolfram and Christian 1976
Woodworth and Salzer 1971
Wroge 1998
Wyatt 1999
Wyatt 2001
Wyatt and Seymour 1999
Yancy 2011
Yang 2004
Zeni and Thomas 1990

Bidialectalism and/or Contrastive Analysis (B)

The references in this category relate in one way or another to the goal of developing bidialectalism in vernacular and standard Englishes, or more precisely, to teaching Standard English as a Second Dialect. Usually, this is advocated or done through the technique of Contrastive Analysis, in which the contrasts between the vernacular or non-standard variety and the standard or mainstream variety are highlighted to accelerate the process of second dialect/language learning.

Work in this area can be divided into two time periods: (1) The 1960s-1980s, in which proposals for using bidialectalism and contrastive analysis were first formulated, as a means of helping vernacular or creole speakers of English do better in schools, after linguists began studying these varieties, often funded by educational agencies or motivated by awareness of educational and socioeconomic disparities; and (2) The 1990s and 2000s, much (but not all) of the interest in this approach revived by the Oakland Ebonics controversy and its aftermath. In the former category, we find early, explicitly argued proposals by Le Page (1968) and D. Craig (1976) for speakers of Caribbean English creoles, by Stewart (1969) and Rentel and Kennedy (1972) for Appalachian English speakers, and by Stewart (1970), Feigenbaum (1970) and others for speakers of African American Vernacular English. Indeed, there were book-length manuals and detailed proposals for developing bidialectalism in specific states or school districts, such as the Standard English Proficiency (SEP) program in California (see Rickford 2002; Secret 1997), and the Psycholinguistics Reading Series in Chicago, Illinois (see Leaverton 1971, 1973), although these are difficult to find in print. One of the most carefully executed book-length manuals of this type is Crowell et al. (1974), which as we note, does not appear to have been formally published and distributed, although it would still be potentially useful, if updated. The only available manuals come from the second period, including self-help books like Berger (1990), which covers pronunciation and grammar, and Wheeler and Swords (2006, 2010) two recent manuals that concentrate on grammatical features, and are intended for use by teachers with speakers of vernacular Englishes.

Arguments for and against bidialectalism and contrastive analysis are set out in Rickford (2002). On the plus side is the fact that this approach acknowledges the vernacular speaker's fluency in a systematic language, and that using the vernacular to teach the standard (to use the title of Rickford 1999) could boost understanding and higher expectations among teachers, and self-esteem and motivation and interest in participation in language arts activities among students. A significant final plus is the fact that studies of experimental bidialectal/CA programs have shown significant improvements over traditional methods in test scores and other performance measures, for instance Taylor (1989) in Chicago, Harris-Wright (1999) in De Kalb county outside Atlanta, Fogel and Ehri (2000) in two Northeastern US cities, Maddahian and Sandamela (2000) on the Academic English Mastery Program in Los Angeles, Sweetland (2006) reporting on an experimental program in Cincinnati, and Wheeler and Swords (2010) reporting on successes in Swords' classroom in Newport News, Virginia.

On the negative side are arguments first formulated by Kochman (1969) and Sledd (1969, 1972) that to claim that increased competence in Standard English will lead to better employment and other individual benefits ignores the potentially greater negative effects of racism and other factors. They also claim that it is hypocritical if not immoral, since we tell students that all dialects are "equal," but then focus their efforts on mastering only the "standard" variety. A second, related critique (cf. Jagger and Cullinan 1974: Craig 1999, p 38) is that some contrastive analysis programs involve practice in translating from the vernacular to the standard, but not the other way around, and not on cognitive development more generally. A third is that the drills often associated with CA can be boring and stultifying, which, however, can be remedied through reducing or eliminating "drill and kill" techniques and increasing the use of literature, song, and other methods (cf. Rickford and Rickford 2007).

One of the most forceful recent critics of the bidialectal approach is Young (2009), who argues (p. 51) that it's a "strategy to negotiate, side-step and ultimately accommodate bias ... and the ongoing racism against the language habits of blacks and other non-white peoples." Instead, Young promotes "code-meshing, the blending and concurrent use of American English dialects in formal, discursive products, such as political speeches, student papers, and media interviews." However, there is no reason why one could not promote both code-switching and code-meshing (for individuals who can master the latter versatile skill), and even studies like Hoover (1978) that show positive attitudes towards the vernacular also show acceptance of the standard and a desire among parents for their children/students to be bidialectal in the vernacular AND the standard. This position is understandable in light of evidence from Charity (2004) and Craig et al. (2009) that competence in Standard English is associated with greater success in reading and school more generally.

Short Citations for Bidialectalism and/or Contrastive Analysis (B)

Aarons et al. 1969
Abrahams and Troike 1972
Adamson 2005
Adger 1993
Adger 1997
Adger 1998
Adger and Christian 2007
Adger et al. 1999
Adler 1978
Afaga and Lai 1994
Ai 2002
Alatis 1970
Allen 1969
Allen 1972

Anderson 1989
Anderson 1990
Anderson 1990
Baker 2002
Ball et al. 1997
Baratz 1970
Baugh 2004
Baxter and Holland 2007
Berger 1990
Blake and Van Sickle 2001
Brown 2006
Brown 2009
Brown 2011
Bruder and Hayden 1973

Bryan 1998
Bryan 2004
Bryan 2010
Bull 1990
Bulletin 1987
Burling 1973
Campbell 1994
Campbell 1997
Cassidy 1970
Cazden 1999
Cheshire et al. 1989
Chisolm and Godley 2011
Christensen 2011
Clachar 2006
Council 2010
Craig 1966
Craig 1976
Craig 1983
Craig 1999
Craig 2006
Craig 2008
Craig et al. 2009
Cronnell 1981
Cronnell 1983
Crotteau 2007
Crowell and Kolba 1974
Crowell et al. 1974
Dandy 1991
Davis et al. 1968
Dean and Fowler 1974
Delpit 1988
Desberg et al. 1979
Devonish and Carpenter 2007
Dillard 1978
Dubois 1978
Eades et al. 2006
Edwards 1981
Elbow 1999
Elifson 1977
Epstein and Xu 2003
Evans 2001
Ezarik 2002
Farr 1986
Farr et al. 2010
Farr et al. 2010
Farrell 1995
Feigenbaum 1970
Feldman et al. 1977
Finegan and Rickford 2004
Fischer 1992
Fishman and Lueders-Salmon 1972
Flanigan 1996
Flynn 2011
Fogel and Ehri 2000
Fogel and Ehri 2006
Funkhouser 1973

Gilyard 1996
Greene and Walker 2004
Grogger 2011
Gupta 1994
Hagemann 2001
Harris et al. 2001
Harris-Wright 1987
Harris-Wright 1999
Hill 2008
Hill 2009
Hollie 2001
Holmes 1999
Hoover 1989
Hoover 1991
Hoover et al. 1996
Jaggar and Cullinan 1974
Johnson 1969
Johnson 1979
Jordan 1989
Kachuck 1978
Kinloch 2005
Kirkland and Jackson 2009
Kochman 1974
Lado 1957
Laffey and Shuy 1973
Le Moine 2001
Le Moine and Hollie 2007
Le Moine and Los Angeles District 1998
Le Page 1968
Lin 1963
Lockwood 1998
Los Angeles District 1998
Los Angeles District 1999
Los Angeles District 2010
Love 1991
Lucas 1997
Luelsdorff 1973
Lyman and Figgins 2005
Maddahian and Sandamela 2000
Malcolm 1995
Malcolm 2000
Malcolm 2007
Malcolm et al. 1999
Malcolm and Königsberg 2007
Mantell 1974
Marckwardt 1974
Matilda 2010
Maxwell 1979
McWhorter 1997
McWhorter 1997
Moore 1999
Morales 2009
Mordaunt 2011
Morren and Morren 2007
Moses et al. 1976
Mufwene 2001

Murray 1997
Murtagh 1982
Musgrave 1962
Nembhard 1983
Nero 1997
Nero 1997
Nero 2000
Nero 2001
Nero 2006
O'Neal and Ringler 2010
O'Neil 1972
Ogbu 2003
Ohannessian and Gage 1969
Oliver et al. 2011
Österberg 1961
Pablo et al. 2001
Padak 1981
Palacas 2001
Palacas 2002
Pandey 2000
Parker and Crist 1995
Perez 2000
Politzer 1993
Politzer and Hoover 1974
Pollard 1998
Pollard 1999
Ramirez et al. 2005
Reaser and Adger 2008
Rentel and Kennedy 1972
Richardson 2003
Rickford and Rickford 2007
Rickford and Rickford 2010
Rickford 1997
Rickford 1999
Rickford 1999
Rickford 1999
Rickford 2002
Rickford 2006
Rickford and Wolfram 2009
Robbins 1989
Roberts 1983
Roberts 2007
Roy 1984
Sato 1989
Schierloh 1991
Schotta 1970
Scott 1997
Scott 1990
Secret 1997
Seymour and Seymour 1979
Sharma 2005
Siegel 1992
Siegel 1999

Siegel 2001
Siegel 2006
Siegel 2008
Siegel 2010
Siegel 2010
Simmons 1991
Simmons-McDonald et al. 1997
Simpkins and Simpkins 2009
Sledd 1969
Sledd 1972
Smith 1979
Smith 1995
Smitherman 1974
Smitherman 1977
Smitherman 2000
Stewart 1964
Stewart 1969
Stewart 1970
Stoller 1975
Tamura 2008
Taylor 1989
Taylor 1975
Taylor 1983
Taylor 1986
Taylor et al. 1983
Tompkins and McGee 1983
Torrey 1971
Troike 1972
Underwood 1974
Valdes et al. 2009
Van Keulen et al. 1998
Wassink 2005
Western Australian Education 2002
Wheeler 2003
Wheeler 2005
Wheeler 2006
Wheeler 2008
Wheeler 2009
Wheeler 2010
Wheeler et al. 2012
Wheeler and Swords 2004
Wheeler and Swords 2006
Wheeler and Swords 2010
Whitney 2005
Wible 2006
Williams 1975
Wolfram 1970
Wolfram 1970
Wolfram 1994
Wolfram 2001
Young 2004
Young 2009

Culture and Curriculum (C)

The references in this topical list grapple, in some way or another, with the question of how to rethink curriculum in light of linguistic and cultural diversity. Early work in this area (e.g., Aarons et al. 1969; Carter 1971; Abrahams & Troike 1972; Chun-Hoon 1973) highlighted the lack of attention to culture in schooling and called for educators to learn about students' culture, analyze their own cultural backgrounds and biases, and work to capitalize on cultural differences as resources to enhance learning rather than problems that prevent learning.

Subsequently, scholars of language and culture developed more detailed questions about how culture is constructed and maintained in interaction, in part due to the contributions of the ethnography of communication approach to analyzing language in use. This methodological approach was notably applied to education in Shirley Brice Heath's (1983) seminal work *Ways with Words* and spawned a wave of research into cultural 'mismatches' between home and school contexts. Michaels 1981 found that the narratives of Black primary students tended to be more 'topic associating' than their White peers' 'topic-centered' stories at sharing time—and that teacher reaction to this difference led to decreased learning opportunities for African American students.

One of the most prolific sites of research on culturally congruent curriculum for vernacular speakers has been Hawai'i, which from 1975 to 2002, received federal Title VII Bilingual Education funding for thirty-five separate direct service projects addressing the unique needs of speakers of Hawaiian Creole English (Pablo et al. 2001). The work of Kathryn Au and her colleagues on Project Holopono in particular has added greatly to the evidence base illustrating the transformative effects of establishing classroom environments that more closely hew to the participation and discourse norms most familiar to children from their community contexts. Smaller bodies of research exist on other vernacular English contexts, including Australia (Eagleson et al. 1982; Malcolm 2000, 2007; Sharifan 2008; Siegel 1992); the UK (Cheshire et al. 1989; Edwards 1979, 1986); and the Caribbean (Christie 1996; Kouwenberg et al. 2011; Nero 2010; Pratt-Johnson 1993, 2006).

In terms of work on culturally congruent curriculum for AAVE speakers, Carol Lee's (1993, 1995) insightful work illustrating how the African American discourse practice of *signifying* could be used in reading comprehension instruction reinvigorated exploration of how to approach the vernacular as a resource rather than a problem. Arnetha Ball (1992, 1995, 2000) extended this approach to African American discourse patterns in the realm of writing. Lee has since built on this type of strategic repurposing of vernacular resources to develop the *cultural modeling* approach to pedagogy (Lee 2007). Other work has illustrated how skillful African American teachers draw strategically on their own cultural and linguistic repertoires to build rapport, model academic expectations, and engage students (e.g., Bohn 2003; Boone 2003; Delpit 1995; Delpit & Dowdy 2002; Irvine 2002; Ladson-Billings 1994, 2000). Yet another line of interest and inquiry has been the need for and effect of literary materials that contain culturally relevant content such as the themes, issues, characters, and problems that students encounter in their daily lives (A. Rickford 1996; Bell & Clark 1998; Meier 2008). Readers interested in culturally relevant literature will find that our bibliography represents only a fraction of the work in this area, and are referred to the field of multicultural children's literature for greater depth. More recently, students' non-academic reading and writing practices, especially those involving digitally mediated language, has become a topic of interest for literacy researchers investigating ways to connect to students' out-of-school lives (Camitta 1993; Carter, 2006; Desai & Marsh 2005).

Short Citations for Culture and Curriculum (C)

Aarons et al. 1969
Abrahams and Troike 1972
Actouka and Lai 1989
Adamson 2005
Afaga and Lai 1994
Alim and Baugh 2007
Allsopp 2000
Amberg and Vause 2009
Au 1980
Au 2008
Au and Kawakami 1985
Au and Kawakami 1991
Balester 1993
Ball 1992
Ball 1994
Ball 1995
Ball 2000
Ball 2000
Ball et al. 1997
Balter and Grossman 2009
Baratz 1969
Baugh 1999
Baugh 2005
Beck 2009
Bell and Clark 1998
Birrell 1995
Blackburn and Stern 2000
Blake and NYU 2009
Boggs 1985
Bohn 2003
Boone 2003
Brathwaite 1985
Brayboy and Castagno 2009
Brod and McQuiston 1997
Brooks 1985
Busch and Ball 2004
Cahnmann 2000
Camitta 1993
Campbell 1994
Campbell 1997
Campbell 2005
Carter 2007
Carter 2011
Carter 1993
Carter 2006
Carter 1971
Castagno and Brayboy 2008
Center for Applied Linguistics 1978
Cheng 1987
Cheshire et al. 1989
Christie 1996
Chun-Hoon 1973
Cook-Gumperz 1993
Corson 1999
Corson 2001

Corson 2003
Courts 1997
Crawford 2001
Cross and Aldrige 1989
Cummins 1986
Dandy 1991
Delain et al. 1985
Delpit 1986
Delpit 1988
Delpit 1995
Delpit and Dowdy 2002
Denham and Lobeck 2005
Denham and Lobeck 2010
Desai and Marsh 2005
Deyhle and Swisher 1997
Dick et al. 1994
Dillard 1970
Dixson and Dingus 2006
Eagleson et al. 1982
Edelsky 1996
Edwards 2010
Edwards 1979
Edwards 1986
Farr et al. 2010
Farr et al. 2010
Fecho 2000
Fecho 2004
Fillmore and Snow 2000
Fordham 1998
Fordham 1999
Foster 1992
Foster 1995
Foster 1999
Foster 2001
Gadsen and Wagner 1995
Galaz 2000
Gee 2007
Gilyard 1991
Gilyard 1996
Gonzalez 1997
Goodman 2003
Greenbaum 1985
Greenbaum and Greenbaum 1983
Gutierrez et al. 2009
Hammond et al. 2005
Harber 1981
Heath 1982
Heath 1983
Hefflin and Barksdale-Ladd 2001
Henry 2000
Herrin et al. 2010
Higgs and Manning 1975
Higgs et al. 1995
Hill 2009
Hilliard 1992

Holt 1975
Hoover 1989
Hoover and Fabian 2000
Horvat and Lewis 2003
Irvine 1990
Irvine 2002
Irvine 2003
Irvine 2003
Kawakami 1999
Kinloch 2005
Kochman 1989
Kouwenberg et al. 2011
Labov and Robins 1969
Ladson-Billings 1992
Ladson-Billings 1994
Ladson-Billings 1995
Ladson-Billings 2000
Ladson-Billings 2001
Ladson-Billings 2002
Lass 1980
Le Moine and Los Angeles District 1998
Leap 1993
Lee 1993
Lee 1995
Lee 1995
Lee 1997
Lee 2006
Lee 2007
Leeper 2003
Malancon and Malancon 1993
Malcolm 1979
Malcolm 1992
Malcolm 1995
Malcolm 2000
Malcolm 2007
Malcolm 2011
Malcolm et al. 1999
Malcolm and Königsberg 2007
Marcuzzi 1986
Matlock 1995
McCarthey 1997
McCarty 2005
McCarty 1980
McDougal 2009
Michaels 1981
Michaels and Collins 1984
Mitchell and Henderson 1990
Moll 1988
Morgan 2010
Nero 2010
Nichols 1989
Ntiri 1990
Ogbu 1991
Ogbu 1992
Ogbu 1999
Ogbu 2003

Osborn 2007
Paris 2011
Patterson 1994
Perry and Delpit 1997
Perry et al. 2003
Pewewardy 1998
Philips 1972
Pratt-Johnson 1993
Pratt-Johnson 2006
Ramirez et al. 2005
Reyhner and Hurtado 2008
Richardson 2008
Rickford 1999
Rickford 2001
Rickford and Rickford 2007
Rickford and Rickford 1995
Roberts 2007
Robinson-Zanartu 1996
Rupley et al. 2008
Rynkofs 2008
Sato 1989
Scott 1990
Scott et al. 2009
Scott et al. 2009
Sealey-Ruiz 2007
Secret 1997
Sharifian 2008
Siegel 1992
Simpkins 2002
Simpkins and Simpkins 1981
Simpkins and Simpkins 2009
Smith 1979
Smitherman and Cunningham 1997
Smitherman and Quartey-Annan 2011
Spack 2006
Speidel 1987
Spolsky and Hult 2008
Starks 1983
Straker 1985
Taylor and Dorsey-Gaines 1988
Taylor 1986
Tett and Crowther 1998
Thomas 1983
Thompson et al. 2008
Troutman 1997
Valdes 2001
Vernon-Feagans 1996
Villegas and Lucas 2002
Waitt 2006
Walker 1992
Washington 2003
Watson-Gegeo and Boggs 1977
Whitney 2005
Whyte 1986
Williams 1975
Williams 1975

Yang 2004   Young 2004
Young et al. 2005   Zephir 1999

Disorders of Speech, Language or Communication (D)

Most of the references included under this topic deal in one way or another with the problem of differentiating between speech and language disorders (for instance, difficulties in
producing sounds or grammatical patterns that match the norms of the community) and
dialect differences between the vernacular and the standard. Suppose, for instance, that
Leroy, an African American boy, regularly pronounces English words ending with a voiceless *th* as though they ended in a voiceless *s* (pronouncing "path" as *pass*), while Anika, an
African American girl, pronounced equivalent English words with a final voiceless *f* (pronouncing "path" as *paf*). Although their teacher might refer both of them to a speech and
language pathologist because their speech differed from the norms of Standard English or
Mainstream American English, an informed clinician might decline to add Anika to her
caseload because her *paf* pronunciations of "path" match the vernacular norms of AAVE.
Leroy's *pass* pronunciations of "path," however, do not match the norms of AAVE or any
other local community, and the speech pathologist should work with him to help him
modify his idiosyncratic pronunciation in line with the norms of AAVE, SE and other local
varieties. Misdiagnosis can have significant negative results, resulting, for instance, in the
over-referral of vernacular English speakers to special education classes

This specific example comes from an interview with Toya Wyatt reported in Banotai
(2006). But the issue has been discussed, especially in the United States, and especially in
relation to speakers of AAVE, for decades (see for instance, Williams 1972; Screen and
Taylor 1972; and Wolfram 1979), usually by scholars who are either speech and language
pathologists (in other countries, sometimes "language therapists"), or linguists, or both.
An important development of the past decade is the creation of the Diagnostic Evaluation of Language Variation (DELV) tests (Seymour et al. 2003a, 2003b, 2005), which are
sensitive to dialect differences, and can measure a child's risk for various kinds of language
disorder. Discussions of the dialect difference/disorder issue since this date (e.g., Craig and
Washington 2006; Stockman 2010; Velleman and Pearson 2010) invariably refer to children's performance on the DELV or related measures.

Largely because speech and language pathology or communication disorders is not a
developed field in Caribbean and other countries in which Anglophone pidgins and creoles are spoken (there are rarely courses in this at local universities, or speech therapists in
local schools), we have no references in this category for such varieties. There are, however, some references (e.g., Bruce and Montgomery 1996; Oetting and McDonald 2001;
Gutierrez-Clellen and Simon-Cereijido 2007) that deal with speech and language disorder
diagnosis among speakers of Latina/o English and Southern White Vernacular English in
the United States.

Short Citations for Disorders of Speech, Language or Communication (D)

Adger 1993   Campbell 1993
Banotai 2006   Campbell 1994
Battle 1993   Champion et al. 2003
Battle 1996   Cole and Taylor 1990
Bland-Stewart 2003   Craig and Washington 2000
Bliss and Allen 1981   Craig and Washington 2002
Bogatz et al. 1986   Craig and Washington 2006
Brice and Montgomery 1996   Craig et al. 2005

Fradd and Weismantel 1989
Gopaul-McNicol et al. 1998
Gutierrez-Clellen and Simon-Cereijido 2007
Hoover et al. 1996
Horton-Ikard 2006
Hwa-Froelich et al. 2007
Jackson and Pearson 2010
Johnson et al. 1998
Jones 1972
Kamhi et al. 1996
Oetting and McDonald 2001
Oetting et al. 2010
Pearson et al. 2009
Pena and Gillam 2000
Pruitt et al. 2010
Rodekohr and Haynes 2001
Seymour 1986
Seymour and Bland 1991
Seymour and Jones 1981
Seymour and Valles 1998
Seymour et al. 1995
Seymour et al. 1998
Seymour et al. 1999

Seymour et al. 2003
Seymour et al. 2003
Seymour et al. 2005
Silliman et al. 2002
Smith et al. 2001
Stockman 1986
Stockman 1996
Stockman 2000
Stockman 2010
Taylor 1972
Taylor 1986
Van Keulen et al. 1998
Vaughn-Cooke 1983
Velleman and Pearson 2010
Washington 1996
Washington and Craig 1992
Washington and Craig 2004
Wilcox and Anderson 1998
Williams 1972
Wolfram 1979
Wolfram 1994
Wyatt 1999

Edited Volumes, Overviews, Reviews, or Other Bibliographies (E)

In this category, we include edited volumes, single or co-authored overviews and collections, reviews and review articles, and other bibliographies. These constitute important reference sources in navigating and synthesizing the many strands of research on vernacular Englishes in education.

The collections focusing on AAVE range from classics like Baratz and Shuy 1969, Fasold and Shuy 1970, and Stoller 1975, to more recent work like Alim and Baugh 2007, Lanehart 2009, Makoni et al. 2003, Norment 2005, Richardson and Jackson 2004, and Smitherman 2000, 2006. Some of the volumes emerged in the wake of important controversies like the 1979 Ann Arbor King decision (e.g., Chambers 1983; Smitherman 1981; and Whiteman 1980) and the 1996 Oakland "Ebonics" controversy (e.g., Adger et al. 1999; Crawford 2001; Johnson and Gopaul-McNicol 1998; Perry and Delpit 1997; Ramirez et al. 2005; and Rickford and Rickford 2000). Others revisit 1974 publication of the CCCC/ NCTE resolution on "Students' Right to their Own Language" (e.g., Cobb et al. 2009; Parks 2000; Smitherman and Villanueva 2003). In general, though, these works run the gamut of important topics such as policy and politics (Makoni and Smitherman 2003; Smitherman and Baugh 2002), language acquisition (Taylor and Leonard 1998), language disorders (Kamhi et al. 1996; Taylor 1986), linguistic interference (Laffey and Shuy 1973), reading (Cullinan 1974; Harber and Bryen 1976; Meier 2008; Snow et al. 1998), and writing (Chesire and Stein 1997).

Among the edited volumes and single-authored overviews and collections, AAVE is most heavily represented, but our list also includes work on Appalachian English (Higgs and Manning 1975, 1995; Leeper 2003), Creole English (Christie 1996; Irish 1995; Migge et al. 2010; Nero 2006; Siegel 1992; Simmons-McDonald and Robertson 2006; Tamura 2008), Latino English (Bixler-Márquez and Ornstein-Galicia 1988), Native American English (Bartelt et al. 1982; Leap 1976; Swisher and Tippeconnic 1999), and other English vernaculars, some including pidgins and creoles (Kachru et al. 2009; Schneider 2007, 2008, 2010; and Schreier 2010).

Finally, bibliographies included under this keyword are Brasch and Brasch 1974 on AAVE, Harris et al. 1995 and Rickford et al. 2004 on AAVE in education, McMillan and

Montgomery 1989 on Southern American English, Herrin et al. 2010 on Appalachian children's literature, and Viereck et al. 1984, which compiles references on a wide variety of English vernaculars.

Short Citations for Edited Volumes, Overviews, Reviews, or Other Bibliographies

Aarons et al. 1969
Abrahams and Troike 1972
Adger et al. 1999
Alatis 1970
Alim and Baugh 2007
Alladina and Edwards 1991
Baratz 1973
Baratz and Shuy 1969
Bartelt et al. 1982
Baugh 1983
Baugh 1999
Baugh 2000
Baugh 2009
Bayley and Bonnici 2009
Bentley and Crawford 1973
Bixler-Màrquez and Ornstein-Galicia 1988
Bolton 2002
Brasch and Brasch 1974
Brooks 1985
Cassidy and Hall 1991
Cassidy and Hall 1996
Castagno and Brayboy 2008
Chambers 1983
Champion and Bloome 1995
Charity Hudley and Mallinson 2011
Cheshire and Stein 1997
Cheshire et al. 1989
Christie 1996
Cook and Lodge 1996
Corson 2001
Craig 1999
Crawford 2001
Cronnell 1981
Cullinan 1974
Delpit and Dowdy 2002
Denham and Lobeck 2005
Denham and Lobeck 2010
DeStefano 1973
Deyhle and Swisher 1997
Eagleson et al. 1982
Egan-Robertson and Bloome 1998
Eggington 1994
Fairclough 1992
Farr 1986
Farr et al. 2010
Fasold and Shuy 1970
Finegan and Rickford 2004
Fought 2006

Gadsen and Wagner 1995
Gee 2007
Glowka and Lance 1993
Görlach and Holm 1986
Görlach and Schneider 1997
Green 2002
Gutierrez et al. 2009
Halasek and Highberg 2001
Hall 2002
Hall 2012
Hall and Turner 1973
Hammond et al. 2005
Harber and Bryen 1976
Harris et al. 1995
Harris et al. 2001
Herrin et al. 2010
Higgs and Manning 1975
Higgs et al. 1995
Hirvela 2010
Irish 1995
Irvine 2002
Jackson and Richardson 2003
Johnson et al. 1998
Jones 1965
Kachru 1997
Kachru et al. 2009
Kamhi et al. 1996
Kirkpatrick 2002
Kleifgen and Bond 2009
Kochman 1972
Kretzschmar 1998
Kymlicka and Patten 2003
Laffey and Shuy 1973
Lanehart 2001
Lanehart 2009
Leap 1976
Leeper 2003
Luke 1986
Makoni et al. 2003
Martin-Jones and Jones 2000
McCarty 2005
McMillan and Montgomery 1989
Meier 2008
Menken 2009
Migge et al. 2010
Morrow et al. 2009
Mufwene et al. 1998
Nero 2006

Norment 2005
Ntiri 1990
Ohannessian and Gage 1969
Osborn 2007
Paulston and McLaughlin 1994
Pendarvis 2010
Perry and Delpit 1997
Pollard 2000
Ramirez et al. 2005
Redd and Schuster Webb 2005
Reyes and Lo 2009
Reyhner 1994
Richardson and Jackson 2004
Rickford and Rickford 2000
Rickford et al. 2004
Roberts 2007
Salaberry 2009
Sandoval et al. 1998
Santa Ana 2004
Schneider 2007
Schneider 2008
Schneider 2010
Schneider and Kortmann 2004
Schreier et al. 2010
Schwartz 1980
Scott and Rogers 1996
Scott et al. 2009
Shankar 2011
Sharma 2010
Shuy 1973
Siegel 1992
Siegel 2010
Simmons-McDonald and Robertson 2006

Smitherman 1977
Smitherman 1981
Smitherman 2000
Smitherman 2006
Smitherman and Baugh 2002
Smitherman and Villanueva 2003
Snow et al. 1998
Somervill 1975
Sperling 1996
Spolsky and Hult 2008
Stewart 1964
Stockman 2010
Stoller 1975
Strickland and Alvermann 2004
Sutcliffe and Wong 1986
Swisher and Tippeconnic 1999
Taavitsainen et al. 1999
Tabouret-Keller et al. 1997
Tamura 2008
Taylor 1986
Taylor and Leonard 1998
Thomas 1983
Trudgill and Hannah 2008
Venezky 1981
Viereck et al. 1984
Washington 1998
Weber 1983
Whiteman 1980
Williams 1970
Williams 1975
Wolfram and Ward 2006
Wolfram et al. 2007
Zentella 2006

Features (F)

This bibliographic resource includes about 325 entries that deal in whole or in part with the linguistic features of the vernacular varieties covered in this volume, most of them written without a view to educational applications. Why do we include these? Because understanding such features and the fact that they're regular and systematic is of great potential importance for teachers of speakers of these varieties, especially if they want to experiment with vernacular literacy, or use contrastive analysis in teaching standard English or other varieties. As Moats (1994) has noted, and as some of us have also noticed in working in schools, teachers' explicit knowledge of the "building blocks of language" (parts of speech, phonemes, morphemes, syllables) can sometimes be quite limited. Hence, the great need for the kinds of resources listed in this category.

At the same time, we could not import every article or book written on every feature of vernacular or creole varieties of English, or the list would overwhelm this bibliography while detracting from its orientation to education. One principle we followed in selecting entries was to opt for works that were general rather than specific or esoteric, and more likely to be accessible to teachers and other readers without a background in linguistics. Sometimes we did include technical works that related to features or approaches that were central to theoretical discussions of one vernacular or another (e.g., Newman 2010; Sharma and Rickford 2009), but we tried to make this the exception rather than the norm.

Second, while there are some excellent books on English varieties, for instance, the general and text series on "Varieties of English Around the World" edited by Manfred Görlach and others, we could not include all of them, but selected typical examples from this series (e.g., Görlach 1986, 1995, 1998, 2002; Sedlatschek 2009; Schneider 2008), hoping that readers, impressed by these, will seek out other volumes in the series on their own.

One resource that many teachers may find useful is *dictionaries*, and our bibliography includes more than a dozen of these (not counting more limited glossaries or word lists, which in general, are omitted). For dictionaries of Anglophone Caribbean varieties, see Allsopp 2003, Allsopp and Allsopp 1996, Cassidy and Le Page 1980, Holm and Shilling 1982, and Winer 2009. For Nigerian and Cameroon English, respectively, see Igboanusi 2002 and Kouega 2006, 2008. For Hong Kong English, see Cummings 2011. For South African Indian English, see Mesthrie 2010. For Melanesian Pidgin English or Tok Pisin as spoken in Papua and New Guinea, see Mihalic 1971. In terms of US varieties, see Montgomery and Hall 2004 for a dictionary of Smoky Mountain English (including Appalachian), Major 1994 and Smitherman 1998 for dictionaries of African American Vernacular English (AAVE), and Cassidy 1985, Cassidy and Hall 1991, 1996, Hall 2002, 2012 for the multi-volume *Dictionary of American Regional English*. Other works that deal with the lexicon or semantics of English vernaculars on a smaller scale or in relation to specific features include Cassidy 1982, Clachar 2003, Dillard 1970, Pollard 1980, Rickford and Greaves 1978, Sharifian 2005, Stewart 2010, and Stockman and Vaughn-Cooke 1992—some of them specifically dealing with lexical or semantic issues that are challenging for students or their teachers in one way or another.

Turning now to descriptions of the grammar and pronunciation of these varieties, the biggest subcategory and the one most likely to be useful to teachers is *general overviews and introductions*. For AAVE, the classic descriptions came out in the 1970s and 1980s (Baugh 1983; Burling 1973; DeStefano 1973; Dillard 1972; Fasold and Wolfram 1970; Labov 1970; 1972; Smitherman 1977), but the overviews from the 1990s and 2000s (Baugh 1999; Dandy 1991; Green 2002, 2004; Rickford 1997, 1999; Rickford and Rickford 2000) include several features that were not covered in earlier overviews. However, Labov et al. 1968 and Wolfram 1969, two of the classic community studies from the earliest decade of modern AAVE research, remain invaluable for their detailed quantitative information on AAVE features, grammatical as well as phonological, and including coverage of variation by social class, gender, age, style, and more. Redd and Schuster (2005) provide a general introduction to AAVE for writing teachers. In terms of US Southern White vernacular varieties of English, Feagin's 1979 study of Alabama English remains an invaluable classic, while Hutchison 2005 and Wolfram et al. 2000 provide excellent introductions to North Carolina varieties. For Appalachian English, see Hackenberg 1972, Mitchell 2005 (short, but geared to writing teachers), and Wolfram and Christian 1976. For Chicano English, the general go-to overview is Fought 2003, but see also her 2006 text on language and ethnicity. For Puerto Rican English, see Wolfram 1974 and Zentella 1997. And for recent discussions of US Latino or Hispanic varieties of English more generally, see Bayley 2008 and Wolfram et al. 2011. For varieties of Native American or American Indian English, see, among others, Bartelt et al. 1982, B. Craig 1991, Flanigan 1987, Hutchison 1999, Leap 1976, 1993, and Wolfram 1980. For Asian American English, see Hanna 1997. Among general introductions to varieties of American English, two recent ones of note are Amberg and Vause (2009) and Wolfram and Schilling-Estes 2006. For highly accessible introductions to American English dialects "coast to coast," see Wolfram and Ward 2006, and the popular videos by Alvarez and Kolker (*American Tongues*, 1987) and MacNeil and Cran (*Do You Speak American*, 2005).

Outside of the United States, the biggest subcategory for which general overviews and introductions are available are Anglophone pidgins and creoles, including Cameroon Pidgin English (Todd 1984), Guyanese Creole (Rickford 1987), Hawaiian Pidgin (Sakoda and Siegel 2003), Jamaican creole (Adams 1991; Cassidy 1982; Christie 1973; Deuber 2009;

Pollard 1993), Nigerian Pidgin (Deuber 2005; Faraclas 1996), and Tok Pisin or Melanesian Pidgin English (Siegel 2009). For British Black English, derived from Caribbean Anglophone creoles, see Sutcliffe 1982. This is just a representative set, since descriptions of several other Anglophone pidgins and creoles could have been included. See Roberts 2007 for a general introduction to West Indian varieties, Kortmann and Upton 2008 for pidgin, creole and vernacular Englishes in the British Isles, Schneider 2008 for similar varieties in the Americas and the Caribbean, Burridge and Kortmann 2008 for similar varieties in the Pacific and Australasia, and Mesthrie 2008 for similar varieties in Africa, South and Southeast Asia. For Hong Kong English, see Bolton 2002 and Setter et al. 2010, and for English in India, see Sedlatschek 2009. For English as spoken by Indians in South Africa, see Mesthrie 1992. For "lesser known" varieties of English, including Newfoundland English, Canada, Anglo-Argentine English, St. Helenian English, Rhodesian English, Eurasian Singapore English, and Norfolk Island and Pitcairn varieties, see Schreier et al. 2010. Finally, for aboriginal and other vernacular varieties in Australia, see Berry and Hudson 1997, and Sharpe 1975.

It would be interesting to compare the features of these vernacular and creole varieties of English in different countries and continents. To a large extent, this has already been done in some of the comprehensive recent overviews of English varieties around the world, such as Kachru et al. 2009, Schneider 2010, Schneider and Kortmann 2004, Trudgill and Hannah 2008.

A number of entries in this category focus only on *grammar* (morphology: the varying forms of words and morphemes or minimum units of meaning, and syntax—how words are put together to form phrases and sentences), for instance Bailey 1966 and Deuber 2009 on Jamaican morphosyntax, Bartels 1982 and Wolfram 1984 on various aspects of tense marking in Native American English, Bayley and Santa Ana 2008 on Chicano English morphology and syntax, Cox 1992 on the Cajun of Louisiana, Huber 1999 on the grammar of Ghanaian English, Mbangwana and Sala 2009 on the grammar of Cameroon English, Sakoda and Tamura on the grammar of Pidgin Hawaiian English.

Others focus on various aspects of *pronunciation,* for instance Chand 2010 on postvocalic *r* (how *r* is pronounced after a vowel, as in *water*) in Indian English, Dubois and Horvath 2003 on vowels in Cajun/Louisiana English, Hall-Lew 2010 on sound change in Asian and other ethnic varieties of English in San Francisco, Irvine 2008, Lacoste 2012, and Meade 2001 on various aspects of pronunciation in Jamaica, Nelson-Barber on pronunciation variation in Pima (Native American) English. Several of the articles in this category deal with the pronunciations of children, or with first language acquisition of English vernacular varieties, for instance Bland-Stewart 2003 on AAVE-speaking two-year olds, and H. Craig et al. 2003, Moran 1993, and Seymour and Seymour 1981 on other aspects of pronunciation among children speaking AAVE. Low and Grabe 1995 and Tarone 1973 are among the only studies in this bibliography that deal with intonation or prosody, the former in Singapore English, the latter in AAVE.

Finally—and this is a category we could have perhaps represented even more fully than we did, but we had to resist our theoretical interests in this area lest they lead us too far from our focus on education—there are references that deal with *social, regional, age or stylistic variation* in these varieties, including Bartelt 2001 on Native American English; and Baugh 1999, Oetting and Garrity 2006, Syrquin 2006, Thomas and Wassink 2010, Van Hofwegen and Wolfram 2010, and Washington et al. 1998 on various kinds of social and stylistic variation in AAVE. Edwards 1983, Roberts 2004 deal with variability in Guyanese Creole and Hawaiian Pidgin English, respectively, while Shankar 2008 deals with varying styles of South Asian English in Silicon Valley, California. Benor 2010 has extended the classic notion of "linguistic repertoire" (the full spectrum of linguistic styles and "means of speaking" that an individual or community might have) to "ethnolinguistic" contexts in particular, stimulating students of ethnic varieties of English and other varieties to pay more attention to this aspect of sociolinguistic competence than they otherwise might.

Short Citations for Features (F)

Aarons et al. 1969
Abrahams and Troike 1972
Adams 1991
Adger 1998
Akande 2010
Alatis 1970
Alford 1982
Alim 2004
Alleyne 1980
Allsopp 2000
Allsopp 2003
Allsopp 2006
Allsopp and Allsopp 1996
Alvarez and Kolker 1987
Alvarez and Kolker 1990
Amberg and Vause 2009
Anderson 2004
Au and Kawakami 1985
Bailey 1965
Bailey 1966
Ball 1992
Ball 1995
Ball and Bernhardt 2008
Bangura 2010
Barbag-Stoll 1983
Bartelt 1981
Bartelt 1982
Bartelt 2001
Bartelt et al. 1982
Battle 1996
Baugh 1983
Baugh 1999
Bayley 2008
Bayley and Santa Ana 2008
Benor 2010
Bentley and Crawford 1973
Berry and Hudson 1997
Blake 1997
Blake and Linguistics, NYU 2009
Bland-Stewart 2003
Bohn 2003
Bolton 2002
Boone 2003
Brown 1968
Brown 1998
Bucholtz 2004
Burling 1973
Burridge and Kortmann 2008
Carrington 1969
Carter 2007
Cassidy 1982
Cassidy 1985
Cassidy and Hall 1991
Cassidy and Hall 1996
Cassidy and Le Page 1980

Chand 2010
Charity 2007
Charity Hudley 2008
Charity Hudley and Mallinson 2011
Cheshire and Stein 1997
Christiansen and Farr 2010
Christie 1996
Christie 2003
Chun 2001
Clachar 2003
Clachar 2005
Clachar 2006
Coelho 1991
Coleman 1997
Connor and Craig 2006
Coupland 2006
Cox 1992
Craig 1991
Craig 1999
Craig and Washington 1994
Craig and Washington 1995
Craig and Washington 2004
Craig et al. 2003
Cran 1986
Cronnell 1981
Dandy 1991
Day-Vines et al. 2009
de Villiers and Johnson 2007
DeStefano 1972
DeStefano 1973
Deuber 2005
Deuber 2009
Deuber and Hinrichs 2007
Devonish 1998
Dillard 1970
Dillard 1972
Dillard and Rivers 1989
Dubois 1978
Dubois and Horvath 2003
Dubois and M. 2003
Durrleman 2008
Eckert 2000
Edwards 1979
Edwards 1980
Edwards 1981
Edwards 1983
Edwards 1986
Edwards 1992
Elugbe and Omamor 1991
Faraclas 1996
Farr and Daniels 1986
Fasold 1972
Fasold 2001
Fasold and Shuy 1970
Fasold and Wolfram 1970

Feagin 1979
Fields 1997
Finegan and Rickford 2004
Flanigan 1985
Flanigan 1987
Flanigan 1990
Flint 1968
Folb 1980
Foreman 2000
Fought 2003
Fought 2006
Funkhouser 1973
Fyle and Jones 1980
Gilyard 1996
Glowka and Lance 1993
Golub 1975
Goodman-France 2008
Görlach 1995
Görlach 1998
Görlach 2002
Görlach and Holm 1986
Görlach and Schneider 1997
Green 2002
Green 2002
Green 2004
Green and Conner 2009
Gupta 1994
Hackenberg 1972
Hall 2002
Hall 2012
Hall and Hall 1969
Hall-Lew 2010
Hall-Lew 2010
Hall-Lew and Starr 2010
Hamilton and Stern 2004
Hanna 1997
Harkins 1994
Harris and Moran 2006
Hazen and Fluharty 2004
Hazen et al. 2010
Higgs and Manning 1975
Higgs et al. 1995
Hirata-Edds 2011
Holm 2000
Holm and Shilling 1982
Holmes 1997
Holton 1984
Huber 1999
Hutcheson 1999
Hutcheson 2000
Hutcheson 2005
Igboanusi 2002
Irvine 2008
Ivy and Masterson 2011
Jackson and Pearson 2010
Jamaican Language Unit 2009

Johnson and de Villiers 2009
Kachru et al. 2009
Keen 1978
Kendall and Wolfram 2009
Kernan-Mitchell 1971
Kirkpatrick 2002
Kochman 1972
Kohn 2008
Kortmann and Upton 2008
Kouega 2006
Kouega 2008
Kuwahara 1998
Labov 1970
Labov 1972
Labov 1980
Labov et al. 1968
Lacoste 2012
Lanehart 2001
Lanehart 2009
Lanehart 2010
Language et al. 1990
Le Page 1981
Leap 1974
Leap 1976
Leap 1982
Leap 1993
Leechman and Hall 1955
Liebe-Harkort 1979
Liebe-Harkort 1983
Low and Grabe 1995
MacNeil and Cran 2005
Major 1994
Makoni et al. 2003
Malcolm 1994
Malcolm et al. 1999
Martin-Jones and Jones 2000
Mbangwana and Sala 2009
McCrum et al. 1986
McDavid 1962
McMillan and Montgomery 1989
McWhorter 1998
Meek 2006
Meier 2008
Mendoza-Denton 1999
Mendoza-Denton 2008
Mendoza-Denton and Iwai 1993
Mesthrie 1992
Mesthrie 2008
Mesthrie 2010
Mihalic 1971
Miller 1967
Mitchell 2005
Moats 1994
Montgomery and Hall 2004
Moran 1993
Morgan 2002

Mufwene et al. 1998
Nelson-Barber 1982
Nero 2006
Newman 2010
Newman and Wu 2011
Norment 2005
Oetting and Garrity 2006
Oh 2002
PACE 1990
Palacas 2002
Penalosa 1980
Politzer et al. 1974
Pollard 1980
Pollard 1993
Pollard 1996
Pollard 2000
Pratt-Johnson 2006
Ray 2009
Redd and Schuster Webb 2005
Renn and Terry 2009
Reyes 2005
Reyhner 1994
Rickford 1987
Rickford 1997
Rickford 1999
Rickford and Greaves 1978
Rickford and Rickford 2000
Roberts 2004
Roberts 2007
Rodriguez et al. 2004
Romaine 1988
Sailaja 2009
Sakoda and Siegel 2003
Sakoda and Tamura 2008
Samant 2010
Santa Ana 1993
Santa Ana and Bayley 2008
Scanlon and Wassink 2010
Schneider 2007
Schneider 2008
Schneider 2010
Schneider and Kortmann 2004
Schreier et al. 2010
Sealey-Ruiz 2005
Sebba 1997
Sedlatschek 2009
Setter et al. 2010
Seymour and Seymour 1981
Shankar 2008
Sharifian 2005
Sharma 2005
Sharma 2005
Sharma 2010
Sharma and Rickford 2009
Sharpe 1979
Shields 1979

Shnukal 2002
Shuy 1970
Siegel 2009
Siegel 2010
Simmons-McDonald 2001
Slomanson and Newman 2004
Smitherman 1977
Smitherman 1997
Smitherman 1998
Smitherman 1998
Smitherman 1998
Smitherman 2000
Smitherman 2000
Smitherman 2006
Spencer 1950
Stewart 2010
Stockman and Vaughn-Cooke 1992
Stout and Erting 1977
Sutcliffe 1982
Sutcliffe and Wong 1986
Syrquin 2006
Tamura 2008
Tarone 1973
Taylor and Leonard 1998
Terry et al. 2010
Terry et al. 2010
Thomas 1999
Thomas 2007
Thomas and Wassink 2010
Todd 1984
Torbert 2002
Troutman 1997
Troutman 1998
Trudgill and Hannah 2008
Van Hofwegen and Wolfram 2010
Washington 1998
Washington 1998
Washington and Craig 2002
Washington et al. 1998
Wassink 2005
Williams 1975
Williamson 1971
Winer 2009
Wolf 2001
Wolford 2006
Wolfram 1969
Wolfram 1974
Wolfram 1980
Wolfram 1984
Wolfram 1991
Wolfram 1994
Wolfram 2004
Wolfram and Christian 1976
Wolfram and Christian 1989
Wolfram and Fasold 1974
Wolfram and Hatfield 1986

Wolfram and Reaser 2005
Wolfram and Schilling-Estes 1997
Wolfram and Schilling-Estes 2006
Wolfram and Ward 2006
Wolfram et al. 1979
Wolfram et al. 2002
Wolfram et al. 2004

Wolfram et al. 2011
Wong 2007
Wong 2007
Wyatt 1995
Yaeger-Dror and Thomas 2010
Zentella 1997

Ideology, Attitudes, and/or Identity (I)

Books and articles topic-coded for "Ideology, Attitudes, and/or Identity" account for almost a *third* of the entries in this bibliography, making it the single biggest topic category, by far. This is not because the topic spans a broad range—the three subcategories are more closely linked than their separate names might suggest. The explanation for the size of this category is that WHAT people think about vernacular or non-standard varieties—e.g., their regularity, legitimacy, expressiveness, and functionality—and their speakers—e.g., their intelligence, capability, moral character, social standing—has a lot to do with their suitability for and role in education. (Attitudes are also crucial for understanding socio-linguistic variation and change, but that's another issue.) In this regard, it almost doesn't matter much whether we're talking about AAVE, Anglophone pidgins and creoles, or ethnic and working class vernaculars. As long as the varieties are regarded as non-standard, and they and their speakers as non-prestigious, issues of attitude, ideology and identity will loom large when we try to understand or change their role in assessment, teaching, and learning. For this reason, we don't need to discuss these varieties separately for this topical overview, as we have for so many of the others.

For instance, it has long been known (Moses et al. 1976 provide evidence from as far back as 1918!) that teachers, like administrators, parents, and members of the general public, tend to have negative attitudes towards AAVE, pidgins and creoles, and vernacular and foreign accented English, and positive attitudes towards Standard or Mainstream English (see for instance, Bakari 2003; Blake and Cutler 2003; Blodgett and Cooper 1973; Cassidy 1970; Covington 1975; DeBose 2005, 2007; Easter et al. 1999; Hosoda et al. 2007; Johnson 1985; Koch et al. 2001; Le Page 1968; Lippi-Green 2012; McLaughlin 2010; McWhorter 1998; Meacham 2000; Meek 2006; Nidue 1992; Piche et al. 1978; Pietras and Lamb 1978; Politzer and Hoover 1974; Rahman 2009; Roberts 2004; Romaine 1999; Siegel 2006; Tamura 1996; Taylor 1973; Tucker and Lambert 1969; Wolfram 1998; Yokota 2008). This often makes it difficult to attempt innovations like dialect readers, bidialectalism via contrastive analysis, or other means of taking vernacular varieties into account in the classroom, as Wolfram et al. 1999, p.155, Simpkins 2002 and others have noted. The extent to which negative attitudes towards vernacular speakers have led to unfair assessments of their abilities or been associated with self-fulfilling negative expectations of their performance is striking and disheartening, especially when clearly connected to ethnic and class stereotypes (see for instance, Cecil 1988; DeMeis and Turner 2004; Labov 1969; Seligman et al. 1972; Shepherd 2011; Smitherman and Scott 1984; Williams 1973, 1976; Williams et al. 1971, 1972; Woodworth and Salzer 1971). And. in the famous *Martin Luther King Junior Elementary School Children et al. v. Ann Arbor School District* decision, Justice Joiner (1979) emphasized that it was not the structure of the AAVE spoken by students that constituted a barrier to equal educational opportunity, but their teachers' limited knowledge of it, and their negative *attitudes* towards it

At the same time, negative attitudes towards pidgin, creole and vernacular varieties on dimensions of legitimacy or prestige are often accompanied by positive attitudes on dimensions of solidarity, dynamism, and sincerity (Barnes 2003; Hoover 1978; Lanehart 2002; Mann 2000; Ohama et al. 2000; Oloruntoba 1992; Rickford 1985; Rickford and Traugott 1985; Rickford and Rickford 2000; Smitherman 1977, 2000; Wassink 1999; Winford 1976). And in a number of cases, especially in pidgin-creole speaking communities in

West Africa and the Caribbean, there have been calls for increased legitimization, use or empowerment of the vernacular (Baldwin 1981; Devonish 2007; Devonish and Carter 2007; Elugbe and Omamor 1991; Gani-Ikilama 1990; Igboanusi 2008; Kephardt 1992; Kouwenberg et al. 2011; Mann 1998, 2000; Mbufong 2001; Neba et al. 2006; Sandred 1996; Wolf 2006; Wolf and Igboanusi 2006).

There have also been a number of notable efforts to improve the attitudes of teachers, counselors, administrators and others towards the vernacular, or at least suggestions about how such efforts should proceed (Bowie and Bond 1994; Charity Hudley and Mallinson 2011; Chen-Hayes et al. 1999; Dundes and Spence 2007; Eades and Siegel 1999; Godley et al. 2006; Higgins 2010; Hoover et al. 1996; Isenbarger and Willis 2006; Katz et al. 2009; Lass 1980; Mallinson and Charity Hudley 2010; Pietras and Lamb 1979; Spanjer and Layne 1983; Sweetland 2010; Wheeler 2010; Williams and Whitehead 1973; Wolfram 2010; Wolfram and Whitehead 1973; Wolfram et al. 2007; Zuidema 2005).

Several entries in this bibliography remind us that the attitudes and ideologies of *students* also matter. Positive integrative attitudes towards target languages or dialects tend to foster successful learning, and hostile or negative attitudes tend to limit successful learning or use. Some of the student attitudes reported in these entries are vigorously *for* the vernacular and *against* the standard and the "establishment" it represents, and to the extent that the vernacular is embraced, through bilingual education and other means, students with more pro-vernacular ideologies may be more engaged and successful (Carpenter and Devonish 2012; Cobb et al. 2009; Delpit 2006; Fordham 1998, 1999; Fordham and Ogbu 1986; Horvat and Lewis 2003; Igoudin 2011; Jordan 1985; Kinloch 2010; Ogbu 1999; Politzer and Hoover 1974; Scoon 1971; Smitherman 1995; Scott et. al 2009; Wassink 2005).

Students' and parents' attitudes to varieties are often linked closely with issues of identity. Among the many entries that deal specifically with identity, many in the context of Latina/o or Native American varieties, are Alim 2003, Carter 2007, Chun 2004, Eades et al. 2006, Farr 2006, Fought 2010, Hanna 1997, Kuwahara 1998, Lanehart 2009, Leap 1974, Nero 2006, Penfield-Jasper 1982, Rampton 1995, Reyes 2007, Tamura 2008, Toribio 2006, Williams and Grantham 1999.

Other issues come up at various points in our entries tagged for this "Attitudes, Ideology and Identity" category, including the relation of academic success to peer group status and functional conflict with the school (Eckert 2000; Labov and Robins 1969), and the association of negative attitudes to vernacular varieties with discrimination in housing (Massey and Lundy 2001) and employment (Grogger 2011; Terrell and Terrell 1983).

Short Citations for Ideology, Attitudes, and/or Identity (I)

Abrahams and Troike 1972
Adger and Christian 2007
Adge et al. 1999
Alim 2003
Allsopp 2000
Alobweede d'Epie 1998
Alvarez and Kolker 1987
Amberg and Vause 2009
Attinasi 1997
Awonusi 1990
Bakari 2003
Baker 1992
Baldwin 1981
Baldwin 1988
Balester 1993
Ball 1997
Ball and Lardner 1997

Ball and Muhammad 2003
Bangura 2010
Baratz 1970
Barnes 2003
Baugh 1988
Baugh 2000
Baugh 2000
Baugh 2005
Baugh 2007
Beck 2009
Becker and Luthar 2002
Berdan 1980
Birch 2001
Birrell 1995
Blake and Cutler 2003
Blodgett and Cooper 1973
Bowie and Bond 1994

Brathwaite 1985
Brown 1968
Brown 2006
Bucholtz 2004
Burling 1973
Cameron 1992
Campbell 1993
Campbell 1994
Cargile 1997
Cargile and Giles 1998
Cargile et al. 2006
Cargile et al. 2010
Carlson and McHenry 2006
Carpenter and Devonish 2010
Carpenter and Devonish 2012
Carrington 1983
Carter 1993
Carter 2007
Carter 2011
Cassidy 1970
Cazden 1970
Cazden 1999
CCCC Committee 2000
Cecil 1988
Champion and Bloome 1995
Cheatham et al. 2009
Chen-Hayes et al. 1999
Cheshire and Edwards 1991
Cheshire et al. 1989
Christiansen and Farr 2010
Chun 2001
Chun 2004
Chun 2009
Clark et al. 1990
Clark et al. 1991
Coelho 1991
Collins 1988
Cook and Lodge 1996
Cooper 1995
Corson 1999
Corson 2001
Coup 2008
Covington 1975
Craig 1983
Crawford 2000
Crawford 2001
Cross et al. 2001
Crowl and Macginitie 1976
Crowley 1989
Crowley 1990
Curzan 2002
Dandy 1991
DeBose 2005
DeBose 2007
Del Torto 2010
Delpit 1988
Delpit 1990

Delpit 2002
Delpit 2006
Delpit and Dowdy 2002
DeMeis and Turner 1978
Denham and Lobeck 2005
Denham and Lobeck 2010
DeStefano 1973
Devonish 2007
Devonish and Carpenter 2007
District 1999
Dowdy 1999
Dundes and Spence 2007
Eades and Siegel 1999
Eades et al. 2006
Easter et al. 1999
Eckert 2000
Edwards 1979
Edwards 1986
Edwards 2010
Egbokhare 2003
Elugbe 1995
Elugbe and Omamor 1991
Evans 2001
Fairclough 1989
Fairclough 1992
Farr 2006
Farr 2011
Farr et al. 2010
Farr et al. 2010
Fasold 2001
Fecho 2000
Fecho 2004
Finegan and Rickford 2004
Fishbein 1973
Fishman 1993
Flanigan 1996
Flower 1996
Flowers 2000
Folb 1980
Fordham 1993
Fordham 1998
Fordham 1999
Fordham and Ogbu 1986
Fought 2003
Fought 2006
Fought 2010
Funkhouser 1973
Gani-Ikilama 1990
Gee 2007
Gere and Smith 1979
Gilmore 1987
Gilyard 1990
Gilyard 1996
Godley and Minnici 2008
Godley et al. 2006
Godley et al. 2007
Goldblatt 1995

Goodman 2003
Green 1963
Green 2002
Greene and Walker 2004
Grogger 2011
Haddix 2008
Haig and Oliver 2003
Haig and Oliver 2003
Hall-Lew and Starr 2010
Hamilton 2005
Hanna 1997
Harris et al. 2001
Higgins 2010
Hilliard 1983
Hilliard 1997
Hilliard 1999
Hinds 1990
Hinton 2001
Hiramoto 2011
Hollie 2001
Holton 1984
Honey 1997
Hoover 1978
Hoover et al. 1995
Hoover et al. 1996
Hopson 2003
Horvat and Lewis 2003
Hosoda 2007
Hutcheson 2005
Igboanusi 2008
Igoudin 2011
Irvine 1990
Irvine 2008
Isenbarger and Smith 1973
Isenbarger and Willis 2006
Jia and Aaronson 2003
Jibril 1995
Johnson 1969
Johnson 1985
Johnson et al. 1998
Joiner 1979
Jordan 1985
Jordan 1989
Jordan 2002
Kachru 1997
Kamhi-Stein 2003
Katz et al. 2009
Kawakami 1999
Kells 2006
Kephart 1992
Kinloch 2010
Kirkland and Jackson 2009
Koch and Gross 1997
Koch et al. 2001
Kochman 1974
Kochman 1981
Kouwenberg et al. 2011

Kretzschmar 1998
Kretzschmar 2008
Kuwahara 1998
Labov 1969
Labov 1970
Labov 1972
Labov 1972
Labov 1982
Labov 1995
Labov and Charity Hudley 2009
Labov and Robins 1969
Lambert and Taylor 1996
Lanehart 1998
Lanehart 2001
Lanehart 2002
Lanehart 2002
Lanehart 2009
Lass 1980
Le Moine and District 1998
Le Page 1968
Leap 1974
Levinson 2005
Linn and Pichè 1982
Linnes 1998
Lippi-Green 2012
Lo and Reyes 2004
Lobeck 2005
Long 1997
Lucas 1997
Luke 1986
Maddahian and Sandamela 2000
Makoni et al. 2003
Mallinson and Charity Hudley 2010
Mann 1996
Mann 1998
Mann 2000
Mann 2009
Marback 2001
Marckwardt 1974
Martinez 2006
Massey and Lundy 2001
Matilda 2010
Mays 1977
Mazrui 2006
Mbufong 2001
McCarty et al. 2010
McCourtie 1998
McDavid 1962
McKay and Wong 1996
McKenry 1996
McLaughlin 2010
McMillan and Montgomery 1989
McRae 1994
McWhorter 1997
McWhorter 1998
Meacham 2000
Meacham 2002

Meek 2006
Meier 1999
Mendoza-Denton and Iwai 1993
Miller and Johnson 1974
Mitchell 2005
Mitchell-Kernan 1972
Mocombe 2006
Mohawk 1985
Mordaunt 2011
Morgan 2002
Moses et al. 1976
Mühleisen 2002
Mufwene 2001
Murray 2001
Murrell 1997
Murtagh 1982
Ndolo 1989
Neba et al. 2006
Neba et al. 2006
Nembhard 1983
Nero 1997
Nero 2000
Nero 2006
Nero 2006
Nichols 1977
Nidue 1992
Ntiri 1990
Oetting and Garrity 2006
Ogbu 1991
Ogbu 1992
Ogbu 1999
Ogbu 2003
Ohama et al. 2000
Oladejo 1991
Oliver and Haig 2005
Oliver et al. 2011
Oloruntoba 1992
O'Neal and Ringler 2010
O'Neil 1972
Orbe 1994
Palacas 2001
Palacas 2002
Paris 2011
Parker and Crist 1995
Parmegiani 2006
Patrick 2006
Patterson 1994
Pavlenko 2004
Penalosa 1980
Penfield-Jasper 1982
Perry and Delpit 1997
Perry et al. 2003
Pewewardy 1998
Piche et al. 1978
Piestrup 1973
Pietras and Lamb 1978
Politzer and Hoover 1974

Pon et al. 2003
Postal 1972
Preston 1991
Purcell-Gates 2002
Rahman 2008
Rampton 1995
Rankie Shelton 2009
Ray 2009
Reaser and Wolfram 2007
Reaser et al. 2005
Reyes 2005
Reyes 2007
Reyes and Lo 2009
Richards and Pratt-Johnson 1995
Richardson 1998
Richardson 2003
Rickford 1985
Rickford 1997
Rickford 1999
Rickford and Rickford 1995
Rickford and Rickford 2000
Rickford and Traugott 1985
Rickford and Wolfram 2009
Roberts 2004
Rodriguez et al. 2004
Romaine 1992
Romaine 1999
Rosenthal 1974
Rosenthal and Jacobson 1968
Rubin 1992
Salaberry 2009
Salomone 2010
Santa Ana 2004
Sato 1985
Schecter and Bayley 1997
Schecter and Bayley 2002
Schröder 2003
Schwartz 1982
Sclafani 2008
Scoon 1971
Scott 1993
Scott and Brown 2008
Scott and Smitherman 1985
Scott et al. 2009
Scott et al. 2009
Sealey-Ruiz 2007
Seligman et al. 1972
Seymour and Seymour 1979
Shafer 2009
Shankar 2008
Shankar 2011
Shapiro 2010
Shepherd 2011
Shin and Kubota 2008
Shuy 1969
Shuy 1970
Shuy 1973

Shuy and Fasold 1973
Siegel 1992
Siegel 2005
Siegel 2006
Siegel 2006
Siegel 2008
Siegel 2009
Siegel 2010
Silverstein 1996
Simmons 1991
Simmons and Baines 1998
Singham 1998
Skutnabb-Kangas et al. 1994
Sledd 1969
Sledd 1996
Smith 1979
Smitherman 1973
Smitherman 1973
Smitherman 1974
Smitherman 1977
Smitherman 1981
Smitherman 1995
Smitherman 1997
Smitherman 2000
Smitherman 2001
Smitherman 2004
Smitherman 2004
Smitherman and Cunningham 1997
Smitherman and Quartey-Annan 2011
Smitherman and Scott 1984
Soukup 2000
Souto-Manning 2009
Spack 2006
Spanjer and Layne 1983
Spolsky and Hult 2008
Steele 1992
Steele 2010
Stewart 1978
Stoller 1975
Stoller 1975
Sutcliffe and Wong 1986
Sweetland 2010
Talmy 2004
Talmy 2009
Talmy 2010
Tamura 1996
Tamura 2002
Tamura 2008
Tapia 1999
Tauber 1997
Taylor 1973
Taylor 1975
Taylor 1983
Taylor 1987
Taylor et al. 1983
Terrell and Terrell 1983
Thomas 1983

Thomas 1999
Thomas and Wassink 2010
Torbert 2002
Toribio 2003
Toribio 2006
Troutman 1998
Troyka 2000
Tucker and Lambert 1969
Urciuoli 1996
Valdes et al. 2009
Van Duinen and Wilson 2008
Van Keulen et al. 1998
Vaughn-Cooke 1999
Venezky 1981
Washington 2001
Wassink 1999
Wassink 2005
Wassink and Curzan 2004
Webster 2010
Weiss 1963
Weldon 2000
Wheeler 2010
Wheeler 2010
Wheeler and Swords 2006
Whiteman 1980
Wiley and Lukes 1996
Williams 1970
Williams 1970
Williams 1973
Williams 1975
Williams 1976
Williams and Whitehead 1973
Williams et al. 1971
Williams et al. 1972
Willinsky 1988
Wilson 2001
Wiltse 2011
Winer 1993
Winer 2006
Winford 1976
Winford 2003
Wolf 2001
Wolf and Igboanusi 2006
Wolff 2006
Wolford and Carter 2010
Wolfram 1991
Wolfram 1993
Wolfram 1998
Wolfram 1998
Wolfram 1999
Wolfram 2001
Wolfram 2001
Wolfram 2004
Wolfram 2010
Wolfram and Christian 1976
Wolfram and Christian 1989
Wolfram and Schilling-Estes 2006

Wolfram et al. 2007
Wolfram et al. 2008
Woodworth and Salzer 1971
Wright 1998
Wynne 2002
Yancy 2011

Yokota 2008
Young 2004
Zentella 2006
Zephir 1999
Zuidema 2005

Controversies about Vernacular Englishes in Schools (K)

The evaluation of language is a central and inescapable element of language in society. At times, everyday evaluation boils over into prolonged and heated public debates. The references in this list explain and comment on one or more controversies concerning the role of vernaculars in education.

Popularly dubbed the "Black English trial," *Martin Luther King Elementary School* vs. *Ann Arbor, Michigan School District* captured the public imagination from 1977–1979. After a two-year trial involving extensive expert testimony from professional linguists, the US District Court of Michigan held that the uninformed attitudes of teachers toward Black students' vernacular had created a barrier to their learning. Chambers 1983, Smitherman 1981, and Whiteman 1980 are invaluable collections of the period's scholarly responses to the *King* decision; other resources and commentary emerging from the *King* trial include Ball and Lardner 1997, Joiner 1979, Labov 1982, Sledd 1982, Smitherman 1981, Smitherman and Baugh 2002, and Starks 1983.

In late 1996, the school board of Oakland, California, adopted a resolution affirming that "Ebonics" was the primary language of its largely African American student population and recommended that this be acknowledged in instructional design. This sparked a national and international furor and also reignited linguists' outreach and research regarding effective pedagogical responses to dialect diversity in the classroom. Book-length works inspired by the Ebonics controversy include Baugh 2000, Crawford 2001, Perry and Delpit 1988, Ramirez et al. 2005, and Rickford and Rickford 2000.

A more recent, mini controversy involving AAVE was triggered by the US Drug Enforcement Agency's call for linguists proficient in Ebonics to assist with interpretation of audio-recordings of African Americans suspected of illicit activity. See Alim and Perry 2001 for a response that frames the issue in light of the educational needs of vernacular-speaking students.

From time to time, there have also been public controversies in creole-speaking contexts about the "bad English" of students and what to do about it, typically involving negative reactions from educators or members of the public to proposals by linguists to recognize the legitimacy and systematicity of the creole vernaculars castigated as "bad English," or to teach the standard variety by contrastive analysis of differences between it and the creole, or, more radically to develop bilingual education in creole and standard English. For discussions of such controversies in the Anglophone Caribbean, see Carpenter and Devonish 2010, Carrington and Borely 1977, Cassidy, F. 1970, and Kouwenberg et al. 2011. For a discussion of such controversies in Hawaii see Roberts 2004, Sato 1989, and Tamura 2002, 2008. Several of Siegel's articles (e.g., 1997, 2007) provide general discussions of the issues around which such controversies revolve.

Short Citations for Controversies about Vernacular Englishes in Schools (K)

Adger et al. 1999
Alim 2005
Alim and Perry 2011
Ball and Alim 2006

Ball and Lardner 1997
Ball et al. 1997
Bangura 2010
Baugh 1999

Baugh 2000
Baugh 2000
Baugh 2004
Burlew 1997
Campbell 2005
Carpenter and Devonish 2010
Carrington and Borely 1977
Cassidy 1970
Cazden 1970
Chambers 1983
Champion and Bloome 1995
Collins 1999
Craig 2006
Crawford 2000
Crawford 2001
C-SPAN 1996
C-SPAN 1997
DeBose 2007
Delpit 2002
Dillard 1972
DoBell 2008
Education 1998
Fields 1997
Finegan and Rickford 2004
Gopaul-McNicol 1998
Greenberg et al. 1984
Hopson 2003
Johnson et al. 1998
Joiner 1979
Journal of Black Psychology 1997
Journal of English Linguistics 1998
Journal of Negro Education 1998
Kouwenberg et al. 2011
Kretzschmar 1998
Kretzschmar 2008
Labov 1982
Lanehart 2001
Le Page 1968
Linguistics 1998
Long 1997
Marback 2001
McWhorter 1997
McWhorter 1997
McWhorter 1998
Monteith 1980
Murray 1997

Nero 2006
Parmegiani 2006
Perry and Delpit 1997
Ramirez et al. 2005
Richardson 1998
Rickford 1997
Rickford 1999
Rickford 1999
Rickford 1999
Rickford 2002
Rickford 2006
Rickford and Rickford 2000
Roberts 2004
Sato 1989
Scholar 1997
Sclafani 2008
Secret 1997
Seymour et al. 1999
Sharma and Rickford 2009
Siegel 1997
Siegel 2007
Sledd 1982
Smitherman 1977
Smitherman 1981
Smitherman 1981
Smitherman 1992
Smitherman 1998
Smitherman 1998
Smitherman 2001
Smitherman and Baugh 2002
Smitherman and Quartey-Annan 2011
Starks 1983
Tamura 2002
Tamura 2008
Taylor 1998
Taylor 1999
Troutman 1998
Troyka 2000
Vaughn-Cooke 1999
Weldon 2000
Whiteman 1980
Williams 1997
Wolfram 1998
Wolfram 1999
Wright 1998
Yancy 2011

Language or Dialect Awareness Approach (L)

The works in this topic center on efforts to share the key insights of the descriptivist approach to language with students, teachers, and educational decision-makers, with the broad goals of fostering greater appreciation for vernacular varieties among the public, and improving educational outcomes for vernacular speakers. The language awareness approach was developed in Britain (where the term is typically capitalized) and refers to primary and secondary curriculum and related initiatives catalyzed by a 1972 national commission into the teaching of literacy in the UK. The resulting reforms included efforts to develop greater sensitivity to language structure and use as a means of improving literacy outcomes. Twenty years later, Norman Fairclough's *Critical language awareness* expanded the boundaries of Language Awareness to include opportunities to grapple with issues of language and power, and with a more explicit goal of achieving greater equity and social justice. The influence of this perspective can be seen in the work of H.S. Alim and Amanda Godley, as well as others (e.g., Cameron 1992; Fecho 2000, 2004). The most common application of critical language awareness approach in the United States has been to engage K-12 students in sociolinguistic research in their own communities.

In the United States, the term *dialect awareness* has been more widely used to refer to efforts to sensitize students, teachers, and the general public to language variation. The work of Walt Wolfram and his students and colleagues (including Kirk Hazen, Christine Mallinson, and Jeff Reaser) exemplifies this engaged scholarship tradition. The North Carolina Language and Life Project has been the most sustained and complex dialect awareness initiative, resulting in the development of elementary and middle school curricula, museum exhibits, language documentaries, and other enterprises aimed at spreading the message that language variation is inherent, natural, and widespread. Initiatives in this vein often avoid ideological critiques of how and why non-prestige varieties are marginalized, preferring instead to take a matter-of-fact stance in presenting evidence that all language varieties are systematic, and work to engage the public in celebrating the role of language in local culture and counteract the most destructive stereotypes and myths regarding vernacular varieties and their speakers. Evaluations of these programs have demonstrated that dialect awareness activities do indeed lead to more tolerant, pluralist attitudes toward sociolinguistic diversity (Reaser 2006; Sweetland 2006).

The literature on engaging schoolchildren in exploring language as an object of study on a broad set of topics strikes us as a lively and innovative area of research. Goodman (2003) outlines a conceptual framework for language study in elementary and middle school and brings it to life with rich examples from classroom practice. Two volumes edited by Denham and Loebeck (2005, 2010) collect a diverse set of "linguistics for kids" initiatives in the US and internationally, including teaching students in the Pacific Northwest about language endangerment and death.

Short Citations for Language or Dialect Awareness Approach (L)

Abrahams and Troike 1972
Adger and Christian 2007
Adger et al. 1999
Alim 2003
Allsopp 2000
Alobweede d'Epie 1998
Alvarez and Kolker 1987
Amberg and Vause 2009
Attinasi 1997
Awonusi 1990
Bakari 2003
Baker 1992
Baldwin 1981
Baldwin 1988
Balester 1993
Ball 1997
Ball and Lardner 1997
Ball and Muhammad 2003
Bangura 2010
Baratz 1970
Barnes 2003
Baugh 1988

Baugh 2000
Baugh 2000
Baugh 2005
Baugh 2007
Beck 2009
Becker and Luthar 2002
Berdan 1980
Birch 2001
Birrell 1995
Blake and Cutler 2003
Blodgett and Cooper 1973
Bowie and Bond 1994
Brathwaite 1985
Brown 1968
Brown 2006
Bucholtz 2004
Burling 1973
Cameron 1992
Campbell 1993
Campbell 1994
Cargile 1997
Cargile and Giles 1998

Cargile et al. 2006
Cargile et al. 2010
Carlson and McHenry 2006
Carpenter and Devonish 2010
Carpenter and Devonish 2012
Carrington 1983
Carter 1993
Carter 2007
Carter 2011
Cassidy 1970
Cazden 1970
Cazden 1999
Cecil 1988
Champion and Bloome 1995
Cheatham et al. 2009
Chen-Hayes et al. 1999
Cheshire and Edwards 1991
Cheshire et al. 1989
Christiansen and Farr 2010
Chun 2001
Chun 2004
Chun 2009
Clark et al. 1990
Clark et al. 1991
Coelho 1991
Collins 1988
Committee 2000
Cook and Lodge 1996
Cooper 1995
Corson 1999
Corson 2001
Coup 2008
Covington 1975
Craig 1983
Crawford 2000
Crawford 2001
Cross et al. 2001
Crowl and Macginitie 1976
Crowley 1989
Crowley 1990
Curzan 2002
Dandy 1991
DeBose 2005
DeBose 2007
Del Torto 2010
Delpit 1988
Delpit 1990
Delpit 2002
Delpit 2006
Delpit and Dowdy 2002
DeMeis and Turner 1978
Denham and Lobeck 2005
Denham and Lobeck 2010
DeStefano 1973
Devonish 2007
Devonish and Carpenter 2007
Dowdy 1999

Dundes and Spence 2007
Eades and Siegel 1999
Eades et al. 2006
Easter et al. 1999
Eckert 2000
Edwards 1979
Edwards 1986
Edwards 2010
Egbokhare 2003
Elugbe 1995
Elugbe and Omamor 1991
Evans 2001
Fairclough 1989
Fairclough 1992
Farr 2006
Farr 2011
Farr et al. 2010
Farr et al. 2010
Fasold 2001
Fecho 2000
Fecho 2004
Finegan and Rickford 2004
Fishbein 1973
Fishman 1993
Flanigan 1996
Flower 1996
Flowers 2000
Folb 1980
Fordham 1993
Fordham 1998
Fordham 1999
Fordham and Ogbu 1986
Fought 2003
Fought 2006
Fought 2010
Funkhouser 1973
Gani-Ikilama 1990
Gee 2007
Gere and Smith 1979
Gilmore 1987
Gilyard 1990
Gilyard 1996
Godley and Minnici 2008
Godley et al. 2006
Godley et al. 2007
Goldblatt 1995
Goodman 2003
Green 1963
Green 2002
Greene and Walker 2004
Grogger 2011
Haddix 2008
Haig and Oliver 2003
Haig and Oliver 2003
Hall-Lew and Starr 2010
Hamilton 2005
Hanna 1997

Harris et al. 2001
Higgins 2010
Hilliard 1983
Hilliard 1997
Hilliard 1999
Hinds 1990
Hinton 2001
Hiramoto 2011
Hollie 2001
Holton 1984
Honey 1997
Hoover 1978
Hoover et al. 1995
Hoover et al. 1996
Hopson 2003
Horvat and Lewis 2003
Hosoda 2007
Hutcheson 2005
Igboanusi 2008
Igoudin 2011
Irvine 1990
Irvine 2008
Isenbarger and Smith 1973
Isenbarger and Willis 2006
Jia and Aaronson 2003
Jibril 1995
Johnson 1969
Johnson 1985
Johnson et al. 1998
Joiner 1979
Jordan 1985
Jordan 1989
Jordan 2002
Kachru 1997
Kamhi-Stein 2003
Katz et al. 2009
Kawakami 1999
Kells 2006
Kephart 1992
Kinloch 2010
Kirkland and Jackson 2009
Koch and Gross 1997
Koch et al. 2001
Kochman 1974
Kochman 1981
Kouwenberg et al. 2011
Kretzschmar 1998
Kretzschmar 2008
Kuwahara 1998
Labov 1969
Labov 1970
Labov 1972
Labov 1972
Labov 1982
Labov 1995
Labov and Charity Hudley 2009
Labov and Robins 1969

Lambert and Taylor 1996
Lanehart 1998
Lanehart 2001
Lanehart 2002
Lanehart 2002
Lanehart 2009
Lass 1980
Le Moine and District 1998
Le Page 1968
Leap 1974
Levinson 2005
Linn and Pich,àö¬Æ 1982
Linnes 1998
Lippi-Green 2012
Lo and Reyes 2004
Lobeck 2005
Long 1997
Los Angeles District 1999
Lucas 1997
Luke 1986
Maddahian and Sandamela 2000
Makon et al. 2003
Mallinson and Charity Hudley 2010
Mann 1996
Mann 1998
Mann 2000
Mann 2009
Marback 2001
Marckwardt 1974
Martinez 2006
Massey and Lundy 2001
Matilda 2010
Mays 1977
Mazrui 2006
Mbufong 2001
McCarty et al. 2010
McCourtie 1998
McDavid 1962
McKay and Wong 1996
McKenry 1996
McLaughlin 2010
McMillan and Montgomery 1989
McRae 1994
McWhorter 1997
McWhorter 1998
Meacham 2000
Meacham 2002
Meek 2006
Meier 1999
Mendoza-Denton and Iwai 1993
Miller and Johnson 1974
Mitchell 2005
Mitchell-Kernan 1972
Mocombe 2006
Mohawk 1985
Mordaunt 2011
Morgan 2002

Moses et al. 1976
Mühleisen 2002
Mufwene 2001
Murray 2001
Murrell 1997
Murtagh 1982
Ndolo 1989
Neba et al. 2006
Neba et al. 2006
Nembhard 1983
Nero 1997
Nero 2000
Nero 2006
Nero 2006
Nichols 1977
Nidue 1992
Ntiri 1990
Oetting and Garrity 2006
Ogbu 1991
Ogbu 1992
Ogbu 1999
Ogbu 2003
Ohama et al. 2000
Oladejo 1991
Oliver and Haig 2005
Oliver et al. 2011
Oloruntoba 1992
O'Neal and Ringler 2010
O'Neil 1972
Orbe 1994
Palacas 2001
Palacas 2002
Paris 2011
Parker and Crist 1995
Parmegiani 2006
Patrick 2006
Patterson 1994
Pavlenko 2004
Penalosa 1980
Penfield-Jasper 1982
Perry and Delpit 1997
Perry et al. 2003
Pewewardy 1998
Piche et al. 1978
Piestrup 1973
Pietras and Lamb 1978
Politzer and Hoover 1974
Pon et al. 2003
Postal 1972
Preston 1991
Purcell-Gates 2002
Rahman 2008
Rampton 1995
Rankie Shelton 2009
Ray 2009
Reaser and Wolfram 2007
Reaser et al. 2005

Reyes 2005
Reyes 2007
Reyes and Lo 2009
Richards and Pratt-Johnson 1995
Richardson 1998
Richardson 2003
Rickford 1985
Rickford 1997
Rickford 1999
Rickford and Rickford 1995
Rickford and Rickford 2000
Rickford and Traugott 1985
Rickford and Wolfram 2009
Roberts 2004
Rodriguez et al. 2004
Romaine 1992
Romaine 1999
Rosenthal 1974
Rosenthal and Jacobson 1968
Rubin 1992
Salaberry 2009
Salomone 2010
Santa Ana 2004
Sato 1985
Schecter and Bayley 1997
Schecter and Bayley 2002
Schröder 2003
Schwartz 1982
Sclafani 2008
Scoon 1971
Scott 1993
Scott and Brown 2008
Scott and Smitherman 1985
Scott et al. 2009
Scott et al. 2009
Sealey-Ruiz 2007
Seligman et al. 1972
Seymour and Seymour 1979
Shafer 2009
Shankar 2008
Shankar 2011
Shapiro 2010
Shepherd 2011
Shin and Kubota 2008
Shuy 1969
Shuy 1970
Shuy 1973
Shuy and Fasold 1973
Siegel 1992
Siegel 2005
Siegel 2006
Siegel 2006
Siegel 2008
Siegel 2009
Siegel 2010
Silverstein 1996
Simmons 1991

Simmons and Baines 1998
Singham 1998
Skutnabb-Kangas et al. 1994
Sledd 1969
Sledd 1996
Smith 1979
Smitherman 1973
Smitherman 1973
Smitherman 1974
Smitherman 1977
Smitherman 1981
Smitherman 1995
Smitherman 1997
Smitherman 2000
Smitherman 2001
Smitherman 2004
Smitherman 2004
Smitherman and Cunningham 1997
Smitherman and Quartey-Annan 2011
Smitherman and Scott 1984
Soukup 2000
Souto-Manning 2009
Spack 2006
Spanjer and Layne 1983
Spolsky and Hult 2008
Steele 1992
Steele 2010
Stewart 1978
Stoller 1975
Stoller 1975
Sutcliffe and Wong 1986
Sweetland 2010
Talmy 2004
Talmy 2009
Talmy 2010
Tamura 1996
Tamura 2002
Tamura 2008
Tapia 1999
Tauber 1997
Taylor 1973
Taylor 1975
Taylor 1983
Taylor 1987
Taylor et al. 1983
Terrell and Terrell 1983
Thomas 1983
Thomas 1999
Thomas and Wassink 2010
Torbert 2002
Toribio 2003
Toribio 2006
Troutman 1998
Troyka 2000
Tucker and Lambert 1969
Urciuoli 1996
Valdes et al. 2009
Van Duinen and Wilson 2008

Van Keulen et al. 1998
Vaughn-Cooke 1999
Venezky 1981
Washington 2001
Wassink 1999
Wassink 2005
Wassink and Curzan 2004
Webster 2010
Weiss 1963
Weldon 2000
Wheeler 2010
Wheeler 2010
Wheeler and Swords 2006
Whiteman 1980
Wiley and Lukes 1996
Williams 1970
Williams 1970
Williams 1973
Williams 1975
Williams 1976
Williams and Whitehead 1973
Williams et al. 1971
Williams et al. 1972
Willinsky 1988
Wilson 2001
Wiltse 2011
Winer 1993
Winer 2006
Winford 1976
Winford 2003
Wolf 2001
Wolf and Igboanusi 2006
Wolff 2006
Wolford and Carter 2010
Wolfram 1991
Wolfram 1993
Wolfram 1998
Wolfram 1998
Wolfram 1999
Wolfram 2001
Wolfram 2001
Wolfram 2004
Wolfram 2010
Wolfram and Christian 1976
Wolfram and Christian 1989
Wolfram and Schilling-Estes 2006
Wolfram et al. 2007
Wolfram et al. 2008
Woodworth and Salzer 1971
Wright 1998
Wynne 2002
Yancy 2011
Yokota 2008
Young 2004
Zentella 2006
Zephir 1999
Zuidema 2005

Materials for Instruction (M)

The works included here are materials useful for implementing linguistically-informed approaches in teaching at the elementary, secondary, or post-secondary levels. Most involve exercises or other activities designed to foster vernacular speakers' acquisition of Standard English features. For instance, Brown (2009) uses literature selections to enhance secondary students' awareness of vernacular features, among other strategies; Wheeler (2010) provides contrastive analysis exercises suitable for the elementary classroom; LeMoine (1998) outlines guiding principles for balanced literacy programs that take the vernacular into account and provides sample curriculum maps, lists of multicultural children's literature, and lesson ideas. Similar collections have been designed for teachers working in Creole contexts (Berry & Hudson 1997; Coelho 1988; 1991; Edwards 1975; Pollard 1993; Simmons-McDonald and Ellis 2002), but as for Appalachian speakers, readily available materials seem to be limited to children's literature reflecting the region's unique culture and language (Pendarvis 2010).

As for reading materials that respond to the unique needs of AAVE speakers, the materials in existence suggest two distinct approaches: the creation of special materials, and the adaptation of published children's literature. In terms of specially-created materials, dialect readers (e.g., Davis et al. 1968; Simpkins & Simpkins 1977) accomplish literacy gains through a developmentally-sequenced transition from vernacular features to corresponding standard features; see Rickford & Rickford 1995 for a review. Linguistically-informed reading materials (Penn Reading Initiative and Labov 2010) use detailed quantitative analysis of vernacular/standard contrasts and reading errors to develop instructional texts that provide targeted practice with specific language features that have proven to be 'sticky spots' for AAVE speakers. Penn's *Reading Road* materials—many of which are available for free download online—also include basic phonics lessons streamlined by linguists and illustrated with graffiti-style illustrations likely to be appealing to urban children. Given the impressive gains in reading skills associated with specially created reading materials, it is unfortunate that so few projects of this type have been pursued. As for the second approach—adapting existing literature that includes vernacular features—while this holds great promise, it is limited by a lack of up-to-date, reliable resource lists. Interested readers cannot use typical library search methods, as catalog entries do not typically make mention of AAVE. When adapting published, commercially available children's literature or poetry, teachers must exercise caution in evaluating resources of this sort to ensure that the representation of the vernacular is accurate and, more importantly, that the selection holds genuine literary merit. See Hoover (1998), Lass (1980), Le Moine and LAUSD (1998) for recommended resources.

Testing instruments are an important resource as well. Seymour et al.'s *Diagnostic Evaluation of Language Variation* instruments represent a much-needed commercially-available tool to help language professionals accurately distinguish between dialect difference and true language disorders. The DELV series builds on earlier work in this vein, such as Hoover (1996).

It is worth noting that the topical list for "Materials" is among the shortest in our bibliographic resource. This is not for a lack of searching. Rather, we believe it reflects two very different sorts of pressures on the publishing environment. One is a reflection of publishers' awareness of the exceedingly politically charged environment that surrounds attempts to acknowledge vernacular varieties in school contexts (cf. Wible 2006). The other is the nature of the incentive system of the academy—and the fact that applied work such as curriculum development is deemed less valuable than 'pure' research or more theoretical approaches. The result of both of these pressures is that teachers who wish to try linguistically-informed approaches must, more often than not, create materials themselves. While this leaves ample room for teacher creativity, we suspect that it also limits to some extent the application of sociolinguistic principles in classrooms.

Short Citations for Materials for Instruction (M)

Alvarez and Kolker 1987
Australia 1994
Berger 1990
Berry and Hudson 1997
Brown 2009
Center for Applied Linguistics 1978
Chisolm and Godley 2011
Coelho 1988
Coelho 1991
Crowell and Kolba 1974
Crowell et al. 1974
Curriculum and Authority 2011
Davis et al. 1968
Education 2002
Edwards 1975
Flynn 2011
Goodman 2003
Haussamen et al. 2003
Hazen 2005
Hoover 1989
Hoover 1998
Hudson 1992
Lass 1980
Le Moine 2001
Le Moine and Los Angeles District 1998

Luelsdorff 1973
MacNeil and Cran 2005
Morrow et al. 2009
Palacas 2002
Pendarvis 2010
Penn Reading Initiative and Labov 2010
Perryman-Clark 2009
Pollard 1993
Reaser and Wolfram 2007
Reaser et al. 2005
Sebba 2002
Seymour et al. 2003
Seymour et al. 2003
Seymour et al. 2005
Simmons-McDonald and Ellis 2002
Simmons-McDonald et al. 1997
Simpkins et al. 1977
Smith 1979
Table 1993
Taylor 1994
Thompson et al. 2008
Wheeler and Swords 2006
Wheeler and Swords 2010
Wolfram and Reaser 2005

Narrative, Discourse, Speech Events or Style (N)

References in this category address, in some way, vernacular features above the level of the sentence, including narratives, discourse, style, and communicative norms. This includes speech events, such as signifying; rhetorical devices such as repetition or rhythm; cultur-ally-specific communicative norms, such as expectations regarding direct/indirect speech; and genres of written or oral communication, such as narratives.

This category overlaps to some extent with *Features (F),* since a complete description of a language variety should include not only its words, pronunciations and grammar, but also its speakers' distinctive conversational patterns and ways of making meaning. Mitchell-Kernan 1971, Kochman 1972, Holt 1975, Labov 1972 and Smitherman 1977 are among the earliest sociolinguistic investigations of distinctively African American discourse features and conversational styles. More recent considerations of discourse in AAVE include Lane-hart 2009 and Morris 2007, both of which look at gendered aspects of discourse.

The classroom implications of this aspect of language variation were recognized almost immediately, as indicated by the appearance of practitioner-oriented works on "Black communication," (Abrahams 1972; Abrahams and Gay 1975; Foster 1986; Taylor and Ort-ney 1980; Kochman 1981). Similar texts intended for teachers of Native American students include Greenbaum and Greenbaum 1983; Phillips 1972; Plank 1994; Scollon and Scollon 1979, 1981; investigations of Hawaiian discourse genres, particularly *talk-story,* include Au 1980 and Watson-Gegeo and Boggs 1977. (See also our treatment of this line of research in *Culture and Curriculum (C).*) Many of these early pedagogical considerations of discourse-level features framed the issue in terms of cultural conflict, highlighting differences in the implicit communicative expectations of mainstream-culture teachers and vernacular-culture students.

Regardless of whether conflict is appealed to specifically, work in this vein has tended to analyze the contrast between Black and White styles as putting AAVE speakers at an educational disadvantage. For instance, Heath 1983 juxtaposed White and African American discourse norms—observing, for instance, ethnically divergent patterns of community expectations regarding the types of questions posed to children—and noted the mismatches between Black language socialization patterns and the communicative norms expected in schools.

Research into narratives has been a significant line of inquiry—in part because of the ubiquity and importance of this genre in primary schooling, in part because Labov's (1972) influential development of a canonical structure for verbal narratives has lent itself to fruitful comparative work, and in part because research has shown that narrative patterns are often a site of counterproductive pedagogical responses to the vernacular (cf Silliman and Champion 2002). Michaels 1981, Michaels and Cazden 1986, and Michaels and Collins 1984 illustrate how African American primary students' topic-associating narratives were misinterpreted by teachers, which ultimately decreased students' access to learning opportunities. Champion 2002 deepens and extends research into African American children's storytelling, developing a typology of a wide range of narrative structures, and connecting African American patterns to their West African parallels. Sherifan et al. 2004 investigate teachers' recall and comprehension of Aboriginal students' narratives. Bayley and Schecter 2005 investigate Mexican American students' written narratives in both English and Spanish; among their conclusions is the finding that Spanish-language maintenance does not undermine English-language skill in narrative construction.

Influenced by the tenets of culturally relevant pedagogy, more recent work has eschewed the tendency to compare-and-contrast and has instead attended specifically to how culturally-specific communicative patterns might serve as instructional resources with their own merits (see especially Ball 1992 et passim and Lee 1993 et passim). Meier 2008 builds on three decades of work on Black discourse to develop a list of linguistic abilities likely to be fostered through language socialization in African American communities, including skill with in-the-moment verbal improvisation, extensive experience in the collaborative construction of narratives and stories, and skill in the construction of imaginative stories with culturally-specific features. For instance, vernacular styles of rhythm and repetition can be used to engage student interest and participation (Bohn 2003; Cahnmann 2000); and African American rhetorical features can serve as the organizing principle for college-level composition courses (Campbell 2005; Gilyard 1996; Richardson and Jackson 2004).

Short Citations for Narrative, Discourse, Speech Events or Style (N)

Aarons et al. 1969
Abrahams and Gay 1975
Abrahams and Troike 1972
Adger 1998
Alim 2003
Alim 2004
Alim 2004
Alim and Baugh 2007
Anderson 1989
Anderson 1990
Au 1980
Au and Kawakami 1985
Ball 1992
Ball 1995
Ball and Lardner 2005
Bartelt 2001
Bayley and Schecter 2005
Birrell 1995
Blake and NYU 2009

Bohn 2003
Boone 2003
Brice and Montgomery 1996
Bryan 2001
Cahnmann 2000
Campbell 1994
Campbell 1994
Campbell 1997
Campbell 2005
Carter 2011
Cazden 1970
Cazden 1988
Cazden 1999
Champion 1998
Champion 2003
Chapman 1994
Christie 1996
Cooper 1995
Dandy 1991

Delain et al. 1985
Delpit and Dowdy 2002
Desai and Marsh 2005
DoBell 2008
Eagleson et al. 1982
Edwards 1979
Edwards and Sienkewicz 1990
Farr 1986
Farr 2005
Farr 2005
Farr 2007
Feagans 1982
Finegan and Rickford 2004
Fordham 1993
Foster 1986
Foster 1989
Foster 1992
Foster 1995
Foster 2001
Gee 1989
Gee 2007
Gonzalez 2006
Goodwin 1990
Green and Conner 2009
Greenbaum 1985
Greenbaum and Greenbaum 1983
Hall and Damico 2007
Hart and Risley 1995
Hart and Risley 2003
Heath 1983
Heath 2000
Hester 1996
Hilliard 1992
Holt 1975
Hoover 1991
Horton-Ikard 2009
Hwa-Froelich et al. 2007
Hyon and Sulzby 1994
Jackson and Richardson 2003
Katz and Champion 2009
Kernan-Mitchell 1971
Kirkland 2010
Kochman 1972
Kochman 1981
Kochman 1989
Kynard 2008
Labov 1969
Labov 1970
Labov 1972
Lanehart 2001
Lanehart 2002
Lanehart 2009
Lee 1993
Lee 1995
Lee 1995
Lee 1997
Lee 2005

Lee 2006
Linn 1995
Lucas and Borders 1994
Mainess et al. 2002
Makoni et al. 2003
Malcolm 1979
Malcolm 1982
Malcolm 1994
Malcolm 2011
Malcolm and Rochecouste 1998
Malcolm et al. 1999
Malcolm et al. 2003
Marcuzzi 1986
Martin-Jones and Jones 2000
McCarty 2005
McCarty and Watahomigie 1998
McKay and Wong 1996
Meier 2008
Michaels 1981
Michaels and Cazden 1986
Michaels and Collins 1984
Mitchell and Henderson 1990
Mocombe 2006
Morgan 2002
Morgan 2010
Morris 2007
Mu"hleisen 2002
Mufwene et al. 1998
Nichols 1989
Norment 1995
Norment 2005
Orbe 1994
Paris 2011
Patterson 1994
Philips 1972
Plank 1994
Pollard 1995
Pollard 1996
Pon et al. 2003
Richardson 2003
Richardson 2008
Richardson and Jackson 2004
Rickford 1999
Rickford and Rickford 2000
Roberts 1983
Robinson-Zanartu 1996
Romaine 1984
Schecter and Bayley 2002
Scollon and Scollon 1979
Scollon and Scollon 1981
Scott 1990
Sealey-Ruiz 2005
Sharifian 2001
Sharifian 2005
Sharifian et al. 2004
Silliman and Champion 2002
Simmons-McDonald and Robertson 2006

Smitherman 1977
Smitherman 1994
Smitherman 2000
Smitherman 2004
Smitherman 2006
Smitherman and Baugh 2002
Souto-Manning 2009
Speidel 1987
Sutcliffe and Wong 1986
Syrquin 2006
Taylor and Matsuda 1988

Taylor and Ortony 1980
Troutman 1998
Urciuoli 1985
Vernon-Feagans 1996
Watson-Gegeo and Boggs 1977
Webster 2010
Williams 1975
Wyatt 1999
Youssef 2006
Zentella 1997
Zentella 2006

Oral and Aural Arts: Speaking and Listening (O)

This category brings together work on the oral and aural components of language. This includes research on oral production and comprehension, as well as instructional advice in speaking and listening, i.e., the "other" language arts, as distinct from the oftentimes more heavily emphasized reading and writing skills.

One strand of research represented here relates to the 1970s "linguistic interference" hypothesis, which held that vernacular speakers are hindered in gaining proficiency in the standard due to important structural differences that hold between their variety and the standard. Experimental work investigating vernacular speakers' ability to produce and comprehend Standard English includes Ames et al. 1971, Frentz 1971, Johnson 1974, and Marwit and Marwit 1976. In a related vein, we include work on the relationship between oral and written language, such as Farr and Janda 1985, Groff 1978, Kennedy 2006, Mayer and New 2010, and Sperling 1996.

A number of references provide instructional advice for increasing proficiency in speaking and listening as language arts skills; these include Berger 1990, Campbell 1994, Cullinan et al. 1974, Elifson 1977, Greene and Walker 2004, Harris-Wright 1999, Mantell 1974, and others. Wheeler and Swords (2004), for example, emphasize the importance of teaching code-switching and contrastive analysis in order to foster students' ability in the standard, with the goal being for students to recognize that both vernacular and standard varieties of English can be appropriate modes of expression depending on the formality of the situation.

References in this category that deal with vernaculars other than AAVE include work on Asian American English (Cheng 1987; Fu 1995; Hosoda 2007; Shin and Milroy 1999), Aboriginal Australian English (Sharifian et al. 2004), Latino English (Wolford 2006), Native American English (Reyhner 1994), and various Creole Englishes (Boggs 1985; Craig 1966; Pratt-Johnson 1993; Reynolds 1999; Richards and Pratt-Johnson 1995; Siegel 1992; Simmons-McDonald and Robertson 2006; Van Sickle et al. 2002; Wheldall and Joseph 1985).

Short Citations for Oral and Aural Arts: Speaking and Listening (O)

Abrahams and Gay 1975
Adger et al. 2007
Ames et al. 1971
Baratz 1969
Baugh 1999
Bayley 2009
Berger 1990
Blake and NYU 2009
Boggs 1985

Brooks 1985
Campbell 1994
Cazden 1999
Cheng 1987
Cole and Taylor 1990
Craig 1966
Craig 1983
Craig et al. 2005
Cullinan et al. 1974

Elifson 1977
Farr and Janda 1985
Feldman et al. 1977
Fillmore and Snow 2000
Foster 1989
Foster 2001
Frentz 1971
Fry and Johnson 1973
Fryburg 1974
Fu 1995
Gay and Tweney 1976
Genshaft and Hirt 1974
Goodwin 1990
Groff 1978
Hall and Turner 1971
Hall et al. 1973
Harris-Wright 1987
Harris-Wright 1999
Hoffman 1992
Hosoda 2007
Isaacs 1996
Johnson 1974
Kachuck 1978
Kennedy 2006
Kochman 1972
Kochman 1981
Kochman 1989
Labov 1969
Labov 1972
Le Moine and District 1998
Lee 1993
Lippi-Green 2012
Luelsdorff 1973
Mantell 1974
Marwit and Marwit 1976

Matlock 1995
Maxwell 1979
Mayer and New 2010
Michaels 1981
Michaels and Collins 1984
Nelson and McRoskey 1978
Plank 1994
Pratt-Johnson 1993
Ray 2009
Reyhner 1994
Reynolds 1999
Richards and Pratt-Johnson 1995
Rickford and Wolfram 2009
Robbins 1989
Scott 1990
Seitz 1975
Sharifian et al. 2004
Shin and Milroy 1999
Shuy 1973
Siegel 1992
Simmons-McDonald and Robertson 2006
Sperling 1996
Sullivan 1971
Talmy 2004
Tarone 1973
Thompson et al. 2004
Treiman 2004
Van Sickle et al. 2002
Washington and Craig 1994
Wheeler 2003
Wheeler and Swords 2004
Wheldall and Joseph 1985
Whitney 2005
Wolford 2006

Politics and Policy (P)

This category overlaps naturally with the topic of *Ideology, Attitudes and Identity (I),* but the references listed here focus more on the policies that schools and school systems adopt with respect to vernacular varieties, and the local, state, and national political contexts in which such policies are negotiated. In addition to explicit executive, legislative, or judicial acts regarding vernacular varieties, issues such as authority, power, public opinion, and individual and group *rights* are related and recurring themes in the references in this topical list.

Two policymaking efforts related to AAVE—the case *Martin Luther King Junior Elementary School Children et al. v. Ann Arbor School District* (1979), and the Oakland school board's 1996 "Ebonics" resolution—each generated a heated public debate. The related sociolinguistic literature is included in this volume's topical list for *Controversies about Vernacular Englishes in Schools (K).* But by and large, AAVE has rarely been a topic of official policymaking. Consequently, the literature on African American language policy consists largely of analyses of missed opportunities and recommendations for possible approaches (cf Baugh 1995, Smitherman 2002). For instance, although the language of African Americans was not a consideration in the landmark 1954 US Supreme Court decision in *Brown v. Board of Education of Topeka* that led to the legal desegregation of public schools, Ball and Alim 2006 and Baugh 2006 consider what might have been if the case had provided remedies related to AAVE. Similarly, DeBose 2005 exhorts engaged scholars to take affirmative steps informed by a language planning perspective—such as corpus planning and status planning—to actively confront widespread and lingering misinformation and negative attitudes toward AAVE.

By contrast, scholars interested in language policy in creole and Native American contexts are able to consider the actual effects of policies as implemented. In pidgin and creole contexts, the issue of orthography and the standardization of spelling has been a policy topic of recurring concern (Crowley 1990; Devonish 1983, 2008; Sala 2009). The affirmation of vernacular varieties as languages of formal instruction is another policy issue of considerable interest: for pidgins and creoles, see Carrington 1976; Craig 1980; and McCourtie 1998, among others; for discussions of Native American languages, see Aguilera and LeCompte 2009; Leap 1978; and Spack 2002.

Corson 1999 provides an excellent starting point for readers in need of an in-depth primer on how to develop a school-level language policy—an activity that could serve as an important leverage point for effecting greater sociolinguistic awareness and justice, and strikes us as having been an underused change tactic in the US context. Rickford and Rickford 2010 and Wheeler 2010 offer insight into navigating the political landscape of local schools or school districts in order to implement sociolinguistic programs.

The Conference on College Composition and Communication's 1974 resolution, "Students' Right to Their Own Language," was intended to directly influence policy and practice in language arts instruction, and scholars inspired by its legacy continue to advocate for explicit policymaking efforts; see Kinloch 2005 et passim; Scott et al. 2009; Smitherman 1999.

Selections which consider the political implications of uncritical, moderate, or critical stances toward Standard English include Alatis 1970; Baratz 1970; Crowley 1989; Curzan 2002; Delpit 1988; Honey 1997; Kochman 1974; Loebeck 2005; Richardson 1998; and Wiley and Lukes 1996.

The No Child Left Behind Act (NCLB)—the George W. Bush administration's version of the Elementary and Secondary Education Act, the major piece of US federal legislation concerning the education of children in public schools—has inspired Balter and Grossman 2009, Baugh and Welborn 2009, and Cleary 2008 to consider the implications of its core policies for vernacular speakers. (Bilingual education issues emerging from NCLB are beyond the scope of this volume, but see Menken 2009 for a review article that includes a partially annotated bibliography of literature on dual language instruction and English Language Learners under NCLB.)

Clark et al. 1990, 1991 critique language awareness policies in the UK. Skutnabb-Kangas et al. 1994 frame language rights issues in a global policy context.

Short Citations for Politics and Policy (P)

Adamson 2005	Baugh 2000
Adger and Christian 2007	Baugh 2006
Adger et al. 1999	Baugh 2006
Aguilera and LeCompte 2009	Baugh 2007
Alatis 1970	Baugh 2009
Alim 2005	Baugh and Welborn 2009
Alim and Baugh 2010	Bereiter and Engelmann 1966
Appel and Verhoeven 1994	Brayboy and Castagno 2009
Attinasi 1997	Bryan 2010
Ball and Alim 2006	Carpenter and Devonish 2010
Balter and Grossman 2009	Carrington 1976
Bangura 2010	Carrington 1983
Baratz 1970	Carrington 1997
Baugh 1995	Carter 1993

Cha and Ham 2008
Chambers 1983
Champion and Bloome 1995
Christie 1996
Clachar 2004
Clark et al. 1990
Clark et al. 1991
Cleary 2008
Clemente 2005
Conference ... Communication 1974
Corson 1999
Corson 2001
Corson 2003
Craig 1971
Craig 1980
Craig 2008
Crawford 2000
Crowley 1989
Crowley 1990
C-SPAN 1996
Curzan 2002
DeBose 2005
DeBose 2007
Delpit 1988
Delpit 1995
Delpit and Dowdy 2002
Denham and Lobeck 2010
Devonish 1983
Devonish 2007
Devonish 2008
Devonish and Carpenter 2007
Deyhle and Swisher 1997
DoBell 2008
Dyson and Smitherman 2009
Eades 2003
Edwards 2010
Eggington 1994
Fairclough 1989
Fairclough 1992
Farr et al. 2010
Farr et al. 2010
Fillmore 2004
Finegan and Rickford 2004
Fishman 1993
Flanigan 1984
Fought 2006
Gilyard 1996
Godley and Minnici 2008
Haddix 2008
Higgins 2010
Holt 1975
Honey 1997
Hoover et al. 1995
Hornberger 2005
Huebner 1985
Hutcheson 1999
Ibukun 2010

Igboanusi 2008
ILEA Afro-Caribbean Language et al. 1990
Johnson et al. 1998
Joiner 1979
Jordan 1985
Jordan 1989
Jordan 2002
Kachru 1997
Kaplan 1994
Kinloch 2005
Kinloch 2009
Kinloch 2010
Kirkland and Jackson 2009
Kirkpatrick 2002
Kleifgen and Bond 2009
Kochman 1974
Koskinen 2010
Kretzschmar 1998
Kretzschmar 2008
Kymlicka and Patten 2003
Labov 1982
Lanehart 1998
Lanehart 2001
Lanehart 2009
Leap 1974
Leap 1978
Leap 1993
Lippi-Green 2012
Lobeck 2005
Makoni et al. 2003
Malcolm 2000
Malcolm 2007
Malcolm and Königsberg 2007
Malcolm et al. 1999
Malcolm et al. 2003
Mann 1996
Mazrui 2006
McCarty 2005
McCarty et al. 2010
McCourtie 1998
McWhorter 1998
Menken 2009
Migge et al. 2010
Migge et al. 2010
Monroy Ochoa and Cadiero-Kaplan 2004
Morgan 2002
Morren and Morren 2007
Murrell 1997
Neba et al. 2006
Nero 2006
Norment 2005
Ntiri 1990
O'Neil 1972
Osborn 2007
PACE 1990
Parks 2000
Parmegiani 2006

Paulston and McLaughlin 1994
Pavlenko 2004
Penfield 1975
Ramirez et al. 2005
Ray 1996
Reyhner and Hurtado 2008
Richardson 1998
Rickford and Wolfram 2009
Roberts 2007
Robertson 1996
Romaine 1992
Sala 2009
Salomone 2010
Santa Ana 2002
Sato 1985
Sato 1989
Saville 1978
Scott et al. 2009
Scott et al. 2009
Sharifian 2008
Shin and Kubota 2008
Shnukal 1992
Siegel 1992
Siegel 1996
Siegel 1999
Siegel 2002
Siegel 2005
Siegel 2005
Siegel 2006
Siegel 2006
Siegel 2007
Siegel 2008
Siegel 2009
Simmons-McDonald 1996
Simmons-McDonald 2004
Simpkins and Simpkins 2009
Skutnabb-Kangas et al. 1994
Sledd 1969
Sledd 1972
Sledd 1982
Smith 1975
Smitherman 1977
Smitherman 1981
Smitherman 1981
Smitherman 1995
Smitherman 1997
Smitherman 1999

Smitherman 1999
Smitherman 2000
Smitherman 2000
Smitherman 2001
Smitherman 2002
Smitherman 2004
Smitherman 2006
Smitherman and Baugh 2002
Smitherman and Quartey-Annan 2011
Smitherman and Villanueva 2003
Spack 2002
Spolsky and Hult 2008
Starks 1983
Stockman 2007
Stoller 1975
Strickland and Alvermann 2004
Stuart 2006
Sutcliffe and Wong 1986
Tamura 1996
Tamura 2002
Tamura 2008
Taylor 1975
Taylor 1998
Taylor 1999
Toribio 2003
Urciuoli 1996
Vaughn-Cooke 1999
Venezky 1981
Washington 1998
Watson-Gegeo 1994
Wheeler 2006
Wheeler 2010
Whiteman 1980
Wible 2006
Wiley and Lukes 1996
Williams 1975
Williams 1975
Willinsky 1988
Wiltse 2011
Winer 2006
Wiruk 2000
Wolford and Carter 2010
Wolfram 2001
Yancy 2011
Young 2009
Zentella 2006

Language Acquisition (Q)

Works in this topical list encompass both first-language acquisition and second-language acquisition, two areas that are related but usually distinguished in terms of the disciplinary "homes" of interested scholars, and corresponding differences in research methods and orientations. Studies of first language acquisition investigate how a child learns his or her native language, and tend to take a descriptive, developmental view, documenting the natural unfolding of language development in the early years. Studies of second language acquisition investigate how a child or adult learns a second (or third, fourth, etc.) non-native language, and as this often (but not always) happens through formal language instruction, instructional methods are of relatively greater interest. Both of these areas have practical importance in education: the former because knowing how speakers of AAVE and other vernaculars acquire their first language is a vital component in distinguishing normal acquisition from possible speech and language disorders, and the latter because research in this domain has a direct bearing on how instructional strategies and materials can be developed for optimal learning of a second language or dialect.

Accordingly, the works listed under this keyword fall into two major categories. The first has to do with first language acquisition for speakers of vernacular Englishes, especially AAVE. Here we find works focusing on acquisition of phonological and grammatical features (Bland-Stewart 2003; H. Craig et al. 2003; Harris and Moran 2006; Seymour and Seymour 1981; Seymour and Ralabate 1985; Stockman 1996), word and sentence structure (H. Craig 2002; H. Craig and Washington 1994; de Villiers and Johnson 2007; Oetting et al. 2010; Seymour and Roeper 1999; Sharma and Rickford 2009; Stockman and Vaughn-Cooke 1992; and Washington and Craig 2002), and discourse structure Craig and Washington 1995; Hester 1996; Craig et al. 1998; Horton-Ikard 2009; Washington and Craig 1994). A number of works also address the relationship between child language acquisition and external factors such as mother-child communication (Blake 1993), socioeconomic status and gender (Washington 1998), family, community and school (Wyatt 2001), and culture and class (Horton-Ikard 2006). For book-length syntheses of this sometimes highly technical literature, we recommend especially *Malik Goes to School: Examining the Language Skills of African American Students from Preschool to Fifth Grade* (Craig 2006) and *Language and the African American Child* (Green 2011). Interested readers are also referred to our topical list for *Communication Disorders (D)* for other relevant work.

The other major category of works included under this topic is second language acquisition of English by speakers of other languages, including Chinese (Jia et al. 2002; Jia and Aaronson 2003), Creole English (Simmons-McDonald 1994), Creole French (Simmons-McDonald 1994, 1998), Korean (Shin and Milroy 1999), Pima (Miller 1977), and Spanish (Valdes 2001). Jia and Aaronson (2003), for example, report on a three-year study of ten Chinese immigrants to the United States between the ages of five and sixteen, finding that the younger children (those aged nine or below at the time of immigration) are generally more rapid in their adoption of English as a preferred language.

We include here as well a number of recent works addressing issues that arise in language contact situations, such as language transfer (Gut 2007; Sharma 2004), language loss and shift (Berlin 2000; Hinton 2001; Torres 2010) and the development of stylized forms of English employed by minority speakers (Del Torto 2010; Samant 2010; Sharma 2011).

Short Citations for Language Acquisition (Q)

Adamson 2005
Anderson 2004
Battle 1996
Baugh 1992
Berlin 2000
Blake 1993
Bland-Stewart 2003
Bogatz et al. 1986
Champion et al. 2003
Chanethom 2010
Charity et al. 2004
Craig 1996
Craig and Washington 1994
Craig and Washington 1995

Craig and Washington 2002
Craig and Washington 2004
Craig and Washington 2004
Craig and Washington 2006
Craig et al. 1998
Craig et al. 1998
Craig et al. 2003
Craig et al. 2003
Craig et al. 2005
Day 1989
de Villiers and Johnson 2007
Del Torto 2010
Feagans 1982
Fish and Pinkerman 2002

Green 2011
Gupta 1991
Gupta 1994
Gut 2007
Harris and Moran 2006
Hart and Risley 1995
Hart and Risley 2003
Hester 1996
Hinton 2001
Horton-Ikard 2006
Horton-Ikard 2009
Ivy and Masterson 2011
Jackson and Pearson 2010
Jia and Aaronson 2003
Jia et al. 2002
Johnson 1974
Johnson et al. 1998
Kamhi et al. 1996
Meade 2001
Meier 2008
Miller 1977
National Research Council 2010
Oetting et al. 2010
Pearson et al. 2009
Rivers et al. 2004
Romaine 1984
Romaine 1988
Romaine 1992
Samant 2010
Seymour and Ralabate 1985
Seymour and Roeper 1999
Seymour and Seymour 1981
Sharma 2005
Sharma 2005

Sharma 2011
Sharma and Rickford 2009
Shin and Milroy 1999
Siegel 2010
Siegel 2010
Silliman et al. 2002
Simmons-McDonald 1994
Simmons-McDonald 1998
Simmons-McDonald 2001
Stockman 1986
Stockman 1989
Stockman 1996
Stockman 2007
Stockman 2010
Stockman and Vaughn-Cooke 1992
Taylor and Leonard 1998
Thomas-Tate et al. 2006
Torres 2010
Troike 1972
Valdes 2001
Valdes et al. 2009
Van Hofwegen and Wolfram 2010
Van Keulen et al. 1998
Vernon-Feagans 1996
Washington 1998
Washington and Craig 1992
Washington and Craig 1994
Washington and Craig 1999
Washington and Craig 2002
Washington et al. 1998
Wyatt 1995
Wyatt 2001
Wyatt and Seymour 1999
Youssef 2006

Reading (R)

As Washington (2003, pp. 1-2) has noted, "Reading undergirds most learning. By implication, reading failure bears a direct relationship to student success in most other subject areas." It is therefore not surprising that reading should receive particular attention from researchers trying to understand and reduce educational disparities in the United States (Jencks and Phillips 1998; Singham 2005; Paige and Witty 2010). And the role that language variation might play in the inequitable reading outcomes among African American and Latino students is an important research question (Snow et al. 1998).

So far as AAVE is concerned, one question that has long been considered is whether the differences between AAVE and standard English might account for the low reading scores of African American students, especially (but not only—see Singham 2002; Ogbu 2003) those in low income or inner city districts. An early suggestion was that teachers should not confuse differences in pronunciation with mistakes in reading (decoding). For instance, as Labov (1967) noted, the child who reads "He passed by both of them" as *He pass' by bof o' dem* may have correctly "read" the printed sentence (i.e., decoded/comprehended all the relevant meanings from the words and inflections), but reproduced it in accord with the pronunciation and grammar rules of his or her spoken dialect. Goodman (1965) made a similar point, and advocated, among other things, that teachers not count dialect-related oral miscues as reading errors. Subsequent researchers (Harber 1982; Craig et al. 2004) found that doing this substantially improved the reading achievement scores of many African American students, but that it was perhaps not the panacea we might have anticipated. For instance, in Harber's study, AAVE speakers continued to underperform Standard English speakers in reading, even when dialect differences were taken into account; and in Craig et al.'s study, modifying scoring protocols for dialect differences improved AAVE speakers' reading accuracy and rate, but not their comprehension.

In general, as Washington and Craig (2001) have noted, the dialect interference hypothesis that more vernacular usage would correlate with greater reading difficulties (Baratz 1969) was not supported in terms of phonological or pronunciation features (Melmed 1970; Rystrom 1970, 1973–74), although the evidence for morphosyntactic or grammatical interference was stronger (Ames et al. 1971; Bartel and Axelrod 1973; Steffensen et al. 1982 supporting it, while Nolen 1972 and Simons and Johnson 1974 disconfirmed it). Some of this literature is relevant to the related issue of whether reading for vernacular speakers should first be taught in the vernacular, via dialect readers—a topic that we consider separately in this volume. It is worth noting here, however, Rickford's (2002) observation that Nolen 1972, Simons and Johnson 1974 and others "are all non-longitudinal one-time studies" that do not consider the pedagogical effect of taking dialect differences into account over time (as in Simpkins and Simpkins 1981). Moreover, as Craig and Washington (2001) have noted, the early studies concentrated on a small set of AAVE features, and were conducted at a time when we knew less about the complexity of AAVE and how student's use of it varies by age and grade level than we do now. Holly Craig and her research team at the University of Michigan have been using more recently a Dialect Density Measure that takes into account more than thirty pronunciation and grammatical features of AAVE (see Craig et al. 2004, 2009), and they have ongoing projects that are considering the role of dialect interference in reading with new experimental data and from fresh perspectives. William Labov, Bettina Baker and other researchers at the University of Pennsylvania have also been doing more detailed linguistic analyses of the reading errors of African American and Latina/o students than were done before (Labov 2001; Labov and Baker 2010), resulting in more refined ways of distinguishing dialect differences from reading errors, and in materials for teaching and tutoring vernacular speakers that appear to be more successful than their predecessors (see Penn Reading Initiative and Labov 2010).

Although it is generally not as informed by theory and practice in the field or reading research as it might be—about phonics, phonemic awareness, whole word approaches, vocabulary knowledge, comprehension strategies and other topics (see for instance, Chall 1996, 2000, Kamil et al. 2011; McCormack and Pasquarelli 2010; Morrow et al. 2009; Snow et al. 1998, 2005)—the literature on AAVE and reading is so deep and varied that it may be helpful to single out some other bibliography items for mention. Washington 2003, cited above for its quotation on the importance of reading, is an impressively concise and informative overview of child-based, home-based, and instruction-based explanations for the reading disparities between African American and White students. Edited volumes that address language and literacy among AAVE speakers include Baratz and Shuy 1969 and Harris et al. 2001. Meier 2008 is a recent book-length overview written for an audience of teachers that relates African American linguistic and rhetorical behavior to reading, with greater focus on comprehension than many other works relating AAVE and reading. Scarborough et al. 2003 is a recent study that returns to the issue of distinguishing dialect differences from reading errors. Drawing on new data from Ohio, Louisiana and Washington, DC, Charity et al. (2004) show that students' use of Standard English correlates with higher reading achievement, and also reveals regional differences in AAVE use in story retellings. Cunningham 1976, an older study, remains valuable for its startling indication that teachers correct dialect-related reading miscues much more often than non-dialect related miscues, even when the former do not affect meaning or interpretation. Labov and Robins (1969), another early study, was one of the first to suggest that functional and cultural conflicts between the school and the street might be more significant than structural difference between AAVE and Standard English in limiting African American students' progress in reading, a conclusion that was reached, in a somewhat different way, by Goodman and Buck 1973 (revising Goodman 1965). A. Rickford 1999, like Carter 1971, Lass 1980, Le Moine 1998 and others, emphasizes the value of culturally congruent reading materials (including African American characters, themes and vernacular language) in maintaining and enhancing reading motivation among African American learners.

Outside of AAVE, we have found relatively little on reading as it relates to dialect variation, and what exists involves less experimental evidence. For English-based *Creoles*, see Au 2008, D. Craig 1999, IDB and CDB 2009, Kephardt 1992, McRae 1994, Simmons-McDonald 2006, and Winer 1999. For *Latina/o and Native American* students and reading, see, among others: Buly 2005, Constantido and Hurtado 2006, Fitzgerald et al. 2008, Mayfield 1985, McCarty and Watahomigie 1998, Miller and Johnson 1974, Narang 1974, Neufeld and Fitzgerald 2001, Neufeld et al. 2006, Reyhner and Hurtado 2008, and Wolfram et al. 1979. For studies of reading involving speakers of *Asian, Asian American and other vernacular Englishes*, including Appalachian, see Gottardo et al. 2001, Hirvela 2010, Leeper 2003, Purcell-Gates 1993, 1995, 1996, Rentel and Kennedy 1972, Stewart 1969a, and Weinstein-Shr 1994.

Short Citations for Reading (R)

Aarons et al. 1969
Abrahams and Troike 1972
Adger et al. 1999
Adger et al. 2007
Alatis 1970
Ames et al. 1971
Au 2008
Bailey 1970
Ball 1994
Baratz 1969
Baratz 1969
Baratz 1970
Baratz 1973
Baratz and Shuy 1969
Bartel and Axelrod 1973
Baugh 1999
Baugh 1999
Bell and Clark 1998
Berdan 1980
Bougere 1981
Brayboy and Castagno 2009
Brock et al. 2009
Brooks 1985
Bulletin 1987
Buly 2005
Burke 1973
Burke et al. 1982
Carter 1971
Chall 1996
Chall 2000
Chall et al. 1990
Charity Hudley 2008
Charity et al. 2004
Connor and Craig 2006
Costantino and Hurtado 2006
Craig 1999

Craig and Washington 2004
Craig and Washington 2004
Craig and Washington 2006
Craig et al. 1998
Craig et al. 2003
Craig et al. 2004
Cross and Aldrige 1989
Cullinan 1974
Cunningham 1976
Delpit 2006
DeStefano 1973
District 1999
Fasold 1969
Fasold and Shuy 1970
Fitzgerald et al. 2008
Flanigan 1985
Francis and Reyhner 2002
Fry and Johnson 1973
Gadsen and Wagner 1995
Gaquin 2006
Gee 2007
Gemake 1981
Gillet and Gentry 1983
Gladney 1973
Goodman 1965
Goodman and Buck 1973
Gottardo et al. 2001
Gunderson 1970
Gutierrez et al. 2009
Hall and Turner 1971
Hall and Turner 1973
Hall et al. 1975
Hammond et al. 2005
Harber 1977
Harber 1981
Harber 1982

Harber and Beatty 1978
Harber and Bryen 1976
Harris et al. 2001
Hart et al. 1980
Hefflin and Barksdale-Ladd 2001
Hirvela 2010
Hockman 1973
Hoover and Fabian 2000
Hunt 1974
IDB and CDB 2009
Isaacs 1996
Jencks and Phillips 1998
Jones 1965
Jones 1979
Kachuck 1978
Kamhi-Stein 2003
Kamil et al. 2011
Kephart 1992
Kirkland 2010
Labov 1967
Labov 1972
Labov 1995
Labov 2001
Labov 2003
Labov and Baker 2010
Labov and Robins 1969
Ladson-Billings 1992
Laffey and Shuy 1973
Lass 1980
Lass 1980
Le Moine and District 1998
Leap 1993
Leaverton 1971
Leaverton 1973
Lee 1993
Lee 1995
Lee 1995
Lee 1997
Lee 2007
Leeper 2003
Lems et al. 2010
Lucas and Singer 1976
Maddahian and Sandamela 2000
Malancon and Malancon 1993
Martin-Jones and Jones 2000
Marwit and Neumann 1974
Mayfield 1985
McCarty 2005
McCarty and Watahomigie 1998
McCormack and Pasquarelli 2010
McCreight 2011
McRae 1994
Meier 2008
Melmed 1971
Melmed 1973
Miller and Johnson 1974
Moats 1994

Monteith 1980
Moore 1999
Morrow et al. 2009
Musgrave 1962
Narang 1974
Nero 2006
Neufeld and Fitzgerald 2001
Neufeld et al. 2006
Nichols 1977
Nolen 1972
Padak 1981
Paige et al. 2010
Penn Reading Initiative and Labov 2010
Potter 1981
Purcell-Gates 1993
Purcell-Gates 1995
Purcell-Gates 1996
Reaser and Adger 2008
Rentel and Kennedy 1972
Reyhner 1994
Reyhner and Hurtado 2008
Rickford 1997
Rickford 1999
Rickford 1999
Rickford 1999
Rickford 2001
Rickford 2002
Rickford 2002
Rickford and Rickford 1995
Rosa 1994
Ruddell 1965
Rystrom 1970
Rystrom 1973
Scarborough et al. 2003
Schwartz 1982
Serwer 1969
Shields 1979
Shuy 1969
Shuy 1973
Silliman et al. 2002
Simmons-McDonald 2006
Simons 1974
Simons 1979
Simons and Johnson 1974
Simpkins 2002
Simpkins and Simpkins 1981
Simpkins et al. 1977
Singham 1998
Singham 2005
Sligh and Conners 2003
Smitherman 1981
Snow et al. 1998
Snow et al. 2005
Somervill 1975
Southard and Muller 1993
Steffensen et al. 1982
Stewart 1969

Stoller 1975
Straker 1985
Strickland and Alvermann 2004
Strickland and Stewart 1974
Tatham 1970
Taylor 1983
Taylor 1987
Taylor 1994
Taylor and Dorsey-Gaines 1988
Terry 2008
Terry et al. 2010
Thompson et al. 2004
Torrey 1970
Troutman and Falk 1982
Venezky 1981
Waitt 2006

Washington 2001
Washington 2003
Washington and Craig 2001
Weber 1973
Weber 1983
Weinstein-Shr 1994
Wheeler et al. 2012
Williams 1970
Winer 1999
Wolfram 1970
Wolfram 1994
Wolfram and Christian 1976
Wolfram and Fasold 1969
Wolfram et al. 1979
Wolfram et al. 2007
Wroge 1998

Strategies for Instruction (S)

What are the implications of language variation for classroom instruction? An early, ubiquitous, and still timely recommendation is for instructors to adopt a descriptive rather than prescriptive approach toward language variation, which entails starting from the premise that all dialects are linguistically equal and thereby rejecting counterproductive myths about the vernacular and its speakers. Allen 1985, Cheatham et al. 2009, Hollie 2001, and Zuidema 2005 elaborate on what instruction embodying the basic premise of awareness and respect might look like. *Dialects in Schools and Communities* (Adger, Wolfram, and Christian 2007), now in its second edition, provides a thorough treatment, at an introductory level, of the practical implications of the descriptive approach in each of the language arts. However, because "thinking like a linguist" is more akin to a broad approach than an instructional strategy per se, see the list for *Ideology, Beliefs, and Attitudes* (I) for a more exhaustive list of works of this type.

Three strategies—*Bidialectalism and Contrastive Analysis* (B), *Language Awareness* (L) and *Vernacular Literacy* (V), have each inspired a significant body of associated literature and have been given their own topic codes in this bibliographic resource; see the introductions to those topics for more information on those particular approaches. Here, it is perhaps worth mentioning that the lines we have drawn between strategies are our own and are therefore often crossed in the actual works themselves. For instance, efforts to add Standard English as a second dialect often crucially involve language awareness activities. Likewise, articles and books that begin with an empirical research question, such as the role of sociolinguistic diversity in test-score gaps, often end by exploring one or more instructional strategies.

The strategies category also overlaps significantly with the lists for assessment, culture and curriculum, reading, and writing, but these topics represent broad instructional design considerations or content areas and are not strategies in themselves, and so this topical list offers a slightly more refined focus.

A linguistically informed approach to assessment might be summed up as follows: Use a detailed, descriptive knowledge of language variation to identify and implement equitable, informed assessment strategies that allow vernacular speakers full access to a challenging curriculum. Depending on the assessment purpose and context, putting this overarching principle into practice may entail distinguishing dialect features from indicators of communicative disorders (Kamhi et al. 1996), distinguishing decoding errors in reading from dialect pronunciations (Goodman 1969, 1997), distinguishing use of vernacular features in writing from errors or lack of writing sophistication (Ball 1995, 1997; Smitherman 2000), and distinguishing differences in vernacular communicative norms such as storytelling or turn-taking from lack of academic aptitude or readiness (Heath 1983; Day Vines et al. 2009). In making these distinctions, the intention is to prevent misdiagnosis of the instructional needs of the vernacular speaker, thus making room for an appropriate pedagogical response rooted in a research-based approach to language variation (Godley et al. 2006).

The rates of reading failure among African American children inspired many early studies of AAVE, and thus, work on related instructional implications date to the 1960s–1980s. The key insight of much of the work of this era advises teachers to distinguish dialect pronunciations from miscues, as noted above, and additionally, to apply knowledge of the linguistic structure to focus phonics instruction on the linguistic environments most likely to cause difficulty for speakers whose dialect differs significantly from print (see Labov 2001, 2003 for empirical work on this issue). As strategies in reading instruction developed over the decades, so did sociolinguistically informed recommendations for adapting reading instruction to the needs of vernacular speakers. Specific strategies advocated by sociolinguistic theory and research include the use of culturally relevant literature, including music lyrics and other nontraditional texts (Baugh 1999; Le Moine and Hollie 2007; Rickford and Rickford 2007); the use of vernacular discourse genres such as signifying to support literary analysis (Anderson 1990; Lee 1993 et passim); and adaptation of questioning strategies to reflect AAVE speakers' dispreference for known-answer questions (Heath 1983; A. Rickford 1999). Meier 2008 is an important and noteworthy addition to the literature on reading instruction in vernacular contexts, as it provides an updated and in-depth consideration of how teachers might modify a wide range of commonly-used instructional strategies in light of research into communicative practices in the African American community.

Perhaps because so much of the research on writing and vernacular varieties is the work of scholars grounded in composition studies rather than linguistics, or perhaps because sociolinguistic interest in writing coalesced later than interest in reading or assessment, a relatively large proportion of the literature on writing is focused on instruction. Farr and Daniels 1986 remains a valuable resource for conceptualizing and implementing linguistically responsive writing instruction for students from a variety of linguistic backgrounds and age levels. Bean et al. 2003, Baker 2002, and Elbow 1999 illustrate, with examples from classroom practice, how teachers can adopt a flexible, pluralistic approach toward Standard English as a means of teaching students the importance of audience and context. More radically, Campbell 2005, Gilyard 1996, and Richardson and Jackson 2004 (among others) advocate de-emphasizing Standard English and centering instruction on the development and use of African American ways with words. Crotteau 2007 offers a detailed description of a thoughtful, and deeply respectful, language awareness intervention with Appalachian high school students struggling to pass writing proficiency exams required for graduation.

Strategies that make use of student culture to shape the classroom's interactional norms are applicable across content areas. Delpit 1990 provides a highly accessible and concrete overview of language instruction strategies compatible with culturally responsive pedagogy. Many studies in this vein point to the positive effect that culturally relevant participation structures can have on student engagement (Au 1980; Bohn 2003; Boone 2003; Foster 2001; Lee 2006; Au and Kawakami 1985; Simpkins and Simpkins 2009).

Short Citations for Strategies for Instruction (S)

Aarons et al. 1969
Abrahams and Troike 1972
Adger 1997
Adger et al. 1992
Adger et al. 1999
Adler 1978
Afaga and Lai 1994

Alexander 1985
Alim and Baugh 2007
Allen 1969
Allen 1972
Amberg and Vause 2009
Anderson 1989
Anderson 1990

Anderson 1990
Au 1980
Au and Kawakami 1985
Australia 1994
Baker 2002
Baldwin 1988
Ball 1995
Ball 1999
Ball 2000
Ball and Lardner 2005
Baratz 1969
Baratz 1969
Baratz 1970
Baugh 1981
Baugh 1999
Baugh 1999
Baugh 2001
Bayley 2009
Becker and Luthar 2002
Bentley and Crawford 1973
Berger 1990
Berry and Hudson 1997
Blake and Van Sickle 2001
Bohn 2003
Boloz and Jenness 1984
Boone 2003
Bougere 1981
Brooks 1985
Brown 2009
Bruder and Hayden 1973
Bryan 2004
Bryan 2010
Bryson and Scardamalia 1991
Bulletin 1987
Burling 1973
Cameron 1992
Campbell 2005
Carpenter and Devonish 2010
Carrington 1983
Carrington and Borely 1977
Cason et al. 1991
Cazden 1988
Center for Applied Linguistics 1978
Chall 2000
Chapman 1994
Charity Hudley and Mallinson 2011
Cheatham et al. 2009
Cheshire and Edwards 1991
Chisolm and Godley 2011
Christensen 2011
Clachar 2004
Coelho 1988
Coelho 1991
Coelho 1991
Cook and Lodge 1996
Courts 1997
Craig 1966

Craig 1969
Craig 1983
Craig 1999
Craig 2008
Cronnell 1981
Crotteau 2007
Crowell and Kolba 1974
Cullinan 1974
Cullinan et al. 1974
Davis et al. 1968
Day-Vines et al. 2009
de Kleine 2009
Delpit 1990
Delpit 2006
Delpit and Dowdy 2002
Denham 2005
Denham 2010
Denham and Lobeck 2005
Denham and Lobeck 2010
Desai and Marsh 2005
District 1998
District 1999
District 2010
Dixson and Dingus 2006
Dundes and Spence 2007
Dyson and Smitherman 2009
Eagleson et al. 1982
Edelsky 1996
Education 2002
Edwards 1979
Edwards 1981
Edwards 1983
Egan-Robertson and Bloome 1998
Elbow 1999
Elifson 1977
Epstein and Xu 2003
Evans 2001
Farr 1986
Farr and Daniels 1986
Farr et al. 2010
Fasold 2001
Fasold and Shuy 1970
Fecho 2004
Feigenbaum 1970
Fillmore and Snow 2000
Fischer 1992
Flint 1968
Flower 1996
Flynn 2011
Fogel and Ehri 2006
Folkes 1995
Foster 2001
Fradd and Weismantel 1989
Funkhouser 1973
Gaquin 2006
Gerbault 1997
Gillet and Gentry 1983

Gilyard 1996
Gladney 1973
Glowka and Lance 1993
Godley et al. 2007
Goodman 1965
Goodman 2003
Goodman and Buck 1973
Greene and Walker 2004
Hagemann 2001
Hall and Hall 1969
Hammond et al. 2005
Harris-Wright 1987
Harris-Wright 1999
Haussamen et al. 2003
Hazen 2005
Heath 1983
Hill 2008
Hill 2009
Hirvela 2010
Hollie 2001
Holmes 1999
Hoover 1989
Hoover 1991
Hoover 1998
Hoover and Fabian 2000
Hudson 1992
Hudson and Taylor 1987
Irish 1995
Irvine 2003
Jackson and Smitherman 2002
Johnson 1969
Johnson 1979
Johnson 1985
Johnson et al. 1998
Jones 1979
Kamhi et al. 1996
Keen 1978
Kirkland and Jackson 2009
Labov 2001
Labov 2003
Lacoste 2007
Lanehart 1998
Lanehart 2002
Le Moine 2001
Le Moine and District 1998
Le Moine and Hollie 2007
Le Page 1981
Lee 1993
Lee 1997
Lee 2007
Lewis and Hoover 1979
Linn 1995
Lockwood 1998
Love 1991
Lyman and Figgins 2005
MacGregor-Mendoza 2005
Malmstrom and Lee 1971

Mantell 1974
Matilda 2010
Matlock 1995
McCormack and Pasquarelli 2010
McCreight 2011
McDavid 1962
McKenry 1996
McRae 1994
McWhorter 1997
McWhorter 1997
Meier 1997
Meier 2008
Michaels and Cazden 1986
Mickan 1992
Migge et al. 2010
Miller and Johnson 1974
Monteith 1980
Mordaunt 2011
Morgan 2010
Mufwene 2001
Murrell 1997
Murtagh 1982
Nembhard 1983
Nero 2000
Norment 2005
Ohannessian and Gage 1969
O'Neal and Ringler 2010
Ovington 1992
Padak 1981
Parker and Crist 1995
Penn Reading Initiative and Labov 2010
Perez 2000
Piestrup 1973
Pollard 1979
Pollard 1993
Pollard 1998
Pollard 1999
Pratt-Johnson 1993
Pratt-Johnson 2006
Reaser 2010
Rentel and Kennedy 1972
Reyhner 1994
Richardson and Jackson 2004
Rickford 1999
Rickford 1999
Rickford and Rickford 2007
Rickford and Rickford 2010
Rickford and Wolfram 2009
Roberts 1994
Roberts 2007
Rosa 1994
Round Table, The 1993
Roy 1984
Scarborough et al. 2003
Schierloh 1991
Schotta 1970
Schwartz 1980

Scott 1990
Scott et al. 2009
Secret 1997
Serwer 1969
Seymour et al. 1995
Siegel 1992
Siegel 1997
Simmons 1991
Simmons and Baines 1998
Simmons-McDonald and Ellis 2002
Simmons-McDonald and Robertson 2006
Simpkins 2002
Simpkins and Simpkins 1981
Simpkins and Simpkins 2009
Simpkins et al. 1977
Sims 1975
Smith 1979
Smitherman 1975
Smitherman 1999
Smitherman 2000
Smitherman 2004
Southard and Muller 1993
Stewart 1964
Stewart 1969
Stewart 1970
Stoller 1975
Tamura 2008

Taylor 1999
Thompson et al. 2008
Tolerance 1996
Tompkins and McGee 1983
Troutman 1998
Venezky 1981
Washington 2003
Washington and Miller-Jones 1989
Wassink 2005
Webber 1985
Wheeler 2003
Wheeler 2008
Wheeler 2009
Wheeler and Swords 2004
Wheeler and Swords 2006
Wheeler and Swords 2010
Whitney 2005
Whyte 1986
Williams 1970
Wolfram 1970
Wolfram 1970
Wolfram 2001
Wolfram and Christian 1989
Wolfram et al. 2007
Young 1968
Young et al. 2005
Zuidema 2005

Teacher Preparation and Practices (T)

When it comes to addressing vernaculars in the classroom, what should teachers know and be able to do? Within educational research, there exists a vast, empirically and theoretically robust literature on teacher education, but few studies focus directly on the issue of vernacular varieties in the classroom. Most of the works listed here therefore emerge from the fields of sociolinguistics or composition studies.

A review of the resources listed here reveals that most articles are programmatic in nature, arguing that teacher education should include, at the very least, basic facts about language variation, and ideally, significant preparation for applying knowledge about student dialect diversity to classroom instruction. Among these, Baugh 1999, Godley et al. 2006, Labov 1995, Meier 1999, 2008 and Moats 1994 outline specific recommendations for the specialized kinds of linguistic knowledge base and training that teachers need to be effective practitioners. For analysis of issues germane to Creoles and other vernaculars, see Koskinen 2010, Malcolm 1995, Nidue 1992, Winford 1976, and Pollard 1983.

Ball and Muhammad (2003) reviewed twenty-five pre-service teacher preparation programs, finding that the extent to which issues of language variation are addressed in teacher education varied widely. The most recent surveys of teacher attitudes toward vernacular varieties indicate both progress in teachers' awareness of language variation and a significant need for even more outreach among practitioners (Blake and Cutler 2003; CCCC Language Policy Committee 2000; Gupta 2010; Katz et al. 2009; Richardson 2003). Many studies of existing teacher practices document, in some way, uninformed or ineffective teacher responses to the vernacular, including unwarranted evaluations of achievement or intellect based on dialect (Crowl and McGintie 1976; Piche et al. 1977; Piche et al. 1978; Shepherd 2011; Tyndall; Woodworth and Salzer 1971; Williams and Whitehead 1972). Studies building on the asset-based approach of culturally responsive pedagogy (Ladson-Billings 1995; Irvine 2002, 2003) focus on the practices of teachers who make effective use of vernacular linguistic resources in the classroom (Bohn 2003; Foster 1989).

The decade of 2000–2010 saw a trend within education research on teachers' dispositions to include investigations of instructional practices that foster changes in pre-service teachers' beliefs about diversity (Bakari 2003). The emerging literature that describes and evaluates sociolinguistic teacher education initiatives suggests a similarly increased focus on applied empirical investigation among scholars of language variation. Wilson 2001 describes how engaging teachers in describing their own participation in language variation can lead to more inclusive attitudes toward student language variation. Haddix 2008 reports on a sociolinguistics class that involved White pre-service teachers in a critical analysis of dominant standard language and color-blind ideologies. Mallinson and Hudley (2010) describe their field-tested framework for using multiple, complementary strategies with in-service educators, including service learning, teaching teachers about the 'privileges of standardized English,' and making sociolinguistic information optimally usable for educators. Sweetland 2010 provides results from an intervention with in-service teachers, illustrating that engaging teachers in applying insights from language variation studies in their classrooms has a greater effect on language attitudes than providing information alone. Wheeler 2010 describes the iterative process of refining teacher professional development lessons for progressively greater impact and fidelity.

Short Citations for Teacher Preparation and Practices (T)

Adamson 2005
Adger 1998
Adger et al. 1992
Adger et al. 1999
Alexander 1985
Alim and Baugh 2007
Anderson 1990
Bakari 2003
Baker 2002
Baldwin 1988
Ball 1997
Ball 2000
Ball 2000
Ball and Lardner 1997
Ball and Lardner 2005
Ball and Muhammad 2003
Baugh 1999
Baugh 2001
Baugh 2006
Berdan 1980
Berlin 2000
Birch 2001
Birrell 1995
Bixler-Màrquez and Ornstein-Galicia 1988
Blackburn and Stern 2000
Blake and Cutler 2003
Blodgett and Cooper 1973
Bohn 2003
Bougere 1981
Bowie and Bond 1994
Brandon et al. 2009
Brooks 1985

Bryan 2001
Bulletin 1987
Campbell 1993
Campbell 1994
Cantoni-Harvey 1974
Cantoni-Harvey 1977
Carter 2006
Cazden 1988
Cazden 1999
CCCC Committee 2000
Cecil 1988
Center for Applied Linguistics 1978
Charity Hudley and Mallinson 2011
Cheng 1987
Cheshire 1982
Cheshire et al. 1989
Cleary 1988
Cook and Lodge 1996
Corson 2001
Craig 1999
Cross 2003
Cross et al. 2001
Crowl and Macginitie 1976
Cunningham 1976
Curzan 2002
Day-Vines et al. 2009
Delpit 1986
Delpit 1988
Delpit 1990
Delpit 1995
Delpit and Dowdy 2002
DeMeis and Turner 1978

Dick et al. 1994
Dixson and Dingus 2006
Dyson and Smitherman 2009
Easter et al. 1999
Edelsky 1996
Fillmore and Snow 2000
Fischer 1992
Fishman and Lueders-Salmon 1972
Flower 1996
Fogel and Ehri 2006
Foster 1986
Foster 1989
Foster 1992
Foster 1995
Foster 1999
Franken and August 2011
Gadsen and Wagner 1995
Gere and Smith 1979
Glowka and Lance 1993
Godley et al. 2006
Godley et al. 2007
Grant et al. 2009
Greene 2005
Gupta 1994
Gupta 2010
Haddix 2008
Haig and Oliver 2003
Haig and Oliver 2003
Harper et al. 1998
Hilliard 1999
Hollie 2001
Hoover 1998
Hoover and Fabian 2000
Hoover et al. 1996
Hoover et al. 1996
Hwa-Froelich et al. 2007
Irvine 1990
Irvine 2002
Irvine 2003
Irvine 2003
Isenbarger and Smith 1973
Isenbarger and Willis 2006
Johnson 1979
Johnson 1985
Johnson et al. 1998
Katz et al. 2009
Koskinen 2010
Labov 1970
Labov 1995
Labov and Charity Hudley 2009
Ladson-Billings 1992
Ladson-Billings 1994
Ladson-Billings 1995
Ladson-Billings 2000
Ladson-Billings 2001
Ladson-Billings 2002
Lass 1980

Le Moine and Hollie 2007
Le Page 1968
Le Page 1981
Lewis and Hoover 1979
Los Angeles District 1999
Love 1991
Lucas and Borders 1994
Luke 1986
Malcolm 1979
Malcolm 1982
Malcolm 1992
Malcolm 1995
Mallinson and Charity Hudley 2010
Marcuzzi 1986
Matilda 2010
McDavid 1962
McKay and Wong 1996
McKenry 1996
Meacham 2000
Meacham 2002
Meier 1999
Michaels and Cazden 1986
Mitchell 2005
Moats 1994
Moats et al. 2006
Moll 1988
Morales 2009
Morgan 2010
Morris 2007
Moses et al. 1976
Murray 2001
Nembhard 1983
Nero 2010
Nichols 1977
Nidue 1992
Oliver and Haig 2005
Oliver et al. 2011
Padak 1981
Palacas 2001
Perry et al. 2003
Piché et al. 1977
Piché et al. 1978
Piestrup 1973
Pietras and Lamb 1978
Plank 1994
Pollard 1980
Pollard 1983
Pollard 1993
Pon et al. 2003
Postal 1972
Purcell-Gates 1995
Purcell-Gates 2002
Ramirez et al. 2005
Ramsey 1985
Rankie Shelton 2009
Reynolds 1999
Richards and Pratt-Johnson 1995

Richardson 2003
Rickford 2002
Rickford and Rickford 2010
Rosenthal and Jacobson 1968
Rupley et al. 2008
Rynkofs 2008
Santa Ana 2004
Schierloh 1991
Schwartz 1980
Scott and Smitherman 1985
Seligman et al. 1972
Shepherd 2011
Shuy 1969
Shuy 1973
Siegel 2005
Simons 1979
Simpson et al. 1999
Sledd 1996
Smith 1979
Smith 1995
Smitherman 1973
Smitherman 1975
Smitherman 1999
Smitherman 2000
Smitherman 2004
Smitherman and Scott 1984
Smitherman and Villanueva 2003
Souto-Manning 2009
Spanjer and Layne 1983

Stewart 1978
Sweetland 2010
Talmy 2004
Talmy 2009
Talmy 2010
Tauber 1997
Taylor 1973
Taylor 1983
Taylor and Matsuda 1988
Tyndall 1991
Van Keulen et al. 1998
Villegas and Lucas 2002
Walker 1992
Washington 2003
Washington and Miller-Jones 1989
Wheeler 2009
Wheeler 2010
Williams 1976
Williams and Whitehead 1973
Williams et al. 1972
Wilson 2001
Winer 1993
Winer 2006
Winford 1976
Wolfram and Christian 1989
Woodworth and Salzer 1971
Wynne 2002
Young et al. 2005

Code Choice (U)

The works included in this category deal in one way or another with code choice: the study of those factors (grammatical, pragmatic, stylistic, social or otherwise) influencing a bilingual or bidialectal speaker's choice to use one language variety over the other. Closely related is the concept of code-switching, the phenomenon whereby a speaker uses two languages or dialects concurrently.

The majority of the seventy-plus works included under this keyword are from the 1990s or later, although a handful of works from the '70s and '80s are found as well, such as Pollard's (1978) study of Jamaica Creole code-switching and Zentella's (1981) study of Puerto Rican code-switching in bilingual classrooms. References related to AAVE code-switching are most numerous in this topical list. One recurrent theme in this literature relates to African American attitudes toward Standard English (Fordham 1998; 1999) and distinctively African American speech styles (Koch et al. 2001; Linnes 2008; Rahman 2008). Another common topic of consideration is whether students have the ability to switch between the vernacular and standard as needed (e.g., between playground and classroom), or how to help them develop this facility. In this connection, readers interested in *Code Choice (U)* should also consult works topic-coded for *Bidialectal Approach (B)*.

References that cover code-switching in other languages and dialects besides AAVE are also included, of course, such as the Jamaica Creole and Puerto Rican studies mentioned above and quite a few more recent works on code-switching among various Latina/o groups (e.g., Baylely and Bonnici 2009; Lambert and Taylor 1996; Mendoza-Denton 1999; Schechter and Bayley 1997; Zentella 1997), as well as among Asian Americans (Reyes and Lo 2009; Shin and Milroy 2000; Walker-Moffat 1995) and Creole speakers (Carpenter and Devonish 2010; Clachar 2005; Labov 1980; Lacoste 2012; Nero 2006; Pollard 1998; Sebba 2000).

A question that commonly arises in investigations of code-switching has to do with the relative contribution of grammatical factors and social factors in influencing the alternation between one language or dialect and the other (Myers-Scotton 2009). According to Koch et al. (2001), the majority of the evidence points toward the conclusion that the primary factors involved are social and have to do with familiarity with the speaker and with the formality of the setting. In this connection, a number of works included here seek to understand code-switching as a stylistic device in the construction of identity (e.g., Alim 2004; Kuwahara 1998; Igoudin 2011; Rampton 1995; Schechter and Bayley 1997; Williams and Grantham 1999). See also Shin and Milroy (2000), who—in their study of Korean-English bilingual children—combat the notion that code-switching in children reflects a deficit in linguistic ability, arguing instead that code-switching functions as a resource for organizing conversation.

Overall, the works in this category help to dispel the mistaken impression of some teachers and observers that students' code-choice, switching or mixing is problematic; while these abilities may need to be extended or developed in some cases, they are usually governed, like so many other aspects of everyday language use, by systematic linguistic and social constraints.

Short Citations for Code Choice (U)

Alim 2004
Amberg and Vause 2009
Baratz 1969
Baugh 1992
Bayley and Bonnici 2009
Bixler-Màrquez and Ornstein-Galicia 1988
Brown 2011
Bucholtz 2004
Burt and Yang 2005
Carpenter and Devonish 2010
Chisolm and Godley 2011
Christensen 2011
Chun 2001
Clachar 2005
Connor and Craig 2006
Craig et al. 2009
DeBose 1992
Dowdy 1999
Dubois 1978
Edelsky 1996
Edwards 1983
Edwards 1992
Edwards 2010
Elbow 1999
Fishman et al. 1971
Flanigan 1996
Flowers 2000
Folb 1980
Fordham 1998
Fordham 1999
Gilyard 1991
Hakimzadeh and Cohn 2007

Igoudin 2011
Jordan 1989
Kinloch 2010
Koch et al. 2001
Kohn 2008
Kuwahara 1998
Labov 1980
Lacoste 2012
Lambert and Taylor 1996
Lanehart 2002
Liebe-Harkort 1979
Linnes 1998
MacGregor-Mendoza 2005
Mayer and New 2010
Mendoza-Denton 1999
Mendoza-Denton 2008
Mitchell-Kernan 1972
Morgan 2002
Myers-Scotton 2009
Nero 2006
Ogbu 2003
Paris 2009
Paris 2011
Penalosa 1980
Pollard 1978
Pollard 1998
Rahman 2008
Rampton 1995
Reaser and Wolfram 2007
Reyes and Lo 2009
Richardson 2003
Rynkofs 2008

Schecter and Bayley 1997
Sebba 2000
Shin and Milroy 2000
Smith 1975
Taylor and Leonard 1998
Thompson et al. 2004
Urciuoli 1985
Vasquez et al. 2008

Walker-Moffat 1995
Wheeler 2005
Youssef 2006
Zentella 1981
Zentella 1997
Zentella 1997
Zentella 2006

Vernacular Literacy or Dialect Readers (V)

The references in this category consider, to varying extents, *vernacular literacy*, which might involve one or more of these strategies: using vernacular reading materials in the classroom; allowing or encouraging students to speak and write in the vernacular; and teaching reading (and other subjects) in the vernacular, rather than or in addition to Standard English. When linguists or educators suggest "taking vernaculars into account" in schools, the general public often assumes that vernacular literacy is what they have in mind, whether the proposals are made in the Caribbean (Carrington and Borely 1976) or the United States (Rickford and Rickford 2000). In actuality, "using the vernacular to teach the standard" (Rickford 1999, p. 23) via Contrastive Analysis or other techniques is proposed much more often. But as the references below indicate, vernacular literacy also has its advocates (and detractors).

The literature on this topic comes almost entirely from work on AAVE or Anglophone pidgins and creoles. In the case of Asian American, Latina/o and Native American students, it is their heritage language (Chinese, Spanish, Navajo or other native language) rather than their vernacular varieties of English that are considered for use in schools, and debate is couched in terms of bilingual rather than bidialectal education. This may be in part because their vernacular varieties of English are considered transitional, interlanguage varieties—stops on the way between fluency in the heritage language and fluency in standard English—although this is certainly not the case for many students in these categories.

The argument for teaching AAVE-speaking students to read initially in their vernacular, and only later transitioning to standard English texts was made first, and in most detail, by Stewart (1969). Stewart pointed out the parallels between AAVE speakers and speakers of West African languages who were first taught to read in foreign languages like English or French—a practice which gives the emergent reader two learning tasks rather than one: learning a second variety as well as learning to read (i.e., decode and extract meaning from written text). Pointing to Österberg's (1961) demonstration that dialect speaking students in Sweden who were initially taught to read in their vernacular went on to perform better in Standard Swedish than their counterparts who were taught to read in Standard Swedish from the start, he advocated a similar strategy for AAVE speaking students, going on to discuss questions about appropriate orthography, phonology and grammar, and illustrating with a short story in dialect, "Shirley and the Valentine Card" (p. 197 ff.). Much of the contemporary literature (e.g., Fasold 1969; Leaverton 1973; Shuy 1969; Wolfram and Fasold 1969) dealt with similar themes. Baratz (1969), a close colleague of and collaborator will William Stewart, indeed put it even more succinctly than he did: "... first teach the child to read in the vernacular, and then teach him to read in standard English" (p. 113). However, then, as now (compare Au 2008 in relation to Hawaiian Creole), not all students and aficionados of the vernacular favored vernacular literacy. Beryl Bailey, whose earlier works (1965, 1966) had distinguished her as an accomplished student and fan of both Jamaican Creole and AAVE, wrote a (1970) article opposing the use of dialect readers to teach initial literacy to AAVE speakers, arguing among other things that it might be counter-productive to delay the teaching of reading in Standard English. Walt Wolfram, whose similar credentials had been established by his (1969) description of AAVE in Detroit and other works, also wrote a (1970) article voicing reservations about dialect readers, not on their intrinsic merits, but on the basis of the strong negative reactions such materials elicited from "the community (i.e., educators in lower-class lack schools, parents and community leaders" (p. 29). Other researchers (e.g., Harber 1977; Marwit and Neumann 1974; McWhorter 1997) have argued that the experimental evidence is either unclear or negative with respect to using dialect readers. However, the nation-wide experiment of Simpkins and his colleagues (Simpkins 2002; Simpkins and Simpkins 1981; Simpkins et al. 1977) with their *Bridge* dialect readers appears to have been strikingly successful. Rickford and Rickford (1995) suggest that other successful experiments with dialect materials continue to make them a viable option. Meier (1997) discusses how to use one popular dialect text, "Flossie and the Fox," and Holly Craig and her colleagues at the University of Michigan are currently doing new research creating and experimenting with reading texts that incorporate various features of AAVE.

Creoles whose vocabulary derives primarily from French, Spanish and Portuguese, have been permitted and/or used for teaching in schools in countries like the Seychelles, Haiti and the Netherlands Antilles for twenty or thirty years, increasingly so and experimentally in other countries over the past ten (Siegel 2010a, p. 389; Simmons-McDonald 2004, and articles by Dijkhoff and Pereira and others in Migge et al. 2010). The only *English*-based pidgin or creole for which this is true is Papua New Guinea, where Tok Pisin has been a choice for formal education since the early 1990s, and is often chosen as the medium of instruction (Ray 1996; Wiruk 2000; Siegel 2010a, p. 389). However, arguments in favor of using creole English materials in Caribbean schools have long been made (cf Kephart 1992), and there has been experimentation with the use of Creole English for vernacular literacy and in bilingual or trilingual education more generally in Jamaica (Carpenter and Devonish 2010, 2012; Devonish and Carpenter 2007) and San Andres, Colombia (Morren 2002), with promising initial results. A bilingual program involving Northern Territory Kriol and English was implemented in Australia, beginning in 1977, but it ended in 1998 (Siegel 1993, 2010a).

Finally, it should be noted that while much of the enthusiasm for vernacular literacy grew out of the often-cited 1953 UNESCO report that extolled the advantages of beginning education in one's vernacular language (see Bull 1955), a more recent re-examination of vernacular literacy by a team of scholars (Tabouret-Keller et al. 1997) has been more balanced, and even critical. At the same time the reservations in the latter seem to have more to do with the sociopolitical contexts in which vernacular literacy is embraced (see Rickford 2011, pp. 263–64) than with the pedagogical value of vernacular literacy itself.

Short Citations for Vernacular Literacy or Dialect Readers (V)

Adger 1993	Charpentier 1997
Anderson 1990	Craig 1980
Appel and Verhoeven 1994	Craig 1999
Au 2008	Craig 2006
Bailey 1970	Craig 2008
Ball and Lardner 2005	Davis et al. 1968
Baratz and Shuy 1969	Devonish 1983
Bean et al. 2003	Devonish and Carpenter 2007
Bixler-Màrquez and Ornstein-Galicia 1988	Engle 1975
Blackburn and Stern 2000	Fasold 1969
Bull 1955	Fasold and Shuy 1970
Camitta 1993	Fischer 1992
Carpenter and Devonish 2010	Fishbein 1973
Carpenter and Devonish 2012	Gerbault 1997
Carrington 1997	Gillet and Gentry 1983
Champion and Bloome 1995	Harber 1977

Harris et al. 2001
Henry 2000
Hinds 1990
Hornberger 2005
IDB and CDB 2009
Jaggar and Cullinan 1974
Kephart 1992
Labov 1995
Lass 1980
Leap 1993
Leaverton 1971
Leaverton 1973
Marwit and Neumann 1974
Matilda 2010
Mbufong 2001
McWhorter 1997
Meier 1997
Migge et al. 2010
Migge et al. 2010
Morren 2002
Mühleisen 2002
Nero 2006
Nolen 1972
Ramirez et al. 2005
Ray 1996
Rickford 1997
Rickford 1999
Rickford 1999
Rickford 1999
Rickford 2011
Rickford and Rickford 1995
Shields 1979
Shuy 1969

Siegel 1992
Siegel 1992
Siegel 1993
Siegel 1997
Siegel 1999
Siegel 2005
Siegel 2006
Siegel 2010
Simmons-McDonald 2004
Simmons-McDonald 2006
Simmons-McDonald and Robertson 2006
Simpkins 2002
Simpkins and Simpkins 1981
Simpkins and Simpkins 2009
Simpkins et al. 1977
Sims 1975
Stewart 1969
Stoller 1975
Stoller 1975
Straker 1985
Strickland and Stewart 1974
Taavitsainen et al. 1999
Tabouret-Keller et al. 1997
Unit 2009
Ure 1981
Williams 1975
Wiruk 2000
Wolfram 1970
Wolfram 1994
Wolfram 2001
Wolfram and Fasold 1969
Wolfram et al. 2007
Wroge 1998

Writing (W)

Sociolinguistic research on writing and vernaculars developed slightly later than similar work on reading. Research conducted in the 1970s and 1980s on the intersection of AAVE and writing focused almost exclusively on the transfer of phonological and morphosyntactic features into writing—that is, determining the extent and nature of influence of dialect on spelling and conventions such as standard subject-verb agreement. The work of Bruce Cronnell (1979 et passim) is a good place to enter the research on this topic; Scott and Rogers (1996) reviews related work; see Nelson (2010) for a more recent study in this vein. Winer 1986 investigates Creole features in the writing of Trinidadian students.

One of the key recommendations emerging from a national scholarly symposium following the *King* decision was a call for greater research into the teaching of writing in African American contexts (cf Smitherman 1981). Farr and Daniels 1985 offers a broad pedagogical framework for teaching writing in linguistically diverse classrooms, integrating methods from the process approach to writing instruction with insights from language variation research. Delpit 1986 raises critical questions regarding the suitability of adopting process writing in diverse classrooms without considering whether and how students' unique cultural and linguistic needs might call for modifications in either instruction or assessment; see also Delpit 1998, Hoover 1991, Spence 2008, Sweetland 2006, and Walker 1992 on this question.

Ball (1992, 1995), Norment (1995) and Smitherman (1992, 1994) were among the first to extend variationist inquiry into the realm of discourse-level features in writing. Subsequently, Campbell 2005, Gilyard 1996, and Richardson and Jackson 2004 have built on research into African American speech acts and communicative norms to develop composition courses rooted in Black rhetorical traditions.

Interest in multiple literacies—the diverse ways in which students access and produce texts—has provided a new scholarly space for research into the writing practices of students who speak a vernacular. Camitta 1993 and Blackburn and Stern 2000 describe the spontaneous vernacular literacy practices of African American youth, which potentially provide fruitful points of departure for engaging students in school-related writing. Hirvela 2010 reviews the literature on multiple literacies among Asian language populations.

Perhaps more so than in other areas of the language arts, research on writing has often noted the desire to maintain and nurture the evocative, authentic qualities of voice available to writers who command a vernacular variety. As such, the issues of code choice have been wrestled with eloquently, and with perhaps greater nuance, than in other areas of inquiry into vernaculars in education (e.g., Ball and Lardner 2005; Elbow 1999).

In contrast to the references collected on reading, which concentrate largely on issues germane to the primary grades, the writing references collected here include a great deal of research and debate about issues at the post-secondary level. The presence and overrepresentation of vernacular speakers in the college basic writing course has inspired many composition instructors to grapple with issues of language, power, and pedagogy. As a result, work emerging from college composition represents the most robust literature on vernacular varieties written by non-linguists and pushes beyond other applied literature and the sociolinguistic literature in terms of theorizing historical, innovative, and potential responses to stigmatized language varieties in educational context. Shaughnessy (1977) is a seminal work in this field; see Halasek and Highberg (2001) for a collection of more recent and notable essays.

The Conference on College Composition and Communication's 1974 resolution, "Students' Right to Their Own Language," set a bold, progressive tone for scholarship on dialects in composition studies; see Cobb et al. 2009 and Smitherman and Villanueva 2003 for recent collections of essays considering the resolution's legacy.

Short Citations for Writing (W)

Adger et al. 1999
Adger et al. 2007
Agnew and McLaughlin 1999
Alatis 1970
Anderson 1990
Balester 1993
Balester and Weber 2002
Balhorn 1999
Ball 1992
Ball 1995
Ball 1997
Ball 1999
Ball and Lardner 1997
Ball and Lardner 2005
Baugh 1981
Baugh 1999
Baxter and Holland 2007
Bean et al. 2003
Blackburn and Stern 2000
Blake and Van Sickle 2001

Boloz and Jenness 1984
Brooks 1985
Brown 2009
Brown 2011
Bruder and Hayden 1973
Bryson and Scardamalia 1991
Bulletin 1987
Busch and Ball 2004
Camitta 1993
Campbell 1994
Campbell 1997
Campbell 2005
Cason et al. 1991
Chaplin 1990
Chapman 1994
Cheshire and Stein 1997
Chiang and Schmida 1999
Christie 1996
Clachar 2003
Clachar 2005

Clachar 2006
Cleary 1988
Coleman 1997
Composition and Communication 1974
Cook-Gumperz 1993
Cronnell 1979
Cronnell 1981
Cronnell 1983
Cronnell 1984
Crotteau 2007
Delpit 1986
Delpit 1988
DeStefano 1972
Devonish 1996
District 1999
Dyche 1996
Dyson and Smitherman 2009
Edwards 1975
Elbow 1999
Farr 1986
Farr and Daniels 1986
Farr and Janda 1985
Fillmore and Snow 2000
Flower 1996
Flynn 2011
Fogel and Ehri 2000
Fox 1994
Francis and Reyhner 2002
Fu 1995
Funkhouser 1973
Gaquin 2006
Gee 2007
Giannasi 1976
Gilyard 1996
Gilyard and Richardson 2001
Goldblatt 1995
Gray-Rosendale et al. 2003
Gregory 1989
Groff 1978
Groff 2004
Gutierrez et al. 2009
Halasek and Highberg 2001
Hall and Damico 2007
Harris et al. 2001
Hartwell 1980
Higgs and Manning 1975
Higgs et al. 1995
Hill 2008
Hirvela 2010
Holmes 1999
Holton 1984
Hoover 1989
Hoover 1991
Hoover and Fabian 2000
Ivy and Masterson 2011
Jackson and Smitherman 2002
Jones 1965

Jordan 1985
Keen 1978
Kells 2006
Kennedy 2006
Kinloch 2005
Kirkland 2010
Kirschner and Poteet 1973
Kynard 2008
Ladson-Billings 2002
Le Moine and District 1998
Leap 1993
Lee 1997
Linn 1995
Malancon and Malancon 1993
Marback 2001
Martin-Jones and Jones 2000
Mayer and New 2010
McCarty 2005
McCarty and Watahomigie 1998
McKay and Wong 1996
McLaughlin 2010
Meier 2008
Miller 1967
Mix 2003
Moats et al. 2006
Morales 2009
Nelson 2010
Nembhard 1983
Nero 1997
Nero 2001
Nero 2006
Nero 2010
Norment 1995
Norment 2005
Palacas 2001
Palacas 2002
Parks 2000
Perryman-Clark 2009
Piche et al. 1977
Piche et al. 1978
Pollard 1999
Purcell-Gates 1993
Purcell-Gates 1995
Purcell-Gates 1996
Ramsey 1985
Redd and Schuster Webb 2005
Richards and Pratt-Johnson 1995
Richardson 2003
Richardson 2008
Richardson and Jackson 2004
Rickford 1999
Rickford 2002
Rickford and Greaves 1978
Rizzo and Villafane 1975
Sala 2009
Schierloh 1991
Schotta 1970

Schwartz 1982
Scott 1993
Scott and Rogers 1996
Sebba 2000
Shaughnessy 1977
Shnukal 2002
Shuy 1973
Simmons-McDonald et al. 1997
Smitherman 1981
Smitherman 1992
Smitherman 1994
Smitherman 1999
Smitherman 2000
Smitherman and Villanueva 2003
Spanjer and Layne 1983
Spence 2008
Spence 2010
Sperling 1996
Sternglass 1974
Stoller 1975
Strickland and Alvermann 2004
Sullivan 1971
Sweetland 2006

Syrquin 2006
Taavitsainen et al. 1999
Taylor 1989
Thiede 1983
Thompson et al. 2004
Troutman 1997
Troyka 2000
Tyndall 1991
Unit 2009
Walker 1992
Weinstein-Shr 1994
Weiss 1963
Whiteman 1981
Whitney 2005
Wible 2006
Williams 1970
Winch and Gingell 1994
Winer 1986
Wolfram and Whiteman 1971
Wolfram et al. 1979
Wolfram et al. 2007
Zeni and Thomas 1990

Language Transfer or Interference (X)

Language transfer (also known as linguistic interference) refers to the phenomenon of a speaker or writer applying knowledge of their native language in a second language context. After foundational variationist research such as Fasold and Wolfram 1970 and Labov 1972 established that the language of Black children was not deficient, but rather systematically different, linguists and psychologists began to inquire into the nature and effects of that difference. The "dialect interference" hypothesis emerged as one alternative explanation for the low literacy attainment among African American children, positing that the vernacular was so structurally divergent that acquisition of oral and written communication in Standard English was necessarily hindered to some degree. Proving or disproving the existence of dialect interference quickly became a hot topic for research, with at least fifty studies published in the 1970s alone. Contemporary reviews of this literature include Baratz 1973; Bougere 1981; Cronnell 1983; Hall and Turner 1973; Hartwell 1980; and Venezky 1981.

Much of this work was experimental and focused on reading. One consistent finding that emerged from this research is that while AAVE phonology does influence children's pronunciation of reading materials, dialect-related pronunciations in oral reading do not indicate a failure to decode the printed word (Baratz 1973; Goodman and Buck 1973; Labov 1967, 1972). As a result, one of the earliest concrete instructional recommendations resulting directly from sociolinguistic research was that reading teachers and reading assessments should distinguish dialect pronunciations from miscues. Unfortunately, research into how and if dialect affected reading comprehension did not produce a similarly clear set of empirical findings or implications for practice, largely because of the difficulty of designing studies with adequate controls. One reviewer noted that "even a cursory examination of the research on dialect interference in the attainment of literacy reveals methodological weaknesses that inhibit the synthesis of findings into justifiable conclusions" (Schwartz 1981, p. 445). More recent work has resolved or sidestepped some of the methodological difficulties by merely seeking to establish correlations rather than causality (e.g., Craig et al. 2009). Charity et al. 2004 inverts the question of interference by investigating and quantifying students' familiarity with school English rather than lack thereof.

Our bibliography includes a diverse set of references on language transfer in pidgin and creole contexts. Based on unique patterns of tense-marking in the writing of Creole-speaking students, Clachar (2004, p. 153) argues that "creole-English speaking students are neither native nor nonnative speakers of English" but rather something in between, and would benefit from literacy instruction designed accordingly. de Kleine 2006 and Winer 1986 look at the transfer of creole features in student writing. Siegel 1999 tackles the issue of interference from a somewhat different perspective, surveying the evidence against the popular viewpoint that the time spent using the vernacular interferes with the acquisition of the standard variety.

Short Citations for Language Transfer or Interference (X)

Alatis 1970
Ames et al. 1971
Balhorn 1999
Ball 1994
Baratz 1969
Baratz 1969
Baratz 1973
Baratz and Shuy 1969
Bartel and Axelrod 1973
Bougere 1981
Brown 1998
Burke 1973
Carrington 1969
Center for Applied Linguistics 1978
Charity et al. 2004
Cheng 1987
Clachar 2003
Clachar 2004
Clachar 2005
Clachar 2006
Cook 1973
Cook and Sharp 1966
Craig 1985
Craig 2008
Craig and Washington 2006
Craig et al. 2009
Cronnell 1979
Cronnell 1983
Cronnell 1984
Cronnell 1985
Cunningham 1976
de Kleine 2006
de Kleine 2009
de Villiers and Johnson 2007
Desberg et al. 1979
DeStefano 1972
Edwards 1979
Farr 1986
Farr and Janda 1985
Fasold 1969
Frentz 1971
Gemake 1981
Gladney 1973

Goodman 1965
Goodman and Buck 1973
Gottardo et al. 2001
Gunderson 1970
Gut 2007
Hall and Turner 1971
Hall and Turner 1973
Hall et al. 1973
Hall et al. 1975
Harber 1981
Harber and Beatty 1978
Harber and Bryen 1976
Hart et al. 1980
Hartwell 1980
Hirata-Edds 2011
Hockman 1973
Johnson 1974
Jones 1979
Kellerman 1995
Kirschner and Poteet 1973
Labov 1967
Labov 1995
Labov 2001
Labov 2003
Labov and Baker 2010
Labov and Charity Hudley 2009
Lado 1957
Laffey and Shuy 1973
Lass 1980
Lucas and Singer 1976
Marwit and Marwit 1976
Marwit and Neumann 1974
Mays 1977
McWhorter 1997
Melmed 1971
Melmed 1973
Mix 2003
Moran 1993
Nelson and McRoskey 1978
Nolen 1972
Odlin 1989
Oetting and Garrity 2006
O'Neil 1990

Orr 1987
Piestrup 1973
Redd and Schuster Webb 2005
Rizzo and Villafane 1975
Roberts 1983
Ruddell 1965
Rystrom 1970
Rystrom 1973
Schwartz 1982
Seitz 1975
Shaughnessy 1977
Shields 1979
Shnukal 2002
Shuy 1969
Shuy 1973
Siegel 1992
Siegel 1997
Siegel 1999
Simons 1974
Simons 1979
Simons and Johnson 1974
Sligh and Conners 2003
Somervill 1975
Sperling 1996

Steffensen et al. 1982
Sternglass 1974
Stewart 1978
Sullivan 1971
Tatham 1970
Terry 2006
Terry 2008
Terry et al. 2010
Terry et al. 2010
Thiede 1983
Torrey 1970
Treiman 2004
Troike 1972
Troutman and Falk 1982
Van Sickle et al. 2002
Venezky 1981
Weber 1973
Wheldall and Joseph 1985
Whiteman 1981
Winch and Gingell 1994
Winer 1986
Wolfram 1970
Wolfram 1984
Wolfram and Whiteman 1971

Video Resources (Z)

We've included in this bibliographic resource just over a dozen videos that deal with ver-nacular varieties of English, primarily for teachers or students who want to hear and see them being spoken, but also for all scholars who want to learn more about their features or history or use in education. Nowadays, one can get samples of virtually any dialect on YouTube, but the samples are usually very brief, and rarely provide any scholarly back-ground on or analysis of the language. By contrast, the videos listed here are longer—half an hour to an hour or more—and they usually feature leading linguistic and other experts providing commentary and analysis, or were made in consultation with such professionals.

Only two of the videos in our list are from outside the United States. Chen and Carper 2005 examine code switching in Hong Kong, and Western Australia Department of Edu-cation 2002 focus on Aboriginal English in Australia.

The others all deal with US varieties of English, including Alvarez and Kolker's 1987 classic, *American Tongues*, and MacNeil and Cran's three part video series, *Do You Speak American?* Both provide overviews of regional and social dialect variation in the United States, and are staples of undergraduate linguistics courses at American universities. The latter is even accompanied by a detailed language awareness curriculum for use in high school or college, much of which is available online via an elaborate and beautifully designed website (see Reaser and Adger 2007, and http://www.pbs.org/speak/). We also include here just three of the several videos available from the North Carolina Language and Life Project (NCLLP) at North Carolina State University: Hutcheson 1999, 2005; and Wolfram et al. 2000. These videos, conceptualized and advised by Walt Wolfram, profes-sor at NC State, represent the most extensive effort by an American scholar to increase awareness and understanding of dialect variation in his or her state or region. Visit http://ncsu.edu/linguistics/talkingnc/titles.php for other titles and more information.

Searider Productions (2009) is the only video in our list that is fully concerned with a pidgin/creole variety, in this case, Hawaiian Pidgin. The other videos about US variet-ies all deal with AAVE, including Cran's (1986) partly historical account (which includes some discussion of Gullah or Sea Island Creole and West African Pidgin English), videos that relate to the Oakland Ebonics controversy of 1996/97 (C-SPAN 1996, 1997), and videos that introduce and exemplify the bidialectal strategies being used in the Academic English Mastery Program (AEMP) in Los Angeles (Los Angeles Unified School District 1998 and 2010). Incidentally, it is worth noting that the Los Angeles school district is much bigger than the Oakland School District, and that the AEMP program, created by former director Noma Le Moine, has escaped the negative publicity Oakland's attempts to recognize Ebonics in 1997 did. This is partly because of the name (who could be against Academic English Mastery?), but also because of the structure of the program, its careful preparation of teachers, and the links Le Moine forged with administrators and policymakers in her district. The videos are worth looking at by others interested in similar innovations elsewhere.

For other potentially relevant videos (dealing with the history or international variability of English, for instance, or with slang and dialect variation in the United States, with Jamaican Creole, or Krio in Australia), see the Teaching resources section of John Rickford's website (www.johnrickford.com).

Short Citations for Video Resources (Z)

Alvarez and Kolker 1987
Alvarez and Kolker 1990
Chen and Carper 2005
Cran 1986
C-SPAN 1996
C-SPAN 1997
Education 2002

Hutcheson 1999
Hutcheson 2000
Hutcheson 2005
Los Angeles District 1998
Los Angeles District 2010
MacNeil and Cran 2005
Productions 2009

BIBLIOGRAPHY

Aarons, Alfred, Barbara Gordon & William Stewart (eds.) 1969. *The Florida FL Reporter Special Anthology Issue: Linguistic-Cultural Differences and American Education.*

1 3 4 5 6 B C E F N R S

Abrahams, Roger D. & Geneva Gay. 1975. Talking Black in the Classroom. In *Black English: Its Background and Its Usage,* ed. by P. Stoller, 158–67. New York: Dell.

1 N O
This chapter examines the power of language among African American youth, noting that verbal skills are highly developed and highly prized among inner city youth—contrary to the widely held belief that many African American students lack communication skills. The authors assert that African American street culture is synonymous with oral culture: "For a member of street culture, language is not only a communicative device but also a mechanism of control and power" (p. 159). They provide examples in which this is precisely the case. Verbal communication caps in the classroom allow students to exercise power over their teachers. Many teachers see verbal skills as indicators of literacy, but Abrahams and Gay argue that there is more to the language of African Americans. For example, members of this community constantly change their language and reverse the meanings of words, thereby showing great competency in communication. The authors conclude that teachers should embrace and understand the importance of Black students' language.

Abrahams, Roger D. & Rudolph C. Troike (eds.) 1972. *Language and Cultural Diversity in American Education.* Englewood Cliffs, NJ: Prentice Hall.

1 4 5 6 B C E F I N R S

Actouka, Melody & Morris K. Lai. 1989. *Project Holopono, Evaluation Report, 1987–1988.* College of Education, University of Hawai'i.

2 C

Adams, L. Emilie. 1991. *Understanding Jamaican Patois: An Introduction to Afro-Jamaican Grammar.* Kingston, Jamaica: LMH Publishing Co.

2 F

Adamson, H. Douglas. 2005. *Language Minority Students in American Schools: An Education in English*. Mahwah, NJ: Lawrence Erlbaum Associates. [Abstract prepared by ERIC and reprinted with permission of the Department of Education from the Education Resources Information Center at eric.ed.gov.]

1 4 B C P Q T
This book addresses the national debate about how to teach the 3.5 million students in American public schools who do not speak English as a native language. This book places this debate and related issues of teaching Standard English to speakers of non-standard dialects, such as Black English, within the larger context of language acquisition theory and current methods of language teaching. Adamson draws from the large body of research and on his own experience as an English teacher in the United States and overseas, to shed light on some of these controversies. Presenting all sides of the issues fairly, he offers a strong endorsement for bilingual and bidialectical education. A strength of the book is the inclusion of original research conducted in a middle school enrolling a majority of Latino students. This research contributes to the field of language education by providing a detailed description of how English language learners study content subjects. Examples from the study are used to illustrate a discussion of Vygotskian learning principles and the relationship between the students' home and school cultures. Following a preface, this book is organized into the following chapters: (1) A Personal Introduction; (2) First and Second Language Acquisition; (3) Language Teaching; (4) Standard and Vernacular English; (5) Learning in a Second Language; (6) School and Family; and (7) Bilingual Education.

Adger, Carolyn, Walt Wolfram, Jennifer Detwyler & Beth Harry. 1992. *Confronting Dialect Minority Issues in Special Education: Reactive and Proactive Perspectives*. Paper presented at the 3rd National Research Symposium on Limited English Proficient Student Issues: Focus on Middle and High School Issues, Washington, D.C.

1 A S T

Adger, Carolyn Temple. 1993. Language Differences: A New Approach for Special Educators. *Teaching Exceptional Children* 21.44–47.

A B D V

Adger, Carolyn Temple. 1997. *Issues and Implications of English Dialects for Teaching English as a Second Language*. Alexandria, VA: TESOL Inc.

2 B S

Adger, Carolyn Temple. 1998. Register Shifting with Dialect Resources in Instructional Discourse. In *Kids Talk: Strategic Language Use in Early Childhood*, ed. by S. Hoyle & C. T. Adger, 151–69. New York: Oxford University Press.

1 B F N T

Adger, Carolyn Temple & Donna Christian. 2007. Sociolinguistic Variation and Education. In *Sociolinguistic Variation: Theories, Methods, and Applications*, ed. by R. Bayley & C. Lucas. Cambridge: Cambridge University Press. [Abstract graciously provided by Carolyn Temple Adger.]

1 6 B I L P
This chapter provides an overview of iconic links between sociolinguistic variation and education initiated in the 1960s and speculates about why its impact on schools is still limited. The relevance of sociolinguistic research to education emerged with articles such as Labov's (1969) "The Logic of Non-Standard English" on the mismatch

between school speech activities and those in which children demonstrated verbal expertise in their communities. Wolfram (1970) showed that tests in the field of speech/language pathology assumed that normal development was marked by Standard English features and that deviation from that norm represented developmental delay. Common to such efforts to influence educational practices is adherence to principles pointing to the researcher's social obligations beyond the research community. Some early efforts to connect sociolinguistic study to education policy and practice have borne fruit. For example, NCTE affirmed the 1974 resolution of the affiliate Conference on College Composition and Communication on students' rights to their own languages and dialects. Some new instructional approaches use vernacular dialects. One approach to Standard English instruction employs contrastive analysis with a vernacular variety (Wheeler and Swords, 2006). A dialect awareness curriculum introduces fundamental sociolinguistic concepts to students in Grade 4 on up (Wolfram and Reaser, 2004). However, disciplinary perspectives and research findings have not been fully integrated into educational processes. Linguists working in education need to recognize the goals and needs of educators and to tailor their applications to the existing educational framework.

Adger, Carolyn Temple, Donna Christian & Orlando Taylor (eds.) 1999. *Making the Connection: Language and Academic Achievement among African American Students.* Washington, D.C.: CAL/Delta.

1 B E I K P R S T W

Adger, Carolyn Temple, Walt Wolfram & Donna Christian. 2007. *Dialects in Schools and Communities – Second Edition.* Mahwah, NJ: Lawrence Erlbaum Associates.

L O R W

Adler, Sol. 1978. *Language Intervention and the Culturally Different Child.* [Abstract prepared by ERIC.]

B S

After describing a variety of compensatory programs that have not been very successful for children who enter school speaking nonstandard dialects, the author describes a bidialectal program that teaches standard usage as "school language" but accepts nonstandard dialects as "everyday language," and makes the differences explicit.

Afaga, Lorna B. & Morris K. Lai. 1994. *Project Akamai, Evaluation Report, 1992–93, Year Four.* College of Education, University of Hawaii.

2 B C S

Agnew, Eleanor & Margaret McLaughlin. 1999. Basic Writing Class of '93 Five Years Later: How the Academic Paths of Blacks and Whites Diverged. *Journal of Basic Writing* 18.40–54.

1 A W

Aguilera, Dorothy & Margaret D. LeCompte. 2009. Restore My Language and Treat Me Justly: Indigenous Students' Rights to Their Tribal Languages. In *Affirming Students' Rights to Their Own Language: Bridging Language Policies and Pedagogical Practices,* ed. by J. C. Scott, D. Straker & L. Katz, 68–84. Urbana, IL: NCTE.

2 6 P

The authors describe Native Hawaiian efforts to restore and sustain their languages, including Hawaiian Creole English, and place these efforts in the context of other indigenous peoples in the United States, including the Yup'ik people of central Alaska.

Ahler, Janet Goldenstein. 1994. The Evolution of Bilingual Education in an American Indian Community: A Decade of Evaluation as Applied Anthropology. *Great Plains Research* 4.293–303.

5

Ai, Xiaoxia. 2002. *Academic English Mastery Program 2000–2001 Evaluation Report*. Los Angeles: Program Evaluation and Research Branch, Los Angeles Unified School District.

1 4 B

Akande, Akinmade. 2010. Is Nigerian Pidgin English English? *Dialectologia et Geolinguistica* 18.3–22.

2 F

Alatis, James (ed.) 1970. Report of the Twentieth Annual Round Table Meeting on Linguistics and Language Studies: Linguistics and the Teaching of Standard English to Speakers of Other Languages or Dialects. Washington, D.C.: Georgetown University Press.

1 2 5 6 B E F P R W X
This is an early but important contribution to the study of vernacular English dialects in schools and their relation to Standard English. Most of the chapters are of interest, but among those especially relevant to this book are: William Labov, "The Logic of Nonstandard English"; Rudolph C. Troike, "Receptive Competence, Productive Competence, and Performance"; Betty W. Robinett, "Teaching Training for English as a Second Dialect and English as a Second Language: The Same or Different"; Eugene J. Briere, "Testing ESL skills among American Indian Children"; Frederic G. Cassidy, "Teaching Standard English to Speakers of Creole in Jamaica, West Indies"; Ralph Fasold, "Distinctive Linguistics Characteristics of Black English"; William A. Stewart, "Historical and Structural Bases for the Recognition of Negro Dialect"; and Walter A. Wolfram, "Linguistic Correlates of Social Differences in the Negro Community."

Alexander, Clara Franklin. 1985. Black English Dialect and the Classroom Teacher. In *Tapping Potential: English and Language Arts for the Black Learner,* ed. by C. Brooks, 20–29. Urbana, IL: NCTE.

1 S T
This is a particularly compelling and comprehensive article-length overview of the implications of Black English dialect in the classroom, comprising the history of the variety, myths and facts, description of some feature, instructional priorities for teachers; the role of dialect in reading and writing, and examples of activities for dialect study. While there are many articles of this type, Allen's broad view of the issues and emphasis on concrete examples set this one apart. The article first appeared in *The Reading Teacher* (33:5) in 1980, shortly after the *King* decision.

Alford, Danny. 1982. Rhetorical Redundancy in Apachean English Interlanguage. In *Essays in Native American English,* ed. by H. G. Bartelt, S. P. Jasper & B. Hoffer, 157–72. San Antonio, TX: Trinity University Press.

5 F

Alim, H. Samy. 2003. "We Are the Streets": African American Language and the Strategic Construction of a Street Conscious Identity. In *Black Linguistics: Language, Society and*

Politics in Africa and the Americas, ed. by S. Makoni, G. Smitherman, A. F. Ball & A. K. Spears, 40–59. London: Routledge.

1 I N

Alim, H. Samy. 2004. Hip Hop Nation Language. In *Language in the USA,* ed. by E. Finegan & J. R. Rickford. Cambridge: Cambridge University Press.

1 N
The article describes Hip Hop Nation Language (HHNL), examining lyrics from prominent rap artists to illuminate the characteristics of HHNL, including its rootedness in African American linguistic practices and regional variability.

Alim, H. Samy. 2004. *You Know My Steez: An Ethnographic and Sociolinguistic Study of Styleshifting in a Black American Speech Community.* Durham, NC: Duke University Press.

1 F N U

Alim, H. Samy. 2005. Critical Language Awareness in the United States: Revisiting Issues and Revising Pedagogies in a Resegregated Society. *Educational Researcher* 34.24–31. [Reprinted with permission of Sage Publications, the publisher, from Educational Researcher 34(7), 24.]

1 K L P
As scholars examine the successes and failures of more than 50 years of court-ordered desegregation since *Brown v. Board of Education of Topeka, Kansas,* and 25 years of language education of Black youth since *Martin Luther King Elementary School Children v. Ann Arbor School District Board,* this article revisits the key issues involved in those cases and urges educators and sociolinguists to work together to revise pedagogies. After reviewing what scholars have contributed, the author suggests the need for critical language awareness programs in the United States as one important way in which we can revise our pedagogies, not only to take the students' language into account but also to account for the interconnectedness of language with the larger sociopolitical and sociohistorical phenomena that help to maintain unequal power relations in a still-segregated society.

Alim, H. Samy & John Baugh (eds.) 2007. *Talkin Black Talk: Language, Education, and Social Change.* New York: Teachers College Press.

1 C E L N S T

Alim, H. Samy & John Baugh. 2010. Ethnosensitivity in Time and Space: Critical Hip Hop Language Pedagogies and Black Language in the US. In *Ethnolinguistic Diversity and Education: Language, Literacy, and Culture,* ed. by M. Farr, L. Seloni & J. Song, 150–66. New York: Routledge.

1 L P

Alim, H. Samy & Imani Perry. 2011. Lost in Translation: Language, Race and the DEA's Legitimization of Ebonics. *Anthropology News* 52.20.

1 K
A brief commentary on the US Drug Enforcement Agency's 2010 call for 'Ebonics translators' to assist with interpreting audiorecordings of AAVE speakers and highlights the discrepancy between law enforcement's willingness to acknowledge the unique nature of AAVE while the educational establishment refuses to legitimize its use as a resource in schools.

Alladina, Safder & Viv Edwards (eds.) 1991. *Multilingualism in the British Isles.* London: Longman.

2 E

Allen, Jeff. 1993. Report on St. Lucia and Dominica. *Pidgins and Creoles in Education (PACE) Newsletter* 4.2–3.

2

Allen, Virginia. 1969. Teaching Standard English as a Second Dialect. *The Florida FL Reporter* 7.123–29.

1 B S

Allen discusses the merits and methods of a contrastive analysis approach to teaching SAE to speakers of nonstandard varieties and documents its success by making reference to the Claflin project (see Lin 1963). The author emphasizes the importance of describing SAE as the variety of English that 'educated' speakers 'habitually' use, as opposed to an inherently superior language. In the approach recommended here, teachers select those SAE constructions that most noticeably differ from their nonstandard counterparts (as opposed to prescriptive rules that are often disregarded in SAE) and help students internalize them one by one through frequent oral repetition. When this method was implemented at Claflin College, students exhibited an increase in self-confidence and motivation. They improved their ability to communicate in SAE and self-correct, and they performed better than the control group in identifying and correcting nonstandard forms on a grammar test. Finally, although the primary focus was on oral speech, students also outperformed the control group on a reading test, and improved their writing ability.

Allen, Virginia. 1972. A Second Dialect Is Not a Foreign Language. In *Language and Cultural Diversity in American Education,* ed. by R. Abrahams & R. Troike, 319–26. Upper Saddle River, NJ: Prentice-Hall, Inc.

1 B S

Alleyne, Mervyn. 1980. *Comparative Afro-American: An Historical-Comparative Study of English-Based Afro-American Dialects of the New World.* Ann Arbor, MI: Karoma Publishers.

1 2 F

Allsopp, Jeannette. 2003. *The Caribbean Multilingual Dictionary of Flora, Fauna and Foods in English, French, French Creole and Spanish.* Kingston, Jamaica: Arawak Publishers.

2 F

Allsopp, Richard. 2000. The Afrogenesis of Caribbean Creole Proverbs. *Society for Caribbean Linguistics Occasional Paper.* 35–53. [Adapted with permission of the Society for Caribbean Linguistics from the original abstract from the Society for Caribbean Linguistics Occasional Paper #34.]

2 C F I

Allsopp points to striking similarities between proverbs from more than twenty-two Sub-Saharan African languages and more than a dozen Caribbean creoles (anglophone and francophone), and argues that the creole speakers have retained—through calquing or systemic transfer—the underlying conceptualization of their African ancestors. These similarities have significant theoretical implications for pidgin and creole linguistics, and Allsopp suggests that scholars should pay more attention to paremiography and paremiology—the collection and study of proverbs—since the latter encapsulate the thinking of our forebears, and preserve the morphology, semantics and idiomaticity of earlier times. He also proposes that the Society for Caribbean Linguistics reach out to teachers and the masses in every Caribbean territory more than it has thus far, supporting and seeking support from them in the study of words, proverbs, and other aspects of language.

Allsopp, Richard. 2006. *The Case for Afrogenesis*. St. Augustine, Trinidad and Tobago: Faculty of Humanities and Education, University of the West Indies.

2 F
Citing the preservation of African linguistic forms in the New World forms of Spanish, Portuguese, French, and English, Allsopp argues for the monogenesis of Caribbean Creoles and Pidgins from West-African languages—a phenomenon he terms *Afrogenesis*. Among the linguistic evidence for Afrogenesis presented in the paper are the phonemic, lexical, and syntactical African linguistic features which remain fundamental linguistic features of New World Spanish, Portuguese, French, and English. Using comparative analysis, the paper repudiates the notion that the primary connection between Caribbean languages is Portuguese; it affirms that the use of direct African vocabulary and the calquing of African idioms in New World dialects and creoles indicate their monogenesis from African languages. Finally, the article cites the uniformity found in the grammatical structure of sentences and word formation as well as the remarkable parallels found in the lexical and syntactical formation of proverbial phrases between African and Caribbean dialects as evidence for the Afrogenesis of pidgin and Creole languages present in both the Caribbean and Africa.

Allsopp, Richard & Jeannette Allsopp. 1996. *Dictionary of Caribbean English Usage*. New York: Oxford University Press.

2 F
This important cross-territorial reference work for the Anglophone Caribbean includes a French and Spanish supplement edited by Jeannette Allsopp, whose 2003 multilingual dictionary of flora, fauna and foods, included in this bibliographic resource, should also be consulted. The *Dictionary of Caribbean English Usage* was reissued in paperback by the University of the West Indies Press, Mona, Kingston, Jamaica, in 2003.

Alobweede d'Epie, C. 1998. Banning Pidgin English in Cameroon? *English Today* 14.54–56.

2 I

Alvarez, Louis & Andrew Kolker. 1987. *American Tongues*. New York: Center for New American Media.

1 F I M Z
Winner of a Peabody Award in 1987, this video, often shown in linguistics courses on university campuses, depicts regional and social variation in the United States, concentrating on words and pronunciations (accents), but also revealing attitudes and prejudices. It includes segments on Southern dialects and on AAVE, with commentary by Walt Wolfram and other academic and public figures.

Alvarez, Louis & Andrew Kolker. 1990. *Yeah You Rite!* New York: The Center for New American Media.

F
"This award-winning film is a fast paced, humorous look at the colorful way the residents of New Orleans express themselves—why they talk the way they do, where the words come from, and what it means to talk with a New Orleans accent." [From the

site: http://www.cnam.com/non_flash/language/yeah.html.] See the accompanying study guide by Walt Wolfram and Lois Refkin, available at http://www.robertapple-ton.com/cnam/downloads/yyr_sg.html, and see the other, even better known video by Louis Alvarez and Andrew Kolker, *American Tongues.*

Amberg, Julie S. & Deborah J. Vause. 2009. *American English: History, Structure, and Usage.* Cambridge: Cambridge University Press.

1 4 5 6 C F I S U
The book offers an overview of the features and history of American English. Especially relevant are chapters 8 ("Variations in American English"), which includes discussion of social and dialect formation and focuses on Chicano and African American English; 9 ("Language, Community, and American Policy"), which mentions US historical policies to speakers of Native American languages, Spanish and Hawai'ian; and 10 ("Conclusion: Language Policy and English Language Learners"), which includes a discussion of bilingual education in California.

Ames, Wilbur, Carl Rosen & Arthur Olsen. 1971. The Effects of Non-Standard Dialect on the Oral Reading Behavior of Fourth Grade Black Children. In *Language, Reading and the Communication Process,* ed. by C. Braun, 63–70. Newark, DE: International Reading Association.

1 O R X
Ames et al. examined dialect interference in the oral reading of Standard English sentences. Twenty-five randomly selected African American inner-city fourth graders were each presented with the fifteen Standard English sentences as developed in Baratz's (1969) bidialectal repetition task. Their oral reading responses were recorded and examined for each of eight key AAVE syntactic and grammatical features. Only four features, specifically those involving zero inflection on nouns and verbs, were observed in the data. Possessive markers, absent 62% of the time, were absent at a significantly greater rate than the other three. The authors note that two limitations of the study were that some of the assumed dialect-based responses could have been decoding miscues, and that subjects unable to read all of the sentences (who may have otherwise exhibited the most dialect features) were replaced. Furthermore, no measures were taken to exclude subjects who did not speak AAVE.

Anderson, Edward. 1989. *Students' Language Rights.* [Abstract prepared by ERIC.]

B L N S
A number of 'motivational' approaches through which students retain the right to their own dialects and language while learning Standard English as a new dialect, including: using a reading program that includes writing models from various heritages and cultures as well as mainstream authors; providing information about the meaning and history of American dialects; discussing and illustrating such verbal and rhetorical strategies as jiving, rapping, and playing the dozens; and role playing in small dramatic situations that require Standard English are described.

Anderson, Edward. 1990. Some Ways to Use the Rhetorical Skills of the Black American Folk Tradition to Teach Rhetoric and Composition *ERIC* ED 328919.

1 B N S

Anderson, Edward. 1990. Teaching Users of Diverse Dialects: Practical Approaches. *Teaching English in the Two-Year College* 17.172–77.

1 B S T V W

Anderson, Raquel. 2004. Phonological Acquisition in Preschoolers Learning a Second Language via Immersion: A Longitudinal Study. *Clinical Linguistics and Phonetics* 18.183–210.

3 6 F Q

Appel, Rene & Ludo Verhoeven. 1994. Decolonization, Language Planning and Education. In *Pidgins and Creoles: An Introduction*, ed. by J. Arends, P. Muysken & N. Smith, 65–74. Amsterdam: John Benjamins.

2 P V

Attinasi, John. 1997. Racism, Language Variety and Urban Minorities: Issues in Bilingualism and Bidialectism. In *Latinos and Education: A Critical Reader*, ed. by A. Darder, R. Torres & H. Gutierrez. New York: Routledge.

4 I P

Au, Kathryn H. 1980. Participation Structures in a Reading Lesson with Hawaiian Children: Analysis of a Culturally Appropriate Instructional Event. *Anthropology and Education Quarterly* 11.91–115.

2 C N S

Au, Kathryn H. 2008. If Can, Can: Hawai'i Creole and Reading Achievement. *Educational Perspectives* 41.66–76. [Abstract prepared by ERIC and reprinted with permission of the Department of Education from the Education Resources Information Center at eric.ed.gov.]

2 C R V
Every multicultural society has a language of power—the language spoken by members of the dominant group or groups—as well as languages that lack power because they are spoken by members of the subordinate group or groups. The ascension of one language over another has long been a source of controversy in Hawai'i, as it has in many parts of the world. In this essay, the author reviews what she has come to understand about Hawai'i Creole (HC) and its relationship to learning to read. The essay is organized around four topics: (1) language, literacy, and power in Hawai'i; (2) HC and literacy learning; (3) resistance to learning literacy in school; and (4) sustained school change to improve the literacy learning of students who speak HC as their primary language.

Au, Kathryn H. & Alice Kawakami. 1985. Research Currents: Talk Story and Learning to Read. *Language Arts* 62. 406–11.

2 C F N S

Au, Kathryn H. & Alice Kawakami. 1991. Culture and Ownership: Schooling of Minority Students. *Childhood Education* 67.280–84.

2 C

Awonusi, Victor O. 1990. Planning for a National (Nigerian) Language. In *Aesthetics and Utilitarianism in Languages and Literatures,* ed. by A. E. Eruvbetine, 113–19. Ojo: Lagos State University, Department of Languages and Literatures.

2 I

Bailey, Beryl. 1965. Toward a New Perspective in Negro English Dialectology. *American Speech* 40.171–77.

1 F

This is an early analysis of AAVE as a separate system from SE, claiming Creole origins and that the deep structure is different from SE's.

Bailey, Beryl. 1966. *Jamaican Creole Syntax: A Transformational Approach*. Cambridge: Cambridge University Press.

2 F

Here is one of the earliest systematic descriptions of the grammar of an English-based creole in a modern theoretical framework and one of the few by a native speaker. The transformational framework is now dated, but the book contains many examples, and provides a relatively complete account of the syntax of the idealized Jamaican basilectal or deepest creole, with some description of its phonology and morphology as well. The book includes a foreword by Robert B. Le Page.

Bailey, Beryl. 1970. Some Arguments against the Use of Dialect Readers in the Teaching of Initial Reading. *The Florida FL Reporter* 8.8, 47.

1 R V

In this short paper, Bailey disagrees with Stewart (1969b), arguing against the use of dialect readers for teaching reading to AAVE speaking children. She argues that (1) although authentic material may be more readily accepted by children 10 to 15 years old, this may not be the case with younger children first learning to read, and what constitutes authenticity in dialect materials is itself unclear; (2) given that Black children have receptive competence both in the standard and their own dialect, reading in the standard would allow competence in that variety to be extended; (3) if children have already acquired the requisite phoneme-grapheme "word attack skills," they would be ready for Standard English reading anyway; (4) it is counter-productive to delay the reading of Standard English, because the purpose of literacy in the United States is to read in Standard English. Although Bailey admits that her viewpoint is not fixed, she raises a number of other cautions, and expresses skepticism about subjecting Black children to "too much and too hastily conceived experimentation in our schools" (p. 47).

Bakari, Rosenna. 2003. Preservice Teachers' Attitudes toward Teaching African American Students: Contemporary Research. *Urban Education* 38.640–54.

1 I T

Baker, Colin. 1992. *Attitudes and Language*. Clevedon, UK: Multilingual Matters Limited.

1 I

Baker, Judith. 2002. Trilingualism. In *The Skin That We Speak*, ed. by L. Delpit & J. K. Dowdy, 49–62. New York: The New Press.

1 4 B S T

Baker, an English teacher in a vocational high school, describes her approach to language instruction. She operates under the assumption that in order to succeed, her students must command not only "formal" (academic) English, but also "home" English and the "professional" English that each of their vocations demands. She establishes respect for the language skills students bring to class by having them examine and present the main salient features of their home dialects, and then facilitates discussion and role-playing activities in order to foster awareness of the appropriateness of different styles of language in different situations. She notes that when students realize that they do not have to abandon or feel ashamed about the way they speak at home, they become more interested in language variation and more willing to learn the mechanics of formal English.

Baldwin, James. 1981. If Black English Isn't a Language, Then Tell Me, What Is? In *Black English and the Education of Black Children and Youth: Proceedings of the National Symposium on the King Decision,* ed. by G. Smitherman, 390–92. Detroit, MI: Center for Black Studies, Wayne State University Press.

1 I
This often cited talk/op-ed by James Baldwin was originally published in the *New York Times,* July 29, 1979.

Baldwin, James. 1988. A Talk to Teachers. In *The Graywolf Annual Five: Multicultural Literacy,* ed. by R. Simonson & S. Walker, 3–12. Saint Paul, MN: Graywolf Press.

1 I S T

Balester, Valerie & Ellen Weber. 2002. Ebonics, Standard American English, and the Power of First-Year Composition. In *Against the Grain: A Volume in Honor of Maxine Hairston,* ed. by M. Hairston, M. Keene, M. Trachsel, R. Joss & D. Jolliffe, 197–210. New York: Hampton.

1 W

Balester, Valerie M. 1993. *Cultural Divide: A Study of African American College-Level Writers.* Portsmouth, NH: Boynton/Cook.

1 C I W

Balhorn, Mark. 1999. Standard Written English and the Language of African Americans. *SECOL Review* 23.124–47.

1 W X

Ball, Arnetha F. 1992. Cultural Preference and the Expository Writing of African American Adolescents. *Written Communication* 9.501–32.

1 C F N W
The following research questions guide Ball's study of the expository writing patterns of African American students: (1) How do preferred organizational patterns vary by ethnic background? (2) What is the ability of these students to identify such patterns? She studies a racially diverse group of students from five urban classrooms, including fifth and sixth grade and high school students. Data collection for the study includes field notes, student writing, and ranking sheets indicating which patterns students prefer. She distinguishes between academic-based (including list patterns, topical nets, hierarchies, and matrices), and vernacular-based (circumlocution, narrative interspersion, and recursion) organizational patterns. All students reported a low preference for using academic patterns for conversational tasks, but African American high school students demonstrated a preference for academic-based patterns 0% of the time for academic written and conversational tasks (p. 518). Furthermore, the findings reveal significant differences between organizational patterns that Black high school students prefer and those preferred by mainstream English conventions. No major difference was found for middle school students. Ball concludes that the language resources of African American English speakers should be used to enhance the learning experience.

Ball, Arnetha F. 1994. Language, Learning, and Linguistic Competence of African American Children: Torrey Revisited. *Linguistics and Education* 7.23–46.

1 C R X

Ball, Arnetha F. 1995. Text Design Patterns in the Writing of Urban African American Students: Teaching to the Strengths of Students in Multicultural Settings. *Urban Education* 30.253–89.

1 C F N S W

Ball, Arnetha F. 1997. Expanding the Dialogue on Culture as a Critical Component When Assessing Writing. *Assessing Writing* 4.169–202. [Abstract prepared by ERIC and reprinted with permission of the Department of Education from the Education Resources Information Center at eric.ed.gov.]

1 I T W

This work reviews findings of an investigation in which four European American teachers assessed fifth and sixth grade students' written texts, and repeats the study using African American teachers assessing the same texts. Findings show that the teachers held consistently different views about assessment. The author presents the voices of the African American teachers, who share their deep-felt concerns and suggestions concerning writing assessment.

Ball, Arnetha F. 1999. Evaluating the Writing of Culturally and Linguistically Diverse Students: The Case of the African American Vernacular English Speaker. In *Evaluating Writing: The Role of Teacher's Knowledge About Text, Learning, and Culture*, ed. by C. Cooper & L. Odell, 225–48. Urbana, IL: National Council of Teachers of English Press.

1 A S W

Ball, Arnetha F. 2000. Empowering Pedagogies That Enhance the Learning of Multicultural Students. *Teachers College Record* 102.1006-34.

1 C S T

Ball, Arnetha F. 2000. Preparing Teachers for Diversity: Lessons Learned from South Africa. *Teacher and Teacher Education* 16.491–509.

1 C T

Ball, Arnetha F. & H. Samy Alim. 2006. Preparation, Pedagogy, Policy, and Power: Brown, the King Case, and the Struggle for Equal Language Rights. *Yearbook of the National Society for the Study of Education* 105.104–24. [Abstract prepared by ERIC and reprinted with permission of the Department of Education from the Education Resources Information Center at eric.ed.gov.]

1 K P

For scholars of literacy and educational linguistics, the years 2004 and beyond have given them cause to not only revisit racial issues fifty years after *Brown v. Board of Education*, but also to revisit twenty-five years of language and racial politics since "the Martin Luther King Black English case." This chapter discusses what needs to happen now—with "more deliberate speed"—as the authors reflect on the years since these two cases were decided and their impact on language education in the United States. As people of color continue to struggle for equal language rights in the United States, the authors call for an agenda that focuses on policy, pedagogy, and preparation. They discuss the historically neglected linguistic dimensions of *Brown* and *King*; and the educational responses to the rulings. In the final section, they consider the challenges that remain to be addressed.

Ball, Arnetha F. & Ted Lardner. 1997. Dispositions toward Language: Constructs of Teacher Knowledge and the Ann Arbor Black English Case. *College Composition and Communication* 48.469–85.

1 I K T W

After reviewing the Ann Arbor Black English case as it relates to teacher attitude, Ball and Lardner present three 'constructs of teacher knowledge' in writing instruction, each of which offers a unique perspective on how teachers transform theory into practice: under 'teacher as technician', teachers simply acquire the necessary sociolinguistic knowledge and adjust accordingly; under 'teacher knowledge as lore', teachers transcend disciplinary knowledge and rely on intuition, and under 'teacher efficacy', teachers operate based on the extent to which they perceive themselves as effective instructors. The authors then discuss implications for teaching writing to African American students, and conclude that instructors would benefit from a knowledge of African American language and culture, in addition to an awareness of how language diversity in the classroom can be an instructional bridge rather than a mere hindrance.

Ball, Arnetha F. & Ted Lardner. 2005. *African American Literacies Unleashed: Vernacular Englishes in the Composition Classroom.* Carbondale: Southern Illinois University.

1 N S T V W

Ball, Arnetha F. & Rashidah Jaami Muhammad. 2003. Language Diversity in Teacher Education and in the Classroom. In *Language Diversity in the Classroom: From Intention to Practice*, ed. by G. Smitherman & V. Villanueva, 76–88. Carbondale: Southern Illinois University Press.

1 4 I T

Ball, Arnetha F., Jilo Williams & Jamal Cooks. 1997. An Ebonics-Based Curriculum: The Educational Value. *Thought & Action* 13.39–50. [Abstract prepared by ERIC and reprinted with permission of the Department of Education from the Education Resources Information Center at eric.ed.gov.]

1 A B C K

The authors examine issues in introduction of an ebonics-based curriculum in public schools in response to the crisis in academic achievement of African American students. They outline the cultural role of African American Vernacular English, concerns about learning levels of students not proficient in Standard English, and implications for supporting diversity in both higher education and elementary and secondary education.

Ball, Jessica & B. May Bernhardt. 2008. First Nations English Dialects in Canada: Implications for Speech-Language Pathology. *Clinical Linguistics & Phonetics* 22.570–88.

5 A F

Balter, Allison & Frank D. Grossman. 2009. The Effects of the No Child Left Behind Act on Language and Culture Education in Navajo Public Schools. *Journal of American Indian Education* 48.19–46.

5 C P

Bangura, Abdul. 2010. *Ebonics Is Good.* San Diego, CA: Cognella.

1 F I K P

Banotai, Alyssa. 2006. Broaden the Language Continuum: Understand Dialect to Boost Diagnostic Skills. *ADVANCE for Speech-Language Pathologists and Audiologists* 16.6–7, 18.

1 6 D

Based on an interview with Toya Wyatt, the author describes why it is important for speech-language pathologists to understand the features of non-Standard English dialects such as AAVE, Appalachian English and Cajun English to avoid misdiagnosing students who use features of those dialects as having a speech-language disorder or abnormality. Among other things, Wyatt emphasizes the value of sampling children's speech in informal as well as formal contexts, and recommends using the Diagnostic Evaluation of Language Variation [DELV] screening test (see Seymour et al. 2003a in this bibliography) to distinguish dialect differences from disorders and identify a child's risk factor for disorder.

Baratz, Joan. 1969. A Bidialectal Task for Determining Language Proficiency in Economically Disadvantaged Negro Children. *Child Development* 40. 889–901.

1 O U X
Baratz combats previous work which argued that because Black children experienced more difficulty repeating back SAE utterances than did White children, they were 'verbally destitute.' Third and fifth graders from two schools in Washington, D.C. were given a repetition task in which fifteen sentences were in SAE and fifteen sentences were in AAVE. Results indicated that White subjects were significantly better at repeating SAE sentences than were Black subjects, especially concerning the third person singular present tense morpheme, if-did constructions, and single negation. On the other hand, Black subjects were significantly better at repeating AAVE utterances than were White subjects, especially concerning did-he constructions and double negation. The author concludes that Black children are generally not bidialectal and experience dialect interference in attempting to produce SAE, and that assessment of language development in Black children should take into account AAVE production in order to be accurate.

Baratz, Joan. 1969. Linguistic and Cultural Factors in Teaching Reading to Ghetto Children. *Elementary English* 46.199–203.

1 C R S X

Baratz, Joan. 1969. Teaching Reading in an Urban Negro School System. In *Teaching Black Children to Read,* ed. by J. Baratz & R. Shuy, 92–116. Washington, D.C.: Center for Applied Linguistics.

1 R S
This includes much of the argumentation and data from Baratz' often-cited (1969) study in Child Development (fully abstracted above) in which she asked African American and White elementary school students to repeat thirty sentences they heard on a tape recording. She found that the African American students did significantly better on the fifteen sentences in AAVE and the White students significantly better on the fifteen sentences in Standard English. In a style similar to that of Labov (1969), Baratz argued that their performance was systematically related to their respective dialects and that contemporary educators and psychologists were wrong in hypothesizing that the language differences and reading difficulties of AAVE-speaking students were indicative of or related to linguistic/cognitive limitations.

Baratz, Joan. 1970. Educational Considerations for Teaching Standard English to Negro Children. In *Teaching Standard English in the Inner City,* ed. by R. Fasold & R. Shuy, 20–40. Washington, D.C.: Center for Applied Linguistics.

1 R S

Baratz, Joan. 1970. Should Black Children Learn White Dialect? *ASHA* 12.415–17.

1 B I P

Baratz, Joan. 1973. Relationship of Black English to Reading: A Review of Research. In *Language Differences: Do They Interfere?*, ed. by J. Laffey & R. Shuy, 101–13. Newark, DE: International Reading Association.

1 E R X

Baratz, Joan & Roger Shuy (eds.) 1969. *Teaching Black Children to Read.* Washington, D.C.: Center for Applied Linguistics.

1 E R V X

Baratz and Shuy present eight papers concerning the possible linguistic causes of low reading achievement among many lower-class African American students. McDavid argues that the more a student's dialect differs from Standard English, the more difficult is the task of learning to read. Goodman takes the same stance, and argues that teachers should allow students to render texts in their own dialects. Labov zeroes in on subtle phonological differences between SAE and AAVE as a source of difficulty. Fasold argues for the use of standard orthography in dialect materials. Baratz presents evidence for linguistic interference and proposes the use of vernacular texts in teaching reading. Shuy further builds on the idea of vernacular texts, and presents ways of making them most effective. Wolfram and Fasold offer three example passages written in AAVE. Finally, Stewart focuses on linguistic interference and warns of possible difficulties associated with the use of vernacular texts.

Barbag-Stoll, Anna. 1983. *Social and Linguistic History of Nigerian Pidgin English.* Tübingen, Germany: Stauffenberg-Verlag.

2 F

Barnes, Sandra. 2003. The Ebonics Enigma: An Analysis of Attitudes on an Urban College Campus. *Race, Ethnicity and Education* 6.247–63.

1 I

Three hundred eighty-nine ethnically diverse students at a southern university filled out a 27-item Likert-type survey regarding their opinions about Ebonics. While overall scores suggested a high degree of variation and ambivalence, analysis of response patterns yielded three prevailing opinions: (1) Ebonics is acceptable and pedagogically useful; (2) Ebonics is neither favorable nor unfavorable, but is associated with socioeconomic disadvantage; and (3) Ebonics is not a legitimate language and impedes learning. The first position correlated positively with liberal political orientation, younger age, lower class ranking, lack of knowledge about the Oakland controversy, and, to a lesser extent, being male. Similarly, (2) was correlated with liberal political orientation and younger age, but also with not voting for Clinton in the 1996 presidential election and with identifying oneself as White. Position (3) was minimally correlated with knowledge of the Oakland controversy. Having uncovered these patterns among a diverse urban community, the author suggests further research regarding the opinions of larger population segments, as well as of lower class African Americans in particular.

Bartel, Nettie & Judith Axelrod. 1973. Nonstandard English Usage and Reading Ability in Black Junior High Students. *Exceptional Children* 39.653–55.

1 R X

Bartel, Nettie, Jeffrey Grill & Diane Bryen. 1973. Language Characteristics of Black Children: Implications for Assessment. *Journal of School Psychology* 11.351–64.

1 A

Bartelt, H. Guillermo. 1981. Semantic Overgeneralizations in Apachean English Interlanguage. *Journal of English Linguistics* 15.10–16.

5 F

Bartelt, H. Guillermo. 1982. Tense Switching in Narrative English Discourse of Navajo and Western Apache Speakers. *Studies in Second Language Acquisition* 4.201–04.

5 F

Bartelt, H. Guillermo. 2001. *Socio- and Stylolinguistic Perspectives on American Indian English Texts.* Lewiston, NY: Edwin Mellen Press.

5 F N

Bartelt, H. Guillermo, Susan Penfield-Jasper & Bates Hoffer (eds.) 1982. *Essays in Native American English.* San Antonio, TX: Trinity University Press.

5 E F

Battle, Dolores. 1993. *Communication Disorders in Multicultural Populations.* Boston, MA: Andover Medical Publishers.

1 2 3 4 5 D

Battle, Dolores. 1996. Language Learning and Use by African American Children. *Topics in Language Disorders* 16.22–37.

1 D F Q

Baugh, John. 1981. Design and Implementation of Language Arts Programs for Speakers of Nonstandard English. In *The Writing Needs of Linguistically Different Students,* ed. by B. Cronnell, 17–43. Los Alamitos, CA: SWRL Educations Research and Development.

1 S W

Baugh, John. 1983. *Black Street Speech: Its History, Structure and Survival.* Austin: University of Texas Press.

1 E F

Baugh, John. 1988. Language and Race: Some Implications for Linguistic Science. In *Language: The Socio-Cultural Context,* ed. by F. J. Newmeyer, 64–74. Cambridge: Cambridge University Press.

1 A I
This article aims to affirm the cognitive equality of people of differing races through linguistics, expanding and updating the Linguistic Society of America's response to Arthur Jensen's (1969) hypothesis about possible genetic causes of low African American scores on standardized tests of intelligence. Addressing Thomas J. Farrell's "IQ and Standard English," Baugh argues that Farrell's reasoning is unconvincing and fails to account for linguistic differences between standard and non-Standard English that lead to achievement gaps between Black and White students on standardized tests. Baugh specifically critiques the notion of oral and literate mentalities differentiating between abstract and non-abstract thought.

Baugh, John. 1992. Hypocorrection: Mistakes in Production of Vernacular African American English as a Second Dialect. *Language & Communication* 12.317–26.

1 Q U

Baugh, John. 1995. The Law, Linguistics, and Education: Educational Reform for African American Language Minority Students. *Linguistics and Education* 7.87–106.

1 P
Baugh critically examines the fact that African Americans are often excluded from receiving funding as a language minority because English is their native language, and says that current linguistic regulations are inconsistent with educational goals for reform. He believes that many African American students are misassigned to incorrect language programs. The native dialect of many students represents a language barrier to full participation in school, and limits their academic and social advancement. Referring to the 1977-79 Black English trial, in which the plaintiffs were the victim of misguided classroom placements, Baugh examines the judge's decision and highlights the fact that he left the issue of linguistic classification unresolved and chose to focus on teacher training. The author gives a legal summary of current regulations that exclude most African American English speakers from funding for language minority students—summarizing Chapter 1, Title VII, and special education and addressing the difficulties with each. He argues that educators should classify and distinguish between students based on linguistic background and suggests that teachers be trained to have a better understanding of the educational consequences of pidginization and creolization. He advocates that instruction be tailored to the linguistic and cultural needs of students.

Baugh, John. 1999. Considerations in Preparing Teachers for Linguistic Diversity. In *Making the Connection,* ed. by C. Adger, D. Christian & O. Taylor, 81–96. Washington, D.C.: CAL/Delta.

1 T

Baugh, John. 1999. *Out of the Mouths of Slaves: African American Language and Linguistic Malpractice.* Austin: University of Texas Press.

1 A C E F K O R S

Baugh, John. 1999. Reading, Writing, and Rap: Lyric Shuffle and Other Motivational Strategies to Introduce and Reinforce Literacy. In *Out of the Mouths of Slaves,* 31–40. Austin: University of Texas Press.

1 R S W
In this paper, originally published under a different title in 1981 in Bruce Cronnell, ed., *The Writing Needs of Linguistically Different Students,* Baugh describes "Lyric Shuffle," a series of games intended to motivate Black children in learning to read by allowing them to select popular song lyrics as reading material. After passing out copies of the lyrics to each student, the instructor plays the song and helps children follow along by using an overhead projector to point to each word as it is sung. Students still new to reading can then play by circling every instance of a predetermined letter, as an exercise in phoneme-grapheme correspondence. More advanced readers, in turn, can play a variety of games that foster both reading and writing skills in which they use vocabulary lists of words taken from their songs to write their own sentences, poems, lyrics or short stories.

Baugh, John. 2000. *Beyond Ebonics: Linguistic Pride and Racial Prejudice.* New York: Oxford University Press.

1 E I K P

Baugh, John. 2000. Oakland's Ebonics Resolutions. In *Beyond Ebonics: Linguistic Pride and Racial Prejudice,* 37–48. New York: Oxford University Press.

1 I K

In Chapter 4 of *Beyond Ebonics*, Baugh presents a brief background to Oakland's Ebonics resolutions and the controversy that followed. He includes the original Policy Statement issued by the African American task force of the Oakland Unified School District, which constitutes "the first formal statement of the controversial interpretation that Ebonics is a language other than English" (p. 38). After outlining the resulting opposition that this caused among linguists, who generally made no distinction between "Ebonics" and "Black English," he then includes the original Ebonics resolution of the Oakland school board, along with the subsequent revision it underwent in light of this opposition. Ultimately, he supports the revision, which implies that "Ebonics" is indeed part of the English speech community, and clarifies that the goal of the educational program should be to use Black English as a bridge for learning Standard English.

Baugh, John. 2001. Applying Linguistic Knowledge of African American English to Help Students Learn and Teachers Teach. In *Sociocultural and Historical Contexts of African American English,* ed. by S. Lanehart, 319–30. Philadelphia: John Benjamins.

1 S T

Baugh addresses the roles of parent, educator, and student in contributing to the success of African American children in school. Parents or other adult advocates are most successful when able to "intercede on behalf of their children in academic settings" (p. 322), which may be difficult for parents who are not proficient in SAE. Educators, in turn, who understand African American culture and value less fortunate children are most likely to be effective. Finally, students must be devoted to their studies and take increased responsibility for their performance as they grow older. The author notes that linguistic stereotypes are still pervasive among teachers and that steps must be taken to ensure that students' home languages are not devalued. To this end, he recommends teacher-training methods that are minimally burdensome on the teachers' time. Aside from linguistic concerns, the author mentions the problem of unequal educational opportunities across the nation's schools, and feels that there must be a balance between minimal national standards and local freedom to shape curriculum. In conclusion he emphasizes that "no child should be made to feel ashamed of his or her native language and culture" (p. 329).

Baugh, John. 2004. Ebonics and Its Controversy. In *Language in the USA,* ed. by E. Finegan & J. R. Rickford, 305–18. Cambridge: Cambridge University Press.

1 B K

Baugh provides an informed perspective on the Ebonics controversy sparked by the Oakland school board's December 1996 resolution to embrace Ebonics as the language spoken by their African American students in an attempt to advance their proficiency in Standard English and increase the level of their academic achievement in all subjects. He examines the origins of Ebonics and its shifting definitions, tracing its journey from "nonstandard Negro English" through "Black English" to "Ebonics." He also considers the international implications inherent in the linguistic legacy that gave birth to the term, acknowledging the multinational and multilingual foundations spawned by the European slave trade that extended from West Africa throughout North and South America and the Caribbean. He discusses the serious educational considerations surrounding the students who speak Ebonics, reflecting on the long-standing academic failure that exists in African American communities like Oakland, and the glaring educational flaws in need of immediate redress. Finally, he urges "fair-minded educators and policymakers" to continue the ongoing quest to make fluency in Standard English a reality for African American students in order to bolster their academic prospects and open avenues to equal educational opportunity.

Baugh, John. 2005. Linguistics and Education in Multilingual America. In *Language in the Schools: Integrating Linguistic Knowledge into K-12 Teaching,* ed. by K. Denham & A. Lobeck, 5–16.

1 C I

Baugh, John. 2006. Linguistic Considerations Pertaining to Brown v. Board: Exposing Racial Fallacies in the New Millennium. *Yearbook of the National Society for the Study of Education* 105.90–103. [Abstract prepared by ERIC and reprinted with permission of the Department of Education from the Education Resources Information Center at eric.ed.gov.]

1 P

Brown v. Board of Education reminds this author, a linguist, of the linguistic diversity among Black Americans, be they descendants of enslaved Africans—as he is proud to be—or Africans who escaped slavery. There is as much linguistic diversity among their race as among any other racial or ethnic group in the United States. When the Supreme Court handed down its landmark decision, *Brown* was hailed as the case that would lead to educational equality for all African Americans. That vision, however, has yet to be realized. In part, that is because, since *Brown,* they have come to understand that racial segregation was only one obstacle standing in their way. This paper seeks to introduce some neglected linguistic dimensions into this realm, with particular attention to the *Brown* ruling and the growing linguistic diversity of Black America.

Baugh, John. 2006. Teaching English among Linguistically Diverse Students. In *English and Ethnicity,* ed. by J. Brutt-Griffler & C. E. Davies, 217–29. New York: Palgrave Macmillan.

1 P T

Baugh, John. 2007. Plantation English in America: Nonstandard Varieties and the Quest for Educational Equity. *Research in the Teaching of English* 41.465–72. [Abstract prepared by ERIC and reprinted with permission of the Department of Education from the Education Resources Information Center at eric.ed.gov.]

1 2 I P

The author shares his experience growing up speaking African American Vernacular English in school and his observations about nonstandard American plantation English. The author's amateur linguistic observations about nonstandard American plantation English gave rise to immediate dialect comparisons between African American Vernacular English (AAVE) and Hawaiian Pidgin English (HPE). Although the Oakland Ebonics controversy attempted to draw strong linguistic parallels between vernacular African American language usage and the acquisition of English as a second language, the author thinks that there are closer linguistic (and educational) parallels between HPE and AAVE situations. However, the plantation vernaculars that emerged in Hawaii and the southern United States have been greatly misunderstood by linguists and educators, to say little of the politicians and pundits who routinely criticize the nonstandard speech of Hawaiians and African Americans who lack fluency in Standard English. Regardless of racial background, speakers of non-Standard English frequently encounter misconceptions about their intellectual ability as well as other stereotypes that devalue the ways in which they use language. Here, the author hopes that these observations may help to clarify the historical relevance of plantation English on the education of many students residing in diverse American communities, including rural Appalachia, America's inner cities, and the islands of Hawaii.

Baugh, John. 2009. Linguistic Diversity, Access, and Risk. *Review of Research in Education* 33.272–82.

1 E P

Baugh, John & Aaron Welborn. 2009. The Hidden Linguistic Legacies of *Brown v. Board* and *No Child Left Behind*. In *Affirming Students' Right to Their Own Language: Bridging Language Policies and Pedagogical Practices,* ed. by J. Cobb Scott, D. Straker & L. Katz, 41–53. New York: Routledge/NCTE.

1 P

The authors review the history and details of "two of the most sweeping Federal measures aimed at providing an equitable education for African Americans and other historically disadvantaged groups" and conclude that each missed opportunities to take language into account in designing educational policies.

Baxter, Milton & Rochelle Holland. 2007. Addressing the Needs of Students Who Speak a Nonstandard English Dialect. *Adult Basic Education and Literacy Journal* 1.145–53. [Reprinted with permission of COABE from the *Adult Basic Education and Literacy Journal* 1(3), 145.]

1 B W

This quasi-experimental study was conducted to assess and address the instructional needs of students who use a nonstandard English dialect for subject-verb agreement in their writing. Fifty-four students of diverse ethnicities in remedial English courses were divided into control and experimental groups. The researchers used four different measurements to assess the students' writing attitudes and to determine their awareness levels for writing Standard English subject-verb agreement. This preliminary study produced strong implications for the teaching of Standard English rules for subject-verb agreement to students who use nonstandard subject-verb agreement while writing English. Further research that implements the instructional methods from this study is needed.

Bayley, Robert. 2008. Latino Varieties of English. In *A Companion to the History of the English Language,* ed. by H. Momma & M. Matto. Oxford: Wiley-Blackwell.

4 F

Bayley, Robert. 2009. Explicit Formal Instruction in Oral Language: English Language Learners. Paper presented at the NRC Workshop on the role of language in school learning: Implications for closing the achievement gap, Menlo Park, CA. See www.nap.edu/catalog.php?record_id=12907

1 4 6 O S

Bayley, Robert & Lisa M. Bonnici. 2009. Recent Research on Latinos in the USA and Canada, Part 1: Language Maintenance and Shift and English Varieties. *Language and Linguistics Compass* 3.1300–13.

4 E U

Bayley, Robert & Otto Santa Ana. 2008. Chicano English: Morphology and Syntax. In *Varieties of English, Vol 2: The Americas and the Caribbean,* ed. by E. Schneider, 572–90. Berlin: Walter de Gruyter.

4 F

Bayley, Robert & Sandra Schecter. 2005. Spanish Maintenance and English Literacy: Mexican-Descent Children's Spanish and English Narratives. In *Language in the Schools:*

Integrating Linguistic Knowledge into K-12 Teaching, ed. by K. Denham & A. Lobeck, 121–38.

4 N
The authors report on an analysis of seventy-one narrative essays (41 in English, 30 in Spanish) produced by Mexican-descent children in grades 4-6. Essays were rated to determine the degree to which children's written narratives adhered to a classic Labovian structure. Overall, there was very little difference in the narrative structure ratings for English and Spanish essays—for both, the mean was between 3 and 4 on a 6-point scale. From this, the authors conclude that these bilingual students command discourse-level features in both Spanish and English. Additionally, the researchers involved bilingual teachers in developing an assessment rubric to evaluate children's narratives—one which weighted higher-order concerns with organization and structure over surface and mechanical features such as spelling and punctuation.

Bean, Janet, Robert Eddy, Rhonda Grego, Patricia Irvine, Ellie Kutz, Paul Kei Matsuda, Maryann Cucchiara, Peter Elbow, Rich Haswell, Eileen Kennedy & Al Lehner. 2003. Should We Invite Students to Write in Home Languages? Complicating the Yes/No Debate. *Composition Studies* 31.25–42. [Abstract prepared by ERIC and reprinted with permission of the Department of Education from the Education Resources Information Center at eric.ed.gov.]

1 4 V W
This is an account of the authors' shared explorations and efforts to name some important variables or criteria that bear on the question of whether or not to invite students to write in a home dialect or language. The author offers conclusions in the form of a list of ten variables to consider.

Beck, Sarah W. 2009. Individual Goals and Academic Literacy: Integrating Authenticity and Explicitness. *English Education* 41.259–80. [Abstract prepared by ERIC and reprinted with permission of the Department of Education from the Education Resources Information Center at eric.ed.gov.]

1 C I
Beck presents a case study of one student's development as a writer in the context of an English classroom in which both curriculum and instruction were strongly influenced by a district-wide context of standards-based reform and the accompanying pressure surrounding high-stakes testing. Sheila, the African American student who is the subject of this study, challenged the values that underlay her teacher's expectations for observing the conventions of Standard English in her writing and, in doing so, contributed to a compelling illustration of the limits of explicitness in the teaching of writing. Interviews with Sheila about her essays offer insight into the sources of motivation that inspired her to develop complex analytical ideas in her essays, even as she maintained her stance on the seeming irrelevance of Standard English as a criterion for a high-quality paper. Drawing on these interviews and samples of her writing, along with teacher interviews and field notes from observations of her English class, the author discusses both her resistance to and her enthusiasm for certain aspects of the writing tasks her teacher set for her, highlighting the significance of points at which the teacher's instruction intersected with her goals and where it did not.

Becker, Bronwyn & Suniya Luthar. 2002. Social-Emotional Factors Affecting Achievement Outcomes among Disadvantaged Students: Closing the Achievement Gap. *Educational Psychologist* 37.197–214.

1 A I S
Although it has no linguistic argumentation or evidence, this article is a useful review of the Black-White achievement gap in US schools, and four social-emotional

components that influence it: academic and school attachment, teacher support, peer values, and mental health. Several school reform models (e.g., Success for All, Direct Instruction) with extensive research bases are reviewed.

Bell, Yvonne & Tangela Clark. 1998. Culturally Relevant Reading Material as Related to Comprehension and Recall in African American Children. *Journal of Black Psychology* 24.455–75.

1 C R
Bell and Clark study story recall and comprehension rates of African American children as a function of the racial imagery and cultural themes of the story. One hundred and nine African American students in grades 1-4 were each presented with one of three story types: Black characters and African American themes, White characters and Euro American themes, and Black characters and Euro American themes. Analysis of recall and comprehension scores showed that the presence of Black characters had a significant and positive effect on comprehension; on recall, however, only third and fourth graders exhibited the effect. Furthermore, presence of African American themes had a significant and positive effect on both recall and comprehension. The authors conclude that their study supports previous research claiming that culturally relevant reading material facilitates information processing, and recommend further research to look for similar effects in other educational resources and in other academic subjects.

Bender, Margaret. 2003. Language and Literacy Teaching for Indigenous Education: A Bilingual Approach. *American Indian Culture and Research Journal* 27.115–17.

5
This is a review article on Francis and Reyhner 2002.

Benor, Sarah Bunin. 2010. Ethnolinguistic Repertoire: Shifting the Analytic Focus in Language and Ethnicity. *Journal of Sociolinguistics* 14.159–83.

1 3 4 F

Bentley, Robert & Samuel Crawford (eds.) 1973. *Black Language Reader.* Glenview, IL: Scott, Foresman.

1 E F S

Berdan, Robert. 1980. Knowledge into Practice: Delivering Research to Teachers. In *Reactions to Ann Arbor: Vernacular Black English and Education,* ed. by M. F. Whiteman. Arlington, VA: Center for Applied Linguistics.

1 I R T
The author discusses effective methods of helping in-service teachers to use linguistics to teach reading in a less intimidating way.

Bereiter, Carl & Siegfried Engelmann. 1966. *Teaching the Disadvantaged Child in the Preschool.* Engelwood Cliffs, NJ: Prentice-Hall.

1 A P

Berger, Mary. 1990. *Speak Standard Too: Add Standard English as a Second Dialect to Your Talking Style.* Chicago: Orchard Books.

1 B M O S
Berger, an experienced speech-language pathologist, presents a guide aimed at teaching SAE to speakers of non-Standard English. The book, written in a straightforward but friendly style, assumes the pragmatic stance that command of SAE is not

a replacement for one's native dialect, but merely a useful additional tool. The first section, Pronunciation Differences, is divided into four chapters (Consonant Clusters, Consonant Sounds, Vowel Sounds, and Word Pronunciation Differences), each of which attends to a variety of relevant contrastive features along with examples and practice drills. The second section, Grammatical Differences, consists of twenty-four lessons aimed at standard usage of verbs, pronouns, prepositions, and more, also with examples and drills.

Berlin, Lawrence N. 2000. The Benefits of Second Language Acquisition and Teaching for Indigenous Language Educators. *Journal of American Indian Education* 39.19–35.

5 Q T

Bernstein, Cynthia Goldin. 2006. Representing Jewish Identity through English. In *English and Ethnicity,* ed. by J. Brutt-Griffler & C. E. Davies, 107–30. New York: Palgrave MacMillan.

6

Berry, Rosaline & Joyce Hudson. 1997. *Making the Jump: A Resource Book for Teachers of Aboriginal Students.* Canberra: Language Australia.

2 6 F M S

Birch, Barbara. 2001. Grammar Standards: It's All in Your Attitude. *Language Arts* 78.535–42.

1 I T
This article, intended for elementary language arts educators, elucidates the assumptions inherent in standard language ideology. Birch distinguishes between the concept of a 'standard grammar' and a 'grammar standard', the latter being a rigid prescriptivist position that fails to take into account language variation and change. A continuum model of language attitudes, with clear examples, ranging from "language equality" to "language prejudice," invites educators to identify and critique their own language perspectives. The author closes by stating that although language equality would be ideal, the realities of language prejudice may necessitate a policy of 'pragmatic prescriptivism,' in which the standard is taught, but not under the presumption that it is in any way inherently superior, and not without a degree of permissiveness toward change.

Birrell, James R. 1995. "Learning How the Game Is Played": An Ethnically Encapsulated Beginning Teacher's Struggle to Prepare Black Youth for a White World. *Teaching and Teacher Education* 11.137–47. [Abstract prepared by ERIC and reprinted with permission of the Department of Education from the Education Resources Information Center at eric.ed.gov.]

1 C I N T
This case study examined how growing up with limited exposure to minority cultures influenced one beginning secondary teacher's first teaching year in multicultural schools. Journal and interview data indicated that his underpreparation for oppositional ethnic behaviors created teacher behavior that diminished Black students' school learning and cultural identity.

Bixler-Márquez, Dennis & Jacob Ornstein-Galicia (eds.) 1988. *Chicano Speech in the Bilingual Classroom.* New York: Peter Lang.

4 E T U V

Black Scholar. 1997. *Special Issues on Ebonics* Vol. 27, No. 1 (Spring) and 2 (Summer).

K

Blackburn, Mollie & Deborah Stern. 2000. Analyzing the Role of the Vernacular in Student Writing: A Social Literacies Approach. *Educational Linguistics* 16.53–69.

1 C T V W

Blake, Ira Kincade. 1993. The Social-Emotional Orientation of Mother–Child Communication in African American Families. *International Journal of Behavioral Development* 16.443–63.

1 Q

Blake, Mary E. & Meta Van Sickle. 2001. Helping Linguistically Diverse Students Share What They Know. *Journal of Adolescent and Adult Literacy* 44.468–75.

1 2 B S W
In this case study, Blake and Van Sickle work with nine African American students from Sea Island High School in South Carolina who had been unable to pass the South Carolina Exit Exam (SCEE). Their goal was to foster the students' abilities to code-switch from their island dialect into Standard English in order to enhance their ability to discuss academic subjects, particularly math and science. By working closely with the students and engaging them in a series of dialogues and writing-workshop sessions in which students talked and wrote about their own personal experiences, the authors gained a greater understanding of the structure of the island dialect and of the nature of language development and code-switching. The students, in turn, improved their ability to code-switch and learned to communicate in Standard English well enough to pass the SCEE. Blake and Van Sickle conclude that an understanding of code-switching and its importance is necessary for both students and teachers in any multi-dialect setting.

Blake, Renee. 1997. Defining the Envelope of Linguistic Variation: The Case of 'Don't Count' Forms in the Copula Analysis of African American Vernacular English. *Language Variation and Change* 9.57–79.

1 F

Blake, Renee & Cecilia Cutler. 2003. AAE and Variation in Teachers' Attitudes: A Question of School Philosophy? *Linguistics and Education* 14.163–94.

1 I T
Eighty-eight teachers at five high schools in New York City completed a 19-point Likert-type survey concerning their attitudes on language variation and instruction. A total of 69% of the respondents viewed AAVE as a form of English, and 55% agreed that it is rule-governed. However, while 52% support bilingual education, only 20% support bidialectal education. Results also indicate that teachers' opinions are significantly affected by the philosophy of the school at which they teach. Teachers at schools that emphasized bilingual education because of their large immigrant population, for example, were more positive in their attitude toward AAVE than are schools with more African American students. The authors conclude that in order to increase sensitivity toward nonstandard varieties of English and educate those children who speak them, educational policies should require teachers to be trained in language diversity.

Blake, Renee & Department of Linguistics at NYU. 2009. *Word: The Online Journal on African American English.* Department of Linguistics, New York University.

1 C F L N O

The website is edited and maintained by Professor Renee A. Blake, other faculty, and students in the Department of Linguistics at New York University. As Blake notes in the "Who we are" section of the website, "This blog was created by Niki Hossack, a graduating senior in my African American English class during Spring 2009. For the final project, I asked students to create something that would aid in educating ourselves about issues pertaining to African American English. Niki followed through with the idea of a blog as a mechanism to share knowledge about African American English with the larger community."

Blake, Renee & Cara Shousterman. 2010. Second Generation West Indian Americans and English in New York City. *English Today* 26.35–43.

2 6

Bland-Stewart, Linda. 2003. Phonetic Inventories and Phonological Patterns of African American Two-Year-Olds: A Preliminary Investigation. *Communication Disorders Quarterly* 24.109–21.

1 D F Q

Bliss, Lynn & Doris Allen. 1981. Black English Responses on Selected Language Tests. *Journal of Communication Disorders* 14.225–33.

1 A D

Blodgett, Elizabeth & Eugene Cooper. 1973. Attitudes of Elementary Teachers toward Black Dialect. *Journal of Communication Disorders* 6.121–33.

1 I T
Survey of 210 elementary teachers in Alabama. Significantly different patterns of responses between Black and White teachers.

Bogatz, Boris, Toshi Hisama, John Manni & Ressa Wurtz. 1986. Cognitive Assessment of Nonwhite Children. In *Treatment of Communication Disorders in Culturally and Linguistically Diverse Populations,* ed. by O. Taylor. San Diego, CA: College Hill Press.

1 A D Q

Boggs, Stephen. 1985. *Speaking, Relating, and Learning: A Study of Hawaiian Children at Home and School.* Norwood, NJ: Ablex Publishing.

2 C O

Bohn, Anita Perna. 2003. Familiar Voices: Using Ebonics Communication Techniques in the Primary Classroom. *Urban Education* 38.688–707.

1 C F N S T
The author presents a case study of an elementary school teacher's pedagogical success in teaching Standard English writing and composition through the utilization of Ebonics features in her classroom. Describing her teaching styles through five vignettes, this article outlines the Ebonics features that the teacher integrates into her teaching lessons and discusses the observed student response to them. The article categorizes the Ebonics communication techniques used by the teacher into the following five groups: tonal semantics through the use of repetitive and rhythmic phrasing, call-and-response exchanges, testifying, signification, and code switching. The author reports that using these five features of Ebonics in the classroom seems to give African American students the psychological confidence in themselves and their culture to become and remain active participants and learners of Standard English in the classrooms. The article also notes that the use of Ebonics features in the classroom

encourages the active participation of and attention from students of diverse non-Ebonics backgrounds. Finally, it ends up sharing the success stories of various teachers who have begun to utilize Ebonics in their classrooms as well.

Boloz, Sigmund A. & Diana Jenness. 1984. The Sun Is Shining in My Eyes: The Navajo Child Enters Kindergarten Expecting to Write and He Can. *Journal of American Indian Education* 23.25–30. [Abstract by ERIC.]

5 S W

The authors describe a successful English writing program for Navajo kindergarten children in Ganado Primary School (Arizona), which encourages children to draw and write in journals. The program indicates that many Navajo students enter school with the capacity to move directly into daily writing and have already formed strong concepts about written language.

Bolton, Kingsley (ed.) 2002. *Hong Kong English: Autonomy and Creativity.* Hong Kong, China: Hong Kong University Press.

6 E F

Bond, Lloyd. 1981. Bias in Mental Tests. In *Issues in Testing: Coaching, Disclosure, and Ethnic Bias,* ed. by B. Green. San Francisco: Jossey-Bass.

1 A

Boone, Patreece. 2003. When the "Amen Corner" Comes to Class: An Examination of the Pedagogical and Cultural Impact of Call-Response Communication in the Black College Classroom. *Communication Education* 52.212–29.

1 C F N S

Boone seeks to discover the significance of call-response on African American students in an educational context. She defines this particular Black English speech pattern as a "reciprocal speech event which serves to unite the speaker and the audience" (p. 213), stressing the importance of the community in the occurrence. She focuses on the popularity of call-response in the church, but argues that it is also present in the classroom. Boone conducts an ethnographic study of a public-speaking class at a Historically Black College and University (HBCU). Her data includes videotapes of the class, one-on-one interviews, and field notes. She focuses on call-response practices initiated by both teacher and students. Furthermore, she provides different instances in which the particular speech pattern is likely to occur, noting a speaker's link to real situations, and a need for support from the audience as eliciting responses. She says that such occurrences create a sense of community within the classroom and preserve the African American culture in the academic setting. Boone's research leads her to conclude that Black speech patterns in the classroom prove beneficial to the academic experience of African American students by fostering motivation via endorsements.

Bougere, Marguerite. 1981. Dialect and Reading Disabilities. *Journal of Research and Development in Education* 14.67–73.

1 R S T X

Bougere discusses several hypotheses regarding the difficulty experienced by many Black children in learning to read. After briefly reviewing research on the discredited hypothesis that cultural and linguistic deprivation is the cause, she cites several studies relevant to the linguistic interference hypothesis, according to which the phonological and grammatical differences between AAVE and Standard English are the greatest hindrance. Finally, she considers evidence that teachers' negative attitudes toward AAVE are often the greater barrier to learning. She concludes by recommending that (1) teachers should be instructed in the systematicity of both Standard English and of

AAVE in order to dispel notions that the latter is merely incorrect English; (2) phonics instruction should consider the difference between Standard English and AAVE; and (3) beginning and remedial reading instruction should incorporate the language experience approach.

Bowie, Robert & Carole Bond. 1994. Influencing Future Teachers' Attitudes toward Black English: Are We Making a Difference? *Journal of Teacher Education* 45.112–18.

1 I T
Seventy-five preservice teachers (overwhelmingly White females) completed a language attitude survey dealing with AAVE. Likert-scale questions returned more negative attitudes than positive, while open-ended responses touched on both the need for students to learn Standard English and the need for teachers to be more sensitive to students' language. Respondents who had been exposed to the topic of AAVE in their preservice education demonstrated more positive attitudes than respondents who had no exposure to issues of language diversity. The authors conclude with a lengthy and thoughtful discussion of the role of knowledge about linguistic diversity in teacher education.

Brandon, LaVada, Denise Marie Taliaferro Baszile & Theodora Regina Berry. 2009. Linguistic Moments: Language, Teaching, and Teacher Education in the U.S. *Educational Foundations* 23.47–66. [Abstract prepared by ERIC and reprinted with permission of the Department of Education from the Education Resources Information Center at eric.ed.gov.]

4 T
In this article, three teacher educators each share a critical linguistic moment, which they frame as critical race counterstories, to make visible the ways in which their own diverse linguistic experiences have shaped their concerns, and efforts as teacher educators. "Linguistic Moments #1: Facing the Power of Language," recounts the experience of a mother/teacher/educator who faces the power of language as her child's teachers attempt to silence and replace her daughter's native tongue with Standard English. "Linguistic Moments #2: "Tu hija tiene mucho poopoo!"," forefronts the efforts of a novice teacher to teach her Spanish-speaking students as they faced down the tyranny of California Proposition 187. Emphasizing both personal and political dynamics of language diversity, a teacher's experience is foregrounded in theoretical frames that support the inextricable links between language and identity. In "Linguistic Moments #3: A Bilingual/Dialectical Dilemma in Teacher Education," the author relives her experience as a woman of color fighting against "stereotypical oppression" while attempting to advocate for a bilingual/bidialectical pre-service teacher in the ivory tower and the schoolhouse.

Brasch, Ila Wales & Walter M. Brasch. 1974. *A Comprehensive Annotated Bibliography of American Black English*. Baton Rouge: Louisiana State University Press.

1 E

Brathwaite, Edward Kamau. 1985. *History of the Voice: The Development of Nation Language in Anglophone Caribbean Poetry*. London: New Beacon Books.

2 C I
In this book, Braithewaite introduces the term *nation language* as a fitting description of the language of the Caribbean, as opposed to *dialect*, which has acquired a negative connotation. After arguing for its legitimacy as a language in its own right, he explains the importance of analyzing its oral literature, given the way prosodic features such as stress and intonation differ in surprising ways from Standard English. He explains that this is part of the total expression of the language, which fully reflects the unique living conditions of the people who speak it.

Brayboy, Bryan McKinley Jones & Angelina E. Castagno. 2009. Self-Determination through Self-Education: Culturally Responsive Schooling for Indigenous Students in the USA. *Teaching Education* 20.31–53.

5 C P R
Outlines culturally responsive schooling (CRS) for Indigenous youth and situates this concept within a larger history of US federal and community-based efforts to educate Indigenous youth in the United States, with a particular focus on language arts outcomes.

Brice, Alejandro & Judy Montgomery. 1996. A Comparison of Latino Students in English as a Second Language and Speech and Language Programs. *Language, Speech, and Hearing Services in Schools* 27.68–81.

4 A D N

Brock, Cynthia H., Gwendolyn Thompson McMillon, Julie L. Pennington, Dianna Townsend & Diane Lapp. 2009. Academic English and African American Vernacular English: Exploring Possibilities for Promoting the Literacy Learning of All Children. In *Handbook of Research on Literacy and Diversity,* ed. by L. M. Morrow, R. Rueda & D. Lapp, 137–57. New York: Guilford Press.

1 R

Brod, Rodney L. & John M. McQuiston. 1983. American Indian Adult Education and Literacy: The First National Survey. *Journal of American Indian Education* 22.1–16.

5

Brod, Rodney L. & John M. McQuiston. 1997. The American Indian Linguistic Minority: Social and Cultural Outcomes of Monolingual Education. *American Indian Culture and Research Journal* 21.125–59.

5 C

Brooks, Charlotte (ed.) 1985. *Tapping Potential: English and Language Arts for the Black Learner.* Urbana, IL: National Council of Teachers of English.

1 C E O R S T W

Brown, Claude. 1968. *The Language of Soul.* In *Esquire,* April, pp. 88, 160-161.

1 F I

Brown, Cynthia. 1998. The Role of the L1 Grammar in the L2 Acquisition of Segmental Structure. *Second Language Research* 14.136–93.

3 6 F X

Brown, David West. 2006. Micro-Level Teaching Strategies for Linguistically Diverse Learners. *Linguistics and Education: An International Research Journal* 17.175–95. [Reprinted with permission of Elsevier from *Linguistics and Education* 17(2).]

1 B I
Language instruction in secondary education is dominated by standard language ideology—a view of language that sanctions one ("standard") variety at the expense of other ("nonstandard") ones. While it is clear that students need access to privileged rhetorical forms, it is similarly clear that most current pedagogies do not facilitate such access for many students, and, in fact, may work to alienate some students from academic processes. Some instructional approaches have been proposed in the past

(i.e., linguistically informed instruction and genre) that offer strategies for more effectively teaching linguistically diverse learners. What is needed is not only a synthesis of the strengths of such approaches, but also an understanding of the fluencies students already possess. Language curricula in secondary schools should intentionally build from the micro- to the macro-level, from the existing linguistic knowledge of students to increased facility with academic and other privileged genres and registers.

Brown, David West. 2009. *In Other Words: Lessons on Grammar, Code-Switching, and Academic Writing*. Portsmouth, NH: Heinemann. [Abstract for *In Other Words* by David West Brown graciously provided by David West Brown.]

1 B M S W

In Other Words provides materials necessary for the implementation of grammar lessons in code-switching and academic language, including background materials for teachers, lesson plans, answer keys, and handouts. Many of the lessons, aimed at middle and high school students, are designed around examples from literature commonly used in schools like *The Adventures of Huckleberry Finn*, *Their Eyes Were Watching God* and *The Piano Lesson*. Similarly, explanations and background materials reference works from authors like Shakespeare, Chaucer and Austin. Using such sources as a point of departure, these lessons are designed to use grammar to explicate clearly and practically some of the features of academic writing, like how sentences are organized, how conjunctive resources can be deployed, and the kinds of linguistic work that different sorts of verbs can do. In addition to the literary references, the lessons make extensive use of examples from music, movies, and other cultural sources that are a part of students' linguistic environment. They are included as illustrations of the systematicity of everyday language and to connect students to the material by taking the real-world language that they encounter in their lives outside of school into the classroom.

Brown, David West. 2011. Dialect and Register Hybridity: A Case from Schools. *Journal of English Linguistics* 39.109–34. [Reprinted with permission of Sage Publications, the publisher, from *Journal of English Linguistics*, 39.]

1 B U W

This case study explores the academic writing practices of some African American English-speaking high school students, focusing in particular on interactions of dialect and register. In some instances, students appear to draw from a range of dialect and register resources and to deploy them in hybridized forms in their compositions. One implication of this hybridity is that it suggests the need to include register analysis as part of linguistically informed approaches to writing instruction (i.e., approaches that apply variationist research and methods to educational settings). Additionally, this case study examines some of the reasons that motivate the production of hybridity, analyzing how the linguistic tasks in which students are asked to engage and students' metalinguistic understandings play a role in the creation of hybridized texts. Finally, this study presents analytic methods that, while not new, are applied in a mixed way that attempts to systematically examine both dialect and register in texts.

Bruder, Mary Newton & Luddy Hayden. 1973. Teaching Composition: A Report on a Bidialectal Approach. *Language Learning* 23.1–15.

1 B S W

Bryan, Beverley. 1998. Some Correspondences between West African and Jamaican Creole Speakers in Learning Standard English. In *Studies in Caribbean Language II*, ed. by P. Christie, B. Lalla, V. Pollard & L. Carrington, 100–11. St. Augustine, Trinidad: Society for Caribbean Linguistics.

2 B

Bryan, Beverley. 2001. Defining the Roles of Linguistic Markers in Manufacturing Classroom Consent. In *Due Respect: Papers on English and English-Related Creoles in the Caribbean in Honor of Professor Robert La Page,* ed. by P. Christie, 79–96. Kingston, Jamaica: University of the West Indies Press.

2 N T

Bryan, Beverley. 2004. Language and Literacy in a Creole-Speaking Environment: A Study of Primary Schools in Jamaica. *Language, Culture and Curriculum* 17.87–96.

[Reprinted with permission of the author from *Language, Culture and Communication* 17(2).]

2 B S

Jamaica is a Creole-speaking environment, where children enter school with a range of varieties, some of which are closely related to English. The expectation is that they will learn English in school. The appropriate language teaching approach, it is argued, is not English as a mother tongue, English as a Second Language or English as a Foreign Language. The paper explores the most appropriate principles and practice for this setting, based on a study of good practice in a selected number of primary schools. The principles of: (1) Immersion; (2) Practice; (3) Scaffolding; and (4) Contrasts are highlighted as particularly relevant. It is hoped that the discussion will be useful to teachers working with Jamaican children in other settings, and will also have relevance for all those who teach children with a language variety different from that of the school.

Bryan, Beverly. 2010. *Between Two Grammars: Research and Practice for Language Learning and Teaching in a Creole-Speaking Environment.* Kingston, Jamaica: Ian Randle Publishers. [Abstract for "Between two Grammars: Research and Practice for Language Learning and Teaching in a Creole-speaking Environment" by Beverly Bryan adapted from an abstract graciously provided by Beverly Bryan.]

2 B P S

This book addresses the challenges facing teachers of English in Caribbean classrooms, identifying some of the core problems for creole-speaking students who struggle to demonstrate English language proficiency at the level required for high stake public examinations. Focusing on Jamaica, the author raises questions about the sociocultural context that the teacher needs to understand, and about what good practice in this context looks like. The research to answer these questions was conducted over several years in different projects, focused on secondary schools, and drawing on historical sources, structured observations, interviews and small scale surveys. The first half of the book presents an enriched view of the multiple meanings of language and English for teaching in the Caribbean, offers a brief description of Jamaican Creole, considers the different ways language is viewed, and analyses the goals for English teaching world-wide. The second half of the book goes beyond the presentation of a single method for achieving proficiency in English. It recognizes that apart from subject knowledge, teachers in a Creole-speaking environment need to understand principles drawn from second language research and practice that are robust enough to generate teacher action at more than one level. Using these principles, the author reviews approaches involving teaching language as communication the use of literature in the language classroom; and language awareness. The author argues that teachers using these principles can make theoretically sound pedagogical decisions about what they offer students, generating ways of working that they, as empowered professionals, can own. In sum: The difficulties of language teaching in a Creole-speaking environment are addressed, and a multi-faceted set of solutions proposed.

Bryson, Mary & Marlene Scardamalia. 1991. Teaching Writing to Students at Risk for Academic Failure. In *Teaching Advanced Skills to at-Risk Students,* ed. by B. Means, C. Chelemer & M. Knapp, 141–67. San Francisco: Jossey-Bass.

S W

Bucholtz, Mary. 2004. Styles and Stereotypes: The Linguistic Negotiation of Identity among Laotian American Youth. *Pragmatics* 14.127–47.

3 6 F I U

Bull, Tove. 1990. Teaching School Beginners to Read and Write in the Vernacular. In *Troms: Linguistics in the Eighties,* 69–84. Oslo, Norway: Novus Press.

1 B

Bull, William E. 1955. Review of Unesco 1953, the Use of Vernacular Languages in Education. *International Journal of American Linguistics* 21.228–94.

1 V

Buly, Marsha Riddle. 2005. Leaving No American Indian/Alaska Native Behind: Identifying Reading Strengths and Needs. *Journal of American Indian Education* 44.29–52.

5 A R

Burke, Carolyn. 1973. Dialect and the Reading Process. In *Language Differences: Do They Interfere?,* ed. by J. Laffey & R. Shuy, 91–100. Newark, DE: International Reading Association.

R X

Burke, Suzanne M., Susanna W. Pflaum & June D. Knafle. 1982. The Influence of Black English on Diagnosis of Reading in Learning Disabled and Normal Readers. *Journal of Learning Disabilities* 15.19–22.

1 A R

Burlew, Ann. 1997. Special Section on Ebonics. *Journal of Black Psychology* 23.205–44.

1 K
This special section includes an editorial introduction by Ann Kathleen Burlew (pp. 205–207) and the following articles: Robert L. Williams "The Ebonics controversy" (pp. 208–214); Lisa M. Koch and Alan Gross, "Children's perceptions of Black English as a variable in interracial perception" (pp. 215–226); Geneva Smitherman and Sylvia Cunningham, "Moving beyond resistance: Ebonics and African American youth" (pp. 227–232); Myrna N. Burnett, Randi Burlew, and Glenetta Hudson, "Embracing the Black English Vernacular: Response to Koch and Gross" (pp. 233–237); Jean T. Pryce, "Similarities between the debates on Ebonics and Jamaican" (pp. 238–241); and Marilyn Lovett and Joneka Neely, "On becoming bilingual" (pp. 242–244).

Burling, Robbins. 1973. *English in Black and White.* New York: Holt, Rinehart and Winston.

1 B F I S
In addition to chapters on the pronunciation, grammar, usage and origins of Black English (and other matters), Burling has three chapters of special relevance to this bibliography: Chapter 6 "Is anything wrong with it?" (pp. 91–110), Chapter 8 "Where did it come from?" (pp. 129–145), and Chapter 9 "Can we help the children toward literacy?" (pp. 146–162).

Burridge, Kate & Bernd Kortmann. 2008. *The Pacific and Australasia*. Berlin: Mouton de Gruyter.

2 6 F

Burt, Susan & Hua Yang. 2005. Growing up Shifting: Immigrant Children, Their Families, and the Schools. In *Language in the Schools: Integrating Linguistic Knowledge into K-12 Teaching,* ed. by K. Denham & A. Lobeck, 29–40.

6 U

Busch, Amy E. & Arnetha F. Ball. 2004. Lifting Voices in the City. *Educational Leadership* 64.64–67.

C W

The article describes urban writing programs in San Francisco, California, Bay Area and writing for empowerment.

C-SPAN. 1996. Ebonics News Conference. C-SPAN. [From the website http://www.c-spanvideo.org/program/77533-1]

1 K P Z

"After their meeting, Ms. Cook and Rev. Jackson briefed reporters on the decision to recognize Ebonics, African American English, in the school system. They stressed that this is simply an extension of already existing practices to help disadvantaged youths of various backgrounds to learn Standard English. Rev. Jackson answered questions from the press."

C-SPAN. 1997. Ebonics in Education. C-SPAN. [From the website http://www.c-span-video.org/program/78237-1]

1 K P Z

"[US Senate] Committee members heard testimony concerning the role of Ebonics, or African-American Vernacular English, in educating African American students. The Oakland school board originally passed a resolution which seemed to call for education of students in Ebonics as a first language and later revised it to call for the recognition of Ebonics as a bridge to learning Standard English. The witnesses included several representatives of the Oakland school district as well as the originator of the term, "Ebonics," and several other language experts. The testimony focused on whether Ebonics is a language, vernacular, dialect or grammatically incorrect English, whether it is the best way for African-Americans to learn Standard English, and whether the program should receive federal funds."

Cahnmann, Melisa. 2000. Rhythm and Resource: Repetition as a Linguistic Style in an Urban Elementary Classroom. *Working Papers in Educational Linguistics* 16.39–52. [Abstract prepared by ERIC.]

1 4 C N

This paper seeks to understand the role of culturally-specific styles of discourse in the classroom. The paper uses and expands upon three categories of classroom language use (control, curriculum, and critique) to present data on how a Puerto Rican American teacher uses repetition and discourse styles that have African and African American origins to perform a variety of classroom functions: to control classroom behavior and talk, to better teach and highlight elements of the curriculum, and to critique the use of Standard English in an elementary classroom context. In the first section, findings are provided on the form and function of repetition in research on African oral traditions and African American language use in church and classroom contexts. The context of the study is described, including the setting, participants, and methods of data collection and analysis. It is concluded that the teacher's use of culturally specific forms of repetition enhanced the way she controlled classroom talk and behavior and increased students' participation and learning of the curriculum.

Cameron, Deborah. 1992. 'Respect, Please!': Investigating Race, Power, and Language. In *Researching Language: Issues of Power and Method,* ed. by D. Cameron, E. Frazer, P. Harvey, M. B. H. Rampton & K. Richardson, 113–30. London: Routledge and Kegan Paul.

2 I L S

Cameron worked with a group of Afro-Caribbean youths at an inner-city youth club in London to discuss racist language and societal attitudes toward the speech of Black British people, and to develop a video documenting some of these discussions and dramatizing their points through role-play for a larger audience. Through these interactions, the author gained new ideas about bidialectalism in this community; for example, she learned that parents were often ashamed of their dialect and delegated their Standard English-proficient children to communicate with 'the authorities.' The young people, in turn, learned about the history of creole varieties and the roots of the prejudice behind them. In light of her experience, the author advocates a style of conducting research in which informants are more directly involved in the research process, so that they not only have the chance to share their own thoughts and opinions but also benefit from expert sociolinguistic knowledge.

Camitta, Miram. 1993. Vernacular Writing: Varieties of Literacy among Philadelphia High School Students. In *Cross-Cultural Approaches to Literacy,* ed. by B. Street, 228–46. Cambridge: Cambridge University Press.

C V W

Campbell, Elizabeth. 1994. *Empowering Students through Bidialectalism: Encouraging Standard English in a Black English Environment.* Fort Meyers, FL: Center for Advancement in Education at Nova University.

1 B M O

The author describes creative modifications to a high school speech and debate class designed to increase students' proficiency in speaking Standard English. The goals of the project were to lead the twenty-one students in the class to "voluntarily decrease their use of Black English in Standard English situations" and to increase participation in debate tournaments. To this end, the curriculum added to the syllabus of a typical speech/debate class, supplementing impromptu speeches, planned speeches, and poetry recitals with exercises focusing on dialect and register, role-playing activities, and individual student-teacher conferences focused on specific AAVE features the teacher had observed during speeches in which Standard English was their target. Several measures of effectiveness—including use of Standard English features, student self-confidence, and parental support for the program—indicated that the course led to positive outcomes for learners.

Campbell, Kermit. 1994. The "Signifying Monkey" Revisited: Vernacular Discourse and African American Personal Narratives. *Journal of Advanced Composition* 14.463–73. [Abstract prepared by ERIC and reprinted with permission of the Department of Education from the Education Resources Information Center at eric.ed.gov.]

1 C N W

Campbell outlines the function of the "signifying monkey" in African American oral traditions. He focuses on vernacular discourse and African American personal narratives to discover linguistic and cultural features of African American students and argues that these identity features be placed at the center of writing instruction for African Americans.

Campbell, Kermit. 1997. "Real Niggaz's Don't Die": African American Students Speaking Themselves into Their Writing. In *Writing in Multicultural Settings,* ed. by C. Severino, J. Guerra & J. Butler, 67–78. New York: Modern Language Association of America.

1 B C N W

Campbell, Kermit. 2005. *Gettin Our Groove On: Rhetoric, Language, and Literacy for the Hip Hop Generation.* Detroit, MI: Wayne State University.

C K N S W
After providing a critical re-evaluation of the Oakland 'Ebonics' controversy, this book outlines how African American rhetorical styles can form the basis of college-level writing and rhetoric instruction. Campbell argues forcefully that a full conception of African American ways with words goes beyond a consideration of morphosyntactic features, but crucially involves an appreciation and analysis of Black discourse styles and rhetorical forms.

Campbell, Lynda. 1993. Maintaining the Integrity of Home Linguistic Varieties: Black English Vernacular. *American Journal of Speech-Language Pathology* 2.11–12.

1 D I T

Campbell, Lynda. 1994. Discourse Diversity and Black English Vernacular. In *School Discourse Problems,* ed. by D. Ripich & N. Creaghead, 93–131. San Diego, CA: Singular Publishing Group, Inc.

1 D I N T

Canagarajah, A. Suresh. 2006. Constructing a Diaspora Identity in English: The Case of Sri Lankan Tamils. In *English and Ethnicity,* ed. by J. Brutt-Griffler & C. E. Davies, 191–216. New York: Palgrave Macmillan.

3 6

Cantoni-Harvey, Gina. 1974. Dormitory English: Implication for the Classroom Teacher. In *Southwest Areal Linguistics,* ed. by G. Bills, 283–92. San Diego, CA: Institute for Cultural Pluralism.

5 T

Cantoni-Harvey, Gina. 1977. Some Observations About Red English and Standard English in the Classroom. In *Studies in Southwestern Indian English,* ed. by W. Leap, 223–33. San Antonio, TX: Trinity University.

5 T

Cargile, Aaron Castelán. 1997. Attidues toward Chinese-Accented Speech: An Investigation in Two Contexts. *Journal of Language and Social Psychology* 16.434–43.

3 I

Cargile, Aaron Castelán & Howard Giles. 1998. Language Attitudes toward Varieties of English: An American-Japanese Context. *Journal of Applied Communication Research* 26.338–56.

3 I

Cargile, Aaron Castelán, Eriko Maeda, Jose Rodriguez & Marc Rich. 2010. "Oh, You Speak English So Well!": U.S. American Listeners' Perceptions of "Foreignness" among Nonnative Speakers." *Journal of Asian American Studies* 13.59–79.

3 I

Cargile, Aaron Castelán, Jiro Takai & Jose I. Rodriguez. 2006. Attitudes toward African-American Vernacular English: A US Export to Japan? *Journal of Multilingual and Multicultural Development* 27.443–56. [Reprinted with permission of the authors from the *Journal of Multilingual and Multicultural Development* 27(6).]

1 I

To the best of our knowledge, this is the first study to examine attitudes towards African can American vernacular English (AAVE) in a setting outside of the United States. Because foreign attitudes toward AAVE can serve as an indirect assessment of a society's racial prejudice, we decided to explore these attitudes in Japan: a country with an intriguing mix of ties that are both close (i.e., politically and economically) and distant (i.e., culturally) vis-a-vis the United States. Considering the ostensible similarities in racial beliefs widely held in both countries, we hypothesized that evaluations of AAVE in Japan would be comparable to those in the United States. We found that the evaluations expressed by a sample of Japanese college students were virtually indistinguishable from the overall pattern of AAVE evaluations made by US citizens and recommend additional research in order to better understand the nature of contemporary Japanese attitudes towards different varieties of English.

Carlson, Holly & Monica McHenry. 2006. Effect of Accent and Dialect on Employability. *Journal of Employment Counseling* 43.70–83.

3 4 6 I

Carpenter, Karen & Hubert Devonish. 2010. Swimming against the Tide: Jamaican Creole in Education. In *Creoles in Education: An Appraisal of Current Programs and Projects,* ed. by B. Migge, I. Leglise & A. Bartens, 167–81. Amsterdam: John Benjamins. [Reprinted with permission of the publisher from *Creoles in education: An appraisal of current programs and projects.* by Migge et. al eds. Amsterdam: John Benjamins.]

2 A I K P S U V

In implementing its Bilingual Education Project (BEP), involving the use of Jamaican Creole and English, the Jamaican Language Unit (JLU) has sought to meet the criteria set out by the Ministry of Education, Youth and Culture in Jamaica for teaching in the home language. The Ministry and the general public needed to be convinced that the pilot BEP did not (1) do academic harm to the children involved, (2) has produced an improvement in the children's competence in English, and (3) has produced improved results in the bilingually taught content subjects. This paper is a midstream evaluation of the success indicators, focusing on the children's performance in standardized tests in both Jamaican and English, and other content subjects.

Carpenter, Karen & Hubert Devonish. 2012. Boys Will Be Boys: Gender and Bilingual Education in a Creole Language Situation. In *Language, Culture and Caribbean Identity,* ed. by J. Allsopp & J. R. Rickford. Mona, Kingston, Jamaica: University of the West Indies Press.

2 A I V

Carrington, Lawrence. 1969. Deviations from Standard English in the Speech of Primary School Children in St. Lucia and Dominica. *International Review of Applied Linguistics* 7.165–84.

2 F X

Carrington, Lawrence. 1976. Determining Language Education Policy in Caribbean Sociolinguistic Complexes. *International Journal of the Sociology of Language* 8.27–44.

2 P

Carrington, Lawrence. 1983. The Challenge of Caribbean Language in the Canadian Classroom. *TESL Talk* 14.15–28.

2 I P S

Carrington, Lawrence. 1997. Social Contexts Conducive to the Vernacularization of Literacy. In *Vernacular Literacy: A Re-Evaluation,* ed. by A. Tabouret-Keller, R. Le Page, P. Gardner-Chloros & G. Varro, 82-92. Oxford: Clarendon Press.

2 P V

In this chapter, Carrington raises a number of background social issues to be considered in attempting to vernacularize literacy, such as whether the non-literate members of a society speak the same language as the literate, whether the community perceives the vernacular as valuable, and whether the vernacular has legal status as a national language. He concludes by offering three general strategies aimed at creating a conducive environment for vernacularization: emphasize the ways in which literacy in the vernacular will benefit the everyday lives of the speakers, emphasize the ways in which the common good brought about by vernacular literacy will be uncontroversial and not threatening to the literate social establishment, and exploit the ways in which the vernacular has seeped into linguistic domains primarily occupied by the official language.

Carrington, Lawrence & C. Borely. 1977. *The Language Arts Syllabus 1975: Comment and Counter-Comment.* University of the West Indies, St. Augustine, Trinidad and Tobago: Multi-Media Production Centre.

2 K S

This is an interesting collection of letters from members of the public and articles (by Carrington and Borely) written in the *Trinidadian Guardian* and *Sunday Guardian* newspapers in 1975 and 1976 in response to the New Primary School Syllabus introduced by the Trinidad and Tobago Ministry of Education and Culture in June 1975. The Syllabus provoked public controversy in part because of its recognition that "the vernacular is a language with an organised system of rules," its observation that "the language spoken by the child when he enters school is, in most cases, structurally different from the English that he is expected to learn in school," and its conclusion that while "The need to teach the English language is still fundamental … the assumptions made by textbooks and English courses designed for native English speakers cannot be accepted in our situation." The public controversy reflected in the newspaper contributions was in some ways similar to the Oakland Ebonics controversy of 1996-97, but in some respects the Trinidadian New Primary School Syllabus was even more radical, in advocating, for instance, that "the teacher must accept the home language of the child as the only means of communication at his disposal. It is only when spontaneity has been achieved that the teaching of English structures should begin. To insist on English standards before that, is to inhibit the class to the extent of preventing discussion altogether."

Carter, Prudence. 2007. *Keepin' It Real: School Success Beyond Black and White.* New York: Oxford University Press.

1 A C

Carter, Phillip M. 2007. Phonetic Variation and Speaker Agency: Mexicana Identity in a North Carolina Middle School. *Penn Working Papers in Linguistics* 13.1–15.

4 F I

Carter, Phillip M. 2011. A Treatise on "Multiculturalism" and Education: A Review of "Language Diversity in the Classroom" by John Edwards. *American Speech* 86.259–63.

1A C I N

Carter, Ronald. 1993. Proper English: Language, Culture, and Curriculum. *English in Education* 27.3–14.

C I P

Carter, Stephanie Power. 2006. "She Would've Still Made That Face Expression": The Use of Multiple Literacies by Two African American Young Women. *Theory Into Practice* 45.352–58. [Reprinted from *Theory Into Practice* 45.]

1 C T
The article discusses a multiple literacies and a traditional approach to literacy by drawing on the experiences of two African American young women in a high school English classroom. The article suggests that teachers who use a more traditional approach to literacy are more apt to view students of color as powerless, failing, struggling, and/or having low literacy abilities; whereas teachers who use a multiple literacies approach are more likely to interrogate power relations, and understand that students of color and students from historically underrepresented groups draw on their social and cultural interpretive frames to make meaning of the world around them and to create spaces of agency within the classroom.

Carter, Thomas. 1971. Cultural Content for Linguistically Different Learners. *Elementary English* 48.162–75.

1 C R

Cason, Nancy, Sandy Tabscott, Joan Thomas & Webster Groves Action Research Team. 1991. Improving Writing of at Risk Students with a Focus on the African American Male. *Bread Loaf News* 5.26–29. [Abstract prepared by ERIC and reprinted with permission of the Department of Education from the Education Resources Information Center at eric.ed.gov.]

1 S W
An action research project designed and evaluated the effectiveness of an instructional strategy to improve the writing of all secondary students (particularly African American males) in the Webster Groves, Missouri, school district. The first year was devoted to an intensive study of African American culture and literature. A list of six principles was developed, supplemented by two more principles developed after the first year: (1) emphasize the writing process; (2) individualize and personalize; (3) encourage cooperative learning; (4) build on strengths; (5) increase engagement with writing; (6) increase control of language; (7) build bridges to more challenging tasks; and (8) use the computer for word processing, editing, and publishing. In the third year, the project expanded to include all at-risk writers. Comparison of pre- and post-assessments indicated that all students improved their scores on district holistic writing tests, and that target students improved their scores even more than the general population. Results also indicated that, of the eight principles, the three most effective were: using the writing process; individualizing and personalizing; and using cooperative learning strategies. Among the changes in their behaviors, the teachers involved in the action

research project gave more time for writing in class, arranged lessons to meet a variety of learning styles, valued ethnic diversity, acted more as facilitators rather than disseminators of knowledge, and became less confrontational in handling discipline. Findings suggest that the teachers' improved rapport with students and students' improved writing skills were worth the commitment of time and energy by the teachers.

Cassidy, Frederic. 1970. Teaching Standard English to Speakers of Creole in Jamaica, West Indies. In *Report of the Twentieth Annual Round Table Meeting on Linguistics and Language Studies: Linguistics and the Teaching of Standard English to Speakers of Other Languages or Dialects*, ed. by J. Alatis, 203–14. Washington, D.C.: Georgetown University Press.

2 B I K
In an effort to draw parallels with the language problem in the United States, Cassidy discusses the language situation in Jamaica in regard to education. After outlining the more salient systematic differences between Standard English and the Jamaican Creole spoken natively by the majority of the population, he explains that public school children are forced into a Standard English environment in which they are unable to cope, because of dry, old-fashioned teaching methods and the way their creole is dismissed as inferior. Teachers, however, often resort to Creole as the only way of communicating with their children. While initial suggestions that Standard English be taught as a foreign language were met with scorn, Cassidy considers this the best method for correcting the situation, and advocates its immediate implementation, under whatever name would be least offensive to the public.

Cassidy, Frederic & Joan Hall (eds.) 1991. *Dictionary of American Regional English, Volume 2 [D-H]*. Cambridge, MA: Belknap Press of Harvard University Press.

6 E F

Cassidy, Frederic & Joan Hall (eds.) 1996. *Dictionary of American Regional English, Volume 3 [I-O]*. Cambridge, MA: Belknap Press of Harvard University Press.

6 E F

Cassidy, Frederic & Robert Le Page. 1980. *Dictionary of Jamaican English*. Cambridge: Cambridge University Press.

2 F
This is the second edition of the *Dictionary of Jamaican English*, first published by Cambridge University Press in 1967. As one of the earliest scholarly, full-length (509 pp.) dictionaries of a Caribbean creole English variety, it has historical significance, and should also be useful to teachers and scholars in Jamaica, the Caribbean, and elsewhere.

Cassidy, Frederic G. 1982. *Jamaica Talk: Three Hundred Years of the English Language in Jamaica*. Kingston, Jamaica: University of the West Indies Press.

2 F
This is a reprint of a classic introduction to Jamaican Creole, first published by Macmillan in 1961.

Cassidy, Frederic G. 1985. *Dictionary of American Regional English*, Volume 1 [A–C]: Cambridge, MA.

6 F
The first volume in a six-volume work scheduled for completion in 2013, this 1985 volume of the Dictionary of American Regional English [DARE] provides a comprehensive overview of the Dictionary, the 1847-item DARE questionnaire on which it was based in part (administered to 2777 informants across the US between 1965 and

1970), and other introductory materials (Guide to Pronunciation, List of Informants, essay on "Language Changes Especially Common in American Folk Speech"), and lexical entries from A to C: a to Czezski. See Cassidy and Hall (1991, 1996), and Hall (2002, 2012) for later volumes of DARE.

Castagno, Angelina E. & Bryan McKinley Jones Brayboy. 2008. Culturally Responsive Schooling for Indigenous Youth: A Review of the Literature. *Review of Educational Research* 78.941–93.

5 C E
The article reviews four decades' worth of literature on culturally responsive schooling (CRS) for Indigenous youth.

Catholic Education Commission of Western Australia. 1994. Feliks: Fostering English Language in Kimberley Schools — a Professional Development Package for Primary Schools. *Aboriginal Child at School* 22.23–24.

2 M S
Briefly describes a bidialectal program used in northern Australia. FELIKS uses the concept of a 'code-switching stairway,' made up of the four 'steps' of awareness; separation of varieties; code-switching; and control of the target variety. See Hudson 1992 and Berry and Hudson 1997 for more information.

Cazden, Courtney. 1970. The Situation: A Neglected Source of Social Class Differences in Language Use. *Journal of Social Issues* 26.35–60.

1 A I K N

Cazden, Courtney. 1988. *Classroom Discourse: The Language of Teaching and Learning.* Portsmouth, NH: Heinemann.

1 N S T

Cazden, Courtney. 1999. The Language of African American Students in Classroom Discourse. In *Making the Connection,* ed. by C. Adger, D. Christian & O. Taylor, 31–52. Washington, D.C.: CAL/Delta.

1 B I N O T

Cecil, Nancy. 1988. Black Dialect and Academic Success: A Study of Teacher Expectations. *Reading Improvement* 25.34–38.

1 A I T

Center for Applied Linguistics. 1978. *Teaching English to Cambodian Students.* Arlington, VA: National Indochinese Clearinghouse, Center for Applied Linguistics.

3 6 C M S T X

Cha, Yun-Kyung & Seung-Hwan Ham. 2008. The Impact of English on the School Curriculum. In *Handbook of Educational Linguistics,* ed. by B. Spolsky & F. Hult, 313–27. Malden, MA: Blackwell.

3 6 P

Chall, Jeanne S. 1996. *Learning to Read: The Great Debate.* Fort Worth, TX: Harcourt Brace College Publishers.

R

Chall, Jeanne S. 2000. *The Academic Achievement Challenge: What Really Works in the Classroom?* New York: Guilford Press.

R S

Chall, Jeanne S., Vicki A. Jacobs & Luke E. Baldwin. 1990. *The Reading Crisis: Why Poor Children Fall Behind.* Cambridge, MA: Harvard University Press.

R

Chambers, John, Jr. (ed.) 1983. *Black English: Educational Equity and the Law.* Ann Arbor, MI: Karoma Publishers.

1 A E K P
Contributors discuss the Ann Arbor "Black English" trial of 1977–1979.

Champion, Tempii. 1998. Tell Me Something Good: A Description of Narrative Structures among African American Children. *Linguistics and Education* 9.251–86.

1 N

Champion, Tempii. 2003. *Understanding Narrative Structures Used among African American Children: A Journey from Africa to America.* Mahwah, NJ: Lawrence Erlbaum Associates.

1 N

Champion, Tempii & David Bloome (eds.) 1995. *Special Issue: Africanized English and Education.* (Linguistics and Education 7).

1 E I K P V

Champion, Tempii, Yvette Hyter, Allyssa McCabe & Linda Bland-Stewart. 2003. "A Matter of Vocabulary": Performances of Low-Income African American Head Start Children on the Peabody Picture Vocabulary Test-III. *Communication Disorders Quarterly* 24.121–27.

1 A D Q

Champion, Tempii, Linda Rosa-Lugo, Kenyatta Rivers & Allyssa McCabe. 2010. A Preliminary Investigation of Second- and Fourth-Grade African American Students' Performance on the Gray Oral Reading Test-Fourth Edition. *Topics in Language Disorders* 30.145–53.

1 A
This study investigated the effectiveness of the Gray Oral Reading Test, fourth edition (GORT-4) in assessing the reading ability of African American English (AAE) dialect speakers. In order to test whether dialect differences affected performance on the GORT-4, twenty second grade and thirteen fourth grade AAE speakers, judged to be typically developing by their teachers, were administered both the GORT-4 and the Diagnostic Evaluation of Language Variation-Screening Test (DELV-ST) to determine if there was a correlation between variation from Mainstream American English (MAE) and performance on the GORT-4. Results showed that most AAE students, although considered typically developing by their teachers, scored below the mean on the GORT-4. However, their scores on comprehension questions were not below the mean. This suggests that the test is inadequate for assessing the reading levels of speakers of dialects divergent from MAE. However, there was a positive correlation between grade level and scores on the GORT-4, suggesting that greater exposure to MAE produces better results on reading assessments. These results suggest that (1) Reading assessment evaluations must incorporate knowledge

of dialectally-conditioned differences in reading, and (2) Exposure to MAE should be readily available in the classroom to speakers of vernacular dialects.

Chand, Vineeta. 2010. Postvocalic (R) in Urban Indian English. *English World-Wide* 31.1–39.

6 F

Chanethom, Vincent. 2010. Influence of American English on Second Generation Lao Immigrant Speakers. *English Today* 26.20–26.

3 Q

Chaplin, M. 1990. A Closer Look at Black and White Students' Assessment Essays. *Iowa English Bulletin* 38.15–27.

1 A W

Chapman, Iris Thompson. 1994. Dissin' the Dialectic on Discourse Surface Differences. *Composition Chronicle* 7.4–7. [Abstract prepared by ERIC and reprinted with permission of the Department of Education from the Education Resources Information Center at eric.ed.gov.]

1 A N S W
Statistics from several southern states show that African American high school students fail their Regents writing exams at a considerably higher rate than do White students. A study evaluated failing Regents essays written by African American high school students in several states to determine what the source of their failure was. Results showed that Black English vernacular accounted for only 15% of the surface errors. Scorers of the exams most commonly cited the essays' failure to provide adequate support for their arguments. They found the essays either illogical, insufficient, unfocused, unclear or repetitious. Therefore, writing teachers have to entertain the notion that development [of voice] is a co-conspirator or co-operant in the failure. What can be done to improve the performance of African American students? The answer is not more drilling of mechanics but some attempt to help them develop a voice in writing. Having been tracked into less demanding classes, they are simply not writing enough. Peter Elbow defines voice as what most people have in their speech but lack in their writing; it brings life to writing; it has the texture and sound of "you." For African American students, finding voice in "talk" or orality has never been a problem. Excerpts from a student's paper show that a real voice resides there.

Charity, Anne. 2007. Regional Differences in Low SES African-American Children's Speech in the School Setting. *Language Variation and Change* 19.281–93.

1 F

Charity, Anne, Hollis Scarborough & Darion Griffon. 2004. Familiarity with School English in African American Children and Its Relation to Early Reading Achievement. *Child Development* 75.1340–56. [Abstract graciously provided by Anne Charity Hudley.]

1 A Q R X
This study examined the sentence imitation and reading skills of 217 African American students in grades K-2 (ages 5 to 8 years) in Cleveland, Ohio, New Orleans, Louisiana, and Washington, D.C. Students used phonological and grammatical features associated with African American English with varying rates. Students' use of Standardized English correlated with higher reading achievement, even when memory ability was held constant through the analysis of the students' retelling of the story. Students in

New Orleans used a greater number of African American English features overall. The study was among the first to establish a correlation between the use of African American English and reading achievement and it also began to establish evidence for regional variation in the use of features of African American English.

Charity Hudley, Anne. 2008. African American English. In *Handbook of African American Psychology,* ed. by H. Neville, B. Tynes & S. Utsey, 199–210. Thousand Oaks, CA: Sage Publications..

1 A F R

Charity Hudley, Anne. 2010. Standardized Assessment of African American Children: A Sociolinguistic Perspective. In *Ethnolinguistic Diversity and Education: Language, Literacy, and Culture,* ed. by M. Farr, L. Seloni & J. Song, 167–92. New York: Routledge.

1 A

After providing an overview of the history of standardized assessments and of sociolinguists' previous efforts to highlight and address linguistic bias in tests, Charity Hudley briefly reviews several contemporary, widely-used tests (Diagnostic Analysis of Nonverbal Accuracy; Dynamic Indicators of Basic Early Literacy Skills; Woodcock Johnson Mastery Tests) and finds culturally or linguistically biased elements in each. The chapter concludes with recommendations for test makers, teachers, and parents.

Charity Hudley, Anne & Christine Mallinson. 2011. *Understanding English Language Variation in American Schools.* New York: Teachers College Press.

1 6 A E F S T

Written in a highly accessible form for educators facing linguistic diversity in the classroom, this book aims to foster teacher awareness about language variation and effective pedagogical strategies for helping students learn to read, write, and communicate effectively in Standard English. The authors (who have also been conducting workshops for teachers) take a multicultural approach, emphasizing the importance (for both students and teachers) of being aware of and appreciating different varieties of English. One chapter each is devoted to three varieties of English: Standard English, Southern English, and African American English. For the latter two varieties, the authors provide phonological and grammatical sketches along with specific strategies educators may use with students coming from these linguistic backgrounds. The book concludes with a chapter on standardized testing and other forms of assessment, focusing on how linguistic and cultural background may influence test-taking ability and suggesting strategies for improving scores.

Charpentier, Jean Michel. 1997. Literacy in a Pidgin Vernacular. In *Vernacular Literacy: A Re-Evaluation,* ed. by A. Tabouret-Keller, R. Le Page, P. Gardner-Chloros & G. Varro, 223–45. Oxford: Clarendon Press.

2 V

Cheatham, Gregory A., Jennifer Armstrong & Rosa Milagros Santos. 2009. "Y'all Listenin?": Accessing Children's Dialects in Preschool. *Young Exceptional Children* 12.2–14. [Abstract prepared by ERIC and reprinted with permission of the Department of Education from the Education Resources Information Center at eric.ed.gov.]

1 2 4 6 A I S

Children come to school with the language of their families and communities. For many children, this means that they speak a nonstandard dialect, an English dialect not used as the primary means of instruction in schools. Examples of dialects include African American English (AAE; i.e., Ebonics), Hawaiian Creole, Hispanic English, and

Southern Mountain English as well as what is considered Standard American English (SAE). Despite the language diversity children bring to school, those who speak non-standard dialects are often penalized for not speaking schools' accepted linguistic code. Often these children are given fewer learning opportunities and are inappropriately assessed and referred for special education placements. In this article, the authors take a culturally and linguistically responsive position to children's nonstandard dialects. They discuss characteristics of dialects and educational implications of nonstandard dialect use and offer recommendations for appropriate instruction, assessment, and program policy.

Chen, Katherine & Gray Carper. 2005. *Multilingual Hong Kong.* New York: Films for the Humanities and Sciences.

6 Z
For further information on this film, which discusses and exemplifies code-switching in Hong Kong, see http://www.foryue.org/index.html.

Chen-Hayes, Stuart F., Mei-whei Chen & Naveeda Athar. 1999. Challenging Linguicism: Action Strategies for Counselors and Client-Colleagues. In *Advocacy in Counseling: Counselors, Clients & Community,* ed. by J. Lewis & L. Bradley, 21–31. Greensboro, NC: ERIC Counseling and Student Services Clearinghouse.

3 I

Cheng, Li-Rong Lily. 1987. *Assessing Asian Language Performance: Guidelines for Evaluating Limited-English-Proficient Students.* Rockville, MD: Aspen.

3 6 A C O T X

Cheshire, Jenny. 1982. Dialect Features and Linguistic Conflict in Schools. *Educational Review* 14.53–67.

6 T

Cheshire, Jenny & Viv Edwards. 1991. Schoolchildren as Sociolinguistic Researchers. *Linguistics and Education* 3.225–49.

6 I L S

Cheshire, Jenny, Viv Edwards, Henk Munstermann & Bert Weltens (eds.) 1989. *Dialect and Education.* Clevedon, UK: Multilingual Matters.

6 B C E I L T
The articles in this volume review connections between language and education in various European countries, including the United Kingdom, the Netherlands, West Germany, Belgium and Denmark. See review by Ntiri (1990) in this volume.

Cheshire, Jenny & Dieter Stein (eds.) 1997. *Taming the Vernacular: From Dialect to Written Standard.* London: Longman.

6 E F W

Chiang, Yuet-Sim D. & Mary Schmida. 1999. Language Identity and Language Ownership: Linguistic Conflicts of First-Year University Writing Students. In *Generation 1.5 Meets College Composition: Issues in the Teaching of Writing to U.S.-Educated Learners of ESL,* ed. by L. Harklau, K. M. Losey & M. Siegal, 81–96. Marwah, N.J: Lawrence Erlbaum Associates.

3 W

Chisolm, James S. & Amanda J. Godley. 2011. Learning About Language through Inquiry-Based Discussion: Three Bidialectal High School Students' Talk About Dialect Variation, Identity, and Power. *Journal of Literacy Research* 43.430–68.

1 B L M S U
How does students' engagement in an inquiry-based discussion about language variation, identity, and power support their sociolinguistic content learning? Drawing on audio recordings of and interviews with African American high school students engaged in an inquiry-based discussion of these themes, Chisolm and Godley add to the emerging empirical literature of sociolinguistic interventions in K-12 school contexts. Students' contributions to the small-group discussion were coded for sociolinguistic content knowledge, identifying each claim or piece of evidence as an utterance about either language variation, identity, or power, and utterances were further assessed for the specificity of support for the claim. The authors yielded three major findings: (1) The content of students' collective argumentation was aligned with current perspectives in the discipline, suggesting that inquiry-based learning is a fruitful instructional mode for content learning about language; (2) the students' deliberations of the discussion questions led to more specific and nuanced understandings of the relationship between language variation and identity and demonstrated their engagement in and contributions to 'real' current debates in sociolinguistics; but (3) the students' discussion only touched on the language ideologies and power structures that shaped their own code-switching practices and the linguistic expectations they faced in academic and professional contexts. An appendix includes an outline of the inquiry-based unit and discussion questions used with secondary students.

Christensen, Linda. 2011. Finding Voice: Learning About Language and Power. *Voices from the Middle* 18.9–17.

B S U
Argues for teaching middle-school students the social and political contexts of "voice," asking critical questions such as whose voices get heard and whose get marginalized. With this critical consciousness, Christensen argues, adolescents who speak vernacular varieties may embrace Standard English as a voice that offers them greater power.

Christiansen, Martha Sidury & Marcia Farr. 2010. Learning English in Mexico: Transnational Language Ideologies and Practices. In *New Literacy Studies in Latin America,* ed. by J. Kalman & B. Street. New York: Routledge.

4 F I

Christie, Pauline (ed.) 1996. *Caribbean Language Issues, Old and New: Papers in Honour of Professor Mervyn Alleyne on the Occasion of His Sixtieth Birthday.* Cave Hill, Barbados: The Press University of the West Indies.

2 C E F N P W

Christie, Pauline. 2003. *Language in Jamaica.* Kingston, Jamaica: Arawak Publications.

2 F

Chun, Elaine. 2001. The Construction of White, Black, and Korean American Identities through African American Vernacular English. *Journal of Linguistic Anthropology* 11.52–64.

1 3 6 F I U

Chun, Elaine. 2004. Ideologies of Legitimate Mockery: Margaret Cho's Revoicings of Mock Asian. *Pragmatics* 14.263–89.

3 I

Chun, Elaine. 2009. Speaking Like Asian Immigrants: Intersections of Accommodation and Mocking at a US High School. *Pragmatics* 19.17–38.

3 I

Chun-Hoon, Lowell. 1973. Teaching the Asian American Experience. In *Teaching Ethnic Studies,* ed. by J. Banks, 118–47. Washington, D.C.: National Council of Social Studies.

3 C

Clachar, Arlene. 2003. Paratactic Conjunctions in Creole Speakers' and ESL Learners' Academic Writing. *World Englishes* 22.271–89.

2 F W X

Clachar, Arlene. 2004. The Construction of Creole-Speaking Students' Linguistic Profile and Contradictions in ESL Literacy Programs. *TESOL Quarterly* 38.153–65.

2 P S X
US public schools typically only distinguish between English for native speakers and English for non-native speakers—with the result that speakers of Caribbean-English Creoles (CEC), for whom Standard English is a second *dialect*, are treated as if they were ESL learners. This study investigates whether students who speak CEC exhibit language acquisition behaviors similar to those of ESL students with respect to the marking of tense and aspect in academic writing. Findings indicated that CEC-speaking students followed a different acquisition path from that of previously researched ESL students. For instance, according to some theories, ESL learners are predicted to mark progressive aspect most often on activity verbs like "play," less often on telic verbs like "build a house," and least often on statives (like "want") and punctuals (like "arrive"). While this (and related predictions for perfective marking) was true for acrolectal CEC speaking students, it was not true for basilectal and mesolectal speaking CEC students. In her discussion, the author notes how intrinsic linguistic features of the creole continuum, representative of CEC-speaking students' linguistic background, may have influenced the patterns found in their writing. And she argues (p. 164) that "their literacy needs cannot be addressed by an ESL curriculum, but rather by one that attends to their specific writing challenges." [Edited version of an abstract provided by the author]

Clachar, Arlene. 2005. Creole English Speakers' Treatment of Tense-Aspect Morphology in English Interlanguage Written Discourse. *Language Learning* 55.275–334.

2 F U W X

Clachar, Arlene. 2006. Re-Examining ESL Programs in Public Schools: A Focus on Creole-English Children's Clause-Structuring Strategies in Written Academic Discourse. *Forum on Public Policy: A Journal of the Oxford University Round Table.*1–38.

2 B F W X

Clark, Romy, Norman Fairclough, Roz Ivanic & Marilyn Martin-Jones. 1990. Critical Language Awareness. Part I: A Critical Review of Three Current Approaches to Language Awareness. *Language and Education* 4.249–60.

I L P

Clark, Romy, Norman Fairclough, Roz Ivanic & Marilyn Martin-Jones. 1991. Critical Language Awareness. Part II: Towards Critical Alternatives. *Language and Education* 5.41–54.

I L P

Cleary, Linda Miller. 1988. A Profile of Carlos: Strengths of a Nonstandard Dialect Writer. *English Journal* 77.59.

1 4 T W

Cleary, Linda Miller. 2008. The Imperative of Literacy Motivation When Native Children Are Being Left Behind. *Journal of American Indian Education* 47.97–117.

5 P

Clemente, Maria de los Angeles. 2005. Review of "America's Second Tongue: American Indian Education and the Ownership of English, 1860–1900". *TESOL Quarterly* 39.787–93.

5 P

Coelho, Elizabeth. 1988. *Caribbean Students in Canadian Schools, Book 1*. Toronto: Carib-Can Publishers.

2 M S

Coelho, Elizabeth. 1991. Caribbean Creole Languages. In *Caribbean Students in Canadian Schools*, 2–41. Markham, Ontario: Pippin Publishing.

2 F I S

This first chapter opens by introducing the concept of language variation and the processes of pidginization and creolization. After explaining the state of Caribbean English Creole in the Caribbean, Coelho explains some of the more salient differences between Caribbean English Creole and Standard English, in terms of lexicon, phonology and grammar. She also includes several anecdotal examples of the misunderstanding that can occur because of false cognates, and provides a short story in Jamaican Creole, along with its Standard English counterpart for comparison. Finally, she discusses prevalent attitudes toward language variation and their implications for education in the Caribbean and in Canada.

Coelho, Elizabeth. 1991. *Caribbean Students in Canadian Schools, Book 2*. Markham, Ontario: Pippin Publishing.

2 M S

Cole, Patricia & Orlando Taylor. 1990. The Performance of Working Class African American Children on Three Tests of Articulation. *Language, Speech and Hearing Services in Schools* 21.171–76.

1 A D O

Coleman, Charles. 1997. Our Students Write with Accents: Oral Paradigms for ESD Students. *College Composition and Communication* 48.486–500.

1 F W

Collins, James. 1988. Language and Class in Minority Education. *Anthropology and Education Quarterly* 19.299–326.

1 5 6 I

Collins, James. 1999. The Ebonics Controversy in Context: Literacies, Subjectivities, and Language Ideologies in the United States. In *Language Ideological Debates*, ed. by J. Blommaert. Berlin: Mouton de Gruyter.

K

CCCC Language Policy Committee. 2000. *Language Knowledge and Awareness Survey, Final Research Report.* National Council of Teachers of English and the Conference on College Composition and Communication.

1 4 5 I T

Conference on College Composition & Communication. 1974. Students' Right to Their Own Language (Special Issue). *College Composition and Communication* 25.

1 4 P W

Connor, Carol McDonald & Holly K. Craig. 2006. African American Preschoolers' Language, Emergent Literacy Skills, and Use of African American English. *Journal of Speech, Language, and Hearing Research* 49.771–92.

1 F R U

Cook, Lenora & Helen Lodge (eds.) 1996. *Voices in English Classrooms: Honoring Diversity and Change.* Urbana, IL: NCTE Press.

6 E I S T

Cook, Mary Jane. 1973. Problems of Southwestern Indian Speakers in Learning English. In *Bilingualism in the Southwest,* ed. by P. R. Turner, 241–49. Tucson: University of Arizona Press.

5 X

Cook, Mary Jane & A. Sharp. 1966. Problems of Navajo Speakers in Learning English. *Language Learning* 1.21–29.

5 X

Cook-Gumperz, Jenny. 1993. Dilemmas of Identity: Oral and Written Literacies in the Making of a Basic Writing Student. *Anthropology and Education Quarterly* 24.336–56.

1 A C W

Cooper, Carolyn. 1995. *Noises in the Blood: Orality, Gender and the "Vulgar" Body of Jamaican Popular Culture.* Durham, NC: Duke University Press.

2 I N

Corson, David. 1999. *Language Policy in Schools: A Resource for Teachers and Administrators.* Mahwah, NJ: Lawrence Erlbaum Associates.

6 C I P
This is a guide for practitioners interested in developing a school-level language policy. It includes chapters on "Critical Language Awareness in School and Curriculum" (pp, 85–134) and "ESL and Minority Languages in Schools and Curriculum" (pp. 171–215).

Corson, David. 2001. *Language Diversity and Education.* Mahwah, NJ: Lawrence Erlbaum Associates.

1 4 5 6 C E I P T
Corson offers a thorough overview and synthesis of decades of research on language diversity in educational context, focusing particularly on policy and ideology. Chapters of special relevance to this book include: 2 "Language, Power and Social Justice in Education"; 3 "Different Cultural Discourse Norms"; 4 "Non-Standard Varieties"; and 5 "Bilingual and English as a Second Language Education."

Corson, David. 2003. *Language, Minority Education, and Gender: Linking Social Justice and Power.* Clevedon, UK: Multilingual Matters.

1 2 3 4 5 C P

Cosden, Merith, Jules Zimmer, Carla Reyes & Maria del Rosario Gutierrez. 1994. Kindergarten Practices and First-Grade Achievement for Latino Spanish-Speaking, Latino English-Speaking and Anglo Students. *Journal of School Psychology* 33.123–41.

4 A

Costantino, Magda & Denny S. Hurtado. 2006. Northwest Native American Reading Curriculum. *Journal of American Indian Education* 45.45–49.

5 R

Coupland, Nikolas. 2006. The Discursive Framing of Phonological Acts of Identity: Welshness through English. In *English and Ethnicity*, ed. by J. Brutt-Griffler & C. E. Davies, 19–48. New York: Palgrave Macmillan.

6 F

Courts, Patrick. 1997. *Multicultural Literacies: Dialect, Discourse, and Diversity.* New York: Peter Lang.

1 6 C S

Covington, Ann. 1975. Teachers' Attitudes toward Black English. In *Ebonics: The True Language of Black Folks*, ed. by R. L. Williams, 40–54. St. Louis, MO: Robert L. Williams and Associates.

1 I

Cox, Juanita. 1992. *A Study of the Linguistic Features of Cajun English.* [microform]. Washington, DC: Distributed by ERIC Clearinghouse. http://www.eric.ed.gov/contentdelivery/servlet/ERICServlet?accno=ED352840

6 F

Craig, Beth. 1991. American Indian English. *English World-Wide* 12.25–61.

5 F

Craig, Dennis. 1966. Teaching English to Jamaican Creole Speakers: A Model of a Multi-Dialect Situation. *Language Learning* 16.49–61.

2 B O S

Craig, Dennis. 1969. *An Experiment in Teaching English.* Mona, Jamaica: Caribbean University Press.

2 S

Craig, Dennis. 1971. Education and Creole English in the West Indies. In *Pidginization and Creolization of Languages*, ed. by D. Hymes, 371–92. Cambridge: Cambridge University Press.

2 P

Craig, Dennis. 1976. Bidialectal Education: Creole and Standard in the West Indies. *International Journal of the Sociology of Language* 8.93–134. [Abstract prepared by ERIC and reprinted with permission of the Department of Education from the Education Resources Information Center at eric.ed.gov.]

2 B

This article discusses language education and the factors that need to be considered in bidialectal education programs in the West Indies such as the relationship between language and the child's natural cultural environment and the role of language in social mobility.

Craig, Dennis. 1980a. Creole Languages and Primary Education. In *Pidgin and Creole Linguistics,* ed. by A. Valdman, 313–32. Bloomington: Indiana University Press.

2 V

Craig, Dennis. 1980b. Models for Educational Policy in Creole-Speaking Communities. In *Theoretical Orientations in Creole Studies,* ed. by A. Valdman & A. Highfield, 245–65. New York: Academic Press.

2 P

Craig, Dennis. 1983. Teaching Standard English to Nonstandard Speakers: Some Methodological Issues. *Journal of Negro Education* 52.65–74.

1 B I O S

Craig argues that instruction in a second dialect involves unique linguistic dynamics to be taken into account in planning methodology. The author cites literature exposing the limitations of the foreign language instruction technique, reminding us of the four classes of language patterns for the learner of a new dialect: (A) those actively used, (B) those used 'only under stress', (C) those understood but not used, and (D) those not yet known at all. Classes C and D require explicit contrastive analytic instruction, while classes A and B do not. In light of this unique schema, teachers should devote a different amount of attention to each pattern type in order to ensure that learners do not overestimate their knowledge of the new dialect. Although evidence shows that even motivated students have difficulty learning a second dialect, the author closes by addressing the language attitude issue, and suggests that teachers diminish the problem by keeping the subject matter interesting and relevant and by keeping the task non-threatening (i.e., by setting realistic goals).

Craig, Dennis. 1985. The Sociology of Language Learning and Teaching in a Creole Situation. In *Language of Inequality,* ed. by N. Wolfson & J. Manes, 273–84. Berlin: Mouton de Gruyter.

2 X

In this paper, Craig begins by discussing the nature of a creole speech community: typically there exists a creole spoken by the majority, a more prestigious standard language reserved for the higher social classes, and also a number of mesolectal varieties that occurs when the middle class mixes the standard with the creole. He then addresses the different kinds of bilingual education systems that might be used in such a community. Instruction in the standard can be problematic for a variety of reasons: (1) if the creole closely resembles the standard, instructors may underestimate the difficulty children will face in learning the standard; (2) children may view the standard negatively, as the language of their oppressors; (3) methodological problems arise when children begin using a variety halfway between their creole and the standard; and (4) children must learn not only a new language, but a new communication format altogether.

Craig, Dennis. 1999. *Teaching Language and Literacy: Policies and Procedures for Vernacular Situations.* Georgetown, Guyana: Education and Development Services.

2 A B E F R S T V

This book, published in Craig's native Guyana five years before his death in 2004, represents his most comprehensive account of the challenges facing creole (e.g., Caribbean) and vernacular (e.g., AAVE) speakers in acquiring literacy, and syllabi and strategies for helping them to that goal. Chapters include: 1—"Relevant situational characteristics"; 2—"The language and literacy education of vernacular speakers"; 3—"Learners' needs and the components of school programmes"; 4—"The background of language-teaching perspectives"; 5—"Literacy in TESORV [Teaching English to Speakers of a Related Vernacular]"; 6—"Procedures for the primary level"; 7—"Procedures for post-primary situations characterised by inadequate primary-level achievement"; 8—"Procedures for the Secondary level; Syllabus Resources,"

Craig, Dennis. 2006. The Use of the Vernacular in West Indian Education. In *Exploring the Boundaries of Caribbean Creole Languages,* ed. by H. Simmons-McDonald & I. Robertson, 99-117. Kingston, Jamaica: University of the West Indies Press.

2 B K V

Craig, Dennis. 2008. Pidgins/Creoles and Education. In *The Handbook of Pidgin and Creole Studies,* ed. by S. Kouwenberg & J. V. Singler. Chichester, UK: Wiley-Blackwell.

2 P V

Craig, Holly K. 1996. The Challenges of Conducting Language Research with African American Children. In *Communication Development and Disorders in African American Children: Research, Assessment and Intervention,* ed. by A. Kamhi, K. Pollock & J. Harris, 1–17. Baltimore: Paul H. Brookes Publishing.

1 A Q

Craig, Holly K. 2008. Effective Language Instruction for African American Children. In *Educating the Other America: Top Experts Tackle Poverty, Literacy, and Achievement in Our Schools,* ed. by S. B. Neumann, 163–84. Baltimore: Paul H. Brookes Publishing.

1 B S X

Craig, Holly K., Carol McDonald Connor & Julie A. Washington. 2003. Early Positive Predictors of Later Reading Comprehension for African American Students: A Preliminary Investigation. *Language, Speech and Hearing Services in Schools* 34.31–43.

1 A Q R

Craig, Holly K., Connie Thompson, Julie A. Washington & Stephanie L. Potter. 2003. Phonological Features of Child African American English. *Journal of Speech, Language, and Hearing Research* 46.623–35.

1 F Q

Craig, Holly K., Connie Thompson, Julie A. Washington & Stephanie L. Potter. 2004. Performance of Elementary-Grade African American Students on the Gray Oral Reading Tests. *Language, Speech and Hearing Services in Schools* 35.141–54.

1 A R

This study examines whether a dialect bias is evident in a commonly used standardized test of reading ability, the Gray Oral Reading Test (GORT-3). Subjects were sixty-five typically developing AAVE speakers, grades 2-5. Children's audiotaped performances of oral reading passages were scored for accuracy twice, once according to the test's standard scoring procedures, and again in a way that gave children credit for variations from print that were attributed to AAVE pronunciations. There were small, but measurable, differences between the two sets of scores. The authors' analysis suggests that these differences are neither statistically nor educationally significant, and the authors conclude that the Gray Oral Reading Test is a valid measure for African American students. It should be noted, however, that for many students, the two sets of scores yielded a change in the classification of reading performances. While standard scoring procedures placed subjects at the boundary between "below average" and "average," the scores adjusted for AAE pronunciations placed performances firmly within the "average" range. The findings also shed light on the relative influence of AAVE on children's reading performance. Most students (94%) produced at least some AAE features in oral reading. However, only 21% of the variations from print produced by these students could be attributed to AAE features (meaning that 79% of their "mistakes" were not dialect-related.) Additionally, the study found that the amount of AAE that children produced *did not* appear to relate to their comprehension scores.

Craig, Holly K. & Julie A. Washington. 1994. The Complex Syntax Skills of Poor, Urban, African American Preschoolers at School Entry. *Language, Speech and Hearing Services in Schools* 25.181–90.

1 A F Q

In a study of forty-five preschool African American children, the authors found a positive relationship between their use of complex syntax and their use of African American Vernacular English. This finding was replicated in their (1995) study of the children, in which they also found a positive relationship between semantic complexity (in prepositional phrases) and the use of AAVE.

Craig, Holly K. & Julie A. Washington. 1995. African-American English and Linguistic Complexity in Preschool Discourse: A Second Look. *Language, Speech, and Hearing Services in Schools* 26.87–93.

1 F Q

Craig, Holly K. & Julie A. Washington. 2000. An Assessment Battery for Identifying Language Impairments in African American Children. *Journal of Speech, Language and Hearing Research* 43.366–79.

1 A D

Craig, Holly K. & Julie A. Washington. 2002. Oral Language Expectations for African American Preschoolers and Kindergartners. *American Journal of Speech-Language Pathology* 11.59–70.

1 A D Q

Craig, Holly K. & Julie A. Washington. 2004. Grade-Related Changes in the Production of African American English. *Journal of Speech, Language and Hearing Research* 47.450–63.

1 F Q R

Describes a study which followed African American students' use of African American English throughout their elementary school years (starting in preschool and ending in the fifth grade) in order to determine a grade-related change in their production of AAE. Each student's use of AAE was determined by the manner in which they described pictures. Data from the study indicated that many African Americans speak African American English at their time of entry into grade school, and there exists an inverse relationship between their use of AAE and their grade. Among the study's findings was that this inverse relationship is initially gradual and then followed by an extreme decline. Researchers call this non-linear change from using AAE to SAE a dialect shift. Students who exhibited a dialect shift were observed to perform significantly better on standardized tests of reading achievement than their peers who were producing higher levels of African American English. Thus the study also discusses the seemingly advantageous nature of dialect shifting from AAE to SAE for reading acquisition.

Craig, Holly K. & Julie A. Washington. 2004. Language Variation and Literacy Learning. In *Handbook of Language and Literacy: Development and Disorders,* ed. by C. A. Stone, E. Silliman, B. Ehren & K. Apel, 228–47. New York: Guilford Press.

1 Q R

Craig, Holly K. & Julie A. Washington. 2006. *Malik Goes to School: Examining the Language Skills of African American Students from Preschool to 5th Grade.* Mahwah, NJ: Lawrence Erlbaum Associates.

1 A D Q R X

Craig, Holly K., Julie A. Washington & Connie Thompson. 2005. Oral Language Expectations for African American Children in Grades 1 through 5. *American Journal of Speech-Language Pathology* 14.119–30.

1 A D O Q

Craig, Holly K., Julie A. Washington & Connie Thompson-Porter. 1998. Average C-Unit Lengths in the Discourse of African American Children from Low-Income, Urban Homes. *Journal of Speech, Language, and Hearing Research* 41.433–44.

1 A Q

Craig, Holly K., Julie A. Washington & Connie Thompson-Porter. 1998. Performances of Young African American Children on Two Comprehension Tasks. *Journal of Speech, Language, and Hearing Research* 41.445–57.

1 A Q R

Craig, Holly K., Lingling Zhang, Stephanie L. Hensel & Erin J. Quinn. 2009. African American English-Speaking Students: An Examination of the Relationship between Dialect Shifting and Reading Outcomes. *Journal of Speech, Language, and Hearing Research* 52.839–55.

1 A B U X
In order to provide evidence for the hypothesis that code-shifting skills help AAVE speakers learn to read, this study examines the relationship between reading scores and the ability to write Standard English. The researchers calculated the Dialect Density Measures (DDMs) for oral and written narratives produced by 165 African American elementary school students. DDMs measure the rate of AAVE features per 100 words. They found a statistically significant difference in mean DDM between oral and written genres, indicating that students are in fact code switching. Controlling for language skill level, they found further that while oral DDM did not significantly predict reading scores, written DDM did. In other words, students who produced more standard written narratives were likely to have higher reading scores. The authors conclude that this provides tentative support for the suggestion that the ability to shift dialects helps AAVE speakers read. However, they warn that their results say nothing about causality; for example, it is also possible that being able to read well makes it easier to acquire Standard English.

Cran, William (director). 1986. *Black on White.* #5 in *The Story of English,* a nine-part television and video series co-produced by MacNeil-Lehrer Productions and the BBC.

1 2 F Z

No. 6 in the videocassette series, "The Story of English," this "Black on White" segment covers the history and features of "Black English" in the United States and related English-based pidgins and creoles in West Africa and the New World, including Gullah on the South Carolina and Georgia coasts. It also explores the use of Black English in music, including Cab Calloway's jive talk of the 1930s, and discusses the *King* court ruling of 1979 in which the city of Ann Arbor was ordered to take Black English into account in its schools. See the corresponding Chapter 6 of the companion book by McCrum, Cran and MacNeil 1986. It was (re)distributed by Public Media, Inc., around 2000.

Crawford, Clinton (ed.) 2001. *Ebonics and Language Education of African Ancestry Students.* New York: Sankofa World Publishers.

1 2 C E I K
This volume considers "Ebonics" to refer generally to language systems used in the African Diaspora. Part I, "The African Origin and Nature of Ebonics," includes chapters by Clinton Crawford, Kimani Nehusi, Ernie Smith, and Aisha Blackshire-Belay. Part II, "Ebonics and Education," includes contributions by Robert Williams, Keith Gilyard, Geneva Smitherman, Arthur K. Spears, and Iona Anderson-Janniere about public opinion regarding Ebonics and school policy. Part III, "Ebonics: Research and Pedagogy," has chapters by John R. Rickford, Carrie M. Jefferson, and Nabeehah Sabree-Shakir, addressing instructional methods for teaching speakers of vernaculars. The book concludes with a selected bibliography for further reading, and recommendations by Crawford and Nehusi for further action toward "correcting a global culture of injustice against Africans" (p. 351).

Crawford, James. 2000. *At War with Diversity: US Language Policy in an Age of Anxiety.* Clevedon, UK: Multilingual Matters.

5 I K P

Cronnell, Bruce. 1979. Black English and Spelling. *Research in the Teaching of English* 13.81–90.

1 W X

Cronnell, Bruce (ed.) 1981. *The Writing Needs of Linguistically Different Students.* Los Alamitos, CA: SWRL Educational Research and Development.

1 4 5 B E F S W

Cronnell, Bruce. 1983. Dialect and Writing: A Review. *Journal of Research and Development in Education* 17.58–64.

4 5 B W X

Cronnell, Bruce. 1984. Black English Influences in the Writing of Third- and Sixth-Grade Black Students. *Journal of Educational Research* 77.233–36.

1 W X

Cronnell, Bruce. 1985. Language Influences in the English Writing of Third- and Sixth-Grade Mexican American Students. *Journal of Educational Research* 78(3), 168-173.

X

Cross, Beverly. 2003. Learning or Unlearning Racism: Transferring Teacher Education to Classroom Practices. *Theory Into Practice* 42.203–09.

1 4 5 T

Cross (2003) presents the results of interviews with twelve White teachers in Milwaukee Public Schools who had graduated from the teacher preparation program at the University of Wisconsin-Milwaukee and had participated in courses designed to prepare them to teach in racially and linguistically diverse classrooms. While the findings are encouraging at first glance—for instance, the necessity of respect for students' language was the most frequently recalled theme of their preparation—Cross suggests that much of the teachers' learning was superficial.

Cross, John, Thomas DeVaney & Gerald Jones. 2001. Pre-Service Teacher Attitudes toward Differing Dialects. *Linguistics and Education* 12.211–27. [Reprinted with permission of Elsevier, the publisher, from *Linguistics and Education* 12(2).]

1 3 4 5 I T
In order to evaluate pre-service teachers' attitudes toward differing dialects, 111 students at a small Alabama university were asked to provide demographic data (including gender, race, age, and socioeconomic status) and to respond to five readers representing a variety of dialects common to the region. Respondents were asked to rate readers on the qualities of intelligence, friendliness, consideration, education, trustworthiness, ambition, honesty, and social status. The results indicate that listeners do evaluate speakers' personal characteristics on the basis of dialect and that race is a factor in the perception of language, since White respondents were most favorable to White speakers and least favorable to Black speakers and Black respondents were most favorable to Black speakers and least to White speakers. Directions for further study are noted.

Cross, Kathy & Jerry Aldrige. 1989. Introducing Southern Dialects to Children through Literature. *Reading Improvement* 26.29–32.

2 6 C R

Crotteau, Michelle. 2007. Honoring Dialect and Culture: Pathways to Student Success on High-Stakes Writing Assessments. *English Journal* 96.27–32. [Reprinted from *English Journal* 96(4) courtesy of NCTE.]

6 A B S W
Honoring students' home dialect is a complex task when preparing them to take state writing tests that require the use of Standard English. Working with students who had failed the test and were in danger of not receiving a diploma, Michelle Crotteau created a supportive learning environment in which students could develop linguistic and mechanical fluency. In the Writing Strategies class, students spoke and wrote about their interests, drew on their dialect (Appalachian English), and learned to recognize audience-appropriate situations for using their dialect and Standard English.

Crowell, Sheila & Ellen Kolba. 1974. Contrastive Analysis in the Junior High School. In *Black Dialects and Reading,* ed. by B. Cullinan, 69–98. Urbana, IL: NCTE.

1 B M S
In this chapter, the authors describe Talkacross (Crowell et al. 1974), a manual and method for helping junior high school students to understand the systematic differences between AAVE and Standard English through contrastive analysis. By listening to dialogue, narration and instruction sequences on tape and completing daily exercises, students cover a variety of topics that contrast the two varieties in a way that remains sensitive to the legitimacy of AAVE. Topics of the course include plurals, possessives, subject-verb agreement, past tense, the use of *be*, negation, and the use of subjects, subject markers (existential *it* vs. *there*, for instance), and relative pronouns (*who* vs. zero, for instance, as subjects, e.g., "I know a girl (who) works in that building." The ultimate goal is for students to be able to speak both varieties of English and switch back and forth between them according to context. The authors make specific

suggestions for using the course (how long to spend on each lesson, how to reinforce the key points, and so on).

Crowell, Sheila, Ellen Kolba, William Stewart & Kenneth Johnson. 1974. *Talk Across: Materials for Teaching Standard English as a Second Dialect.* Montclair, NJ: Caribou Associates.

1 B M

This excellent contrastive analysis program consists of a 69-page teacher's manual and a 193-page student activity book. But the only copy we've ever seen is a typescript, and it doesn't appear to have been formally published and distributed.

Crowl, Thomas & Walter Macginitie. 1974. Influence of Students' Speech Characteristics on Teachers' Evaluations of Oral Answers. *Journal of Educational Psychology* 66.3:304-308.

1 I T

In this matched-guise experiment, Black and White ninth grade males provided oral answers to social studies questions. "Mirror" tapes were made—if a Black student performed a particular answer on Tape A, a White student performed that answer on Tape B. White teachers enrolled in graduate level professional courses (n = 62) were randomly assigned to listen and evaluate one of the two tapes. The difference between subjects' ratings of the same answer spoken by Black students (M = 5.48; SD = 2.60) and by White students (M = 5.82; SD = 2.59) was statistically significant. Additionally, the effect of answer quality was investigated, and it appeared (p. 306) that "inherently superior answers spoken by Black students were not perceived as any better than inherently inferior answers spoken by White students; or conversely, inherently inferior answers spoken by White students were perceived as being as good as inherently superior answers spoken by Black students."

Crowley, Terry. 1989. *Standard English and the Politics of Language.* Urbana: University of Illinois Press.

I P

Crowley, Terry. 1990. The Position of Melanesian Pidgin in Vanuatu and Papua New Guinea. In *Melanesian Pidgin and Tok Pisin,* ed. by J. W. M. Verhaar. Amsterdam: John Benjamins.

2 I P

Crowley addresses the status of Bislama in Vanuatu and contrasts it to that of the mutually intelligible Tok Pisin in Papua New Guinea. In Papua New Guinea, Tok Pisin is regarded as 'regional' while English enjoys national status. In Vanuatu, on the other hand, despite the official status of English and French as the languages of education, it is Bislama that has become the language of national identity, used in the national newspaper, on currency, and on the radio. Research attributes this to the 1970's release of a Bislama translation of the New Testament and many popular hymns, and to the great political involvement of the ni-Vanuatu. As a result of the relatively rapid rise in status of the language, however, no standardized orthography had been fully disseminated, resulting in much variability in spelling. Current local efforts around the time of the writing of this paper included the development of a committee to standardize vocabulary and orthography, the development of a Bislama-language grammar textbook, the establishment of a Pacific Languages Unit at the University of the South Pacific, and the training of primary and pre-school teachers in bilingual education.

Cullinan, Bernice (ed.) 1974. *Black Dialects and Reading.* Urbana, IL: NCTE.

1 E R S

Cullinan, Bernice, Angela Jagger & Dorothy Strickland. 1974. Language Expansion for Black Children in the Primary Grades. *Young Children* 24.98–112.

1 O S

Cummings, Patrick Jean. 2011. *A Dictionary of Hong Kong English: Words from the Fragrant Harbor.* Hong Kong: Hong Kong University Press.

6F

Cummins, Jim. 1986. Empowering Minority Students: A Framework for Intervention. *Harvard Educational Review* 56.18–36.

1 3 4 5 A C

Cunningham, Patricia. 1976. Teachers' Correction Responses to Black-Dialect Miscues Which Are Non-Meaning-Changing. *Reading Research Quarterly* 12.637–53.

1 R T X
Found that teachers across the United States were more likely to correct dialect-related miscues (*Here go a table* for *Here is a table*) than those that were not dialect related (*Here is a table* for *There is a table*). A total of 78% of dialect-related miscues were corrected; only 27% of non-dialect related miscues were corrected.

Curzan, Anne. 2002. Teaching the Politics of Standard English. *Journal of English Linguistics* 30.339–52.

1 I P T

Da Pidgin Coup. 2008. Pidgin and Education: A Position Paper. *Educational Perspectives* 41.30–39. [Abstract prepared by ERIC and reprinted with permission of the Department of Education from the Education Resources Information Center at eric.ed.gov.]

2 A I
This article presents an adaptation of a position paper written by DaPidginCoup, a group of concerned faculty and students in the Department of Second Language Studies (SLS). In fall 1999, the group became concerned about a statement made by the chairman of the Board of Education implicating Pidgin in the poor results of the students of Hawai'i on national standardized writing tests. The group's discussions led to the writing of this position paper. Their aim was to provide well-researched advice about the complex relationship between Pidgin and English, and the issues involved in discussing the role of Pidgin in education.

Dalphinis, Morgan. 1985. *Caribbean and African Languages: Social History, Language, Literature, and Education.* London: Karia Press.

2

Dandy, Evelyn. 1991. *Black Communication: Breaking Down the Barriers.* Chicago: African-American Images.

1 B C F I N

Davis, Olga, Mildred Gladney & Lloyd Leaverton. 1968. *The Psycholinguistics Reading Series.* Chicago: Chicago Board of Education.

1 B M S V

Day, Richard. 1989. The Acquisition and Maintenance of Language by Minority Children. *Language Learning* 29.295–303.

2 Q

Day-Vines, Norma L., Heather H. Barto, Beverly L. Booker, Kim V. Smith, Jennifer Barna, Brian S. Maiden, Linda Zegley & Monique T. Felder. 2009. African American English: Implications for School Counseling Professionals. *Journal of Negro Education* 78.70–82. [Reprinted with permission of the journal from the *Journal of Negro Education* 78(1), 70.]

1 F S T

African American English (AAE) refers to the systematic, rule-governed linguistic patterns of found among African Americans. This article provides an overview of AAE. More specifically, the article enumerates the historical underpinnings associated with AAE, identifies a representative set of AAE characteristics, reviews relevant research, and addresses implications for school counselors who work with AAE speakers.

de Kleine, Christa. 2006. West African World English Speakers in U.S. Classrooms: The Role of West African Pidgin English. In *Dialects, Englishes, Creoles and Education,* ed. by S. Nero. Mahwah, NJ: Lawrence Erlbaum Associates.

2 A X

This essay aimed to investigate the key factors which may contribute to the seemingly paradoxical underachievement of Anglophone West-African Students in the US public school systems. West-African students are often placed into ESL classes where they are marked as having limited proficiency in the English language. However, their limited English proficiency testing stands in contrast to the significant exposure to Standard English, which they often indicate having had since elementary school years. After analyzing the writing samples of a group of West-African ESL students in Washington D.C., the author notes the students' systematic tendencies to make similar grammatical mistakes, and suggests that they are due to interference from their West-African Pidgin English (WAPE). The essay then discusses how these systematic grammatical errors in SAE reflect grammatical structures of WAPE. The essay ends by indicating a bias of the accepted English proficiency tests and highlighting the need for more accurate indicators of a student's academic ability.

de Kleine, Christa. 2009. Sierra Leonean and Liberian Students in ESL Programs in US Classrooms: The Role of Creole English. In *The Languages of Africa and Diaspora: Educating for Language Awareness,* ed. by J. A. Kleifgen & G. Bond, 178–98. Bristol, UK: Multilingual Matters.

2 S X

de Villiers, Jill & Valerie Johnson. 2007. The Information in Third-Person /S/: Acquisition across Dialects of American English. *Journal of Child Language* 34.133–58. [Copyright © 2007 Cambridge University Press. Reprinted with permission of Cambridge University Press from *Journal of Child Language,* 3(1).]

1 F Q X

The production of third-person /s/ on English verbs seems to be ahead of comprehension. Mainstream American English (MAE) is contrasted with African American English (AAE), in which /s/ is rarely supplied. Two studies explored what information children get solely from /s/ on the end of a verb. Sixty-five MAE- and sixty-five AAE-speaking four- to seven-year-olds participated in one of two experimental picture-choice comprehension studies. Neither group of four-year-olds could use the /s/ to determine if the event was generic rather than past tense on a verb (e.g., "cuts/ cut"), or whether it was a verb or a noun compound as in "The penguin dresses"/"The penguin dress". MAE-speakers do not use the information in third-person /s/ alone until age five, and not reliably until age six years. In keeping with AAE production, AAE-speaking children do not use the information in /s/ at all in this age range.

Dean, Mary & Elaine Fowler. 1974. An Argument for Appreciation of Dialect Differences in the Classroom. *Journal of Negro Education* 43.302–09.

1 B

DeBose, Charles. 1992. Codeswitching: Black English and Standard English in the African American Linguistic Repertoire. *Journal of Multilingual and Multicultural Development* 13.157–67.

1 U
DeBose, treating AAVE and SAE as two separate linguistic systems, provides evidence that educated, middle-class African Americans can be fully fluent in both systems and codeswitch between them according to context. An individual named P., a college-educated African American woman with southern roots, was recorded conversing with her husband, daughter, and two researchers. During the first few minutes, P. conversed with a researcher using SAE only. As the other participants began to speak, P. responded to them in AAVE. When P. narrated a story, she did so primarily in SAE, but with some AAVE, especially in giving direct quotations. In a second session, she used AAVE consistently in a casual conversation with both her husband and the researchers. The author, combating the assumption that AAVE is mainly spoken by the poor and uneducated, suggests that bilingualism is prominent among African Americans who grow up in a lower-class setting speaking AAVE and who then learn SAE as they achieve middle class. SAE then becomes the "mainstream" language while AAVE remains the "ingroup" language.

DeBose, Charles. 2005. *The Sociology of African American Language: A Language Planning Perspective*. Basingstoke: Palgrave Macmillan. [Abstract adapted from an abstract graciously provided by Charles DeBose.]

1 I P
The body of linguistic scholarship on African American Language (AAL) and critical responses to it by educators, policymaker and the general public is amenable to study from a language planning and policy perspective. Such a perspective not only includes decisions by judges, legislators or educators regarding the place of AAL in the class-room, and in society; but also decisions of linguists about the variety that are contrary to common sense. Major issues of AAL studies such as whether or not it has the same underlying structure as other varieties of American English qualify as corpus plan-ning issues insofar as they entail claims about the grammatical structure of a variety defined in the real world as lacking structure. Other issues such as what AAL should be called and whether it is a dialect or a separate language, qualify as status planning issues insofar as the variety is constructed in the real world as "bad" English. A soci-ology of knowledge framework is used to underscore the social construction of real world knowledge and define the Ebonics Phenomenon as consisting of three bodies of knowledge: The real world of everyday experience; linguistic scholarship; and Ebon-ics scholarship. Differences among them are explained with reference to two crucial variables: the stigmatization of AAL, and the hegemony of Standard English. Chapter 9, "Ebonics and Black School Achievement: The Language Difference Hypothesis," discusses the African American Literacy and Culture Project funded through a con-gressional appropriation in the wake of the Oakland Ebonics controversy, and argues against the assumption that African American language is a barrier to the acquisition of literacy. A pervasive theme of the book is the extent to which academic research is affected by the social location of the scholar.

DeBose, Charles. 2007. The Ebonics Phenomenon, Language Planning, and the Hege-mony of Standard English. In *Talkin Black Talk: Language, Education and Social Change*, ed. by H. S. Alim & J. Baugh, 30–42. New York: Teachers College Press.

1 I K P

Del Torto, Lisa M. 2010. 'It's So Cute How They Talk': Stylized Italian English as Socio-linguistic Maintenance. *English Today* 26.55–62.

6 I Q

Delain, Marsha Taylor, P. David Pearson & Richard C. Anderson. 1985. Reading Comprehension and Creativity in Black Language Use: You Stand to Gain by Playing the Sounding Game! *American Educational Research Journal* 22.155–73.

1 C N

The authors found that African American children who are better at signifying also have greater skill at figurative language comprehension. No similar effect was found for White kids.

Delpit, Lisa. 1986. Skills and Other Dilemmas of a Progressive Black Educator. *Harvard Educational Review* 56.379–86.

1 A C T W

Delpit, Lisa. 1988. The Silenced Dialogue: Power and Pedagogy in Educating Other People's Children. *Harvard Educational Review* 58.280–98.

1 B C I P T W

Delpit, Lisa. 1990. Language Diversity and Learning. In *Perspectives on Talk and Learning,* ed. by S. Hynds & D. L. Rubin, 247–66. Urbana, IL: NCTE.

1 6 I S T

This is a good outline for how to present the basic issues to teachers new to linguistics. Discusses the affective filter and notes that form shouldn't be over-emphasized. Includes a nice vignette of an Athabaskan teacher's highlighting of "Heritage Language" and "Formal Language."

Delpit, Lisa. 1995. *Other People's Children: Cultural Conflict in the Classroom.* New York: W. W. Norton.

1 C P T

Delpit, Lisa. 2002. No Kinda Sense. In *The Skin That We Speak: Thoughts on Language and Culture in the Classroom,* ed. by L. Delpit & J. K. Dowdy, 31-48. New York: The New Press.

1 I K

Delpit, Lisa. 2006. What Should Teachers Do? Ebonics and Culturally Responsive Instruction. In *Dialects, Englishes, Creoles, and Education,* ed. by S. Nero, 93–101. Mahwah, NJ: Lawrence Erlbaum Associates.

1 I R S

"What must teachers do?" is the central question Delpit addresses. She focuses on group identity, strategies for integrating linguistic diversity, attitudes towards Ebonics, and reading. She cites a study by Nelson-Barber on the Pima Indian language, in which young children who were capable of speaking in the standard dialect chose to adopt the dialect of their environment to fit in with the larger group; Delpit implies that a similar phenomenon is occurring among African American youth. For this reason, she says that teachers should be cognizant of the fact that students' language directly relates to their background and loved ones. At the same time, however, teachers must strike a balance between this reality and the fact that children who are not exposed to the "politically popular dialect" (p. 95) remain less likely to succeed. Delpit argues that students must learn that different contexts require different forms of communication; she mentions role play and creating bilingual dictionaries as methods that teachers can utilize. Her central message is that teachers must provide access to the standard dialect while celebrating the native dialect of students. She leaves readers with this final thought, "Access to standard language may be necessary, but it is definitely not sufficient to produce intelligent, competent caretakers of the future" (p. 100).

Delpit, Lisa & Joanne Kilgour Dowdy (eds.) 2002. *The Skin That We Speak: Thoughts on Language and Culture in the Classroom.* New York: The New Press.

1 A C E I N P S T

DeMeis, Debra K. & Ralph R. Turner. 1978. Effects of Students' Race, Physical Attractiveness, and Dialect on Teachers' Evaluations. *Contemporary Educational Psychology* 3.77–86.

1 I T

Denham, Kristin. 2005. Teaching Students About Language Change, Language Endangerment, and Language Death. In *Language in the Schools: Integrating Linguistic Knowledge into K-12 Teaching,* ed. by K. Denham & A. Lobeck, 149–60.

1 L S

Denham, Kristin. 2010. Linguistics in a Primary School. In *Linguistics at School: Language Awareness in Primary and Secondary Education,* ed. by K. Denham & A. Lobeck, 189–203.

S

Denham, Kristin & Anne Lobeck (eds.) 2005. *Language in the Schools: Integrating Linguistic Knowledge into K-12 Teaching.* Mahwah, NJ: Lawrence Erlbaum Associates.

2 4 C E I S
The authors examine the role of linguistic knowledge in classrooms from kindergarten to high school, from a range of perspectives (twenty chapters). Some chapters describe ideas for lessons that would benefit all learners (such as ideas for exploring the dictionary in a linguistically-savvy way). Of particular interest are the following chapters: 1—"Linguistics and Education in Multilingual America," by John Baugh; 2—"Embracing Diversity through the Understanding of Pragmatics," by Jin Sook Lee; 3—"Growing Up Shifting: Immigrant Children, Their Families, and the Schools," by Meredith Burt and Hua Yang; 5—"'My Teacher Says:': Mastery of English and the Creole Learner," by Alicia Wassink; 8—"A Critical Approach to Standard English," by Anne Lobeck; 10—"Spanish Maintenance and English Literacy: Mexican-Descent Children's Spanish and English Narratives," by Robert Bayley and Sandra Schecter; 12—"Teaching Students About Language Change, Language Endangerment, and Language Death," by Kristin Denham; 13—"Language as a Reflection of Our Social and Physical World: What Students Can Learn From Metaphor," by Janet Higgins; 14—"Contrastive Analysis and Codeswitching: How and When to Use the Vernacular to Teach Standard English," by Rebecca Wheeler; and 15—"English LIVEs: Language in variation exercises for today's classrooms," by Kirk Hazen.

Denham, Kristin & Anne Lobeck (eds.) 2010. *Linguistics at School: Language Awareness in Primary and Secondary Education.* New York: Cambridge University Press.

1 6 C E I L P S
This volume focuses on ways to improve K-12 education about language, and how linguists can make a difference in this regard. Part I, "Linguistics from the top down:

encouraging institutional change," includes eight examples of how linguists have collaborated with schools, districts, or states to catalyze greater language awareness in curricula both in the United States and abroad. Part II, "Linguistics from the Bottom Up: Encouraging Classroom Change" includes seven examples of linguists working directly with classroom teachers or students around issues of linguistics or language variation. The volume concludes with eight vignettes written by classroom teachers who are incorporating language awareness activities into their teaching. Particularly relevant are the following chapters: 2—"Bringing Linguistics into the School Curriculum: Not One Less," by Wayne O'Neil; 7—"Developing Sociolinguistic Curricula that Help Teachers Meet Standards," by Jeffrey Reaser; 9—"From Cold Shoulder to Funded Welcome: Lessons from the Trenches of Dialectally Diverse Classrooms," by Rebecca Wheeler; 11—"Fostering Teacher Change: Effective Professional Development for Sociolinguistic Diversity," by Julie Sweetland; 13—"Linguistics in a Primary School," by Kristin Denham; and 17—"Code Switching: Connecting Written and Spoken Language Patterns," by Karren Mayer and Kirstin New.

Desai, Shiv Raj & Tyson Marsh. 2005. Weaving Multiple Dialects in the Classroom Discourse: Poetry and Spoken Word as a Critical Teaching Tool. *Taboo: The Journal of Culture and Education* 9.71–90. [Abstract prepared by ERIC and reprinted with permission of the Department of Education from the Education Resources Information Center at www.eric.ed.gov.]

1 4 C N S
Spoken word is a form of poetry that utilizes the strengths of the communities: oral tradition, call-and-response, home languages, storytelling, and resistance. Spoken word poetry is usually performed for an audience and must be heard. The authors are interested in investigating how spoken word can be utilized as a critical teaching tool that can be employed to foster critical consciousness, dialogue, and action. In other words, how students can reflect and articulate their lived experiences while envisioning new possibilities. In this paper, the authors provide an overview of some of the key ideas and concepts of Critical Pedagogy, Critical Race Theory, and Critical Literacy studies. Through an examination of the major components of Critical Pedagogy, they evidence the libratory potential of spoken word. In offering an overview of Critical Race Theory, they highlight the practice of counter-storytelling as a central theme of spoken word. An analysis of Critical Literacy studies provides insights into the reading of the word and the world and the multiple discourses employed and elicited in spoken word. Following this analysis, the authors draw upon their work at LAX High School (Los Angeles), where they have employed poetry and spoken word poetry to connect with their students.

Desberg, Peter, George Marsh, Lee Ann Schneider & Caroline Duncan-Rose. 1979. The Effects of Social Dialect on Auditory Sound Blending and Word Recognition. *Contemporary Educational Psychology* 4.140–44.

1 B X

DeStefano, Johanna. 1972. Productive Language Differences in Fifth-Grade Black Students' Syntactic Forms. *Elementary English* 47.552–58.

1 F W X

DeStefano, Johanna. 1973. *Language, Society and Education: A Profile of Black English.* Worthington, OH: Jones Publishing.

1 E F I R

Deuber, Dagmar. 2005. *Nigerian Pidgin in Lagos: Language Contact, Variation and Change in an African Urban Setting.* London: Battlebridge.

2 F

Deuber, Dagmar. 2009. 'The English We Speaking': Morphological and Syntactic Variation in Educated Jamaican Speech. *Journal of Pidgin and Creole Languages* 24.1–52.

2 F

Deuber, Dagmar & Lars Hinrichs. 2007. Dynamics of Orthographic Standardization in Jamaican Creole and Nigeria Pidgin. *World Englishes* 26.22–47.

2 F

Devonish, Hubert. 1983. Towards the Establishment of an Institute for Creole Language Standardization and Development in the Caribbean. In *Studies in Caribbean Language,* ed. by L. Carrington, 300–16. St. Augustine, Trinidad: Society for Caribbean Linguistics.

2 P V

Devonish, Hubert. 1996. Vernacular Languages and Writing Technology Transfer: The Jamaican Case. In *Caribbean Language Issues, Old and New: Papers in Honour of Professor Mervyn Alleyne on the Occasion of His Sixtieth Birthday,* ed. by P. Christie, 101–11. Cave Hill, Barbados: The Press University of the West Indies.

2 W

Devonish, Hubert. 1998. On the Existence of Autonomous Language Varieties in 'Creole Continuum Situations'. In *Studies in Caribbean Language II,* ed. by P. Christie, B. Lalla, V. Pollard & L. Carrington, 1–12. St. Augustine, Trinidad, West Indies: Society for Caribbean Linguistics.

2 F

Devonish, Hubert. 2007. *Language and Liberation: Creole Language Politics in the Caribbean.* Kingston, Jamaica: Arawak Press. [Abstract for *Language and Liberation: Creole Language Politics in the Caribbean* by Hubert Devonish graciously provided by Hubert Devonish.]

2 I P
The 1986 first edition of this work sought to explain the language question to those involved in the fight to free the populations of the Creole-speaking Caribbean from external political and economic control. It demonstrated that diglossia has been an inherent part of the history of state structures as diverse as Ancient Egypt, Ancient China, eighteenth century France and a full range of situations in the modern and not so modern Creole-speaking Caribbean, from Grenada to the Atlantic Coast of Nicaragua, from Guyana to Haiti. It presented evidence for diglossia being both a cause and a source of the economic, social and political inequalities in human societies. A critical institution for reproducing diglossia, the work argues, is the educational system. True democracy and genuine social equality and justice require the abolition of diglossia and a revision of the language education policies and practices which underpin it. For the Creole-speaking Caribbean, this means the widespread use of the majority Creole languages for all functions, private and public, informal and formal, non-official and official, and as media of instruction and literacy in the formal education system. The second edition of 2007 incorporates, without change, all of the first edition, but includes a new, extended chapter, 'The Historical Present', which brings the reader up to date with the developments in language policy and practice within the Creole-speaking Caribbean, and provides a revised approach to the concept of diglossia. The

chapter documents the increased level of linguistic assertiveness and self-confidence amongst Creole-speakers in the Caribbean. Unsurprisingly, the education system has been the site of much of this assertiveness, from Haiti, through Curacao to Jamaica. This linguistic assertiveness is linked to the development of a grass roots sense of national identity at odds with the post-colonial states and their inherited education systems, which still prevail in the region. The new edition casts itself in the role of documenting and theorizing about a struggle which is continuing.

Devonish, Hubert. 2008. Language Planning in Pidgins and Creoles. In *The Handbook of Pidgin and Creole Studies,* ed. by S. Kouwenberg & J. V. Singler, 615–36. Chichester, UK: Wiley-Blackwell.

2 P

Devonish, Hubert & Karen Carpenter. 2007. Towards Full Bilingualism in Education: The Jamaican Bilingual Primary Education Project. *Social and Economic Studies* 56.277–303. [Reprinted with permission of Social and Economic Studies 56(1-2).]

2 B I P V
This paper examines the attempts to address the rights of the speakers of Creole vernacular language varieties within the mainstream education system with a focus on the Caribbean. In particular the paper describes the Ministry of Education Youth & Culture (MOEYC) approved Bilingual Education Project (BEP) currently being piloted in Jamaica. The BEP and more recent research exploring the outlook of the general public towards the use of Jamaican challenge accepted notions of language attitudes toward speakers of vernacular languages and the learning and teaching of literacy skills at the primary school level. The results show that children in grades one and two of a government primary school acquire literacy in both Jamaican and English simultaneously and can readily distinguish between the two language varieties both orally and in writing. The objections to teaching in Jamaican raised in the past, such as lack of public acceptance and lack of a standard writing system need revisiting given both the success of the BEP and the shift in public opinion.

Deyhle, Donna & Karen Swisher. 1997. Research in American Indian and Alaska Native Education: From Assimilation to Self-Determination. In *Review of Research in Education,* ed. by M. W. Apple, 113–94. Washington, D.C.: American Educational Research Association.

5 C E P

Dick, Galena Sells, Dan W. Estell & Teresa L. McCarty. 1994. Saad Naakih Bee'enootiilji Na'alkaa: Restructuring the Teaching of Language and Literacy in a Navajo Community School. *Journal of American Indian Education* 33.31–46.

5 C T

Dillard, Joseph. 1970. *Lexicon of Black English*. New York: Random House.

1 C F

Dillard, Joseph. 1972. *Black English: Its History and Usage in the United States*. New York: Random House.

1 F K

Dillard, Joseph. 1978. Bidialectal Education: Black English and Standard English in the United States. In *Case Studies in Bilingual Education,* ed. by B. Spolsky & R. Cooper, 298–311. Rowley, MA: Newbury House.

1 B

Dillard presents a review of literature concerning bidialectalism. The author found a general consensus, despite past debate, that dialect differences correlate with ethnic affiliation and not just geographic affiliation, and that SAE and AAVE differ not only phonologically but also syntactically. Still, the question of whether these differences cause significant miscomprehension remained unresolved. Proponents of bidialectal education advocated either SESD (Standard English as a second dialect), or the use of dialect readers. SESD approaches typically relied on some form of repetition drills, such as those outlined in Feigenbaum (1970). Ultimately, Dillard concludes that, due in part to the widespread stigma against nonstandard language, no research to date provided conclusive evidence regarding the effectiveness of bidialectal education.

Dillard, J. L. & Shirley A. Rivers. 1989. Dialectology in Our Time? The English of the Cajuns. In *English across Cultures, Cultures across English: A Reader in Cross-Cultural Communication,* ed. by O. Garcia & R. Otheguy, 305–18. Berlin: New York: Mouton.

6 F

Dixson, Adrienne & Jeannine Dingus. 2006. Personal Investments, Professional Gains: Strategies of African American Women Teacher Educators. *Mid-Western Educational Researcher* 19.36–40.

1 C S T
The article includes a discussion of the use of AAVE as one of several pedagogical and curriculum strategies discussed.

DoBell, Daniel. 2008. Thirty Years of Influence: A Look Back at Geneva Smitherman's Talkin and Testifyin. *Journal of Negro Education* 77.157–67. [Reprinted with permission of the journal from the *Journal of Negro Education* 77(2), 157.]

1 K N P
Thirty years after its publication, Geneva Smitherman's seminal work, "Talkin and Testifyin" continues to influence scholars, policymakers and practitioners. This article takes a look at Smitherman's work by first providing an overview of the sociolinguistic theoretical foundations that led to its publication. This is followed by a reception history of "Talkin and Testifyin"; first in general terms as a scholarly work followed by an examination of Smitherman's impact on a select group of disciplines. Finally, conclusions are presented that demonstrate how this important work has not only bridged scholarly disciplines, but also, extended the understanding of African American English to the world at large.

Dowdy, Joanne Kilgour. 1999. Doublespeak. *Caribbean Quarterly* 45.52–63.

2 I U
A shortened version of this paper, written by a professor of literacy reflecting (inter alia) on the angst of choosing between Creole and Standard English (White) styles of expression in her native Trinidad, is reprinted in Delpit and Dowdy (2002), *The skin that we speak.*

Dubois, Betty Lou. 1978. A Case Study of Native American Child Bidialectalism in English: Phonological, Morphological, and Syntactic Evidence. *Anthropological Linguistics* 20.1–13.

5 B F U

Dubois, Sylvie & Barbara M. Horvath. 2003. Creoles and Cajuns: A Portrait in Black and White. *American Speech* 78.192–207.

2 6 F

Dubois, Sylvie & Horvath Barbara M. 2003. The English Vernacular of the Creoles of Louisiana. *Language Variation and Change* 15.255–88.

6 F

Dundes, Lauren & Bill Spence. 2007. If Ida Known: The Speaker Versus the Speech in Judging Black Dialect. *Teaching Sociology* 35.85–93. [Abstract prepared by ERIC and reprinted with permission of the Department of Education from the Education Resources Information Center at eric.ed.gov.]

1 I S

While students generally recognize that racism exists on an individual level, the instructor's challenge is to both elucidate patterns of discrimination and to expose their corollary: unearned and unrecognized systemic privilege of the dominant group. Unaware that their sense of entitlement advantages them at the expense of people of color, some students may resent discussion of the pervasive yet invisible systems that afford supremacy to the group in power. The exercise presented in this article examining Black dialect (BD) provides a thought-provoking demonstration of this social inequity that promotes critical self-examination. Although most students are aware of the range of dialects found in the United States, few have contemplated if there are compelling reasons to vilify BD, a variety of English also known as Black English, African American English, or Ebonics in the popular media, and used in varying degrees by African Americans in writing and speech. The class lesson described represents a synthesis of arguments advanced by a number of linguistics scholars that demonstrates that BD is a unique but not inferior system of English grammar with variations that convey distinct nuances of meaning that can enhance discussions of social inequality and racial bias. While other exercises help broaden students' perspective on social inequality, this exercise offers advantages that other lessons often lack: (1) Unusual approach: Students are intrigued by how deconstructing BD in a sociology class can reflect the broader power structure; (2) Non-threatening way of teaching about social inequality: The exercise takes students through a series of steps where they draw their own conclusions that culminate in implications about cultural hegemony. It provides a solid illustration of discrimination in which contentious questions of an oppressed individual's effort and ability are irrelevant; and (3) Direct reflection of reality: Compared to simulations where instructors face the significant challenge of convincing students that the game mirrors real life, BD is concrete with tangible social consequences. The goal of this teaching note is to demonstrate that while a single standard for speech may be functional, dialects that differ from those used by the people in power have come to reflect inferiority, regardless of their actual merit. Who makes the judgment and about whom can affect the perceived worth of a particular practice. The authors also explore how BD elucidates the operation of dominance and privilege in other areas of social life.

Durrleman, Stephanie. 2008. *The Syntax of Jamaican Creole: A Cartographic Perspective.* Amsterdam: John Benjamins.

2 F

Dyche, Caroline. 1996. Writing Proficiency in English and Academic Performance: The University of the West Indies, Mona. In *Caribbean Language Issues Old & New,* ed. by P. Christie, 143–62. Kingston, Jamaica: The Press University of the West Indies.

2 W

Dyson, Anne Haas & Geneva Smitherman. 2009. The Right (Write) Start: African American Language and the Discourse of 'Sounding Right'. *Teachers College Record* 111.973–98. [Reprinted with permission of the journal from *Teachers College Record* 111(4).]

1 P S T W
In early literacy studies, communicative disconnects between teachers and children have been discussed primarily in relation to reading. Dyson and Smitherman focus on teacher-student interactions about children's writing, that is, about their efforts to make a voice visible on paper. Writing is a rich context for studying how AAL figures into early literacy teaching and learning. Teachers urge children to listen to how their words sound in order to compose their message. But what sounds "right" to young children will vary for developmental, situational, and, as emphasized herein, sociocultural reasons. Drawing on data collected in an ethnographic project on child writing, the authors illustrate how, in the course of teacher-student interaction, young children's major resources for learning to write—their very voices—may become a source of problems. One important pedagogical site for teaching basic literacy skills in the observed first grade was teacher-led editing conferences, in which the classroom teacher focused on written conventions, including standardized usage.

Eades, Diana, Suzie Jacobs, Ermile Hargrove & Terri Menacker. 2006. Pidgin, Local Identity, and Schooling in Hawai'i. In *Dialects, Englishes, Creoles, and Education,* ed. by S. Nero, 139–63. Mahwah, NJ: Lawrence Erlbaum Associates.

2 B I
Surveys Hawai'i's movement toward Pidgin as the predominant language, chronicling the shift from the historical prohibition of Pidgin in Hawai'an classrooms to its recent, increased acceptance in the educational arena. It then describes Hawai'i's development of small experimental programs attempting to deal with the individual needs of Pidgin-speaking students; Hawai'i has uniquely secured Title VII Bilingual Education funds for teaching English to Pidgin speakers. The authors applaud the Hawai'ian Board of Education for their efforts to address learning issues that distinctively apply to Pidgin speakers, but question the attempts to address Pidgin through ESL-like programs, arguing that addressing Pidgin as a second language rather than an English dialect fails to pedagogically capitalize on the existing English skills that many Pidgin speakers have already developed through their understanding of the dialect.

Eades, Diana & Jeff Siegel. 1999. Changing Attitudes Towards Australian Creoles and Aboriginal English. In *Creole Genesis, Attitudes and Discourse,* ed. by J. R. Rickford & S. Romaine, 265–78. Philadelphia: John Benjamins.

2 I

Eagleson, Richard, Susan Kaldor & Ian Malcolm (eds.) 1982. *English and the Aboriginal Child.* Canberra, Australia: Curriculum Development Centre.

2 6 C E N S

Easter, Linda, Eileen Shultz, T. Kelley Neyhart & U. Mae Reck. 1999. Weighty Perceptions: A Study of the Attitudes and Beliefs of Preservice Teacher Education Students Regarding Diversity and Urban Education. *The Urban Review* 31.205–20.

1 3 4 5 I T
Among other things, the authors report that 26% of White teachers interviewed felt that their students speaking a different dialect than they were presented a potential 'problem.'

Eckert, Penelope. 2000. *Linguistic Variation as Social Practice.* Malden, MA: Blackwell.

6 F I

Edelsky, Carole. 1996. *With Literacy and Justice for All: Rethinking the Social in Language and Education*. New York: Taylor and Francis.

1 4 C S T U

Edwards, John. 2010. *Language Diversity in the Classroom*. Bristol, UK: Multilingual Matters.

1 6 C I P U

Edwards, Viv. 1979. *The West Indian Language Issue in British Schools*. London: Routledge and Kegan Paul.

2 6 C F I S X
An early, book-length study of the educational under-performance of "West Indian" children in England (children born in England to West Indian immigrants) and its connection to their vernacular speech, heavily influenced by their families' English creoles (from Jamaica and other Caribbean territories). The focus of the chapters is as follows: 1—"West Indians in Britain"; 2—"West Indian Creole"; 3—"Verbal skills in West Indians"; 4—"Creole Interference"; 5—"Language attitudes and educational success"; 6—"Practical approaches to language"; 7—"Curriculum change for a multicultural society."

Edwards, Viv. 1983. *Language in Multicultural Classrooms*. London: Batsford Academic and Educational Ltd.

2 S

Edwards, Viv. 1986. *Language in a Black Community*. Clevedon, UK: Multilingual Matters.

2 C F I

Edwards, Viv & Thomas Sienkewicz. 1990. *Oral Cultures Past and Present: Rappin' and Homer*. Oxford: Blackwell.

1 N

Edwards, Walter F. 1975. A Guided Composition Course for Form I Children in Guyana. *English Language Teaching* XXIX.197–206.

2 M W

Edwards, Walter F. 1979. The Sociolinguistic Significance of Some Guyanese Speech Acts. *International Journal of the Sociology of Language*.79–102.

2 N

Edwards, Walter F. 1980. Varieties of English in Guyana: Some Comparisons with BEV. *Linguistics* 18.289–310.

2 F

Edwards, Walter F. 1981. Problems of Teaching English to Amerindian Children in Guyana. *English Language Teaching* XXXV.338–45.

5 S

Edwards, Walter F. 1981. Two Varieties of English in Detroit. In *Black English and the Education of Black Children and Youth,* ed. by G. Smitherman, 393–408. Detroit, MI: Center for Black Studies, Wayne State University.

1 B F

Edwards, Walter F. 1983. Code Selection and Shifting in Guyana. *Language in Society* 12.295–311.

2 F U

Edwards, Walter F. 1992. Sociolinguistic Behavior in a Detroit Inner-City Black Neighborhood. *Language in Society* 21.93–115.

1 F U

Egan-Robertson, Ann & David Bloome (eds.) 1998. *Students as Researchers of Culture and Language in Their Own Communities.* Creskill, NJ: Hampton Press.

6 E L S

Egbokhare, Francis O. 2003. The Story of a Language: Nigerian Pidgin in Spatiotemporal, Social and Linguistic Context. In *Studies in African Varieties of English,* ed. by P. Lucko, L. Peter & H.-G. Wolf, 21-40. Frankfurt, Germany: Lang.

2 I

Eggington, William. 1994. Language Policy and Planning in Australia. *Annual Review of Applied Linguistics* 14.137–55. [Abstract prepared by ERIC.]

2 E P

A discussion of language policy formation and planning in Australia covers the following: the development of the national policy on languages, and the Australian Language and Literacy Policy and its four goals related to English language and literacy, languages other than English, aboriginal and Torres Strait Islander languages, and language/literacy services.

Elbow, Peter. 1999. Inviting the Mother Tongue: Beyond "Mistakes," "Bad English," and "Wrong Language". *JAC: A Journal of Composition Theory* 19.359–88.

B S U W

In this thoughtful essay by a major voice in composition theory, Peter Elbow explores the issues a writing instructor must grapple with in order to create a classroom environment where students feel safe enough to write in their 'home voices' as well as in Standard Written English. In a novel addition to debates on how and how much to focus on conventions, Elbow resolves the dilemma between teaching Standard English and students' right to their own language by focusing his instruction in conventions on instilling within students the habit of accessing resources on Standard English when needed for copyediting.

Elifson, Joan. 1977. Teaching to Enhance Bidialectalism: Some Practical and Theoretical Concerns. *English Education* 9.11–21.

1 B O S

Elifson draws on language acquisition research to motivate a curriculum that capitalizes on children's developing awareness of stylistic and social variation in language. The author outlines a secondary-level curriculum that promotes bidialectal skills in speaking, in which students gradually move from passive understanding of a new dialect into active production. In the initial stages, students are exposed to contrasting patterns through oral drills. Students then memorize and perform play passages to begin using new language features. In subsequent lessons, students begin to plan and produce their own original speech with more and more emphasis on content over form until finally, they practice communicating spontaneously in the new dialect. Ultimately the author maintains that although the decision of whether or not to pursue bidialectalism belongs to each individual, there is enough interest among students to warrant promoting the idea to legislatures and school boards, and refining teaching strategies.

Elugbe, Ben. 1995. Nigerian Pidgin: Problems and Prospects. In *New Englishes: A West African Perspective,* ed. by A. Bamgboṣe, A. Banjo & A. Thomas, 284–99. Ibadan, Nigeria: Mosuro.

2 I

Elugbe, Ben & Augusta Omamor. 1991. *Nigerian Pidgin: Background and Prospects.* Ibadan, Nigeria: Heinemann.

2 F I

Engle, Patricia Lee. 1975. *The Use of Vernacular Languages in Education: Language Medium in Early School Years for Minority Language Groups.* Washington, D.C.: Center for Applied Linguistics.

6 V

Epstein, Ruth I. & Lily X. J. Xu. 2003. *Roots and Wings: Teaching English as a Second Dialect to Aboriginal Students—a Review of the Literature.* [Abstract prepared by ERIC.]

5 B S
Education plays a primary role in ensuring language maintenance and school success in Saskatchewan, Canada, and around the world. Language includes both "standard-ized" language and vernacular dialects. This document reviews the literature related to teaching English as a Second Dialect in school. The review covers information on the problems and challenges faced by speakers of minority languages including social and cultural processes and implications of language maintenance as well as how languages are taught and learned in school. It also includes literature on best practices in teaching English as a Second Dialect (ESD). Contains ninety-nine references.

Evans, Hyacinth. 2001. *Inside Jamaican Schools.* Kingston: University of the West Indies Press.

2 B I S
Set in the larger context of a discussion of students, teachers and the curriculum in Jamaica schools, Chapter 6, "Language in the Classroom" describes a 1989 "Opera-tion English" project involving Grade 7 high school students, in which the author served as consultant and evaluator. She describes the methodology and principal results as follows (p. 108): "Creole—the students' language—was respected and vali-dated, teaching/learning materials encouraged student expression, students' language and experience were respected and the students were encouraged to use SJE (Stan-dard Jamaican English) in meaningful contexts. The results show that students learn to speak and write SJE when such teaching methods are used. In this study, most Creole-speaking students improved their ability to speak and write SJE, though the gains within the short time span [year one of a three-year project] were modest and sometimes inconsistent. Moreover, some students developed a more positive attitude toward SJE; their ability to speak SJE significantly enhanced their self-esteem. The results, however, indicate that changes in language use from Creole to SJE must be seen in the long term."

Ezarik, Melissa. 2002. A Time and a Place. *District Administration: Education Leadership, Curriculum, Technology & Trends* 38.5 (May):38-42.

1 B

Fagundes, Deana, William Haynes, Nancy Haak & Michael Moran. 1998. Task Variability Effects on the Language Test Performance of Southern Lower Socioeconomic Class African American and Caucasian Five-Year-Olds. *Language, Speech and Hearing Services in Schools* 29.148-57.

1 A

Fairclough, Norman. 1989. *Language and Power.* London: Longman.

1 I P

Fairclough, Norman (ed.) 1992. *Critical Language Awareness.* London: Longman.

1 E I L P

Faraclas, Nicholas. 1996. *Nigerian Pidgin.* London: Routledge.

2 F

Farr, Marcia. 1986. Language, Culture, and Writing: Sociolinguistic Foundations of Research on Writing. *Review of Research in Education* 13.195–223.

1 4 5 B E N S W X

Farr, Marcia. 2005. ¡A Mí No Me Manda Nadie! Individualism and Identity in Mexican Ranchero Speech. In *Latino Language and Literacy in Ethnolinguistic Chicago*, ed. by M. Farr, 34–65. Mahwah, NJ: Lawrence Erlbaum Associates.

4 N

Farr, Marcia. 2005. *Latino Language and Literacy in Ethnolinguistic Chicago.* Mahwah, NJ: Lawrence Erlbaum Associates.

4 N

Farr, Marcia. 2006. *Rancheros in Chicagoacán: Language and Identity in a Transnational Community.* Austin: University of Texas Press.

4 I

Farr, Marcia. 2007. Literacies and Ethnolinguistic Diversity: Chicago. In *Encyclopedia of Language and Education, Vol. 2: Literacy,* ed. by B. Street. Heidelberg, Germany: Springer-Verlag.

4 N

Farr, Marcia. 2011. Urban Plurilingualism: Language Practice, Policies, and Ideologies in Chicago. *Journal of Pragmatics* 43.1161–172. [Reprinted with permission of Elsevier, the publisher, from the *Journal of Pragmatics* 43(5).]

4 I

Plurilingual language practices in Chicago are examined using the notions of linguistic markets and language ideologies. Plurilingualism encompasses bi/multilingualism and bidialectalism, or both, in dynamic use. Chicago always was and is plurilingual; traders speaking Haitian Creole, French, and English confronted speakers of indigenous Checagou languages in the late eighteenth century, and the enormous nineteenth century migration brought German and other European languages. Twentieth century migration brought Asian and other world languages and, notably, Spanish. Ethnographic research in homes, workplaces, schools, and religious organizations illustrates vibrant contemporary plurilingualism. Both historical and contemporary plurilingualism are embedded in a larger context of competing language ideologies that explain the persistence of plurilingual practices and the ambivalent history of official language policy in Illinois. Although dominant ideologies valorize a mono-glot Standard English, plurilingual practices evidence a persistent valuing of non-(standard) English language. For example, the official language policy of the Chicago Public Schools promotes (Standard) English at the expense of students' community languages, whereas the grass-roots Multilingual Chicago Initiative promotes Chicago's plurilingualism. Dominant ideologies that link a codified "standard" with modernity, clarity and rationality and vernacular varieties with lack of education and irrationality explain the former, whereas local linguistic markets explain the latter.

Farr, Marcia & Harvey Daniels. 1986. *Language Diversity and Writing Instruction*. Urbana, IL: National Council of Teachers of English.

1 F S W

Farr, Marcia & Mary Ann Janda. 1985. Basic Writing Students: Investigating Oral and Written Language. *Research in the Teaching of English* 19.62-83.

1 O W X

Farr, Marcia, Lisya Seloni & Juyong Song (eds.) 2010. *Ethnolinguistic Diversity and Education: Language, Literacy, and Culture*. New York: Routledge.

1 2 6 A B C E I P S
The editors' introduction (Chapter 1) to this book discusses ethnolinguistic diversity in language and literacy education, and provides a conceptual framework for under-standing. Part I consists of four chapters, each of which addresses a different eth-nolinguistic population. Part II consists of six chapters that discuss ways in which sociolinguistic research can contribute to the improvement of language and literacy education for these linguistic minority students. Chapter 7 (H. Samy Alim & John Baugh) attempts to sensitize the reader to the tensions that marginalized students who embrace critical hip hop and Black language pedagogies confront. Finally, Chapter 11 (Angela E. Rickford & John R. Rickford) offers suggestions for improving linguists' contributions to the literacy education of vernacular and creole speakers.

Farr, Marcia, Lisya Seloni & Juyoung Song. 2010. Introduction: Ethnolinguistic Diversity in Language and Literacy Education. In *Ethnolinguistic Diversity and Education: Language, Literacy, and Culture*, ed. by M. Farr, L. Seloni & J. Song, 1–20. New York: Routledge.

2 A B C I P

Farrell, Thomas. 1983. IQ and Standard English. *College Composition and Communication* 34.470–84. [Abstract graciously provided by Thomas Farrell.]

1 A
This paper is a follow up to, but a significant departure from, Farrell's "Literacy, the Basics, and All That Jazz" in the January 1977 issue of College English (pp. 443-459). Drawing on the thinking of Walter J. Ong (e.g., *Interfaces of the Word*, 1982) in both articles, Farrell argues that Black inner-city youth come primarily from an oral and White youth from a literate culture. In his 1977 article Farrell downplayed the importance of grammar instruction ("the basics"), but in his 1983 article he draws on Eric Havelock's work (e.g., *Preface to Plato*, 1982) to stress the importance of grammar instruction, especially learning the standard forms of the verb "to be." Agreeing with him that the source of those is genetic rather than environmental, Farrell hypothesizes that learning the standard forms of the verb "to be" would help Black vernacular speakers actuate the potential for what Jensen refers to as Level II cognitive development, and, more

generally, that "the mean IQ scores of black ghetto students will go up when they learn to speak and write Standard English" (p. 481). Farrell claims that his hypothesis is testable and urges studies to test it. As of 2011, he regrets that he did know about nor mention the Bridge approach to reading instruction developed by Simpkins, Simpkins and Holt (1977). [See Baugh 1983 for a critical view, and Greenberg et al. (1984) and Farrell (1995) for a response to some of his critics.]

Farrell, Thomas. 1995. A Defense for Requiring Standard English. In *Rhetoric: Concepts, Definitions, Boundaries,* ed. by W. Covino & D. Jolliffe, 667–78. Boston: Allyn and Bacon.

1 A B
Originally published in 1987 in *PRE/TEXT: An Inter-disciplinary Journal of Rhetoric,* 7(3–4), 165–79

Fasold, Ralph. 1969. Orthography in Reading Materials for Black English Speaking Children. In *Teaching Black Children to Read,* ed. by J. Baratz & R. Shuy, 68–92. Washington , D.C.: Center for Applied Linguistics.

1 R V X

Fasold, Ralph & Roger Shuy (eds.) 1970. *Teaching Standard English in the Inner City.* Washington, D.C.: Center for Applied Linguistics.

1 E F R S V

Fasold, Ralph & Walt Wolfram. 1970. Some Linguistic Features of Negro Dialect. In *Teaching Standard English in the Inner City,* ed. by R. Fasold & R. Shuy, 41–86.

1 F

Fasold, Ralph W. 1972. *Tense Marking in Black English; a Linguistic and Social Analysis.* Arlington, VA: Center for Applied Linguistics.

1 F

Fasold, Ralph W. 2001. Ebonic Need Not Be English. In *Language in Our Time: Bilingual Education and Official English, Ebonics and Standard English, Immigration and the Unz Initiative (Georgetown University Round Table on Language and Linguistics 1999),* ed. by J. E. Alatis & A.-H. Tan, 262–80. Washington, D.C.: Georgetown University Press.

1 F I S

Feagans, Lynne. 1982. The Development and Importance of Narratives for School Adaptation. In *The Language of Children Reared in Poverty: Implications for Evaluation and Intervention,* ed. by L. Feagans & D. Farran, 19–52. New York: Academic Press.

1 N Q

Feagin, Crawford. 1979. *Variation and Change in Alabama English: A Sociolinguistic Study of the White Community.* Washington, D.C.: Georgetown University Press.

6 F
This book is a useful description of one variety of White Southern American vernacular English, and one that is sensitive and accountable to variability (through its extensive use of frequencies) by language internal and external factors.

Fecho, Bob. 2000. Critical Inquiries into Language in an Urban Classroom. *Research on the Teaching of English* 34.368–95.

1 C I

Fecho, Bob. 2004. *Is This English? Race, Language, and Culture in the Classroom*. New York: Teachers College Press.

1 C I S

Feigenbaum, Irwin. 1970. The Use of Nonstandard in Teaching Standard: Contrast and Comparison. In *Teaching Standard English in the Inner City*, ed. by R. Fasold & R. Shuy, 87–104.

1 B S

After establishing that the difference between standard and nonstandard English is not in "correctness" but rather in appropriateness (each one being appropriate in different situations), Feigenbaum argues for the value of a contrastive analysis approach for training students to recognize and exploit the syntactic and phonological differences between AAVE and SAE. Feigenbaum explains and exemplifies three types of oral drills that may be useful in heightening students' facility with spoken SAE. In discrimination drills, the teacher reads pairs of sentences, which may or may not demonstrate syntactic differences between the two varieties, and students respond "same" or "different" accordingly. In identification drills, the teacher reads sentences and students respond with "nonstandard" or "standard." In translation drills, students translate the teacher's sentences into and out of AAVE, and in response drills, students practice responding to a given question using the same variety in which it was asked. The author recommends engaging in these fast-paced drills for ten to fifteen minutes per class period using natural, rapid English for maximum effectiveness.

Feldman, Carole, Addison Stone & Bobbi Renderer. 1990. Stage, Transfer, and Academic Achievement in Dialect-Speaking Hawaiian Adolescents. *Child Development* 61.472–85.

2 A

An experimental study that uses modified Piagetan tasks to illustrate that Hawaiian Creole-speaking students are capable of abstract thinking that they do not demonstrate on standardized assessments of literacy.

Feldman, Carol Fleishman, Addison Stone, James Wertsch & Michael Strizich. 1977. Standard and Nonstandard Dialect Competencies of Hawaiian Creole English Speakers. *TESOL Quarterly* 11.41–50.

2 B O

Fields, Cheryl. 1997. Ebonics 101: What Have We Learned? *Black Issues in Higher Education* 13.18–21, 24–28.

1 F K

This article offers good coverage of the 1996/97 Ebonics controversy in Oakland, California, with a timeline. Lots of the key players are quoted.

Fillmore, Lily Wong. 2004. Language in Education. In *Language in the USA*, ed. by E. Finegan & J. R. Rickford, 339–60. Cambridge: Cambridge University Press.

6 P

Fillmore, Lily Wong & Catherine Snow. 2000. *What Teachers Need to Know About Language*. Washington, D.C.: ERIC Clearinghouse on Languages and Linguistics.

1 4 C O S T W

Finegan, Edward & John R. Rickford (eds.) 2004. *Language in the USA*. Cambridge: Cambridge University Press.

1 B E F I K N P
This collection provides an in-depth look at language issues in the United States from the perspectives of some of its leading scholars. The book is broken down into three parts, "American English," "Other Language Varieties," and "The Sociolinguistic Situation." While all three components provide good insight into the world of language, the last proves to be most useful when discussing AAVE. This section includes a chapter from John Baugh entitled, "Ebonics and its controversy," and one by H. Samy Alim on "Hip Hop Nation Language." For further detail on the two, please see their respective abstracts in this bibliography.

Fischer, Katherine. 1992. Educating Speakers of Caribbean English Creole in the United States. In *Pidgins, Creoles, and Nonstandard Dialects in Education*, ed. by J. Siegel, 99–123.

2 B S T V
Fischer describes her implementation of the Caribbean Academic Program (CAP) aimed at fostering proficiency in Standard English among students whose native language is Caribbean English Creole (CEC). By teaching students relevant linguistic theory and conveying to them that they are learning a foreign language rather than merely having their speech corrected, motivation increases, and children learn to embrace both their native language and the English they are trying to learn. An essential part of demonstrating the legitimacy of the children's native language is teaching them basic literacy in CEC using an adapted orthography. After outlining the basic curriculum (including language theory and related issues, writing in Creole, English grammar, and translation exercises) and providing a brief case study involving one of her students, Fischer concludes that the program is a success. Also included are appendices containing log entries, class transcripts and student evaluations of the program.

Fish, Margaret & Brenda Pinkerman. 2002. Language Skills in Low-SES Rural Appalachian Children: Kindergarten to Middle Childhood. *Journal of Applied Developmental Psychology* 23.

6 A Q
Reports on a longitudinal study in which the language skills of 113 low-SES rural children from West Virginia were assessed at nine months, fifteen months, four years old, and prior to kindergarten entry. Findings indicate that while children typically developed communicative language sufficient for the home and community environment, a majority of the children had low language skills according to standardized measures that predict achievement in school settings.

Fishbein, Justin. 1973. A Nonstandard Publisher's Problems. In *Language Differences: Do They Interfere?*, ed. by J. Laffey & R. Shuy, 163–70.

I V

Fishman, Joshua, Robert Cooper & Roxanne Ma. 1971. *Bilingualism in the Barrio*. Bloomington: Indiana University Press.

4 U

Fishman, Joshua & Erika Lueders-Salmon. 1972. What Has the Sociology of Language to Say to the Teacher? On Teaching the Standard Variety to Speakers of Dialectal or Sociolectal Varieties. In *Functions of Language in the Classroom*, ed. by C. Cazden, V. John & D. Hymes. New York: Teachers College, Columbia University.

6 B T

Fishman, Joshua A. 1993. In Praise of My Language. *Working Papers in Educational Linguistics* 9.1–11. [Abstract prepared by ERIC.]

I L P

This paper highlights a new approach to the topic of language consciousness. Although a good deal has already been learned about the topic in connection with such questions as: "When and among whom does language consciousness arise?"; "When is it stronger and when is it weaker?"; and "What does it lead its adherents to do on behalf of their own beloved language and in opposition to completing language?" one element has been missing, namely, an approach that would enable scholars to capture and appreciate the world view, the belief system, and the emotional motivational readiness for overt behavior that language so often entails. The paper discusses the tendency of ethnic and national groups to cultivate and advocate "my" language over all others in terms of the focus on the internal emotional and historical resources of a given culture.

Fitzgerald, Jill, Steven Amendum & Karren Guthrie. 2008. Young Latino Students' English-Reading Growth in All-English Classrooms. *Journal of Literacy Research* 40.59–94.

4 R

Flanigan, Beverly. 1981. *American Indian English in History and Literature: The Evolution of a Pidgin from Reality to Stereotype.* Bloomington: Indiana University Press.

5

Flanigan, Beverly. 1984. Bilingual Education for Native Americans: The Argument from Studies of Variational English. In *On TESOL '83: The Question of Control,* ed. by J. Handscombe, R. Orem & B. Taylor, 81–93. Washington, D.C.: Teachers of English to Speakers of Other Languages.

5 P

Flanigan, Beverly. 1985. American Indian English and Error Analysis: The Case of Lakota English. *English World-Wide* 6.217–36.

5 F R

Flanigan, Beverly. 1987. Language Variation among Native Americans: Observations on Lakota English. *Journal of English Linguistics* 20.181–99.

5 F

Flanigan, Beverly. 1990. Heckewelder and the Ohio Valley Indians: Language and Culture on the American Frontier. *Ohio University Working Papers in Linguistics and Language Teaching* 11.45–54.

5 F

Flanigan, Beverly Olson. 1996. I Might Could Be Polylectal: Report from the Mid-American Field. *Ohio Working Papers in Linguistics and Language Teaching* 15.103–21.

5 B I U

Flanigan, Beverly Olson. 2004. Languages and Dialects in the Midwest. In *The Midwest: The Greenwood Encyclopedia of American Regional Cultures,* ed. by J. W. Slade & J. Y. Lee, 323–48. Westport, CT: Greenwood Press.

5

Flint, E. H. 1968. Aboriginal English: Linguistic Description as an Aid to Teaching. *English in Australia* 6.3–21.

6 F S

Flower, Linda. 1996. Negotiating the Meaning of Difference. *Written Communication* 13.44–92.

1 I S T W

Flowers, Doris. 2000. Codeswitching and Ebonics in Urban Adult Basic Education Classrooms. *Education and Urban Society* 32.221–36.

1 I U

Flynn, Jill Ewing. 2011. The Language of Power: Beyond the Grammar Workbook. *English Journal* 100.27–30.

B L M S W

The author describes an eighth-grade language unit that helps students understand the value of dialects and standardized English, in part by being explicit about the 'language of power.'

Fogel, Howard & Linnea Ehri. 2000. Teaching Elementary Students Who Speak Black English Vernacular to Write in Standard English: Effects of Dialect Transformation Practice. *Contemporary Educational Psychology* 25.212–35.

1 B W

Fogel and Ehri compare the effects of different instructional approaches in strengthening students' use of SAE forms in writing. Twelve intact third and fourth grade classes were randomly assigned to one of three treatment conditions. In Condition "E", students were exposed to six targeted Standard English grammatical forms through listening to two stories read by the teacher. Subjects in group "ES" received exposure to text as well as explicit instruction in strategies depicting the rules of SAE. The third treatment condition, "ESP," received exposure, strategy instruction, and guided practice in applying the strategies in sentence-translation tasks. Results indicated that "students in the ESP groups made significantly greater gains from pretest to posttest than students in the ES and E conditions, which did not differ from each other" (p. 222). The ESP group similarly used significantly more SAE forms when writing a story. Furthermore, on the story writing task, the ES group wrote shorter stories and created less opportunities for using the targeted features in their writing. According to the authors, this suggests that these students were "actively inhibiting their use" of targeted forms, possibly because the instruction they received made them more aware of potential mistakes but didn't give them the tools to avoid them (p. 225).

Fogel, Howard & Linnea Ehri. 2006. Teaching African American English Forms to Standard American English-Speaking Teachers: Effects on Acquisition, Attitudes, and Responses to Student Use. *Journal of Teacher Education* 57.464–80. [Reprinted with permission of Sage Publications, the publisher, from *Journal of Teacher Education* 57(5), 464.]

1 B S T

Many US students speak nonstandard forms of English, yet dialect issues are slighted in teacher education programs and literacy courses. In this study, classroom teachers who spoke Standard American English (SE) were familiarized with seven syntactic features characterizing African American English (AAE). Three approaches to instruction based on a cognitive view of self-regulated learning were compared: exposure to the features by reading AAE text (E); exposure plus explanation of dialect transformation strategies (ES); and exposure, strategy explanation, and guided practice transforming sentences from SE to AAE (ESP). On posttests, all forms of instruction improved teachers' knowledge and positive attitude toward AAE. However, ESP instruction proved more effective in teaching teachers how to translate sentences into AAE and to use AAE in writing stories. Results support the value of implementing self-regulated learning theory and reveal effective ways to teach dialect features to teachers so they can help AAE-speaking students learn SE.

Folb, Edith. 1980. *Runnin Down Some Lines: The Language and Culture of Black Teenagers.* Cambridge, MA: Harvard University Press.

1 F I U

Folkes, Karl. 1995. Development of an Experimental Language Arts Program for Speakers of Caribbean English Creole (CEC): Approach and Rationale. In *Caribbean Students in New York: Occasional Paper #1,* ed. by J. A. G. Irish, 40–57. Brooklyn, NY: Caribbean Diaspora Press.

2 S

Fordham, Signithia. 1993. 'Those Loud Black Girls': (Black) Women, Silence, and Gender 'Passing' in the Academy. *Anthropology and Education Quarterly* 24.3–32.

1 A I N
Fordham examines the role of gender in academic achievement, considering in particular the case of African American girls. Using observation and interview data obtained from an ethnographic study of twelve under-achieving and twelve high-achieving students at a high school in Washington, D.C., she examines the role of being female in the school system. She finds that many of the high-achieving girls obtained academic success by remaining silent, and thereby resisting the image of the "loud Black girl." Fordham concludes by posing questions about how to deal with gender inequity in the academic world.

Fordham, Signithia. 1998. Speaking Standard English from Nine to Three: Language as Guerrilla Warfare at Capital High. In *Kids Talk: Strategic Language Use in Later Childhood,* ed. by S. Hoyle & C. Edger, 205–16. New York: Oxford University Press.

1 C I U
In the study reported on here, Fordham spent several years at a predominantly African American high school in Washington, D.C., where she observed that Standard English is stigmatized among students, who consider it a sign of "acting White." Some academically motivated students, however, adopt the practice of "renting" (as Fordham calls it) Standard English for use in the classroom, and then use AAVE as their standard language in all other contexts. At the heart of this kind of behavior is a linguistic "guerrilla warfare" unconsciously adopted by students and reinforced by their parents and teachers. Although Fordham does not have the ultimate solution, she concludes that before addressing academic issues, "we must first understand the meaning of the linguistic practices of African American adolescents" (p. 214).

Fordham, Signithia. 1999. Dissin' "the Standard": Ebonics and Guerrilla Warfare at Capital High. *Anthropology and Education Quarterly* 30.272–93.

1 A C I U
Based on an ethnography of 'Capital High,' a predominantly African American high school in Washington, D.C., Fordham notes that among the students, AAVE has become the standard language, and Standard English has become the stigmatized vernacular. While students largely refuse to adopt Standard English because they associate

it with 'acting White' and capitulating to their perceived oppressors while losing their own identity, most learn to 'borrow' Standard English for use within the classroom. Low-achieving students appear to be motivated by a desire to maintain their Black identity through the avoidance of work, while high-achieving students recognize Standard English as a necessary instrument in the classroom, and still consistently maintain AAVE as their standard in social circles. The author concludes that continuing to examine the cultural significance inherent in students' discourse practices is the first step toward planning effective policy.

Fordham, Signithia & John Ogbu. 1986. Black Students' School Success: Coping with the "Burden of 'Acting White'". *The Urban Review* 18.176–206.

1 A I
Fordham and Ogbu posit that Black student underachievement is partially the result of an 'oppositional social identity' whereby Black students discourage each other from succeeding academically because it is perceived as 'acting White.' After laying a theoretical framework, the authors illustrate the phenomenon through a case study of thirty-three Black students at a predominantly Black high school in Washington, D.C. Students who are capable yet unsuccessful admit that they are driven by desire for peer acceptance and fear of being called a 'brainiac'. High-achieving students, on the other hand, disguise their classroom success by being as inconspicuous as possible about it and/or by adopting an alternate jokester or athlete persona in front of friends. Furthermore, because using Standard English (SE) is another sign of 'acting White,' students refrain from using SE when outside the classroom. The authors conclude that the solution to this problem will be in (1) making more opportunities available to African Americans to combat the perception that success is only for White people; (2) removing any bias in the way schools distinguish between White and Black students' abilities; and (3) raising awareness of the problem among schools so that corrective policies and programs can be implemented.

Foreman, Christina. 2000. Identification of African-American English from Prosodic Cues. *Texas Linguistic Forum* 43.57–66.

1 F

Foster, Herbert. 1986. *Ribbin', Jivin', and Playin' the Dozens: The Persistent Dilemma in Our Schools*. Cambridge, MA: Ballinger.

1 N T

Foster, Michele. 1989. 'It's Cookin' Now': A Performance Analysis of the Speech Events of a Black Teacher in an Urban Community College. *Language in Society* 18.1–29.

1 N O T

Foster, Michele. 1992. Sociolinguistics and the African-American Community: Implications for Literacy. *Theory Into Practice* 31.303–11.

1 C N T

Foster, Michele. 1995. Talking That Talk: The Language of Control, Curriculum, and Critique. *Linguistics and Education* 7.107–28.

1 C N T

Foster, Michele. 1999. Teaching and Learning in the Contexts of African American English and Culture. *Education and Urban Society* 31.177–89.

1 A C T

Foster, Michele. 2001. Pay Leon, Pay Leon, Pay Leon Paleontologist: Using Call-and-Response to Facilitate Language Acquisition among African American Students. In *Sociocultural and Historical Contexts of African American English,* ed. by S. Lanehart, 281–98. Philadelphia: John Benjamins.

1 C N O S
Foster examines the role of call-and-response in the classroom. She begins by expanding on Smitherman's 1977 definition of call-and-response. Foster provides an example of call-and-response in which a teacher uses familiar intonation and rhythmic patterns to help a student achieve the unfamiliar. Foster also reviews early research that alludes to the utility of using call-and-response in the classroom. Data for Foster's study consist of 100 call-and-response sequences that were recorded at two predominately African American schools in San Francisco, California. Analysis of these data suggests that the sequences vary in the following ways: (1) code, the system of communication; (2) function, what they express; (3) initiator, who initiates the call-and-response; and (4) mode, how the sequence is performed. While Foster admits that it is not possible to definitively describe the role of call-and-response in the classroom, she does say that evidence reveals positive effects of the technique. She claims that this pedagogy is useful because it draws on what students already know, to teach them what they need to learn.

Fought, Carmen. 2003. *Chicano English in Context.* Basingstoke, UK: Palgrave.

4 F I
Drawing primarily on her own fieldwork in the Los Angeles Chicano community, Fought discusses in turn, the "Social Context" (Chapter 2); "Phonology of Chicano English" (Chapter 3); "Syntax and Semantics of Chicano English" (Chapter 4); "Sociolinguistics of Chicano English I: Phonetic Variation" (Chapter 5); "Sociolinguistics of Chicano English II: Syntactic Variation" (Chapter 6); "Bilingualism and Spanish Fluency" (Chapter 7); "Language Attitudes" (Chapter 8); and "Conclusions: The Future of Research on Chicano English" (Chapter 9).

Fought, Carmen. 2006. *Language and Ethnicity.* Cambridge: Cambridge University Press. [Abstract for Fought, Carmen. 2006. *Language and Ethnicity* graciously provided by Carmen Fought.]

1 4 E F I P
This book draws on sociolinguistic research from a wide range of different ethnic groups around the world, in order to explore the social and psychological processes that are involved in the construction of ethnic identity. It features separate chapters on AAVE and Latino Englishes. It looks generally at different interactional styles in the classroom, and provides a summary of research on using vernacular varieties to teach a standard variety. This book is intended for linguistics students at the graduate and advanced undergraduate levels, for scholars in other fields, and for anyone interested in communication in multiethnic settings.

Fought, Carmen. 2010. Language as a Representation of Mexican American Identity. *English Today* 26.44–48.

4 6 I

Fox, Thomas. 1994. Repositioning the Profession: Teaching Writing to African American Students. In *Composition Theory for the Postmodern Classroom,* ed. by G. A. Olson & S. I. Dobrin. Albany, NY: SUNY Press.

W

Fox argues that taking African American language into account in the composition classroom must go beyond a 'narrow' understanding of 'dialect interference' to include a complex analysis of the cultural, historical, and rhetorical contexts of African American writers. Using the literary concept of 'position' can avoid "reductive and simplistic accounts of African American writing."

Fradd, Sandra & M. Jeanne Weismantel. 1989. *Meeting the Needs of Culturally and Linguistically Different Students: A Handbook for Educators*. Boston: Little Brown.

1 D S

Francis, Norbert & Jon Reyhner. 2002. *Language and Literacy Teaching for Indigenous Education: A Bilingual Approach*. Bristol, UK: Multilingual Matters.

5 R W

Franken, Margaret & Matilda August. 2011. Language Use and the Instructional Strategies of Grade 3 Teachers to Support "Bridging" in Papua New Guinea. *Language and Education* 25.221–39. [Reprinted from *Journal of Applied School Psychology* 25(2).]

2 T

For over a decade, the Department of Education in Papua New Guinea (PNG) has adopted vernacular education as a way of ensuring that the educational experiences of children in schools draw on the cultural and linguistic knowledge they bring to the classroom. In PNG, there are many potential vernaculars—apart from the local languages, there are Tok Pisin and Hiri Motu. The policy advocates "bridging" as an instructional strategy. While the term is used extensively by teachers, it is unclear what teachers think it entails and how they enact bridging. This small-scale exploratory study documents the views of a group of Grade 3 teachers in the East New Britain region and provides observations of their bridging strategies. While the teachers are not particularly supportive of vernacular education, they report on and use instructional strategies that include translation, metalinguistic comparison, contrast and elaboration. The teachers make much use of elicitation to encourage children to articulate their understanding of English, and they demonstrate flexible and dynamic use of languages in their classrooms. The fact that the study recorded no use of the local languages suggests that systematic follow-up of policy in practice is much needed, together with more in-depth research.

Frentz, Thomas. 1971. Children's Comprehension of Standard and Negro Nonstandard English Sentences. *Speech Monographs* 38.10–16.

1 O X

Fry, Maurine A. & Carole Schulte Johnson. 1973. Oral Language Production and Reading Achievement among Selected Students. *Journal of American Indian Education* 13.22–27.

5 A O R

Fryburg, Estelle. 1974. Ways of Evaluating Children's Oral Language. In *Black Dialects and Reading,* ed. by B. Cullinan, 21–39. Urbana, IL: NCTE.

1 A O

Fu, Danling. 1995. *My Trouble Is My English: Asian Students and the American Dream*. Portsmouth, NH: Boynton/Cook: Heinemann.

3 O W

Funkhouser, James. 1973. A Various Standard. *College English* 34.806–27.

1 B F I S W

Reporting on the author's approach of addressing AAVE features in the writing of college-level students, Funkhouser goes into some detail on the constraints of the features which appeared in student writing most frequently: the inflectional suffixes *-ed* and *-s*. The author also gives thoughtful consideration to how to introduce a bidialectal approach to postsecondary students, and acknowledges the thorny issues of language and power throughout.

Fyle, Clifford N. & Eldred D. Jones. 1980. *A Krio—English Dictionary*. Oxford: Oxford University Press.

2 F

Gadsen, Vivian & Daniel Wagner. 1995. *Literacy among African American Youth: Issues in Learning, Teaching, and Schooling*. Creskill, NJ: Hampton.

1 A C E R T

Galaz, Ruth. 2000. The Borders of Our Minds: The Issue Is Curriculum. *Active Learner: A Foxfire Journal for Teachers* 5.32–34. [Abstract prepared by ERIC.]

5 C
A teacher recalls how the first years of Foxfire coincided with her first years of teaching Kiowa students in Oklahoma. A curriculum derived from the region, inspired by ideas that became known as the Foxfire core practices, and delivered via small group work and facilitative teaching, generated student interest, innumerable activities, school-community connections, and improved attitudes about schoolwork.

Gani-Ikilama, T. O. 1990. Use of Nigerian Pidgin in Education? Why Not? In *Multilingualism, Minority Languages, And language Policy in Nigeria,* ed. by N. E. Emenanjo, 219–27. Agbor: Central Books.

2 I

Gaquin, Sheila. 2006. The Year of Writing. *Educational Leadership* 63.80–81. [Abstract prepared by ERIC and reprinted with permission of the Department of Education from the Education Resources Information Center at eric.ed.gov.]

5 R S W
In this column, the author relates her experience as a teacher in a K-12 school in Point Hope, Alaska, where most of the students spoke "Village English," a form of non-standard English mixed with the village's native language of Inupiaq. She notes that the students' reading test scores, which had been below the twenty-fifth percentile, were increased by instruction which included a combination of guided reading, shared reading, vocabulary development, explicit phonics, literacy groups, flexible grouping, team teaching, and parent involvement. The focus then turned to improving writing scores. Using daily writing exercises, along with having the students evaluate others' writing, resulted in significant improvement by year-end.

Garcia, Ofelia. 2011. Latino Language Practices and Literacy Education in the U.S. In *Ethnolinguistic Diversity and Education: Language, Literacy, and Culture,* ed. by M. Farr, L. Seloni & J. Song, 193–211. New York: Routledge.

4 A

Garcia, Ofelia & Kate Menken. 2006. The English of Latinos from Plurilingual Transcultural Angle: Implications for Assessment and Schools. In *Dialects, Englishes, Creoles, and Education,* ed. by S. Nero, 167–84. Mahwah, NJ: Lawrence Erlbaum Associates.

4 A

Gay, Judy & Ryan Tweney. 1976. Comprehension and Production of Standard and Black English by Lower-Class Black Children. *Developmental Psychology* 12.262–68.

1 A O

Gee, James. 1989. Two Styles of Narrative Construction and Their Linguistic and Educational Implications. *Discourse Processes* 12.263–65.

1 N

Gee, James P. 2007. *Social Linguistics and Literacies: Ideology in Discourses (Fourth Edition).* London: Falmer Press.

A C E I N R W

In its first edition, *Social Linguistics and Literacies* emerged as one of the founding texts of the `New Literacy Studies' approach to sociocultural analysis of language and literacy. Now in its fourth edition, this influential text has been updated to include contemporary issues such as digital literacies. Gee explicates complex theoretical constructs such as ideology and discourse in a highly accessible form, using concrete examples from classroom dilemmas to great effect. The problem of responding equitably to vernacular speakers is a theme addressed directly and indirectly throughout the book.

Gemake, Josephine. 1981. Interference of Certain Dialect Elements with Reading Comprehension for Third Graders. *Reading Improvement* 18.183–89.

1 R X

Gemake examines the effect of dialect interference on reading comprehension as a function of sentence complexity. Subjects consisted of three groups of eighteen third-graders each, matched for reading scores: one group of monodialectal AAVE-speakers, one group of monodialectal SAE-speakers, and one group of bidialectal speakers. Each student read aloud a booklet containing twenty-four SAE sentences (eight simple, eight compound, and eight complex) and answered two comprehension questions after each sentence. Results indicated that although the monodialectal AAVE speakers and the bidialectal speakers exhibited omission of inflectional endings during oral reading, comprehension was not affected. Furthermore, analysis of comprehension responses among all three groups of children indicated that sentence complexity did not affect comprehension. Analysis within the group of monodialectal AAVE speakers, however, indicated that this group had significantly more incorrect responses regarding complex sentences than regarding simple or compound sentences. The author concludes that dialect-related responses should not be treated as reading errors since they do not affect comprehension, and suggests further investigation on the effect of complex sentence patterns on comprehension rate.

Genshaft, Judy & Michael Hirt. 1974. Language Differences between Black Children and White Children. *Developmental Psychology* 10.431–56.

1 A O

Gerbault, Jeannine. 1997. Pedagogical Aspects of Vernacular Literacy. In *Vernacular Literacy: A Re-Evaluation,* ed. by A. Tabouret-Keller, R. Le Page, P. Gardner-Chloros & G. Varro, 142–85. Oxford: Clarendon Press.

6 S V

Gere, Anne Ruggles & Eugene Smith. 1979. *Attitudes, Language and Change.* Urbana, IL: NCTE.

1 I T

Giannasi, Jenefer. 1976. Dialects and Composition. In *Teaching Composition: Ten Bibliographical Essays,* ed. by G. Tate, 275–304. Fort Worth: Texas Christian University Press.

1 W

Gillet, Jean Wallace & J. Richard Gentry. 1983. Bridges between Nonstandard and Standard English with Extensions of Dictated Stories. *Reading Teacher* 36.360–64.

2 R S V

Gilmore, Perry. 1987. Sulking, Stepping, and Tracking: The Effects of Attitude Assessment on Access to Literacy. In *Literacy and Schooling,* ed. by D. Bloome, 99–120. Norwood, NJ: Ablex.

A I

Gilyard, Keith. 1990. Genopsycholinguisticide and the Language Theme in African-American Literature. *College English* 52.776–86.

1 I

Gilyard, Keith. 1991. *Voices of the Self: A Study of Language Competence.* Detroit. MI: Wayne State University Press.

1 C U

Gilyard, Keith. 1996. *Let's Flip the Script: An African American Discourse on Language, Literature and Learning.* Detroit, MI: Wayne State University Press.

1 B C F I P S W

Gilyard, Keith & Elaine Richardson. 2001. Students' Right to Possibility: Basic Writing and African American Rhetoric. In *Insurrections: Approaches to Resistance in Composition Studies,* ed. by A. Greenbaum. Albany, NY: SUNY Press.

1 W

Gladney, Mildred. 1973. Problems in Teaching Children with Nonstandard Dialects. In *Language Differences: Do They Interfere?,* ed. by J. Laffey & R. Shuy, 40–46. Newark, DE: International Reading Association.

1 R S X

Glowka, Wayne & Donald Lance (eds.) 1993. *Language Variation in North American English: Research and Teaching.* New York: Modern Language Association.

1 2 4 6 E F S T

Godley, Amanda J., Brian D. Carpenter & Cynthia A. Werner. 2007. "I'll Speak in Proper Slang": Language Ideologies in a Daily Editing Activity. *Reading Research Quarterly* 42.100–31.

1 I S T

Godley, Amanda J. & Angela Minnici. 2008. Critical Language Pedagogy in an Urban High School English Class. *Urban Education* 43.319–46.

1 I L P The purpose of this study was to examine how classroom conversations about diverse dialects of English can provide a useful foundation for critical language and literacy instruction for students who speak African American Vernacular English (AAVE) and other stigmatized dialects. This article describes a weeklong unit on language variety that implemented what we call "critical language pedagogy" in three predominantly African American, 10th-grade English classes. Analyses of class discussions, interviews, and pre- and post-questionnaires demonstrate that the unit helped students critique dominant language ideologies, become more conscious of their own code-switching, and view dialect variation as natural and desirable.

Godley, Amanda J., Julie Sweetland, Rebecca Wheeler, Angela Minnici & Brian D. Carpenter. 2006. Preparing Teachers for Dialectally Diverse Classrooms. *Educational Researcher* 35.30–37. [Reprinted with permission of Sage Publications from *Educational Researcher* 35(8), 30.]

1 I T

Scholarship on dialect diversity in classrooms has yielded two seemingly incompatible lines of research. Although numerous pedagogical approaches have been shown to provide productive alternatives to traditional responses to stigmatized dialects, research on public perceptions and teachers' attitudes suggests that negative beliefs about stigmatized dialects and the students who speak them are deeply entrenched in US society. The authors argue that teacher preparation grounded in sociolinguistic understandings of dialect diversity can help teachers develop productive pedagogical responses to students' language choices. Drawing on previous research and their own work with teachers, the authors present a framework for preparing teachers for dialectally diverse classrooms. Recommendations include anticipating resistance, addressing issues of identity and power, and emphasizing pedagogical applications of sociolinguistic research.

Goldblatt, Eli. 1995. 'Round My Way: Authority and Double-Consciousness in Three Urban High School Writers. Pittsburgh, PA: University of Pittsburgh Press.

1 4 I W

Golub, Lester. 1975. English Syntax of Black, White, Indian, and Spanish-American Children. *The Elementary School Journal* 75.323–34.

1 4 5 6 F

Gonzalez, Gilbert. 1997. Culture, Language, and the Americanization of Mexican Children. In *Latinos and Education: A Critical Reader*, ed. by A. Darder, R. Torres & H. Gutierrez. New York: Routledge.

4 C

Gonzalez, Norma. 2006. *I Am My Language: Discourses of Women and Children in the Borderlands*. Tucson: University of Arizona Press.

4 N

Goodman, Kenneth S. 1965. Dialect Barriers to Reading Comprehension. *Elementary English* 42.853–60.

1 R S X

In this article, reprinted in Baratz and Shuy (1969, pp. 14-8), Goodman hypothesizes that the more a student's dialect differs from Standard English, the more difficult is the task of learning to read (this hypothesis is later rejected/revised, see Goodman et al. 1997). The author explains that divergent dialects are fully expressive and rule-governed, but that the systematic ways in which they differ from Standard English interfere with the process of reading standard texts. The main kinds of phonological and syntactic points of divergence among dialects are outlined and exemplified. Ultimately, Goodman concludes that the most practical approach for teaching reading to speakers of nonstandard dialects is to give children material written in Standard English, but allow them to read it in their own dialect. Among the key aspects of this approach, it is emphasized that teachers must focus on fostering reading skills rather than trying to alter students' speech; when children have confidence in their own language, they can better use it as a base for building literacy.

Goodman, Kenneth S. & Catherine Buck. 1973. Dialect Barriers to Reading Comprehension Revisited. *The Reading Teacher* 27.6–12.

1 R S X
Goodman and Buck, revising/rejecting an earlier hypothesis in Goodman 1965, draw on several years of research to conclude that speakers of low-status dialects face no special barriers in learning to read other than teachers' confusion and negative attitudes regarding linguistic difference. First, they reject the notion that nonstandard pronunciations (e.g., he'p for "help") constitute reading miscues, since it is to be expected that children will pronounce words in accordance with the phonology of their own dialect. In a recent study on dialect-related miscues in reading, the authors found that no subjects were completely consistent in their use of dialect-based shifts; in fact, only seven subjects out of the ninety-four showed more than 20% dialect-related miscues. While all seven were Black, many Black subjects exhibited few miscues, or none at all. Furthermore, it was found that even subjects with no miscues often used dialect features when asked to retell the story they read. The authors conclude that although less proficient readers do show increased dialect use, these are not necessarily causally linked, and moreover, dialect-related miscues do not hinder the reading process. This article was reprinted in *The Reading Teacher* in 1997 (50.6, pp. 454-60), with a brief introduction by John G. Marnitz, a few months after the Oakland Ebonics resolutions generated national and international controversy.

Goodman, Yetta M. 2003. *Valuing Language Study: Inquiry into Language for Elementary and Middle Schools.* Urbana, IL: NCTE.

L M S
This is a highly practical guide to integrating language study into language arts classes, rich with concrete examples from classrooms. Goodman's conceptual framework for language study experiences includes 'critical moment teaching,' strategy lessons, and thematic units.

Goodman-France, Shelome. 2008. Review of Dagmar Deuber, "Nigerian Pidgin English: Language Contact, Variation and Change in an African Urban Setting". *Language in Society* 37.131–33.

2 F

Goodwin, Marjorie Harness. 1990. *He-Said-She-Said: Talk as Social Organization among Black Children.* Bloomington: Indiana University Press.

1 N O

Gopaul-McNicol, Sharon-Ann. 1998. Guest Editorial: African American Education and the Ebonics Issue. *Journal of Negro Education* 67.2–4.

1 K

Gopaul-McNicol, Sharon-Ann, Grace Reid & Cecilia Wisdom. 1998. The Psychoeducational Assessment of Ebonics Speakers: Issues and Challenges. *Journal of Negro Education* 67.16–24.

1 A D

Among the issues the article explores is the inability of standardized tests to appreciate and adequately account for the diverse, nonstandard dialects and cultural experiences of students. This article explains that psycho-educational assessments' disregard for nonstandard English use and experiences is especially true regarding the testing of Ebonics-speaking students. Expected psychometric test performance scores are normalized on Standard English speaking students' performance; therefore Ebonics speakers are often wrongfully assessed as low-achievers when they do not meet these normalized scores. A study discussed in this article indicates the narrowing and often elimination of these observed achievement gaps when members of each group were given tests that were linguistically and culturally appropriate. The article concludes with a discussion of ways to remedy this problem and move towards improved testing.

Görlach, Manfred. 1995. *More Englishes: New Studies in Varieties of English, 1988–1994.* Amsterdam: John Benjamins.

6 F

Görlach, Manfred. 1998. *Even More Englishes: Studies, 1996–1997.* Amsterdam: John Benjamins.

6 F

Görlach, Manfred. 2002. *Still More Englishes.* Amsterdam: John Benjamins.

2 6 F

Görlach, Manfred & John A. Holm (eds.) 1986. *Focus on the Caribbean.* (Varieties of English around the World. General Series.) Amsterdam: John Benjamins.

2 E F

Görlach, Manfred & Edgar W. Schneider (eds.) 1997. *Englishes around the World: Studies in Honor of Manfred Görlach.* (Varieties of English around the World. General Series.) Amsterdam: John Benjamins.

2 6 E F

Gottardo, Alexandra, Bernice Yan, Linda Siegel & Lesly Wade-Woolley. 2001. Factors Related to English Reading Performance in Children with Chinese as a First Language: More Evidence of Cross-Language Transfor of Phonological Processing. *Journal of Educational Psychology* 93.530–42.

3 6 R X

Grant, Sycarah, Evelyn Oka & Jean Baker. 2009. The Culturally Relevant Assessment of Ebonics-Speaking Children. *Journal of Applied School Psychology* 25.113–27. [Reprinted from *Journal of Applied School Psychology* 25(2).]

1 A T
Professional organizations and federal legislation stipulate that assessments of all students must be fair and unbiased. Although these entities provide guidance, there continues to be a gap between guidelines and practice. This article examines the nature of culturally competent practice with Ebonics-speaking youth. Many school psychologists face challenges such as large caseloads, lack of knowledge about Ebonics, and limited access to culturally appropriate assessment materials. The present article fills this gap by providing practitioners with information on the history of Ebonics, implications for the students they assess, and practical ways to address these issues with limited resources.

Gray-Rosendale, Laura, Loyola K. Bird & Judith F. Bullock. 2003. Rethinking the Basic Writing Frontier: Native American Students' Challenge to Our Histories. *Journal of Basic Writing* 22.71–106.

5 W

Green, Gordon C. 1963. Negro Dialect, the Last Barrier to Integration. *Journal of Negro Education* 32.81–83.

1 I

Green, Lisa. 2002. A Descriptive Study of African American English: Research in Linguistics and Education. *International Journal of Qualitative Studies in Education* 15.673–90.

1 F

Green, Lisa. 2002. *African American English: A Linguistic Introduction.* Cambridge: Cambridge University Press.

1 E F I

This book provides a thorough and technical description of the main features of African American English [AAE] by an African American native speaker from Louisiana who is also a formal syntactician. In addition to the detailed description of the vocabulary, pronunciation and grammar of AAE, the book covers pragmatic/ speech event use, and discusses other relevant aspects of the variety. Chapters include: 1—"Lexicons and meaning"; 2—"Syntax part 1: Verbal markers in AAE"; 3—"Syntax part 2: Syntactic and morphosyntactic properties in AAE"; 4—"Phonology of AAE"; 5—"Speech events and rules of interaction in AAE"; 6—"AAE in literature"; 7—"AAE in the media"; 8—"Approaches, attitudes and education."

Green, Lisa. 2004. African American English. In *Language in the USA,* ed. by E. Finegan & J. R. Rickford, 76–91. Cambridge: Cambridge University Press.

1 F

Green, Lisa. 2011. *Language and the African American Child.* Cambridge: Cambridge University Press.

1 Q

Green, Lisa & Tracy Conner. 2009. Rhetorical Markers in Speech of Girls Developing African American Language. In *African American Women's Language: Discourse, Education and Identity,* ed. by S. Lanehart. Newcastle upon Tyne, UK: Cambridge Scholars Press.

1 F N

The authors report on a study of the use of preverbal markers in the speech of young African American girls acquiring language in vernacular speech communities. They find that the use of preverbal markers such as preverbal *had* event marking and remote *BIN* are attested in some girls' speech by four years of age, and that girls use these syntactic resources to achieve pragmatic effects such as aggrandizement.

Greenbaum, Paul E. 1985. Nonverbal Differences in Communication Style between American Indian and Anglo Elementary Classrooms. *American Educational Research Journal* 22.101–15. [Abstract prepared by ERIC.]

5 C N

Nonverbal behaviors associated with classroom conversation in Choctaw Indian and White middle-class public schools were videotaped with two cameras providing a view of the teacher and class and the listener-gaze of individual students. Results indicated cultural differences in nonverbal behavior were associated with classroom interaction.

Greenbaum, Paul E. & Susan D. Greenbaum. 1983. Cultural Differences, Nonverbal Regulation, and Classroom Interaction: Sociolinguistic Interference in American Indian Education. *Peabody Journal of Education* 61.16–33. [Abstract prepared by ERIC.]

5 C N
Various studies of interaction between teachers and American Indian students indicate that nonverbal behaviors interfere with classroom communication and educational performance. American Indian children exhibit such behaviors as less talking, low voice tones, and averted gaze during conversations. These behaviors seem to hinder students in the learning process.

Greenberg, Karen, Patrick Hartwell, Margaret Himley, R. E. Stratton & Thomas Farrell. 1984. Responses to Thomas J. Farrell, 'Iq and Standard English'. *College Composition and Communication* 35.455–78.

1 A K

Greene, Deric & Felicia Walker. 2004. Recommendations to Public Speaking Instructors for the Negotiation of Code-Switching Practices among Black English-Speaking African American Students. *Journal of Negro Education* 73.435–42. [Reprinted with permission of the journal from *Journal of Negro Education* 73(4-11), 435.]

1 B I S
This article offers six recommendations that instructors can employ to encourage effective classroom code-switching practices among Black English-speaking students in the basic communication course: (1) reconsider attitudes, (2) communicate expectations, (3) demonstrate model language behavior, (4) affirm students' language, (5) create culturally reflective assignments, and (6) develop assessment methods.

Greene, Nicole Pepinster. 2005. Cajun, Creole, and African American Literacy Narratives. *Multicultural Perspectives* 7.39–45. [Reprinted from *Multicultural Perspectives* 7(4).]

1 2 6 T
This article examines students' narrative responses to reading professional literacy histories. Demonstrating the importance of narrative as a way of learning, it shows how elementary education majors of diverse backgrounds explore their relation with language in a traditional grammar class. Cajun, Creole, and African American students recover their literacy histories and articulate the relation between the loss of language and the loss of culture and heritage. Drawing on the parallels between their discourse histories and the discourse histories of other cultures, these narratives also suggest that the students are now able to establish their linguistic identity and develop a greater sensitivity to the situations of their own students in the multicultural classrooms of southwest Louisiana.

Gregory, George Ann. 1989. Composing Processes of Native Americans: Six Case Studies of Navajo Speakers. *Journal of American Indian Education* 28.1–6.

5 W

Groff, Cynthia. 2004. Language and Literacy Teaching for Indigenous Education: A Bilingual Approach. *Language in Society* 33.301–03.

5 W
This is a review article on Francis and Reyhner 2002.

Groff, Patrick. 1978. Children's Oral Language and Their Written Composition. *Elementary School Journal* 78.180–91.

O W

Grogger, Jeffrey. 2011. Speech Patterns and Racial Wage Inequality. *Journal of Human Resources* 46.1–25. [Abstract prepared by ERIC.]

1 B I
Investigates the relationship between use of AAVE and wages; found that even after controlling for measures of skill and family background, Black speakers whose voices were distinctly identified as Black by anonymous listeners earn about 12% less than Whites with similar observable skills. Indistinctly identified Blacks earn essentially the same as comparable Whites.

Gunderson, Doris. 1970. *Language and Reading*. Washington, D.C.: CAL.

3 R X

Gupta, Abha. 2010. African-American English: Teacher Beliefs, Teacher Needs and Teacher Preparation Programs. *The Reading Matrix* 10.152–64.

T
The author reports on a survey completed by approximately 150 K-12 teachers regarding their knowledge and beliefs and training regarding AAVE. Although more than two-thirds of the teachers surveyed indicated a need to learn strategies and ways to address AAVE in the classroom, less than one-third of the survey respondents reported that their teacher preparation program trained them to address the linguistic needs of students speaking AAVE.

Gupta, Anthea Fraser. 1991. Acquisition of Diglossia in Singapore English. In *Child Language Development in Singapore and Malaysia,* ed. by A. Kwan-Terry, 119–45. Singapore: Singapore University Press.

6 Q

Gupta, Anthea Fraser. 1994. *The Step-Tongue: Children's English in Singapore*. Clevedon, UK: Multilingual Matters.

6 B F Q T

Gut, Ulrike. 2007. First Language Influence and Final Consonant Clusters in the New Englishes of Singapore and Nigeria. *World Englishes* 26.346–59.

6 Q X

Gutierrez, Kris D., P. Zitlali Morales & Danny C. Martinez. 2009. Re-Mediating Literacy: Culture, Difference, and Learning for Students from Nondominant Communities. *Review of Research in Education* 33.212–45.

C E R W
A sophisticated review article which traces the "intellectual trails" of competing explanations of, and responses to, culturally diverse learners in US schools from deficit approaches, and cultural mismatch approaches, to contemporary transformative approaches which build on nondominant students' cultural and linguistic assets.

Gutierrez-Clellen, Vera & Gabriela Simon-Cereijido. 2007. The Discriminant Accuracy of a Grammatical Measure with Latino English-Speaking Children. *Journal of Speech and Language Hearing Research* 50.968–81.

4 A D

Hackenberg, Robert. 1972. *A Sociolinguistic Description of Appalachian English*. Washington, D.C.: Georgetown University.

6 F

Haddix, Marcelle. 2008. Beyond Sociolinguistics: Towards a Critical Approach to Cultural and Linguistic Diversity in Teacher Education. *Language and Education* 22.254–70. [Reprinted from *Language and Education* 22(5).]

1 I P T
The author shares findings from a qualitative study of White, monolingual preservice teachers enrolled in a sociolinguistics course that examines the interplay of language and ethnicity in the United States. The primary aims of the study were to learn more about the preservice teachers' awareness of their cultural and linguistic backgrounds and to explore how they felt their new understandings about linguistic diversity would impact their future practice as teachers. In this paper, the author examines the cultural and linguistic identity work of two White, monolingual preservice teachers initiated by their participation in this course. Findings from interview and archival data suggest that while teacher education grounded in sociolinguistic research and principles can impact teachers' attitudes and practices towards linguistic diversity, teacher education that engages a critical approach to understanding language and ethnicity can encourage teachers' interrogation of their own cultural and linguistic location and challenge dominant standard language and color-blind ideologies.

Hagemann, Julie. 2001. A Bridge from Home to School: Helping Working Class Students Acquire School Literacy. *The English Journal* 90.74–81.

1 4 B S
Hagemann demonstrates the importance of using one's home language to master written school language by describing the tactic she used with three students, one southern White, one African American, and one Chicano, who spoke mutually intelligible but somewhat different English vernaculars. Citing Siegel (1999), she argues that successfully learning a second dialect and learning a second language are similar in that both require learners to form different mental representations for each system. However, learning a second dialect is in some ways more difficult since students may not be aware of the specific differences. For this reason, the best way to help vernacular English speakers master Standard English, is to implement a pedagogy of overt comparison, in which students are first taught to notice a specific feature, then compare it with "their existing knowledge of English" (p. 77), and finally, to integrate it into their daily routines. The article basically offers a brief introduction to contrastive analysis, but one that teachers might find attractive because it is written in relatively non-technical language, considers motivation as well as mechanics, and has practical suggestions.

Haig, Yvonne & Rhonda Oliver. 2003. Is It a Case of Mind over Matter? Influences on Teachers' Judgements of Student Speech. *Australian Review of Applied Linguistics* 26.55–70. [Abstract prepared by ERIC.]

6 I T
The authors suggest that while language variation is widespread and natural, it is subject to judgment and that where a standard has developed other varieties are judged against the standard. They investigate how teachers judge the speech of school-aged students and what influences that judgment. Results show teachers' perceptions of speech were most strongly influenced by students' use of nonstandard varieties of English.

Haig, Yvonne & Rhonda Oliver. 2003. Language Variation and Education: Teachers' Perceptions. *Language and Education* 17.266–80. [Abstract prepared by ERIC.]

I T
This article investigates how teachers perceive the speech of school-aged children and whether the socioeconomic status or level of schooling of the students influences these perceptions. Findings suggest that teachers' judgments of what is problematic and their perception of what causes these problems may differ according to the socioeconomic status of their students and to the year level being taught.

Hakimzadeh, Shirin & D'Vera Cohn. 2007. *English Usage among Hispanics in the United States.* Washington, D.C.: Pew Hispanic Center.

4 U

Halasek, Kay & Nels Pearson Highberg (eds.) 2001. *Landmark Essays on Basic Writing).* New York: Routledge.

E W
Since its inception, instructors of Basic Writing field have confronted issues of non-standard language in the classroom, and have been among the most productive scholars in both theory and practice. This volume reprints several essays which address AAVE and other vernaculars, including "Teaching Language in Open Admissions" by Adrienne Rich; "The Silenced Dialogue: Power and Pedagogy in Educating Other People's Children" by Lisa Delpit; and "Literacies and Deficits Revisited" by Jerrie Cobb Scott.

Hall, Darryl Ted & James Damico. 2007. Black Youth Employ African American Vernacular English in Creating Digital Texts. *The Journal of Negro Education* 76.80–88.

N W
This analysis of high school students' use of AAVE discourse features (tonal semantics, sermonic tone, call and response, and signifying) in digital written texts.

Hall, Joan (ed.) 2002. *Dictionary of American Regional English, Vol. 4: P–Sk.* Cambridge, MA: Belknap Press of Harvard University Press.

6 E F

Hall, Joan (ed.) 2012. *Dictionary of American Regional English, Vol. 5, Sl–Z.* Cambridge, MA: Belknap Press of Harvard University Press.

6 E F

Hall, R. M. R. & Beatrice Hall. 1969. The "Double" Negative: A Non-Problem. *The Florida FL Reporter* 7.113–15.

1 F S
Hall and Hall dispel myths that double negation is merely an illogical error, and give a brief background to the logic behind it and to the history of its stigmatization in Standard English. The authors then explain some of the idiosyncrasies of Standard English negation rules and suggest a method for teaching them to AAVE-speakers through a variety of transformational exercises (e.g., "Robinson Crusoe saw someone on the beach." —> "Robinson Crusoe didn't see anyone on the beach.") that gradually introduce more and more complex structures.

Hall, Vernon & Ralph Turner. 1971. Comparison of Imitation and Comprehension Scores between Two Lower-Class Groups and the Effects of Two Warm-up Conditions on Imitation of the Same Groups. *Child Development* 42.1735–50.

1 O R X

Hall, Vernon & Ralph Turner. 1973. The Validity of the 'Different Language Explanation' for Poor Scholastic Performance by Black Students. *Review of Educational Research* 44.69–81.

1 E R X

Hall, Vernon, Ralph Turner & William Russell. 1973. Ability of Children from Four Subcultures and Two Grade Levels to Imitate and Comprehend Crucial Aspects of Standard English: A Test of the Different Language Explanation. *Journal of Educational Psychology* 64.147–58.

1 O X

Hall, William, Stephen Reder & Michael Cole. 1975. Story Recall in Young Black and White Children: Effect of Racial Group Membership, Race of Experimenter, and Dialect. *Developmental Psychology* 11.628–34.

1 R X
Hall et al. examine story recall as a function of the dialect of the story, the race of the subject, and the race of the experimenter. Sixteen Black children and sixteen White children, aged 4.5 years, were each presented with four short stories, two in AAVE and two in SAE. Stories were presented over the course of two sessions so that each child had one White experimenter and one Black experimenter, and each session contained two stories, one in each dialect. Analysis of recall scores showed that White students performed better than Black students in recalling SAE stories, Black students performed better than White students in recalling AAVE stories, and Black students performed as well with AAVE stories as White students performed with SAE stories. The race of the experimenter had no effect. The authors conclude that their research supports the 'language difference' hypothesis, and that subjects likely experienced 'mnemonic interference' in recalling stories that were presented in a dialect different from their own.

Hall-Lew, Lauren. 2010. Ethnicity and Sociolinguistic Variation in San Francisco. *Language and Linguistics Compass* 4.458–72. [Reprinted from *Language and Linguistics Compass* with permission of the author.]

3 F
California's San Francisco Bay Area has long been one of the most ethnically diverse areas of the United States, and ethnicity is an integral aspect of any research on language use in the region. This article gives a brief social history of San Francisco with respect to settlement patterns since the 1850s' gold rush, paying particular attention to Chinese Americans, who are argued to play an especially distinctive role in the city's history and current social landscape. This article also reviews the sociolinguistic research on language and ethnicity in and around San Francisco, with a focus on studies on variation and change in English, noting the relative lack of attention to Asian American ethnicities and calling for increased scholarship on the linguistic construction of Asian identities in the San Francisco area.

Hall-Lew, Lauren. 2010. Ethnicity and Sound Change in San Francisco English. In *Proceedings of the Thirty-Fifth Annual Meeting of the Berkeley Linguistics Society, February*

14–16, 2009: General Session and Parasession on Negation, ed. by I. Kwon, H. Pritchett & J. Spence, 111–22. Berkeley, CA: Berkeley Linguistics Society.

3 6 F

Hall-Lew, Lauren & Rebecca Starr. 2010. Beyond the Second Generation: English Use among Chinese Americans in the San Francisco Bay Area. *English Today* 26.12–19.

3 6 F I

Hamilton, Greg & Ruthie Stern. 2004. English in the City: Wass'up, Mrs. Stern? *English Journal* 93.89–92. [Abstract prepared by ERIC and reprinted with permission of the Department of Education from the Education Resources Information Center at eric. ed.gov.]

1 F
This article focuses on the particular challenges, choices, and celebrations relevant to teaching in an urban setting. The speech of African American students is described as rich and reflective of the African American oral tradition. The article also discusses the meaning, rules and the evolution of African American English.

Hamilton, Kendra. 2005. The Dialect Dilemma: Whether One Is Speaking Ebonics or Appalachian English, Sociolinguists Say All Dialects Are Created Equal. *Black Issues in Higher Education* 22.34. [Abstract prepared by ERIC and reprinted with permission of the Department of Education from the Education Resources Information Center at eric.ed.gov.]

1 6 I
This document shares Dr. Walt Wolfram's views on African American Dialect. He states that the most elementary principle is that all language is patterned and rule-governed, and one can apply that principle to African American English, Appalachian English, and to every other dialect that is examined.

Hammond, Bill, Mary Rhodes Hoover & Irving P. McPhail (eds.) 2005. *Teaching African American Learners to Read: Perspectives and Practices*. Newark, DE: International Reading Association.

C E R S

Hanna, David. 1997. Do I Sound 'Asian' to You? Linguistic Markers of Asian American Identity. In *Proceedings of the 21st Annual Penn Linguistics Colloquium,* ed. by A. Dimitriadis, L. Siegel, C. Surek-Clark & A. Williams. Philadelphia: Department of Linguistics, University of Pennsylvania.

3 6 F I

Harber, Jean R. 1977. Influence of Presentation Dialect and Orthographic Form on Reading Performance of Black, Inner-City Children. *Educational Research Quarterly* 2.9–16. [Abstract prepared by the author in conjunction with ERIC and reprinted with permission of the Department of Education from the Education Resources Information Center at eric.ed.gov.]

1 A R V
Equivalent forms of listening comprehension, oral reading, and oral reading comprehension tasks in (1) Standard English, (2) Black English, standard orthography, and (3) Black English, nonstandard orthography were administered to Black, inner-city children. Subjects scored highest on Black English, standard orthography and lowest on Black English, nonstandard orthography on both types of reading tasks.

Harber, Jean R. 1981. The Effect of Cultural and Linguistic Differences on Reading Performance. In *The Social Psychology of Reading,* ed. by J. Edwards, 173–92. Silver Spring, MD: Institute of Modern Languages, Inc.

1 C R X

Harber reviews literature concerning the effects of cultural and linguistic differences on reading performance. Possible environmental factors that hinder reading performance include low-quality instruction and materials, lack of cognitive stimulation during preschool years, and negative self-concept brought about by past failures. Furthermore, studies have shown that teachers often have negative attitudes toward speakers of nonstandard dialects, and the resulting low teacher expectancy may translate into low student performance. Turning to linguistic factors, the author reviews research concerning dialect interference in listening comprehension, oral reading, oral reading comprehension and silent reading comprehension. Given the number of contradictory results and methodological problems, further research is suggested. To this end the author makes several suggestions for future studies, and also urges the development of dialect-appropriate assessment material given the Standard English bias of currently available instruments.

Harber, Jean R. 1982. Accepting Dialect Renderings of Extant Materials on Black-English Speaking Children's Oral Reading Scores. *Education and Treatment of Children* 5.271–82.

1 A R

Harber, Jean R. & Jane R. Beatty. 1978. *Reading and the Black English Speaking Child.* Newark, DE: International Reading Association.

1 R X

Harber, Jean R. & Diane N. Bryen. 1976. Black English and the Task of Reading. *Review of Educational Research* 46.387–405.

1 E R X

Harber and Bryen review the literature concerning the extent to which dialect interference hinders Black children learning to read. Although it is safe to conclude that dialect interference does affect oral reading ability, the authors find numerous contradictory results and methodological errors in studies concerning reading and listening comprehension. They then cite a number of unresolved issues concerning the use of special beginning reading materials that utilize AAVE: there is no conclusive evidence that it is more effective than traditional approaches, officials have been reluctant to accept the use of written nonstandard language, there is as yet no suitable orthography, teachers must still be trained in the details of AAVE, and there are many Black children who do not speak AAVE. The authors conclude that further research should be done to address these issues before the implementation of any new educational programs.

Harkins, Jean. 1994. *Bridging Two Worlds: Aboriginal English and Cross-Cultural Understanding.* St. Lucia, Australia: University of Queensland Press.

6 F

Harper, Frederick D., Kisha Braithwaite & Ricardo D. LaGrange. 1998. Ebonics and Academic Achievement: The Role of the Counselor. *Journal of Negro Education* 67.25–34.

1 A T

Harris, Joyce, Alan Kamhi & Karen Pollock (eds.) 2001. *Literacy in African American Communities*. Mahwah, NJ: Lawrence Erlbaum Associates.

1 B E I R V W

Harris, Kandis & Michael Moran. 2006. Phonological Features Exhibited by Children Speaking African American English at Three Grade Levels. *Communication Disorders Quarterly* 27.195–205. [Reprinted with permission of Sage Publications, the publisher, from Communication Disorders Quarterly 27(4), 195.]

1 F Q

This study compared phonological features of African American English speakers at three grade levels: preschool, elementary school, and middle school. The phonological features exhibited at all three grade levels were quite similar. The frequency of usage, determined by the percentage of speakers exhibiting the feature and by the mean number of occurrences of the feature, varied. The frequency of occurrence of some features decreased as grade level increased, the frequency of others remained the same, and the frequency of others was quite variable at the different grade levels. We noted one unusual feature ("bazin" for "bathing") among several younger speakers.

Harris, Ovetta, Vicki Anderson, David Bloome & Tempii Champion. 1995. A Select Bibliography of Research on Africanized English and Education. *Linguistics and Education* 7.151–56.

1 E

Harris-Wright, Kelli. 1987. The Challenge of Educational Coalescence: Teaching Nonmainstream English-Speaking Students. *Journal of Childhood Communication Disorders* 11.209–13.

1 B O S

Harris-Wright describes a training sequence for helping students distinguish between "home language" and "school language" as developed by DeKalb County School System (Decatur, GA). In order to increase awareness of the need for the ability to use language for different purposes and of the various implications of unproductive communication skills, and in order to allow students to practice mainstream English while not entirely dismissing their "home language," students are videotaped while engaged in oral reading or conversation. After the students are shown videotapes that demonstrate the difference between unproductive and productive communication styles, they view their own taped material in order to judge their personal communicative effectiveness in Standard English. Then, after a number of activities aimed at increasing awareness of the difference between home and school languages, the students are once again videotaped and then shown these new tapes so that they can assess their improvement in using Standard English. Harris-Wright reports that fourteen of the fifteen participants "demonstrated the ability to discriminate between 'home communication' and 'school communication' " and "90% of the student participants have demonstrated use of standard English dialect as an additional communicative style" (p. 212). Based on these encouraging results, the program was expanded in subsequent years. Additional results of DeKalb County's Bidialectal Communication Program are available in Rickford (2001), who presents the reading composite scores of participating students and a control group on the Iowa Test of Basic Skills, noting that students in the bidialectal group made bigger relative reading composite gains than students in the control group.

Harris-Wright, Kelli. 1999. Enhancing Bidialectalism in Urban African American Students. In *Making the Connection,* ed. by C. Adger, D. Christian & O. Taylor, 53–60. Washington, D.C.: CAL/Delta.

1 B O S

Hart, Betty & Todd R. Risley. 1995. *Meaningful Differences in the Everyday Experience of Young American Children.* Baltimore: Paul H. Brookes Publishing. [Abstract prepared by ERIC.]

1 A N Q
Noting the scientifically substantiated link between children's early family experience and their later intellectual growth, this book describes a longitudinal study of the circumstances of early language learning and the central role of home and family in the emergence of language and word learning. The vocabularies of forty-two children were studied from the time they first began to say words at about one year until they were about three years old. The study also observed the children's interactions with other persons in their families, which formed the contexts for their word learning. Results indicated that the most important factors in language acquisition are the economic advantages of children's homes and the frequency of language experiences. The basic findings from the study are that children who were born into homes with fewer economic resources learn fewer words, have fewer experiences with words in interactions with other persons, and acquire a vocabulary of words more slowly. Five parenting features that predicted future achievement were: (1) language diversity; (2) feedback; (3) guidance style; (4) language emphasis; and (5) responsiveness. The book concludes by outlining an agenda for intervention that would begin in the home and very early in a young child's life, with a focus on the social influences on language and its acquisition within the cultural context of the family. Two appendices contain a table of quality features of parent language and interaction, and twenty figures of data.

Hart, Betty & Todd R. Risley. 2003. The Early Catastrophe. The 30 Million Word Gap. *American Educator* 27.4–9.

1 A N Q
These authors report on a study concluding that by age three, children from privileged families have heard 30 million more words than children from underprivileged families. While not about AAVE per se, this research is about language socialization in African American families. The startling (but perhaps misleading) statistic of the '30 million word gap' has been influential in educational circles, especially within nonprofit and charter organizations focused on addressing the inequities in educational outcomes between African American students and their White or more affluent counterparts.

Hart, Jane, John Guthrie & Linda Winfield. 1980. Black English Phonology and Learning to Read. *Journal of Educational Psychology* 72.636–46.

1 R X

Hartwell, Patrick. 1980. Dialect Interference in Writing: A Critical View. *Research in the Teaching of English* 14.101–18.

1 W X

Haussamen, Brock, Amy Benjamin, Martha Kolln & Rebecca Wheeler. 2003. *Grammar Alive! A Guide for Teachers.* Urbana, IL: National Council of Teachers of English.

1 M S

Hazen, Kirk. 2005. English LIVES: Language in Variation Exercises for Today's Classrooms. In *Language in the Schools: Integrating Linguistic Knowledge into K-12 Teaching*, ed. by K. Denham & A. Lobeck, 181–9. Mahwah, NJ: Lawrence Erlbaum Associates.

6 L M S

Hazen, Kirk, Paige Butcher & Ashley King. 2010. Unvernacular Appalachia: An Empirical Perspective on West Virginia Dialect Variation. *English Today* 26.13–22.

6 F

The authors present an accessible overview of English in West Virginia, followed by an empirical examination of ten dialect features. Five were found to be used less frequently: leveled *was* (e.g., *We was there*), demonstrative *them* (e.g., *She bought them berries*), *a*-prefixing (e.g., *She's a- working*), the *for-to* infinitive (e.g., *It wasn't for me to play sports*), perfective *done* (e.g., *He done washed the dishes*). The other five dialect features are being maintained by West Virginians at the same levels or at increased rates: the alveolar form of *-ing* (e.g., *We were walkin'*), consonant cluster reduction (e.g., *past* as *pas'*), vowel mergers (e.g., *pin/pen* with the same vowel), pleonastic pronouns (e.g., *My sister, she is a doctor*) and quotative *like* (e.g., *He was like, 'I'm not going'*).

Hazen, Kirk & Ellen Fluharty. 2004. Defining Appalachian English. In *Linguistic Diversity in the South: Changing Codes, Practices and Ideology*, ed. by M. Bender, 50-65. Athens, GA: University of Georgia Press.

6 F

Heath, Shirley Brice. 1982. What no bedtime story means: Narrative skills at home and school. *Language in Society* 11.1:49-76.

1 6 C N O

Heath, Shirley Brice. 1983. *Ways with Words: Language, Life and Work in Communities and Class Rooms*. New York: Cambridge University Press.

1 C N S

Heath, Shirley Brice. 2000. Linguistics in the Study of Language in Education. *Harvard Educational Review* 70.49–59.

N

Hefflin, Bena & Mary Barksdale-Ladd. 2001. African American Children's Literature That Helps Students Find Themselves: Selections for Grades K-3. *The Reading Teacher* 54.810–19.

1 C R

Henry, William. 2000. The Use of Creole Alongside Standard English to Stimulate Students' Learning. *Forum* 42.23–27.

2 C V

Herrin, Roberta T., Sheila Quinn Oliver & George Ella Lyon. 2010. *Appalachian Children's Literature: An Annotated Bibliography*. Jefferson, NCL McFarland.

6 C E

This is a annotated compilation of over 2000 children's books set in the thirteen-state region of Appalachia, indexed by author, title, illustrator, and subject matter.

Hester, Eva Jackson. 1996. Narratives of Young African American Children. In *Communication Development and Disorders in African American Children: Research, Assessment and Intervention,* ed. by A. Kamhi, K. Pollock & J. Harris, 227–45. Baltimore: Paul H. Brookes Publishing.

1 N Q

Higgins, Christina. 2010. Raising Critical Language Awareness in Hawai'i at Da Pidgin Coup. In *Creoles in Education: An Appraisal of Current Programs and Projects,* ed. by B. Migge, I. Leglise & A. Bartens, 118-36. Amsterdam: John Benjamins.

2 I P

Higgs, Robert & Ambrose Manning (eds.) 1975. *Voices from the Hills: Selected Readings of Southern Appalachia.* New York: Frederick Ungar Publishing.

6 C E F W

Higgs, Robert, Ambrose Manning & Jim Wayne Miller (eds.) 1995. *Appalachia inside Out: A Sequel to Voices from the Hills.* Knoxville: University of Tennessee Press.

6 C E F W

Hill, K. Dara. 2008. Providing Access to Standard and Nonstandard Writing Conventions: How a Teacher Encouraged His Students' Use of Literate Identity. *Penn GSE Perspectives on Urban Education* 5. [Reprinted with permission of the Penn Graduate School of Education from *Perspectives on Urban Education,* 5(2).]

1 6 B S W
Grounded in integrated and excerpt style (Emerson et al., 1995), this article chronicles Mr. Lehrer, an English teacher who provides his students access to standard and nonstandard writing conventions. Student writing samples and discursive practices illustrate enhanced awareness of distinctions between nonstandard language (African American Vernacular English and European American Vernacular English) and Standard English, against the backdrop of a suburban school experiencing problems of residency. Also examined is the historical construct that shapes current conditions and disparities between neighboring urban and suburban boundaries. In a climate where many teachers assume the home language of working-class Detroit children is deficient, Mr. Lehrer's practices are improvisational, based on changing demography in his classroom, for he assumes competence and a space for all students to recognize that they appropriate a deviation from Standard English.

Hill, K. Dara. 2009. Code-Switching Pedagogies and African American Student Voices: Acceptance and Resistance. *Journal of Adolescent & Adult Literacy* 53.120–31.

1 B S

Hill, Marc Lamont. 2009. *Beats, Rhymes and Classroom Life: Hip Hop Pedagogy and the Politics of Identity.* New York: Teachers College Press.

1 C

Hilliard, Asa. 1983. Psychological Factors Associated with Language in the Education of the African American Child. *Journal of Negro Education* 52.24–34.

1 A I

Hilliard, Asa. 1992. Behavioral Style, Culture, and Teaching and Learning. *Journal of Negro Education* 61.370–77.

1 C N

Hilliard, Asa. 1997. Language, Culture, and the Assessment of African-American Children. In *Assessment for Equity and Inclusion: Embracing All Our Children,* ed. by A. L. Goodwin, 229–38. New York: Routledge.

1 A I

Hilliard, Asa. 1999. Language, Diversity, and Assessment: Ideology, Professional Practice, and the Achievement Gap. In *Making the Connection,* ed. by C. Adger, D. Christian & O. Taylor, 125–36. Washington, D.C.: CAL/Delta.

1 A I T

Hinds, Suzanne Francis. 1990. Facing up to Home Truths: Use of Local Dialect in Jamaican Schools. *Times Educational Supplement.*16.

2 I V

Hinton, Leanne. 2001. Involuntary Language Loss among Immigrants: Asian-American Linguistic Autobiographies. In *Language in Our Time: Bilingual Education and Official English, Ebonics and Standard English, Immigration and the Unz Initiative (Georgetown University Round Table on Language and Linguistics 1999),* ed. by J. E. Alatis & A.-H. Tan, 203–52. Washington, D.C.: Georgetown University Press.

3 I Q

Hiramoto, Mie. 2011. Consuming the Consumers: Semiotics of Hawai'i Creole in Advertisements. *Journal of Pidgin and Creole Languages* 26.247–75.

2 I

Hirata-Edds, Tracy. 2011. Influence of Second Language Cherokee Immersion on Children's Development of Past Tense in Their First Language, English. *Language Learning* 61.700–33.

5 F X

Hirvela, Alan. 2010. Diverse Literacy Practices among Asian Language Populations: Implications for Theory and Pedagogy. In *Ethnolinguistic Diversity and Education: Language, Literacy and Culture,* ed. by M. Farr, L. Seloni & J. Song, 99–126. New York: Routledge.

3 E R S W
A cogent and comprehensive review article that surveys several strands of literature on Asian students: 'key perspectives' that frame contemporary studies of literacy; formal heritage language learning; school-based literacy; and out-of-school literacy contexts.

Hockman, Carol. 1973. Black Dialect Reading Tests in the Urban Elementary School. *Reading Teacher* 26.581–83.

1 A R X

Hoffman, Edwina. 1992. Oral Language Development. In *Teaching American Indian Students,* ed. by J. Reyhner, 132–42. Norman: University Oklahoma Press.

5 O

Hollie, Sharroky. 2001. Acknowledging the Language of African American Students: Instructional Strategies. *English Journal* 90.54-59.

1 B I S T
Hollie discusses the Linguistic Affirmation Program (LAP), a research-based language awareness program used in Los Angeles which has been successful in raising

achievement rates among minority students. Hollie explains that the classification of AAVE as a West African language, a dialect of English, or a Creole is unimportant. All that matters for classroom instruction is an acknowledgment that it is different from English but not deficient. Furthermore, research has shown that nonstandard language awareness is effective in raising literacy rates. Based on an implementation study, the author attributes the success of LAP to the combined use of instructional strategies within six key focus areas: Second Language Methodology (e.g., use of collaborative grouping), Building on Learning Styles and Strengths (e.g., presenting the same material to all students without watering it down), Cultural Awareness (e.g., use of culturally relevant literature), Balanced Literacy (e.g., contrastive phonetic analysis), Linguistic Awareness (e.g., introducing students to SAE vocabulary), and Classroom Learning Environment (e.g., classroom libraries with culturally conscious literature). The author concludes that systematization of LAP teaching will require that teachers receive professional development in the six focus areas, and that policy makers give the program an opportunity to work.

Holm, John. 2000. *An Introduction to Pidgins and Creoles.* Cambridge: Cambridge University Press.

2 F

Holm, John A. & with Alison Watt Shilling. 1982. *Dictionary of Bahamian English.* Cold Spring, NY: Lexik House.

2 F

Holmes, David G. 1999. Fighting Back by Writing Black: Beyond Racially Reductive Composition Theory. In *Race, Rhetoric and Composition,* ed. by K. Gilyard, 186-213. Portsmouth, NH: Boynton/Cook.

1 B S W

Holmes, Janet. 1997. Maori and Pakeha English: Some New Zealand Social Dialect Data. *Language in Society* 26.65–101.

6 F

Holt, Grace. 1975. Black English: Surviving the Bastardization Process. In *Ebonics: The True Language of Black Folk,* ed. by R. L. Williams, 64–74. St. Louis, MO: Robert L. Williams and Associates.

1 P

Holt, Grace. 1975. Metaphor, Black Discourse Style, and Cultural Reality. In *Ebonics: The True Language of Black Folks,* ed. by R. L. Williams, 86-95. St. Louis, MO: Robert L. Williams and Associates.

1 C N

Holton, Sylvia Wallace. 1984. *Down Home and Uptown: The Representation of Black Speech in American Fiction.* Rutherford, NJ: Fairleigh Dickinson University Press.

1 F I W

Honey, John. 1997. *Language Is Power: The Story of Standard English and Its Enemies.* London: Faber and Faber.

6 I P

Hoover, Mary. 1978. Community Attitudes toward Black English. *Language in Society* 7.65–87.

1 I
Eighty African American adults in East Palo Alto and Oakland, California, who had children in first or sixth grade, were interviewed regarding their attitudes toward their children using and being exposed to vernacular Black English versus standard Black English in a variety of social contexts. Attitudes were elicited by playing recorded speech samples and providing written samples, and then asking the respondents whether they would object to their children speaking/hearing/writing/reading in that way in the home/school/community. Over all, 85% of the respondents reported accepting the standard in all contexts and accepting the vernacular in informal contexts. Parents who commanded the standard were more accepting of their children being exposed to the vernacular than those parents who spoke only the vernacular themselves. Likewise, parents with more positive feelings toward their ethnicity were also positive toward the vernacular. The author concludes that the results do not indicate cultural self-rejection as previous work suggested, but rather that a dispreference for the vernacular in certain settings is a response to racism.

Hoover, Mary. 1989. *The 1-2-3 Method: A Writing Process for Bidialectal Students*. Edina, MN: Bellwether Press.

1 B C M S W

Hoover, Mary. 1991. Using the Ethnography of African-American Communications in Teaching Composition to Bidialectal Students. In *Languages in Schools and Society: Policy and Pedagogy*, ed. by M. McGroarty & C. Faltis, 465–85. Berlin: Walter de Gruyter.

1 B N S W

Hoover, Mary. 1998. A Recommended Reading List for Teachers of African American Students Who Speak Ebonics. *Journal of Negro Education* 67.43–47.

1 M S T

Hoover, Mary & E. Marsha Fabian. 2000. A Successful Program for Struggling Readers. *Reading Teacher* 53.474–76.

1 C R S T W
In this short paper, Hoover and Fabian describe a successful literacy program based on their years of work with struggling readers. First, they outline the characteristics of a successful school: the involvement of a strong administrator, emphasis on motivation and high expectation, extensive staff development, monitoring of student progress and considerable time devoted to reading and language arts, and the use of a structured phonic/linguistic approach to teaching reading. A sample lesson plan is then provided, illustrating some of the teaching techniques used in the program. The day begins with a brief daily affirmation. An exercise in phonemic awareness is then followed by a review of past material. After the new material is introduced, a variety of games are used as reinforcement activities. Next, texts are presented using only previously introduced patterns to give students practice reading. As the next component, teachers read aloud to their students in order to expose them to good literature. Finally, in writers' workshop, students then have the chance to produce their own material. The authors also emphasize the importance of stressing reading in the other subject areas for students in upper grades.

Hoover, Mary, Shirley Lewis, Robert Politzer, James Ford, Faye MacNair-Knox, Shirley Hicks & Darlene Williams. 1996. Tests of African American English for Teachers of Bidialectal Students. In *Handbook of Tests and Measurements for Black Populations,* ed. by R. Jones, 367–81. Hampton, VA: Cobb and Henry.

1 A T

Hoover, Mary, Faye McNair-Knox, Shirley Lewis & Robert Politzer. 1996. African American English Attitude Measures for Teachers. In *Handbook of Tests and Measurements for Black Populations,* ed. by R. L. Jones, 383–93. Hampton, VA: Cobb & Henry.

1 A I T

Hoover, Mary, Robert Politzer & Orlando Taylor. 1995. Bias in Reading Tests for Black Language Speakers: A Sociolinguistic Perspective. In *Testing African American Students: Special Reissue of the Negro Educational Review,* ed. by A. Hilliard, 51–68. Chicago: Third World Press.

1 A I P

Hoover, Mary Rhodes, Robert Politzer, Dwight Brown, Shirley Lewis, Shirley Hicks & Faye McNair-Knox. 1996. African American English Tests for Students. In *Handbook of Tests and Measurements for Black Populations,* ed. by R. L. Jones, 353–66. Hampton, VA: Cobb & Henry.

1 A B D

Hopson, Rodney. 2003. The Problem of the Language Line: Cultural and Social Reproduction of Hegemonic Linguistic Structures for Learners of African Descent in the USA. *Race, Ethnicity and Education* 6.227–45.

1 I K

Hornberger, Nancy. 2005. Special Issue: Heritage/Community Language Education: US and Australian Perspectives. *International Journal of Bilingual Education and Bilingualism* 8.

2 6 P V

Horton-Ikard, RaMonda. 2006. The Influence of Culture, Class, and Linguistic Diversity on Early Language Development. *Zero to Three* 27.6–12.

1 D Q
Effective intervention for early language delay in minority and poor children is difficult to provide because we know so little about its prevention, assessment, and treatment. This article provides an overview of an "integrative model of minority child development" that considers the influence of social factors such as race and class to explore how cultural and economic differences influence the processes of language development and the language skills of African American toddlers from poor backgrounds. The authors share findings from several studies that examine African American toddlers' performance on a variety of scales: measuring early language and grammatical abilities; the use of cultural dialect, known as African American English; and the influence of socioeconomic status on their vocabulary and word-learning abilities. The findings suggest that African American children demonstrate unique developmental trends in their processes of language acquisition while at the same time they demonstrate similar levels of language ability to that of the same-aged, White, Standard American English-speaking peers. Furthermore, standardized vocabulary measures provide an isolated and limited view of young African American children's true language learning abilities.

Horton-Ikard, RaMonda. 2009. Cohesive Adequacy in the Narrative Samples of School-Age Children Who Use African American English. *Language, Speech, and Hearing Services in Schools* 40.393–402.

1 N Q
Language samples from thirty-three African American children, aged seven to eleven years, were analyzed for AAE use and indicators of cohesion such as personal reference, demonstrative reference, lexical, and conjunctive markers. The study concluded that typically developing African American children used the same category types of cohesive devices observed among children who speak Standard American English.

Horvat, Erin McNamara & Kristine Lewis. 2003. Reassessing the "Burden of 'Acting White'": The Importance of Peer Groups in Managing Academic Success. *Sociology of Education* 76.265–80.

1 A C I
Challenging the 'acting White' hypothesis presented in Fordham and Ogbu 1986, Horvat and Lewis present case studies of eight academically successful female African American high school students. They find that these students, rather than living in constant fear of being accused of 'acting White', are actually quite confident within their social groups. When socializing with peers who do not value academics, they do try to downplay their success, but do so not for fear of ostracism, but rather to avoid making their friends feel uncomfortable. Furthermore, there is enough diversity among Black social groups that these young women have managed to find groups of highly supportive, like-minded students who embrace success and consider it in harmony with their African American heritage. Although the research presented here does not cover male students or academically unsuccessful students, the authors deem this "positive power found in some Black peer groups" (p. 276) to be worthy of follow-up in addressing the Black-White achievement gap.

Hosoda, Megumi. 2007. Listeners' Cognitive and Affective Reactions to English Speakers with Standard American English and Asian Accents. *Perceptual and Motor Skills* 104.307–26.

3 6 I O

Huber, Magnus. 1999. *Ghanaian Pidgin English in Its West African Context: A Sociohistorical and Structural Analysis.* Amsterdam: John Benjamins.

2 F

Hudson, Joyce. 1992. Fostering English Language in Kimberly Schools: An in-Service Course for Teachers. In *Pidgins, Creoles and Nonstandard Dialects in Education, Applied Linguistics Association of Australia Occasional Paper Number 12,* ed. by J. Siegel, 124–26.

2 M S

Hudson, Joyce & A. Taylor. 1987. Teaching English to Kriol Speakers: Where on Earth Do I Start? *The Aboriginal Child at School* 15.3–19.

2 S

Huebner, Thom. 1985. Language Education Policy in Hawaii: Two Case Studies and Some Current Issues. *International Journal of Society and Language* 56.29–49.

2 P

Hunt, Barbara Carey. 1974. Black Dialect and Third and Fourth Graders' Performance on the Gray Oral Reading Test. *Reading Research Quarterly* 1.103–23.

1 A R

Hutcheson, Neal. 1999. *Indian by Birth: The Lumbee Dialect*. Raleigh: The North Carolina Language and Life Project.

6 F P Z
"Stripped of their heritage language generations ago, the Lumbee Indians of Southeaster North Carolina carved out a unique dialect of English to maintain their distinctive cultural identity." [From the website http://ncsu.edu/linguistics/talkingnc/products/indianbybirth.php] Professor Walt Wolfram is the creator and executive producer of the North Carolina Language and Life Project [NCLLP] at North Carolina State University.

Hutcheson, Neal. 2000. *The Ocracoke Brogue: A Portrait of Hoi Toider Speech*. Raleigh: North Carolina Language and Life Project. North Carolina Language and Life Project.

6 F Z
"In *The Ocracoke Brogue*, native islander share their stories and explain many of the words and phrases in the local dialect." [From the website http://ncsu.edu/linguistics/talkingnc/products/ocracokebrogue.php] Ocracoke is an island off the coast of North Carolina. Professor Walt Wolfram is the creator and executive producer of the North Carolina Language and Life Project [NCLLP] at North Carolina State University, under whose auspices this video was produced.

Hutcheson, Neal. 2005. V*oices of North Carolina: Language, Dialect, and Identity in the Tarheel State*. Raleigh: The North Carolina Language and Life Project.

6 F I Z
"Cherokees, Lumbees, rural and urban African Americans, Spanish-speaking immigrants, and the new generation of southerners in metropolitan areas all reveal how their way with words communicates their identity." [From the website, http://ncsu.edu/linguistics/talkingnc/products/voicesofnc.php] Professor Walt Wolfram is the creator and executive producer of the North Carolina Language and Life Project [NCLLP] at North Carolina State University. See Wolfram and Schilling-Estes' 1997 book on the Ocracoke Brogue, also in this bibliography.

Hwa-Froelich, Deborah, Dania C. Kasambira & Amy Marie Moleski. 2007. Communicative Functions of African American Head Start Children. *Communication Disorders Quarterly* 28.77–91.

1 A D N T

Hyon, S. & E. Sulzby. 1994. African American Kindergartners' Spoken Narratives: Topic Associating and Topic Centered Styles. *Linguistics and Education* 6.121–52.

1 N

Ibukun, Yinka. 2010. Nigeria Harnesses Pidgin English Power. In *The Guardian Weekly*. UK.

2 P

IDB & CDB. 2009. *Literacy and Numeracy in the Caribbean: A Subregional Meeting*. Washington, D.C.: Inter-American Development Bank.

2 R V

This report of a December 2008 Caribbean subregional meeting on literacy and numeracy in the Caribbean sponsored by the Inter-American Development Bank (IDB) and Caribbean Development Bank (CDB) contains interesting data on literacy achievement and improvement in several Caribbean countries (see especially the overview by Ana Cristina Accioly de Amorim), and relevant papers by Hazel Simmons-McDonald, Stafford Griffith and others. It is available online at: http://tinyurl.com/dyzck2e or https://www.caribank.org/titanweb/cdb/webcms.nsf/AllDoc/D5D3BBE A4581915C042577A7005F56D7/$File/IDB_CDB_Barbados_Report3%20with%20 IDB%20and%20CDB%20last%20version.pdf

Igboanusi, Herbert. 2002. *A Dictionary of Nigerian English Usage*. Ibadan: Enicrownfit.

2 F

Igboanusi, Herbert. 2008. Empowering Nigerian Pidgin: A Challenge for Status Planning? *World Englishes* 27.68–82.

2 I P

Igoudin, Lane. In preparation. Asian American Girls Who Speak African American English: A Subcultural Language Identity. In *Multilingual Identities: New Global Perspectives*, ed. by I. DuBois & N. Baumgarten. Berlin: Mouton.

1 3 I U

This study investigates language attitudes and practices of three Asian American adolescent girls enrolled in a Southern California high school who use elements of African American Vernacular English (AAVE) in their everyday speech. The study confirms the presence of a variety of phonological, morphosyntactic, and lexical features of AAVE in the subjects' speech. Cognizant of AAVE's stigma and their use of it, the girls nonetheless express affinity for it. They also show varying degrees of ability to codeswitch between AAVE and Standard American English. The study establishes the connection between the subjects' language code choice and their identity construction, primarily as a means to acquire membership in their multicultural peer group by using the target group's code of choice. The use of AAVE in this context provides an opportunity to gain the subcultural capital and access the desired personal power and prestige among peers. The variance between these girls' anticipated social identities and their code choice actually helps them attain the benefits of crosscultural socialization.

ILEA Afro-Caribbean Language and Literacy Project in Further & Adult Education. 1990. *Language and Power*. London: Harcourt Brace Jovanovich.

2 F L P

Irish, J. A. George. 1995. *Caribbean Students in New York*. New York: Caribbean Diaspora Press.

2 E S

Irish, J. A. George & Coleen Clay. 1995. *Assessment of Caribbean Students: A Guide for Assessing Children from Caricom Nation States and Dependent Territories*. Brooklyn: Caribbean Diaspora Press (Medgar Evers College).

2 A

Irvine, Alison. 2008. Contrast and Convergence in Standard Jamaican English: The Phonological Architecture of the Standard in an Ideologically Bidialectal Community. *World Englishes* 27.9–25.

2 F I

Irvine, Jacqueline Jordan. 1990. *Black Students and School Failure: Policies, Practices, and Prescriptions.* Westport, CT: Greenwood Press.

1 A C I T

Irvine, Jacqueline Jordan (ed.) 2002. *In Search of Wholeness: African American Teachers and Their Culturally Specific Classroom Practices.* New York: Palgrave.

1 A C E T

Irvine, Jacqueline Jordan. 2003. *Educating Teachers for Diversity: Seeing with a Cultural Eye.* New York: Teachers College Press.

1 A C T

Irvine, Jacqueline Jordan. 2003. The Education of Children Whose Nightmares Come Both Day and Night. In *Educating Teachers for Diversity,* ed. by J. J. Irvine, 1–14. New York: Teachers College Press.

1 A C S T

Irvine outlines four proposed theories for explaining the achievement gap: the socio-economic, claiming that low family income and status correlate to low achievement; the sociopathological, claiming that cultural disadvantage is to blame; the (refuted) genetic, claiming that African Americans are inherently less intelligent, despite ample evidence to the contrary, and the cultural-incongruence, which posits that the cultural differences between home and school life cause misunderstanding and hostility. Building on this latter theory, Irvine is convinced that the solution lies in educating teachers to be sufficiently compassionate and understanding, and to treat minority children with dignity.

Isaacs, Gale. 1996. Persistence of Non-Standard Dialect in School-Age Children. *Journal of Speech and Hearing Research* 39.434–41.

1 6 A O R

Isenbarger, Joan & Veta Smith. 1973. How Would You Feel If You Had to Change Your Dialect? *English Journal* 62.994–96. [Abstract prepared by the author and reprinted with permission of the author from the Educational Resources Information Center at eric.ed.gov.]

I T

The authors provide a short, qualitative description of an experimental workshop for White pre-service teachers in which the positions of AAVE and Standard English were reversed. They conclude that the experiential nature of the lesson provoked aspiring teachers to think more carefully about the "psychological aspects" of dialect change.

Isenbarger, Lynn & Arlette Ingram Willis. 2006. An Intersection of Theory and Practice: Accepting the Language a Child Brings into the Classroom. *Language Arts* 84.125–35.

1 I T

This article draws from the experiences of a European American classroom teacher, her African American teacher educator, the classroom teacher's interactions with an African American family, and her conversations with her African American aide. It answers the call to speak to the everyday experiences of teachers who seek to acknowledge and address the linguistic and cultural understandings that students bring with them to our classrooms and explores the tension a teacher experiences as she navigates between theories she is reading and discussing in her university coursework and the expectations and understandings of the parents and aide of an African American male who is a student in her classroom. In addition, the teacher educator makes recommendations for applying theory and research in multilingual and multicultural classrooms.

Ivy, Lennette J. & Julie J. Masterson. 2011. A Comparison of Oral and Written English Styles in African American Students at Different Stages of Writing Development. *Language, Speech, and Hearing Services in Schools* 42.31–40.

F Q W
Fifteen African American third graders and fifteen African American eighth graders were asked to respond to interview questions and complete retellings both verbally and in writing. Using a dialect density measure, the rates of six distinctive AAVE features in speaking and in writing were compared. Results revealed that while AAVE usage was similar in speaking and in writing for third graders, eighth graders used more AAVE in speaking than in writing.

Jackson, Austin & Geneva Smitherman. 2002. 'Black People Tend to Talk Eubonics': Race and Curricular Diversity in Higher Education. In *Strategies for Teaching First-Year Composition,* ed. by D. H. Roen, V. Pantoja, L. Yena, S. K. Miller & E. Waggoner, 46–51. Urbana, IL: National Council of Teachers of English.

1 S W

Jackson, Janice & Barbara Pearson. 2010. Variable Use of Features Associated with African American English by Typically Developing Children. *Topics in Language Disorders* 30.135–44.

1 D F Q

Jackson, Ronald & Elaine Richardson (eds.) 2003. *Understanding African American Rhetoric.* New York: Routledge.

1 E N

Jaggar, Angela & Bernice Cullinan. 1974. Teaching Standard English to Achieve Bidialectalism: Problems with Current Practices. *Florida FL Reporter* 12.63–70.

1 B V
Jaggar and Cullinan outline four major concerns with trends in bidialectal education, centered around the theme that hasty implementation has obscured the true nature and goals of bidialectalism. First, misguided instruction may result when teachers, based on misinterpretation of research findings, view AAVE as a foreign language rather than a dialect mutually intelligible with English, and fail to see the continuum of variability existing between them. Second, research suggests that AAVE-speaking children already possess considerable productive and receptive competence in SAE, yet many programs in bidialectalism do not take this into account. Third, for the sake of expediency, several important practices are left out of programs: initial diagnosis of students' competence and subsequent evaluation of progress, focus on communicative competence (i.e., knowledge of when to use each dialect) rather than mere linguistic competence, and focus on the most important contrastive features before moving onto the less important ones. Finally, explicit instruction in the structural differences between the two dialects may be too artificial to be effective; research shows that code-switching is a natural phenomenon, and therefore students would benefit from more natural, experience-based techniques.

Jamaican Language Unit. 2009. *Writing Jamaican the Jamaican Way / Ou Fi Rait Jamiekan.* Kingston, Jamaica: Arawak Publications.

2 F V W

Jencks, Christopher & Meredith Phillips. 1998. *The Black-White Test Score Gap.* Washington, D.C.: Brookings Institution Press.

A R

Jia, Gisela & Doris Aaronson. 2003. A Longitudinal Study of Chinese Children and Adolescents Learning English in the United States. *Applied Psycholinguistics* 24.131–61.

3 6 I Q

Jia, Gisela, Doris Aaronson & Yanhong Wu. 2002. Long-Term Language Attainment of Bilingual Immigrants: Predictive Variables and Language Group Differences. *Applied Psycholinguistics* 23.599–621.

3 6 Q

Jibril, Munzali. 1995. The Elaboration of the Functions of Nigerian Pidgin. In *New Englishes: A West African Perspective,* ed. by A. Bamgboṣe, A. Banjo & A. Thomas, 232–47. Ibadan: Mosuro.

2 I

Johnson, Helen. 1985. Tips for Language Teaching: Teacher Attitude and Ghetto Language. In *Tapping Potential: English and Language Arts for the Black Learner,* ed. by C. Brooks, 75–77. Urbana, IL: NCTE.

1 I S T

Johnson, Kenneth. 1969. Pedagogical Problems of Using Second Language Techniques for Teaching Standard English to Speakers of Nonstandard Negro Dialect. *Florida FL Reporter* 7.75–87, 154.

1 B I S
Although convinced that second language techniques are more effective than traditional methods in teaching SAE to speakers of AAVE, Johnson offers several caveats that must be considered before adopting this approach. First, teachers' negative attitudes toward AAVE have a detrimental effect on student performance, and in order to become successful instructors they must first be trained in the systematicity of AAVE. Moreover, students may have little motivation for learning SAE; they are proud of their distinctive language and may view learning SAE as a capitulation to White culture. Some students see no advantage in learning it and risk ostracism for using it in their social circles. The relative similarity between AAVE and SAE can also cause problems: differences between the two dialects are often so subtle that children may produce AAVE forms without realizing that they are nonstandard. Johnson cautions against repetitive drilling in SAE: it may be too tedious since children already have competence in the standard. Finally, decontextualized drills may alienate children who already "speak English." Johnson suggests that students first be taught about the nature of dialects in order to accept instruction in SAE.

Johnson, Kenneth. 1974. A Comparison of Black-Dialect Speaking Children and Standard English-Speaking Children and Their Ability to Hear Final Consonant Stops. *TESOL Quarterly* 3.375–87.

1 O Q X

Johnson, Kennneth. 1979. Teaching Mainstream American English: Similarities and Differences with Speakers of Ebonics and Speakers of Foreign Languages. *Journal of Black Studies* 9.11–22.

1 B S T

Johnson, Sylvia, Sharon-Ann Gopaul-McNicol & Frederick Harper (eds.) 1998. *Special Focus Section: African American Education and the Ebonics Issue.* (*Journal of Negro Education* 67).

1 A D E I K P Q S T

Johnson, Valerie & Jill de Villiers. 2009. Syntactic Frames in Fast Mapping Verbs: Effect of Age, Dialect, and Clinical Status. *Journal of Speech, Language & Hearing Research* 52.610–22.

1 F

Joiner, Charles. 1979. *The Ann Arbor Decision: Memorandum Opinion and Order and the Educational Plan.* Washington, D.C.: Center for Applied Linguistics.

1 I K P

Jones, Allen (ed.) 1965. *Language Teaching, Linguistics, and the Teaching of English in a Multilingual Society.* Kingston, Jamaica: University of the West Indies, Faculty of Education.

2 E R W

Jones, Dalton. 1979. Ebonics and Reading. *Journal of Black Studies* 9.423–48.

1 R S X

Jones draws on previous work to raise three potential obstacles faced by AAVE-speakers learning to read: teachers unfamiliar with AAVE may misinterpret pronunciation differences as reading errors, students' lack of familiarity with SAE structure may hinder fluent reading, and younger students who have not yet internalized receptive competence in the phonology of SAE may have trouble learning with the phonics approach. The author considers evidence from reading theory as supportive of the appropriateness of beginning reading materials written in the children's dialect, but points out that this method has its drawbacks given the question of transfer, the variability within each child's speech and from child to child, and the possible lack of social acceptance. Finally, the author describes a curriculum used over a three-year period with pre-schoolers which emphasizes inductive rather than deductive learning, attempting to exploit the children's natural learning style. Before being formally introduced to the alphabet or phonics, children participated in activities aimed at helping them understand the concept of reading and detect the structural patterns inherent in the orthography. Through these and other motivational techniques, all the five year olds in the program were reading by the end of the year, and eight of the ten who moved onto first grade were placed in advanced or second grade reading groups.

Jones, Shirley. 1972. The role of the public school speech clinician with the inner-city child. *Journal of Language, Speech, and Hearing Services in Schools* 3 (2): 20–29.

1 D

Jordan, June. 1985. Nobody Mean More to Me Than You and the Future Life of Willie Jordan. In *On Call: Political Essays*, 157–73. Boston: South End Press.

1 I P W

This classic essay by author and poet June Jordan is essentially about attitudes towards American Black English. It begins with the discomfort expressed by students in one of her college classes, most of whom were African American, about the vernacular language in Alice Walker's book, *The Color Purple.* ("Why she have them talk so funny? It don't sound right." p. 159.) In response, Jordan gets them to translate Walker's dialogue into Standard English, and in the wake of the ludicrousness and hilarity this produces, she goes on to help them understand the systematic rules of Black English, and to continue translating back and forth between Standard English and Black English. This would have been interesting enough in itself, but there was more. Reggie Jordan, the brother of one of the students in the class, Willie Jordan, was murdered by Brooklyn police, and the class, moved and incensed, wanted to write a series of condolences to Willie's family, and a series of messages to the police. They also wanted to get the condolences and messages published in *Newsday*, preceded by an explanatory paragraph. But the question then arose about whether this should be written in Standard English (to increase the probability of getting published) or in Black English (to best serve the memory of Willie's brother and to remain true to their identities). In the end, they decided to write in Black English. But neither *Newsday* nor the *Village Voice* nor other news outlets published or responded to the piece, and the essay leaves readers to debate whether this was because of the language, the content, or other considerations.

Jordan, June. 1989. White English/Black English: The Politics of Translation. In *Moving Towards Home: Political Essays*. London: Virago.

1 B I P U

Jordan, June. 2002. Problems of Language in a Democratic State. In *Some of Us Did Not Die: New and Selected Essays of June Jordan*, 223–32. New York: Basic.

1 I P

Journal of Black Psychology 23.3. 1997. *Special Section on Ebonics.*

1 K

Journal of English Linguistics 32.3. 1998. *Special Issue: Ebonics.*

1 K

Journal of Negro Education 67.1. 1998. *Special Focus Section: African American Education and the Ebonics Issue.*

1 K

Kachru, Braj B. 1997. World Englishes and English-Using Communities. *Annual Review of Applied Linguistics* 17.66–87. [Abstract prepared by ERIC.]

6 E I P
A review of literature since 1990 on world English focuses on theoretical, conceptual, descriptive, ideological, and power-related issues, including: types of diaspora; English-using communities; dynamics of those communities; monolingual paradigms and heteroglossic English forms; transcultural literary creativity; codification and authentication of English; convention in usage; the roles of English; and language attitudes. A nine-item annotated bibliography is included.

Kachru, Braj B., Yamuna Kachru & Cecil L. Nelson (eds.) 2009. *The Handbook of World Englishes*. (Blackwell Handbooks in Linguistics). Malden, MA: Oxford: Blackwell.

E F

Kachuck, Beatrice. 1978. Black English and Reading: Research Issues. *Education and Urban Society* 10.385–98.

1 A B O R
In light of the low reading achievement among AAVE-speaking children, Kachuck reviews the relevant literature and examines it within a framework of reading theory. Several conclusions are drawn. First, by the first grade, Black children have an active vocabulary corresponding well to that of first-grade basal readers, and exhibit some

degree of bidialectalism. However, the research suggests that the label "bidialectal" itself may be problematic, since the rate at which children use dialect features varies depending on the sampling method (with spontaneous production yielding higher dialect feature rates than sentence repetition). Second, the existing research has shown that reading comprehension is only weakly correlated with oral productive and receptive competence of Standard English. Since the results of many studies may have been skewed by the exclusion of nonreaders, studies taking place at the reading acquisition stage are recommended. It is also suggested that future studies might benefit from taking into account cognitive and affective variables, and from examining which specific dialect features produced by children affect reading comprehension.

Kamhi, Alan, Karen Pollock & Joyce Harris (eds.) 1996. *Communication Development and Disorders in African American Children: Research, Assessment, and Intervention.* Baltimore: Paul H. Brookes Publishing.

1 A D E Q S

Kamhi-Stein, Lia. 2003. Reading in Two Languages: How Attitudes toward Home Language and Beliefs About Reading Affect the Behaviors of "Underprepared" L2 College Readers. *TESOL Quarterly* 37.35–71.

4 I R

Kamil, Michael L., P. David Pearson, Elizabeth Birr Moje & Peter P. Afflerback. 2011. *Handbook of Reading Research*, Volume IV. New York: Routledge.

R

Kaplan, Robert B. 1994. Language Policy and Planning in New Zealand. *Annual Review of Applied Linguistics* 14.156–76. [Abstract prepared by ERIC.]

2 P

A discussion of language policy formation and planning in New Zealand focuses on the need for a national languages policy and governmental human resource development planning. It includes "unplanned" language planning; the multilingual/multicultural situation, including Maori, Pacific Islands, other, international, and English languages; and other sociocultural issues influencing the language situation.

Katz, Laurie & Tempii Champion. 2009. There's No "1" Way to Tell a Story. In *Affirming Students' Right to Their Own Language: Bridging Language Policies and Pedagogical Practices*, ed. by J. Cobb Scott, D. Straker & L. Katz, 192–205. New York: Routledge/National Council of Teachers of English.

1 N

Katz, Laurie, Jerrie Cobb Scott & Xenia Hadjioannou. 2009. Exploring Attitudes toward Language Differences: Implications for Teacher Education Programs. In *Affirming Students' Right to Their Own Language: Bridging Language Policies and Pedagogical Practices*, ed. by J. Cobb Scott, D. Straker & L. Katz, 99–116. New York: Routledge/National Council of Teachers of English.

1 I T

Kawakami, Alice. 1999. Sense of Place, Community, and Identity: Bridging the Gap between Home and School for Hawaiian Students. *Education and Urban Society* 32.18–40.

2 C I

Kawakami explains how the colonization of Hawaii and subsequent reforms left the indigenous people with an educational system that alienated them from their traditional cultural values, resulting in underachievement. Based on interviews with Hawaiian educators, it was concluded that a successful education experience would have to take place in a culturally authentic environment and include hands-on activity, and recent attempts at reform have focused on fostering new kinds of learning communities that correlate traditional values (devotion to family and community, love of the land, etc.) with educational points. After outlining a number of recent initiatives in this vein, the author concludes that the learning community model is a success, and that new policies, provisions and programs should be enacted to ensure its expansion and endurance.

Keen, John. 1978. *Teaching English: A Linguistic Approach*. London: Methuen & Co Ltd.

F S W

Kellerman, Eric. 1995. Crosslinguistic Influence: Transfer to Nowhere? *Annual Review of Applied Linguistics* 15.125–50. [Abstract prepared by ERIC.]

X

Reviews recent research on crosslinguistic influence, focusing on the part played by knowledge of one's first language in the acquisition of a second language (L2). It is also argued that there can be transfer that is not licensed by similarity to the L2, and where the way the L2 works may largely go unheeded.

Kells, Michelle Hall. 2006. Tex Mex, Metalingual Discourse, and Teaching College Writing. In *Dialects, Englishes, Creoles, and Education*, ed. by S. Nero, 185–201. Mahwah, NJ: Lawrence Erlbaum Associates.

4 I L W

Kendall, Tyler & Walt Wolfram. 2009. Local and External Language Standards in African American English. *Journal of English Linguistics* 37.305–30.

1 F

Kennedy, Eileen. 2006. Literacy Development of Linguistically Diverse First Graders in a Mainstream English Classroom: Connecting Speaking and Writing. *Journal of Early Childhood Literacy* 6.163–89. [Reprinted with permission of Sage Publications from *Journal of Early Childhood Literacy* 6(2), 163.]

1 2 6 O W

Children who speak different home languages and dialects in a monolingual classroom often carry the challenge of having to develop literacy in a different language. This article presents a qualitative study of five first graders who speak different home languages in an inner city mainstream English classroom. Through interviews, classroom writing, field notes, and recorded classroom interaction, Kennedy presents findings that indicate that writing in mainstream English can be problematic cognitively and emotionally for these children. Kennedy also offers some ways to foster an intercultural space for these children in a monolingual classroom and help find a way of validating diverse students' language and culture.

Kephardt, Ronald. 1992. Reading Creole English Does Not Destroy Your Brain Cells. In *Pidgins, Creoles and Nonstandard Dialects in Education*, ed. by J. Siegel, 67–84.

2 I R V

In this revision of a paper originally presented at a TESOL meeting in April 1987, Kephart describes his development of a phonemic orthography for Carriacou Creole English (CCE), which he then introduced to a treatment group of twelve year olds in

Carriacou (Grenada, West Indies) who used it to practice reading in their native language for two to three sessions per week. These students, along with a control group of comparable students who continued to be instructed in Standard English only, were tested regularly in their ability to read in Standard English. While the results were not conclusive enough to state that reading practice in CCE improved the students' abilities to read in Standard English, it was not shown to be detrimental. Because of this, and the "enjoyment and enthusiasm" observed among the students while reading in CCE, Kephart concludes that students should be allowed to gain literacy in their native language as well as in Standard English.

Kernan-Mitchell, Claudia. 1971. *Language behavior in a Black urban community.* Monographs of the Language-Behavior Laboratory, Volume 2. University of California, Berkeley.

Kinloch, Valerie. 2005. Poetry, Literacy, and Creativity: Fostering Effective Learning Strategies in an Urban Classroom. *English Education* 37.96–114. [Abstract prepared by ERIC and reprinted with permission of the Department of Education from the Education Resources Information Center at eric.ed.gov.]

1 4 C W
In this essay, the author argues for a democratized way of developing a consciousness of differences by describing two abbreviated creative writing classroom experiences with urban sixth grade middle school students during the 2002-2003 academic year. She draws on Tony Medina's (2001) claim that poetry and writing weave people and worlds together as she highlights how students' interaction with one another and with her, based on reciprocal and mutual exchanges, heightens their speaking, writing, and literacy skills. The goals of this essay are: (1) to highlight democratic prospects of literacy for sixth grade middle school poet-learners in an alternative, twenty-eight-week creative writing program; (2) to illustrate how creative strategies can "promote writing as act of change" (Kinloch, 2002, p. 10); and (3) to offer implications of creativity on student authorization to use original ideas, "word habits" (Jordan, 1985, p.123), and multiple perspectives to enhance academic and personal identities. The author begins with a brief description of the creative writing program, and then discusses how specific creative strategies, exchanges, and student writings contribute to a call for consciousness of differences of urban sixth grade middle school students who represent diverse heritages (e.g., Mexican, Bosnian, African, and African American).

Kinloch, Valerie. 2005. Revisiting the Promise of "Students' Right to Their Own Language": Pedagogical Strategies. *College Composition and Communication* 57. 83–113. [Reprinted from *College Composition and Communication* 57(1).]

1 4 B P
The implications of the "Students' Right to Their Own Language" resolution on classroom teaching and practices point to a continual need to reevaluate how communicative actions—linguistic diversities—of students are central aspects of the work within composition courses. This article revisits the historical significance and pedagogical value of the resolution in its critique of student-teacher exchanges, in its advancement of strategies that invite language variations into composition courses, and in its proposal to support the expressive rights of students.

Kinloch, Valerie. 2009. Power, Politics, and Pedagogies: Re-Imagining Students' Right to Their Own Language through Democratic Engagement. In *Affirming Students' Right to Their Own Language: Bridging Language Policies and Pedagogical Practices,* ed. by J. Cobb Scott, D. Straker & L. Katz, 85–98. New York: Routledge/National Council of Teachers of English.

1 P

Kinloch, Valerie. 2010. "To Not Be a Traitor of Black English": Youth Perceptions of Language Rights in an Urban Context. *Teachers College Record* 112.103–41. [Adapted from the original abstract with permission of the journal from *Teachers College Record* 112(1).]

1 I P U
Using an ethnographic approach, this study details how youth perceive language rights in their academic and community lives, particularly in relation to what they name "Black English" and "Academic English." Data for this ethnographic project, which derive from a larger ongoing multiyear study on youth representations of community and literacy, were collected from two African American teenage males who reside in or near New York City's Harlem community. The article uses a case study design to examine youth perceptions of language in their struggle to acquire academic success.

Kirkland, David. 2010. English(Es) in Urban Contexts: Politics, Pluralism, and Possibilities. *English Education* 42.293–306. [Abstract prepared by ERIC and reprinted with permission of the Department of Education from the Education Resources Information Center at eric.ed.gov.]

1 N R W
This article draws on data taken from two studies conducted on literacy and urban youth—"Boys in the Hood" and "Literacies in Online Social Communities" projects. In the "Boys in the Hood" project, the author examined how six young Black men practiced literacy from 2003 to 2006. In the "Literacies in Online Social Communities" project, a study spanning more than two years, the author examined the discourses of urban youth in online social communities. These empirical contexts undergird an analysis of the question: How do urban youth use languages for social, cultural, and political purposes? The author analyzed data, using ethnographic and critical discourse approaches. Blending the two approaches, he explored emergent patterns in the data to chart the expansion and intensification of variance in the youths' language practices. Implications for English education research, policy, and practice are presented.

Kirkland, David & Austin Jackson. 2009. Beyond the Silence: Instructional Approaches and Students' Attitudes. In *Affirming Students' Right to Their Own Language: Bridging Language Policies and Pedagogical Practices,* ed. by J. Cobb Scott, D. Straker & L. Katz, 132–50. New York: Routledge/National Council of Teachers of English.

1 B I P S

Kirkpatrick, Andy (ed.) 2002. *Englishes in Asia: Communication, Identity, Power and Education.* Melbourne, Australia: Language Australia Ltd.

3 6 E F P

Kirschner, Samuel & G. Howard Poteet. 1973. Nonstandard English Usage in the Writing of Black, White, and Hispanic Remedial English Students in an Urban Community College. *Research in the Teaching of English* 7.351–55.

1 4 W X
The authors examine the writing of 109 low-income remedial English students at a community college, and conclude that there are no significant differences between non-standard usage of Blacks, Whites, and Hispanics. Coding categories are not transparent and titles (e.g., wrong word) suggest that the coding was not linguistically informed.

Koch, Lisa & Alan Gross. 1997. Children's Perceptions of Black English as a Variable in Intraracial Perception. *Journal of Black Psychology* 23.215–26. [Reprinted with permission of Sage Publications, the publisher, from *Journal of Black Psychology* 23(3), 215.]

1 I

The purpose of this investigation is to examine African American children's perceptions of those African Americans who use Black English (BE) in contrast to those who use Standard English (SE). Previous studies examining adult perceptions revealed that as middle-class African Americans move more toward the mainstream of American culture, their perceptions of African Americans who speak BE have become more negative. However, previous research with children indicates that children may in fact view BE as more positive than SE. In the present study, African American male and female junior high students were exposed to an audiotaped male speaking in either BE or SE. Participants were then asked to rate the speaker on a number of personality characteristics. Results indicated that contrary to the literature with African American adults, African American children rated the BE model as more likable and competent than the SE model.

Koch, Lisa, Alan Gross & Russell Kolts. 2001. Attitudes toward Black English and Codeswitching. *Journal of Black Psychology* 27.29–42.

1 I U

Using the matched guise technique, the authors asked 102 African American undergraduates at a predominantly White southeastern US university to evaluate audiotapes of an African American speaking in an informal (conversations with a friend) and formal (job interview) context in one of four guises: Black English (BE) in both contexts, Standard English (SE) in both, appropriate code switching (ACS)—SE in the formal, BE in the informal context, and inappropriate code switching (ICS)—BE in the formal, SE in the informal context. Subjects rated the "speaker" they heard on a Speech Dialect Attitudinal Scale with twelve pairs of adjectives in three groups: socio-intellectual status (e.g., literate/illiterate), aesthetic quality (e.g., pleasing/displeasing) and dynamism (e.g., strong/weak). The SE and ACS speakers were rated higher on socio-intellectual status than the BE and ICS ones. Subjects also felt that the SE and ACS speakers would be more desirable work partners than the BE or ICS ones, but said they would like to get to know the BE speaker as much as the SE or ACS speakers, suggesting that BE was "not viewed as inherently negative" (p. 40), but as inappropriate in formal contexts. The authors suggest directions for further research, including replication with non-students.

Kochman, Thomas (ed.) 1972. *Rappin' and Stylin' Out: Communication in Urban Black America*. Urbana: University of Illinois Press.

1 E F N O

An important reader in its day, this edited volume on the language and discourse styles of African Americans contains several articles that are still worth reading for those working with speakers of AAVE in schools, including: Benjamin G. Cooke, "Nonverbal communication among African Americans: An initial classification"; Claude Brown, "The language of soul"; Grace Sims Holt, "'Inversion' in Black communication"; Roger D. Abrahams, "Joking: The training of the man of words in talking broad"; Thomas Kochman, "Toward an ethnography of Black American speech behavior"; William Labov, "Rules for ritual insults"; and Claudia Mitchell-Kernan, "Signifying, loud-talking and marking".

Kochman, Thomas. 1974. Standard English Revisited, or, Who's Kidding/Cheating Who(M)? *The Florida FL Reporter* 12.31–44, 96.

1 B I P

Kochman, Thomas. 1981. *Black and White Styles in Conflict*. Chicago: University of Chicago Press.

1 I N O

Drawing on the literature on vernacular communicative norms and his experience as an instructor in racially integrated secondary and post-secondary settings, Kochman describes a set of linguistic behaviors and expectations that "reveal or clarify cultural reasons for communication difficulty." Chapters include "Classroom Modalities," "Fighting Words," "Boasting and Bragging," and "Information as Property," among others.

Kochman, Thomas. 1989. Black and White Cultural Styles in Pluralistic Perspective. In *Test Policy and Test Performance: Education, Language and Culture,* ed. by B. Gifford, 259–96. Boston: Kluwer.

1 C N O

Kohn, Mary Elizabeth. 2008. *Latino English in North Carolina: A Comparison of Emerging Communities.* Raleigh: North Carolina State University.

4 F U

Kortmann, Bernd & Clive Upton. 2008. *The British Isles.* Berlin: Mouton de Gruyter.

2 6 F

Koskinen, Arja. 2010. Kriol in Caribbean Nicaragua Schools. In *Creoles in Education: An Appraisal of Current Programs and Projects,* ed. by B. Migge, I. Leglise & A. Bartens, 133-66. Amsterdam: John Benjamins.

2 P T

Kouega, Jean-Paul. 2006. *Aspects of Cameroon English Usage: A Lexical Appraisal.* Munich, Germany: Lincom Europa.

2 6 F

Kouega, Jean-Paul. 2008. *A Dictionary of Cameroon Pidgin English Usage: Pronunciation, Grammar and Vocabulary.* Munich, Germany: Lincom Europa.

2 F

Kouwenberg, Silvia, Winnie Anderson-Brown, Terri-Ann Barrett, Shyrel-Ann, Dean Tamirand De Lisser, Havenol Douglas, Marsha Forbes, Autense France, Lorna Gordon, Byron Jones, Novelette McLean & Jodianne Scott. 2011. Linguistics in the Caribbean: Empowerment through Creole Language Awareness. *Journal of Pidgin and Creole Languages* 26.387–403.

2 C I K

Kretzschmar, William (ed.) 1998. *Special Issue: Ebonics. Journal of English Linguistics* 26.

1 E I K P

Kretzschmar, William. 2008. Public and Academic Understandings About Language: The Intellectual History of Ebonics. *English World-Wide* 29.70–95.

1 I K P

Kuhlman, Natalie & Milo Kalecteca. 1982. Assessing Indian English. In *Essays in Native American English,* ed. by H. G. Bartelt, S. Penfield-Jasper & B. Hoffer, 195–217. San Antonio, TX: Trinity University.

5 A

Kuwahara, Yuri. 1998. *Interactions of Identity: Inner-City Immigrant and Refugee Youths, Language Use, and Schooling*: Stanford University. [Abstract for Kuwahara, Yuri. 1998. *Interactions of Identity: Inner-City Immigrant and Refugee Youths, Language Use, and Schooling* graciously provided by Yuri Kuwahara.]

1 3 6 F I U
This two-year ethnographic study explores the lives of immigrant and refugee youths—Cambodian, Mien, Vietnamese, Thai, Chinese, and Mexican—as they negotiate their identities in an urban setting in California. The youths' use of features of their native languages, Standard English, and African American Vernacular English (AAVE) are examined as symbolic, constitutive indexes of their shifting identities over time. The study found that the youths' acculturation into differing segments of society was conditioned ideologically by the norms and values shaping global and local structuring and practice, which determine and maintain the social order. Ethnically resilient youths from intact families used their cultural values and histories to achieve academically, with greater use of Standard English, while youths who became disintegrated in the social orders of their schools actively differentiated themselves from both "mainstream" America and their traditional cultures, acquiring instead AAVE and the norms of "gangsta" rap culture.

Kymlicka, Will & Alan Patten. 2003. Language Rights and Political Theory. *Annual Review of Applied Linguistics* 23.3–21.

2 E P
The article discusses research on language contact according to political philosophy. Elucidates many of the approaches to the determination of linguistic rights possible within a normative theory.

Kynard, Carmen. 2008. Writing While Black: The Colour Line, Black Discourses and Assessment in the Institutionalization of Writing Instruction. *English Teaching: Practice and Critique* 7.4–34. [Reprinted with permission of the journal from *English Teaching: Practice and Critique* 7(2), 4.]

1 A N W
Student essays for a college-level, department-wide final examination are scrutinized to represent the ways that students, who consciously employ rhetorical and intellectual traditions of Black discourses, get penalized according to limited notions of academic writing. A dynamic intersection is examined to show how this particular group of students are understood and discarded via: (1) the larger arena of race and literacy/education in elementary and secondary settings; (2) the history and institutionalization of freshman composition in college English departments; and (3) the racialized, punitive, anti-literacy nature of institutional writing assessment and programming.

Labov, William. 1967. Some Sources of Reading Problems for Speakers of the Black English Vernacular. In *New Directions in Elementary English,* ed. by A. Frazier, 140–67. Champaign, IL: NCTE.

1 A R X
Labov zeroes in on subtle phonological differences between SAE and AAVE as one of the sources of difficulty facing AAVE-speaking children and their teachers in beginning reading instruction. Several phonological processes produce sets of homonyms in AAVE which may not be present in the teacher's speech, e.g., r-lessness (guard = god), l-lessness (toll = toe), simplification of consonant clusters (past = pass), and weakening of final consonants (road = row). When these phonological processes correspond to an apparent absence of inflectional morphemes such as past tense -ed or possessive -s, it can become unclear whether such morphemes are part of the children's grammar.

Quantitative linguistic analysis can be used to show which changes indicate true grammatical difference, which changes indicate phonological difference at the lexical level, and which changes indicate mere surface phonetic transformation. (The latter is often the case.) Labov recommends that teachers learn to make such distinctions so that they do not confuse different pronunciations with true reading errors, and so that they can judge, for example, whether the reading of "passed" as "pass" indicates a lack of understanding of the morpheme -ed and/or the pronunciation of the graph -ed, or a correct reading with alternate pronunciation.

Labov, William. 1969. *The Logic of Nonstandard English*. In James E. Alatis, ed., Monograph Series on Languages and Linguistics No. 22 [20th Annual Round Table: Linguistics and the Teaching of Standard English to Speakers of Other Languages or Dialects], 1-43. Washington, D.C.: Georgetown University Press.

1 A I N O
This classic work attacks the then-dominant misconception among educational psychologists that inner city African American students' academic failure was due to verbal deficit and linguistic deprivation. Labov explains that threatening test situations often prevent researchers from seeing the full extent of African American children's verbal ability, because children respond by being defensive and taciturn. In more relaxed settings, such children are much more verbal. Another difficulty is that researchers confuse the verbosity of middle class speakers with logic. Labov shows that the vernacular discourse of Larry, an inner-city African American teenage speaker of AAVE encodes logical structure and abstract ideas effectively and is also forceful, cogent, and clear. By contrast, the Standard English speech of Charles M., a middle-class speaker, is marred by repetition, hedging, and big words designed to impress the listener rather than clarify his ideas. Labov then shows that some of the features of inner city children's discourse that are misinterpreted as illogical or as evidence that they do not think in complete thoughts involve processes of ellipsis that are common in Standard English and other languages. And he argues that the grammar of AAVE is systematic and equally capable of expressing complex propositions. Finally, he discusses the negative impact of the misconceived notion of linguistic deprivation. Because this and the associated concept of cultural deprivation theory blame children and their homes rather than schools, it allows society to ignore needed reforms in schooling. And because the problem is misdiagnosed, the proposed solutions are likely to fail, leading to even more misguided and racist assumptions (e.g. about genetic or intellectual inferiority). As Labov forcefully concludes (p. 34): "That educational psychology should be strongly influenced by a theory so false to the facts of language is unfortunate; but that children should be the victims of this ignorance is intolerable."

Labov, William. 1970. *The Study of Nonstandard English*. Champaign, IL: NCTE.

1 F I N T

Labov, William. 1972. Academic Ignorance and Black Intelligence. *Atlantic Monthly* 229.59–70.

1 I O

Labov, William. 1972. *Language in the Inner City: Studies in the Black English Vernacular*. Philadelphia: University of Pennsylvania Press.

1 E F I N R

Labov, William. 1976. Systematically Misleading Data from Test Questions. *The Urban Review* 9.

1 A

Labov, William. 1980. Is There a Creole Speech Community? In *Theoretical Orientations in Creole Studies,* ed. by A. Valdman, 369–88. New York: Academic Press.

2 F U

Labov, William. 1982. Objectivity and Commitment in Linguistic Science. *Language in Society* 11.165–201.

1 I K P

Labov, William. 1995. Can Reading Failure Be Reversed? A Linguistic Approach to the Question. In *Literacy among African American Youth,* ed. by V. Gadsden & D. Wagner, 39–68. Creskill, NJ: Hampton Press.

1 I R T V X

Labov reviews research concerning AAVE as it pertains to improving literacy rates among African American youths. Early work suggested that although some points of contrast between AAVE and SAE may present interference in learning to read, failure rates were largely due to teachers' negative attitudes toward AAVE. BRIDGE, a program designed to help students transition from AAVE to SAE in a culturally and linguistically sensitive way, was demonstrated to be effective in increasing reading ability, but ultimately shelved because of parents' and teachers' objections to its use of AAVE. Labov discusses the strengths and weaknesses of the program, and outlines five basic principles to be incorporated into any language arts program aimed at assisting speakers of nonstandard English. Recent evidence for the increasing divergence of AAVE from SAE is taken as indicative of an even greater need for integrated classrooms and BRIDGE-like programs.

Labov, William. 2001. Applying Our Knowledge of African American English to the Problem of Raising Reading Levels in Inner City Schools. In *Sociocultural and Historical Contexts of African American English,* ed. by S. Lanehart, 299–317. Philadelphia: John Benjamins.

1 R S X

Labov explains the importance of linguistic theory in shedding light on the difficulty with which many African American students learn to read and in offering relevant solutions. He reports on work with inner-city children in grades 2-5 who were one to two years behind in reading ability. Trained tutors were able to isolate the specific grapheme environments in which each student exhibited difficulty, and then administer customized corrective reading material. While improvement in some areas were noted and most students progressed to the Basic level of reading ability (but not the Advanced or Proficient level), most students still demonstrated considerable difficulty with final consonant clusters, most likely because of the surface-structure transformations they often undergo in AAVE. Labov takes this as evidence that AAVE grammar must be considered when teaching reading to AAVE-speakers, and concludes that further research will benefit from greater structural knowledge of AAVE.

Labov, William. 2003. When Ordinary Children Fail to Read. *Reading Research Quarterly* 38.128–31.

1 A R S X

Labov notes that despite the considerable progress in treating reading disorders, little has been done to reverse the consistently high rate at which perfectly healthy minority children fail at reading. He zeroes in on linguistic interference as one of the causes, arguing that the mismatch between the home language and the language of reading instruction is greater for minority children than for mainstream children. Working toward a solution, he states that we must "understand what it is like not to be able to read," (p. 129), given the complex phonemic analysis involved in decoding text (e.g., it may not be obvious to a beginner that the /l/ in *leap* is the same as the /l/ in *tool*, especially for AAVE-speakers who increasingly vocalize /l/ in certain contexts). As a first step, then, one must "assess what these struggling readers do or do not know about sound-to-letter correspondences" (p. 130). Based on initial research, the author lists four generalizations gleaned so far about reading behavior among struggling children (e.g., children largely understand the alphabetic principle but have trouble when there is a one-to-many or many-to-one correspondence between sound and letter). The author concludes that because of the heterogeneous nature of our society, reading research must focus on language diversity.

Labov, William & Bettina Baker. 2010. What Is a Reading Error? *Applied Psycholinguistics* 31.735–57.

1 4 A R X
In order to investigate the influence of dialect differences on oral reading proficiency, this study hypothesizes that a true reading error (misreading of the writer's intent) will cast a semantic shadow on and increase the likelihood of errors in subsequent words in a clause. Six hundred and twenty-seven poor readers in inner-city elementary schools in Pennsylvania, Georgia and California were administered a multi-faceted oral reading test. Subjects were African American, European American, or Latinos who either learned to read in English or Spanish first. Each deviation from the reading passage was labeled either a clear error (e.g., reading "blood" as "boat") or a dialectically determined potential error (e.g., reading "played" as "play"). To determine the effect of a clear or potential error, the number of errors in the clause following each clear error, potential error, and correct reading was calculated. Results showed that potential errors tended to behave more like correct readings for the African American subjects, causing few subsequent reading errors in the clause, while potential errors behaved more like clear errors for Latinos who learned to read Spanish first, causing more subsequent errors and revealing a deeper unfamiliarity with English grammar. Because the potential errors were dialect variants more common to African American Vernacular English, these results suggest that potential errors that are known variants of a speaker's dialect should be considered separately from clear errors in studies of reading competency.

Labov, William & Anne Charity Hudley. 2009. *Symbolic and Structural Effects of Dialects and Immigrant Minority Languages in Explaining Achievement Gaps*. Paper presented at the NRC Workshop on the role of language in school learning: Implications for closing the achievement gap, Menlo Park, CA. See www.nap.edu/catalog.php?record_id=12907

1 A I T X

Labov, William, Paul Cohen, Clarence Robbins & John Lewis. 1968. *A Study of the Non-Standard English of Negro and Puerto-Rican Speakers in New York City. Final Report, Cooperative Research Project 3228*. Philadelphia: US Regional Survey.

1 4 F

Labov, William & Clarence Robins. 1969. A Note on the Relation of Reading Failure to Peer-Group Status in Urban Ghettoes. *The Teachers College Record* 70.395–405.

1 A C I R

Lacoste, Veronique. 2007. Modelling the Sounds of Standard Jamaican English in a Grade 2 Classroom. *Caribbean Journal of Education* 29.290–326.

2 S

Lacoste, Veronique. 2012. *Phonological Variation in Rural Jamaican Schools*. Amsterdam: John Benjamins.

2 F U

Lado, Robert. 1957. *Linguistics across Cultures: Applied Linguistics for Language Teachers*. Ann Arbor: The University of Michigan Press.

1 2 B X
Although clearly dated, this is a classic textbook for those interested in contrastive analysis as a basis for developing bidialectalism, e.g., between Creole English or AAVE and Standard English.

Ladson-Billings, Gloria. 1992. Liberatory Consequences of Literacy: A Case of Culturally Relevant Instruction for African-American Students. *Journal of Negro Education* 61.378–91.

1 C R T
Ladson-Billings argues for a 'literacy for liberation' approach to teaching reading. She notes that despite prevailing counter-sentiments in the United States, there exists among African Americans a strong and unified cultural consciousness. She likewise observes that in movements in some developing nations, literacy is seen as a matter of political and cultural empowerment, whereas in the United States, it is often seen as the maintenance of the status quo. Based on a case study of an effective White teacher of African American elementary school students, the author presents six tenets of holistic, culturally relevant instruction (e.g., "Teachers and students are engaged in collective struggle against the status quo" (p. 388). She concludes by emphasizing the importance of instilling in teachers that African Americans have a long history of resilience and are fully capable of learning.

Ladson-Billings, Gloria. 1994. *The Dreamkeepers: Successful Teachers of African American Children*. San Francisco: Jossey-Bass.

1 C T

Ladson-Billings, Gloria. 1995. Toward a Theory of Culturally Relevant Pedagogy. *American Educational Research Journal* 32.465–91.

1 5 C T

Ladson-Billings, Gloria. 2000. Fighting for Our Lives: Preparing Teachers to Teach African Americans. *Journal of Teacher Education* 51.206–14.

1 C T

Ladson-Billings, Gloria. 2001. *Crossing over to Canaan: The Journey of New Teachers in Diverse Classrooms*. San Francisco: Jossey-Bass.

1 C T

Ladson-Billings, Gloria. 2002. I Ain't Writin' Nuttin': Permissions to Fail and Demands to Succeed in Urban Classrooms. In *The Skin That We Speak*, ed. by L. Delpit & J. K. Dowdy, 107-20. NJ: New Press.

1 C T W

Laffey, James & Roger Shuy (eds.) 1973. *Language Differences: Do They Interfere?* Newark, DE: International Reading Association.

1 B E R X

Lambert, Wallace & Douglas Taylor. 1996. Language in the Lives of Ethnic Minorities: Cuban American Families in Miami. *Applied Linguistics* 17.477–500.

4 I U

Lanehart, Sonja. 1998. African American Vernacular English and Education: The Dynamics of Pedagogy, Ideology, and Identity. *Journal of English Linguistics* 26.122–36.

1 I P S

Lanehart, Sonja (ed.) 2001. *Sociocultural and Historical Contexts of African American English.* Philadelphia: John Benjamins.

1 E F I K N P

Lanehart, Sonja. 2002. Goals and Teaching English Language Classes. *Journal of English Linguistics* 30.328–38.

1 I S

Lanehart, Sonja. 2002. *Sista, Speak!: Black Women Kinfolk Talk About Language and Literacy.* Austin: University of Texas Press.

1 I N U
Lanehart examines the language and literacy identities of four African American women across three generations of one family (hers). The author uses both the sociocultural and historical contexts of the participants to help define their language and literacy identities. The various entities within their sociocultural and historical contexts (family, community, and work) are integrated with the goals and possible selves that emerge within them. As a group, their language significantly differs between the kitchen talk and interview talk contexts. These narratives reveal beliefs about correct and incorrect speech grounded in ideological perspectives that are points of contention for the participants.

Lanehart, Sonja (ed.) 2009. *African American Women's Language: Discourse, Education, and Identity.* Newcastle upon Tyne: Cambridge Scholars Publishing. [Abstract graciously provided by Sonja Lanehart.]

1 2 E F I N P
This book brings together new research on African American Women's Language, from diverse disciplinary perspectives: Lisa Green and Tracy Conner, "The Way I Can Speak for Myself": The Social and Linguistic Context of Counseling Interviews with African American Adolescent Girls in Washington, D.C.; Alicia Beckford Wassink, Two Black Women Growing Up with Two "Black Languages": Kinship and Attitudes toward Jamaican Creole and African American Language; Stand Up and Speak Out: "Oppositional Talk" in the Discourse of African American Girls; Into the Breach: Representing the Messy Truths of Black Women's Hair and Language Practices; Charles E. De Bose, Church Lady Talk: African American Women's Language in the Church; and Elaine Richardson, Gender Ideologies in Hip Hop Feminism and Performances of Black Womanhood.

Lanehart, Sonja. 2010. African American Language. In *The Handbook of Language and Ethnic Identity, 2nd ed.,* ed. by J. Fishman & O. Garcia, 340–52. New York: Oxford University Press.

1 F

Lass, Bonnie. 1980. Improving Reading Skills: The Relationship between the Oral Language of Black English Speakers and Their Reading Achievement. *Urban Education* 14.437–48.

1 I R T X

Lass examines the relation between students' language and their reading comprehension rates. Seventy-two AAVE-speaking students in grades 2, 4, 6 and 8 each completed two speaking tasks, one designed to elicit AAVE and thus measure dialect variety, and one designed to elicit SAE and thus measure code-switching ability. Each speech sample was rated based on a list of thirty-two features that contrast AAVE and SAE. Scores were correlated with raw scores from a standardized reading test. Although it was hypothesized that students who spoke varieties of AAVE more similar to SAE and students who were more adept at code-switching would both have significantly higher reading scores, no significant correlations were found. The author discusses four possible factors contributing to these results, and ultimately considers it most likely that the hypotheses were incorrect. Lass concludes that attempts to alter either the language of the student or the language of the reading material will not improve reading skills, and that instead, teacher attitudes need to be changed.

Lass, Bonnie. 1980. Trade Books for Black English Speakers. *Language Arts* 57.413–19.

1 C M R V

Lawerence, Gay. 1978. Indian Education: Why Bilingual-Bicultural? *Education and Urban Society* 10.305–20.

5

Le Moine, Noma. 2001. Language Variation and Literacy Acquisition in African American Students. In *Literacy in African American Communities,* ed. by J. Harris, A. Kamhi & K. Pollock, 169–94. Mahwah, NJ: Lawrence Erlbaum Associates.

1 A B M S

After briefly outlining different hypotheses concerning the origin of AAVE, Le Moine draws on personal experience to discuss the advantages of six nontraditional approaches for facilitating literacy instruction among African American SELLs (Standard English Language Learners). She recommends that teachers: (1) learn about nonstandard language and nonstandard language speakers; (2) integrate this knowledge into instruction; (3) employ second-language acquisition techniques; (4) balance instruction with language experience, whole language/access to books, and phonics; (5) integrate the history and culture of the students; and (6) build on the learning styles and strengths already present within the students. The author concludes that African American SELLs will benefit from a mixture of both traditional and nontraditional literacy approaches, and closes with bulleted lists outlining instructional materials and strategies.

Le Moine, Noma & Los Angeles Unified School District. 1998. *English for Your Success: A Language Development Program for African American Children Grades Pre-K-8.* Maywood, NJ: The People's Publishing Group.

1 B C I M O R S W

Le Moine, Noma & Sharroky Hollie. 2007. *Developing Academic English for Standard English Learners.* New York: Teachers College Press.

B S T

Le Page, Robert. 1968. Problems to Be Faced in the Use of English as the Medium of Education in Four West Indian Territories. In *Language Problems of Developing Nations,* ed. by J. A. Fishman, C. A. Ferguson & J. D. Gupta, 431–42. New York: John Wiley and Sons.

2 A B I K T

Le Page explores the language situation in the West Indian territories of Jamaica, British Honduras, Guyana and Trinidad and Tobago, where most people speak some variety of creolized English. Although Standard English was the gateway to higher education and career success, the failure rate on the English-language sections of the two Great Britain-based standardized examinations employed in the West Indies was between 70 and 90%. The education system, unfortunately, did not recognize language interference factors; refused to consider the legitimacy of Creole as a language in its own right, and teachers even failed to recognize Creole aspects of their own speech. Students who were best at imitating standard forms were the ones who succeeded, while many otherwise talented students did not. As a remedy, Le Page recommends that teachers be trained in Standard English, that teaching materials be prepared that are sensitive to the West Indies environment and make use of contrastive analysis, that current teachers be retrained in these new ideas, and that radio and television language teaching programs be set up for use within schools.

Le Page, Robert. 1981. *Caribbean Connections in the Classroom: A Pamphlet of Guidance for Teachers Concerned with the Language Problems of Children of Afro-Caribbean Descent*. York: University of York.

2 F S T

Leap, William. 1974. Ethnics, Emics, and the New Ideology: The Identity Potential of Indian English. In *Social and Cultural Identity: Problems of Persistence and Change*, ed. by T. Fitzgerald, 51–62. Athens: University of Georgia Press.

5 I P

Leap, William. 1974. On Grammaticality in Native American English: The Evidence from Isleta. *Linguistics* 128.79–89.

5 F

Leap, William. 1976. *Studies in Southwestern Indian English*. San Antonio, TX: Trinity University Press.

5 E F

Leap, William. 1978. American Indian English and Its Implications for Bilingual Education. In *Georgetown Round Table on Languages and Linguistics 1978: International Dimensions of Bilingual Education*, ed. by J. Alatis, 657–69. Washington, D.C.: Georgetown University Press.

5 P

Leap, William. 1982. The Study of Indian English in the U.S. Southwest: Retrospect and Prospect. In *Bilingualism and Language Contact: Spanish, English, and Native American Languages*, ed. by F. Barkin, E. Brandt & J. Ornstein-Galicia, 101–19. New York: Teachers College.

5 F

Leap, William. 1993. *American Indian English*. Salt Lake City: University of Utah Press.

5 F

Leap, William L. 1982. Roles for the Linguist in Indian Bilingual Education. In *Language Renewal among American Indian Tribes: Issues, Problems, and Prospects*, ed. by R. St. Clair & W. L. Leap, 19–30. Rosslyn, VA: National Clearinghouse for Bilingual Education.

5

Leaverton, Lloyd. 1973. Dialectal Readers: Rationale, Use and Value. In *Language Differences: Do They Interfere?*, ed. by J. Laffey & R. Shuy, 114-26. Newark, DE: International Reading Association.

1 R V
Leaverton's study, appearing in a collection of articles titled *Language Differences: Do They Interfere?* (Laffey & Shuy 1973) was the first experimental attempt to examine the usefulness of instructional materials developed with linguistic insights in mind. Specifically, his study set out to investigate, by means of a small controlled comparison, whether beginning texts "phrased in the actual word patterns and grammatical structure used by the children in their oral speech" helped dialect-speaking children learn to read more quickly, and whether reading a nonstandard passage first helped the child learn to read an equivalent standard passage (p. 116). Two sets of seven minimally-differing stories were developed, which were introduced to the children as "Everyday Talk" and "School Talk" versions. These materials, called the Psycholinguistic Reading Series (Davis, Gladney, & Leaverton 1968), were tested in a public inner-city elementary school in Chicago. Leaverton notes that "there was a definite trend in favor of the experimental group" (p. 122). Specifically, the experimental group made significantly fewer errors on an oral reading test, and children in the experimental condition ranked higher on the speed measure significantly more often than children in the control group.

Lee, Carol. 1993. *Signifying as a Scaffold for Literary Interpretation: The Pedagogical Implications of an African American Discourse Genre*. Urbana, IL: NCTE.

1 C N O R S

Lee, Carol. 1995. A Culturally-Based Cognitive Apprenticeship: Teaching African American High School Students Skills in Literary Interpretation. *Reading Research Quarterly* 30.608–30.

1 C N R

Lee, Carol. 1995. Signifying as a Scaffold for Literary Interpretation. *Journal of Black Psychology* 21.357–81.

1 C N R
In what proved to become a seminal contribution to the field, Lee investigates whether the study of signifying (a speech event popular among African Americans involving the use of innuendo and metaphor) can improve literary interpretation skills. For a six-week period at two predominantly African American high schools with low achievement rates, two control classes continued with their normal curriculum, while four experimental classes practiced analyzing dialogues involving signifying and then applying these skills to the interpretation of African American literary texts. Analysis of pre- and post-tests taken by the six classes indicated that the experimental group improved their literary interpretation skills over the six weeks to a significantly greater degree than did the control group. Furthermore, additional tests taken by the experimental group indicated that those students with more skill in signifying and more prior social knowledge relevant to the texts performed significantly better on both the pre- and posttests. The author concludes that the present study documents the value of cultural material in helping students generate "abstract metacognitive strategies" (p. 379), and suggests further research to explore this idea further.

Lee, Carol. 1997. Bridging Home and School Literacies: A Model of Culturally Responsive Teaching. In *A Handbook for Literacy Educators: Research on Teaching the Commu-*

nicative and Visual Arts, ed. by J. Flood, S. B. Heath & D. Lapp, 330–41. New York: Macmillan.

1 C N R S W

Lee, Carol. 2006. "Every Good-Bye Ain't Gone": Analyzing the Cultural Underpinnings of Classroom Talk. *International Journal of Qualitative Studies in Education (QSE)* 19.305–27. [Reprinted from *International Journal of Qualitative Studies in Education* 19(3).]

1 C N

This article explicates the Cultural Modeling Framework for designing robust learning environments that leverage everyday knowledge of culturally diverse students to support subject-matter-specific learning. It reports a study of Cultural Modeling in the teaching of response to literature in an urban underachieving high school serving African American students from low-income communities who are also speakers of African American English. The study is situated in the history of research on African American English as a resource for academic learning, particularly in relation to literacy. Results document the ways that African American rhetorical features served as a medium for complex literary reasoning and provided contextualization cues to enhance participation.

Lee, Carol. 2007. *Culture, Literacy, and Learning: Taking Bloom in the Midst of the Whirlwind.* New York: Teachers College Press.

1 C R S

Making ample and excellent use of vignettes from urban classrooms, Lee outlines the Cultural Modeling Project, which draws on student competencies in AAVE and hip hop culture to tackle complex problems in the study of literature.

Lee, Jin Sook. 2005. Embracing Diversity through the Understanding of Pragmatics. In *Language in the Schools: Integrating Linguistic Knowledge into K-12 Teaching,* ed. by K. Denham & A. Lobeck, 17–28. Mahwah, NJ: Erlbaum Associates.

N

Leechman, Douglas & Robert A. Hall, Jr. 1955. American Indian Pidgin English: Attestations and Grammatical Peculiarities. *American Speech* 30.163–71.

2 5 F

Leeper, Angela. 2003. The "Other America": Looking at Appalachian and Cajun/Creole Resources. *Multicultural Review* 12.34–32.

2 6 C E R

Lems, Kristin, Leah Miller & Terena Soro. 2010. *Teaching Reading to English Language Learners: Insights from Linguistics.* New York: Guilford Press.

4 R

Levinson, Kenneth. 2005. At the Crossroads of Language Variation: Urban College Students Learn About Sociolinguistics. *Teaching English in the Two-Year College* 33.198–210. [Abstract prepared by ERIC and reprinted with permission of the Department of Education from the Education Resources Information Center at eric.ed.gov.]

I L

Learning about how language works not only gives students a better grounding in English; it also provides insights into the nature of what it means to be human. Language is both universal and a key element of human diversity. In becoming schooled in linguistic aspects of diversity, students become aware of their own language choices and the possibilities of expanding those choices, opening the door to interactions with different communities socially, academically, and professionally. In this article, the author discusses Language in the Multicultural Setting, a linguistics course that offers students the fundamentals of linguistics in the context of a survey of sociolinguistics. The author also describes some of the course topics like child language development, gender and language, and bilingualism, among other things, and includes examples of student writing from both native and nonnative developmental writers in addition to student writing from those who did not require developmental courses.

Lewis, Shirley & Mary Hoover. 1979. *Teacher Training Workshops on Black English and Language Arts Teaching.* Stanford, CA: Center for Educational Research at Stanford.

1 S T

Liebe-Harkort, Marie-Louise. 1979. Bilingualism and Language Mixing among the White Mountain Apaches. *Folia Linguistica* 13.345–56.

5 F U

Liebe-Harkort, Marie-Louise. 1983. A Note on the English Spoken by Apaches. *International Journal of American Linguistics* 2.207–08.

5 F

Lin, San-Su. 1963. An Experiment in Changing Dialect Patterns: The Claflin Project. *College English* 24.644–47.

B

Linn, Michael. 1995. Stylistic Variation in Vernacular Black English and the Teaching of College Composition. In *Composing Social Identity in Written Language,* ed. by D. L. Rubin, 33–46. Hillsdale, NJ: Lawrence Erlbaum Associates. [Reprinted in Michael D. Linn, ed., 1998. *Handbook of Dialectics and Language Variation, 2nd ed.,* 515–528. New York: Academic Press.]

1 N S W

Linn, Michael & Gene Piché. 1982. Black and White Adolescent and Preadolescent Attitudes toward Black English. *Research in the Teaching of English* 16.53–69. [Reprinted from *Research in the Teaching of English,* 16(1).]

1 I

This study describes the attitudes of Black and White, male and female, middle and lower class adolescents and preadolescents in response to tape-recorded samples of Standard English (SE) and Black English (BE). Using the matched guise technique, the BE version approximated the percentage of actual versus potential occurrence, as they were found in Wolfram's Detroit study, of these features: nonoccurrence of the copula, nonoccurrence of the third person singular {Z}, nonoccurrence of the plural {Z}, nonoccurrence of the possessive {Z}, and the occurrence of multiple negation. In addition there was one occurrence of invariant be in the BE sample. The results indicate that BE is no longer considered the "shuffling speech of slavery" by either White or Black grade school or high school students. Complicated aspects of social change over the past two decades have created a greater feeling of pride among the Blacks and some changes in regard for Blacks by Whites. This study also demonstrates that children reach the zenith of ethnic identity about the beginning of puberty.

Linnes, Kathleen. 1998. Middle-Class AAVE Versus Middle-Class Bilingualism: Contrasting Speech Communities. *American Speech* 73.339–68.

1 I U

Direction of likely language shift in two ethnic communities is predicted on the basis of sociolinguistic interviews with 30 middle-class African Americans and thirty middle-class German-English bilinguals. While adult African Americans in this community were college-educated and primarily used Standard English, their speech evidenced some distinct features of AAVE. Discussion of ethnic topics (as opposed to mainstream topics) elicited higher frequencies of some AAVE features, especially for speakers under thirty. Speakers aged thirty to fifty-four were less likely to employ AAVE features than either younger or older speakers. When the interviews with German-English bilingual speakers were subjected to similar analyses, no clear code-switching preferences emerged; speakers were comfortable discussing ethnic topics in English. The author concludes by suggesting that whereas German-English bilingual speakers, in the absence of social discrimination, are headed toward English monolingualism, the bidialectal African American speakers will likely continue to preserve certain AAVE features.

Lippi-Green, Rosina. 2012. *English with an Accent* (2nd ed.) New York: Routledge.

1 3 4 A I O P

Lo, Adrienne & Angela Reyes. 2004. Relationality: Discursive Constructions of Asian Pacific American Identities. A Special Double Issue of *Pragmatics*. 14.

3 6 I

Lobeck, Anne. 2005. A Critical Approach to Standard English. In *Language in the Schools: Integrating Linguistic Knowledge into K-12 Teaching,* ed. by K. Denham & A. Lobeck, 97–108.

I P

Lockwood, Michael. 1998. *Practical Ways to Teach Standard English and Language Study.* Reading, UK: Reading and Language Information Centre.

B S

Long, Edgarita & John Christensen. 1998. Indirect Language Assessment Tool for English-Speaking Cherokee Indian Children. *Journal of American Indian Education* 38.1–14.

5 A

Long, Michael. 1997. Ebonics, Language, and Power. *Social Anarchism* 24.5–29.

1 I K

Los Angeles Unified School District. 1998. *An Overview of the Academic English Mastery Program: Empowerment through Communication.* In *AEMP Video Series.* Los Angeles, CA: Los Angeles Unified School District, Division of Instruction, Language Acquisition Branch.

1 B S Z

Los Angeles Unified School District. 1999. *Linguistic Affirmation Program: Program Overview and Instructional Framework.* Los Angeles, CA: Los Angeles Unified School District.

1 B I R S T W

The Academic English Mastery Program, developed by Noma LeMoine for the Los Angeles Unified School District, is also depicted more briefly in MacNeil and Cran's 2005 video, *Do you Speak American?*

Los Angeles Unified School District. 2010. *Instructional Strategies for the AEMP [Academic English Mastery Program] Classroom*. Los Angeles, CA: Los Angeles Unified School District, Division of Instruction, Language Acquisition Branch.

1 4 B S Z

Love, Theresa A. 1991. *A Guide for Teaching Standard English to Black Dialect Speakers*.

1 B S T

Low, Ee Ling & Esther Grabe. 1995. Prosodic Patterns in Singapore English. In *Proceedings of the Xiiith International Congress of Phonetic Sciences: Icphs 95; Stockholm, Sweden, 13–19 August 1995*, ed. by K. Elenius & P. Branderud, 636–39. Stockholm: KTH and Stockholm University.

3 6 F

Lucas, Ceil. 1997. Ebonics and ASL [American Sign Language]: Teaching Our Children the Codes of Power. *Perspectives in Education and Deafness* 15.12–13.

1 6 B I

Lucas, Ceil & Denise Glyn Borders. 1994. *Language Diversity and Classroom Discourse*. Norwood, NJ: Ablex Publishing Corporation.

1 N T

Lucas, Marilyn & Harry Singer. 1976. Dialect in Relation to Oral Reading Achievement: Recoding, Encoding, or Merely a Code? In *Theoretical Models and Processes of Reading*, ed. by H. Singer & R. B. Ruddell, 429–39. Newark, DE: International Reading Association.

4 R X
Note: Reprinted from *Journal of Reading Behavior* 7/2, Summer 1975, 137–48.

Luelsdorff, Philip. 1973. *Standard English for Urban Blacks: Pronunciation*. Madison: University of Wisconsin Press.

1 B M O

Luke, Allan. 1986. Linguistic Stereotypes, the Divergent Speaker and the Teaching of Literacy. *Journal of Curriculum Studies* 18.397–408.

1 E I T

Lum, Darrell H. Y. 2008. What School You Went? Local Culture, Local Identity, and Local Language: Stories of Schooling in Hawai'i. *Educational Perspectives* 41.6–16. [Abstract prepared by ERIC and reprinted with permission of the Department of Education from the Education Resources Information Center at eric.ed.gov.]

2
In this article, the author explores local culture and local cultural practices in an attempt to understand the forces and influences that have affected the development of a local identity as well as the persistence of Pidgin (Hawai'i Creole) as its language. The author begins with an introductory discussion of themes that emerge in two short stories, (1) "What School You Went?"; and (2) "No Pass Back," narrated in Pidgin by a young narrator describing his school experiences during the 1950s and 60s. The vignettes in the first story demonstrate the clear distinctions between the mainstream adult culture and that of the students. The second story "No Pass Back" is an exploration of power and resistance and of how change can occur from within a community.

Together they paint a picture of local Hawai'i culture and of the narrator's growing understanding of his place in the world. The stories are fitting examples of the ways in which literature can illuminate the complexities of identity formation in the context of family, friends, classmates, and teachers.

Lyman, Huntington & Margo Figgins. 2005. Democracy, Dialect, and the Power of Every Voice. *English Journal* 94.40–47. [Reprinted from *English Journal* 95(4).]

1 B S

Beginning with the belief that students' proficiency with both Standard English and their home language is essential, Lyman and Figgins show how "rich experiences in the exploration of dialect serve as a precursor to mastering Standard English" (p. 45).

MacGregor-Mendoza, Patricia. 2005. Bilingualism: Myths and Realities. In *Language in the Schools: Integrating Linguistic Knowledge into K-12 Teaching,* ed. by K. Denham & A. Lobeck, 109–20.

S U

MacNeil, Robert & William Cran. 2005. *Do You Speak American?* Arlington, VA: MacNeil-Lehrer Productions.

1 6 F L M Z

A three-part (three hour) documentary series, originally aired on PBS (Public Broadcasting Service), which explores language variation in the United States. The Academic English Mastery Program in Los Angeles, led by Noma LeMoine, is highlighted as an example of how knowledge of vernacular language varieties can enhance language arts instruction. See Reaser et al. (2005) for an accompanying curriculum appropriate for high school, college, or teacher education settings.

Maddahian, Ebrahim & Ambition Padi Sandamela. 2000. *Academic English Mastery Program- 1998–99 Evaluation Report.* [Abstract prepared by ERIC and reprinted with permission of the Department of Education from the Education Resources Information Center at eric.ed.gov.]

1 A B I R

This document evaluates the effectiveness of the Los Angeles Unified School District's Academic English Mastery Program, a program designed to serve students whose lack of proficiency in Standard American English is an impediment to academic performance. This study used random sampling, experimental and control groups, and three principle data collection instruments (writing and speaking language assessment measures, teacher surveys, and observation checklists). Three main conclusions are drawn: The Academic English Mastery program is an effective program for improving academic use of the English language for African American speakers of non-mainstream English; better utilization of the program improved student progress, and program effectiveness can be improved if teachers are motivated to implement and utilize program principles to their fullest extent; and teachers with more experience and education are more successful in improving student achievement. Given these results, recommendations are made for expanding the program, including focusing on other nonstandard English language minorities in future program evaluations and conducting longitudinal studies to examine the long-term impact of the program. Included are an executive summary, several tables, an explanation of purposes and methods, a summary of findings, conclusions and recommendations, two appendices (the teacher survey and the observation matrix), and extensive references.

Mainess, Karen, Tempii Champion & Allyssa McCabe. 2002. Telling the Unknown Story: Complex and Explicit Narration by African American Preadolescents. *Linguistics and Education* 13.151–73.

1 N

Major, Clarence. 1994. *Juba to Jive: A Dictionary of African-American Slang.* New York: Penguin.

1 F

Makoni, Sinfree, Geneva Smitherman, Arnetha Ball & Arthur K. Spears (eds.) 2003. *Black Linguistics: Language, Society, and Politics in Africa and the Americas.* New York: Routledge.

1 6 E F I N P
This volume, which includes studies by Black linguists of Black Languages in Africa and the Western Hemispheric Diaspora, is divided into three parts: Ideological practices in research on Black languages, Conceptualization and status of Black languages, and Inclusion and exclusion through language. AAVE, a major focus of this bibliography, is discussed in part 1 in Don Winford's chapter on language ideology and H. Samy Alim's chapter on African American language and street conscious identity, and in part 3 in chapters by John Baugh ("Linguistic profiling"), Awad El Karim M. Ibrahim ("Black English as a symbolic site of identification and language learning"), and Arnetha F. Ball ("US and South African teachers' developing perspectives on language and literacy"). Velma Pollard's chapter in part 1 deals with the language of the Rastafari in Jamaica and its philosophical, social and cultural context. The chapters in part 2, by Zaline M. Roy-Campbell, Hassana Alidou, Nkhelebeni Phaswana, and Sinfree Makoni, deal with Black languages in Africa, including their status and use in schools and government bodies in countries ranging from Burkina Faso, Mali, Mozambique, and Niger to South Africa.

Malancon, Richard & Mary Jo Malancon. 1993. Language, Literacy and the Image of the Child in American Indian Classrooms. *Language Arts* 70.182–92.

5 C R W

Malcolm, Ian. 1979. The West Australian Aboriginal Child and Classroom Interaction: A Sociolinguistic Approach. *Journal of Pragmatics* 3.305–20.

6 C N T

Malcolm, Ian. 1982. Verbal Interaction in the Classroom. In *English and the Aboriginal Child*, ed. by R. Eagleson, S. Kaldor & I. Malcolm, 165–92. Canberra, Australia: Curriculum Development Centre.

6 N T

Malcolm, Ian. 1992. English in the Education of Speakers of Aboriginal English. In *Pidgins, Creoles and Non-Standard Dialects in Education (Occasional Paper No. 12)*, ed. by J. Siegel, 14–41. Melbourne: Applied Linguistics Association of Australia.

6 C T

Malcolm, Ian. 1994. Aboriginal English inside and Outside the Classroom. *Australian Review of Applied Linguistics* 17.147–80.

6 F N

Malcolm, Ian. 1995. *Teacher Development for Bidialectal Education.* Paper presented to the International Conference on Language Development, Denpasar, Bali.

6 B C T
Describes a teacher training curriculum in use at Edith Cowan University in Australia.

Malcolm, Ian. 2000. English and Inclusivity in Education for Indigenous Students. *Australian Review of Applied Linguistics* 22.51–66.

6 B C P

Malcolm, Ian. 2007. Cultural Linguistics and Bidialectal Education. In *Applied Cultural Linguistics,* ed. by F. Sharifian & G. Palmer, 53–63. Amsterdam: John Benjamins.

6 B C P

Malcolm, Ian. 2011. Learning through Standard English: Cognitive Implications for Post-Pidgin/-Creole Speakers. *Linguistics and Education* 22.3:261-72.

2 C N

Malcolm, Ian, Yvonne Haig, Patricia Königsberg, Judith Rouchecouste, Glenys Collard, Alison Hill & Rosemary Cahill. 1999. *Two-Way English: Towards More User-Friendly Education for Speakers of Aboriginal English.* Perth: Western Australia Department of Education.

6 B C F N P

Malcolm, Ian & Patricia Königsberg. 2007. Bridging the Language Gap in Education. In *The Habitat of Australia's Aboriginal Languages: Past, Present and Future,* ed. by G. Leitner & I. Malcolm, 267–97. Berlin: Mouton de Gruyter.

6 B C P

Malcolm, Ian, Terry Kessaris & Janet Hunter. 2003. Language and the Classroom Setting. In *Reform and Resistance in Aboriginal Education,* ed. by Q. Beresford & G. Partington. Crawley, Australia: University of Western Australia Press.

6 N P

Malcolm, Ian & Judith Rochecouste. 1998. *Australian Aboriginal Students in Higher Education.* Perth, Australia: National Centre for English Language Teaching and Research, Macquarie University, in association with the Centre for Applied Language Research at Edith Cowan University.

6 N

Mallinson, Christine & Anne Charity Hudley. 2010. Communicating About Communication: Multidisciplinary Approaches to Educating Educators About Language Variation. *Language and Linguistics Compass* 4.245–57.

1 4 6 I T

Malmstrom, Jean & Janice Lee. 1971. *Teaching English Linguistically: Principles and Practices for High School.* New York: Appleton-Century-Crofts.

L S
This book has a great list of 'literary selections illustrating US dialects' (p. 151). It is dated, but still useful.

Mann, Charles. 1996. Anglo-Nigerian Pidgin in Nigerian Education: A Survey of Policy, Practice, and Attitudes. In *Language, Education and Society in a Changing World,* ed. by T. Hickey & J. Williams. Dublin, Ireland: Multilingual Matters.

2 I P

Mann, Charles. 2009. Attitudes Towards Anglo-Nigerian Pidgin in Urban, Southern Nigeria: The Generational Variable. *Revue Roumaine de Linguistique* 54.349–64.

2 I

Mann, Charles C. 1998. Language, Mass Communication and National Development: The Role, Perceptions and Potential of Anglo-Nigerian Pidgin in the Mass Media. In *Language in Development: Access, Empowerment and Opportunity,* 136–44. Kuala Lumpur, Malaysia: National Institute of Public Administration.

2 I

Mann, Charles C. 2000. Reviewing Ethnolinguistic Vitality: The Case of Anglo-Nigerian Pidgin. *Journal of Sociolinguistics* 4.458–74.

2 I

Mantell, Arlene. 1974. Strategies for Language Expansion in the Middle Grades. In *Black Dialects and Reading,* ed. by B. Cullinan, 55–68. Urbana, IL: NCTE.

1 B O S

Marback, Richard. 2001. Ebonics: Theorizing in Public Our Attitudes toward Literacy. *College Composition and Communication* 53.11–32.

1 I K W

Marckwardt, Albert. 1974. Issues in the Teaching of Standard English. *The Florida FL Reporter* 12.21–24, 94.

6 B I

Marcuzzi, Rose. 1986. Urban Education of Native/Indian Children. *Canadian Journal of Native Education* 13.27–31. [Abstract prepared by ERIC.]

5 C N T
The author considers the cultural background and language patterns of Indian children and the difficulties they are likely to encounter in the urban classroom. Emphasizes that teacher attitudes are important in helping Indian children achieve in school.

Martin-Jones, Marilyn & Kathryn Jones (eds.) 2000. *Multilingual Literacies.* Amsterdam: John Benjamins.

2 6 E F N R W

Martinez, Glenn. 2006. *Mexican Americans and Language: Del Dicho Al Hecho.* Tucson: University of Arizona Press.

4 I

Marwit, Samuel & Karen Marwit. 1976. Black Children's Use of Nonstandard Grammar: Two Years Later. *Developmental Psychology* 12.33–38.

1 O X
The authors expand on a previous study that examined Black and White second-graders' ability to inflect nonsense nouns and verbs. Here, the same task is given to those

115 subjects out of the original pool of 201 who were still in the same school system, now in the fourth grade. The previous study had shown that White students supplied significantly more standard forms and Black students supplied significantly more non-standard forms. The present study found the same results, and found that all students supplied significantly more standard forms and significantly fewer nonstandard forms in fourth grade than they did in second grade.

Marwit, Samuel & Gail Neumann. 1974. Black and White Children's Comprehension of Standard and Nonstandard English Passages. *Journal of Educational Psychology* 66.329–32.

1 R V X
Marwit and Neumann examine reading comprehension rates of Black and White students as a function of the dialect of the reading material and the race of the examiner. Sixty Black and fifty-three White second graders each completed the Reading Comprehension section of the California Reading Test (translated into nonstandard for half of the students). Although it was hypothesized that Black students would better comprehend nonstandard material and White students would better comprehend standard material, it was found that White students received significantly higher comprehension scores than Black students on both standard and nonstandard formats. Furthermore, all subjects performed significantly better on the standard format than on the nonstandard format, and Black subjects performed significantly better on the standard format when tested by a White examiner than when tested by a Black examiner. The authors conclude that their findings provide additional evidence against the linguistic interference stance, and suggest that Black students' unexpected better performance with the standard format may be a result of their perception that the standard is the language of the classroom or of their distrust of nonstandard in an environment where it is not typically rewarded.

Massey, Douglas & Garvey Lundy. 2001. Use of Black English and Racial Discrimination in Urban Housing Markets: New Methods and Findings. *Urban Affairs Review* 36.452–69.

1 I

Matilda, August. 2010. *Supporting English Language Learning by Bridging from Children's First Languages in Papua New Guinea: An Analysis of Grade 3 Teachers' Conceptions and Practices.* Hamilton, New Zealand: University of Waikato.

2 B I S T V

Matlock, Marci. 1995. Sa'ah Naaghai Bik'eh Hozhoon: Tapping into the Power of Words. *Journal of Navajo Education* 12.19–24. [Abstract prepared by ERIC.]

5 C O S
The article describes a postsecondary speech communications course that combines traditional course content with Navajo philosophy by teaching college students how to organize formal speeches through a culture-based process involving thinking, planning, taking action, and developing confidence and competence. Includes student perceptions of this approach to teaching speech communications.

Maxwell, Donald. 1979. Green English: Spoken Standard English as a Second Dialect. *TESOL Newsletter* 13.13.

B O

Mayer, Karren & Kirstin New. 2010. Code Switching: Connecting Written and Spoken Language Patterns. In *Linguistics at School: Language Awareness in Primary and Secondary Education,* ed. by K. Denham & A. Lobeck, 240–43.

6 O U W

Mayfield, Margie I. 1985. Parents, Children and Reading: Helping Canadian Native Indian Parents of Preschoolers. *The Reading Teacher* 39.301–05.

5 R

Mays, Luberta. 1977. *Black Children's Perception of the Use of Their Dialect.* San Francisco, CA: R&E Research Associates, Inc.

1 I X

Mazrui, Alamin A. 2006. A Sociolinguistics of "Double-Consciousness": English and Ethnicity in the Black Experience. In *English and Ethnicity,* ed. by J. Brutt-Griffler & C. E. Davies, 49-74. New York: Palgrave Macmillan.

1 I P

Mbangwana, Paul N. & Bonaventure M. Sala. 2009. *Cameroon English Morphology and Syntax: Current Trends in Action.* Munich, Germany: Lincom Europa.

2 F

Mbufong, Paul. 2001. Pidgin English in Anglophone Cameroon Education. *English Today* 17.52–54.

2 I V

McCarthey, Sarah. 1997. Connecting Home and School Literacy Practices in Classrooms with Diverse Populations. *Journal of Literacy Research* 29.145–82.

C

McCarty, Teresa (ed.) 2005. *Language, Literacy, and Power in Schooling.* Mahwah, NJ: Lawrence Erlbaum Associates.

C E N P R W

McCarty, Teresa, Mary Eunice Romero-Little, Larisa Warhol & Ofelia Zepeda. 2010. "I'm Speaking English Instead of My Culture": Portraits of Language Use and Change among Native American Youth. In *Ethnolinguistic Diversity and Education: Language, Literacy, and Culture,* ed. by M. Farr, L. Seloni & J. Song, 69–98. New York: Routledge.

5 6 I P

McCarty, Teresa & Lucille Watahomigie. 1998. Language and Literacy in American Indian and Alaska Native Communities. In *Sociocultural Contexts of Language and Literacy,* ed. by B. Perez, 69–98. Mahwah, NJ: Lawrence Erlbaum Associates.

5 N R W

McCarty, Teresa L. 1980. Language Use by Yavapai-Apache Students: With Recommendations for Curriculum Design. *Journal of American Indian Education* 20.1–9.

5 C

McCormack, Rachel L. & Susan Lee Pasquarelli. 2010. *Teaching Reading: Strategies and Resources for Grades K-6*. New York: Guilford Press.

R S

McCourtie, Lena. 1998. The Politics of Creole Language Education in Jamaica: 1891–1921 and the 1990s. *Journal of Multilingual and Multicultural Development* 19.108–27. [Reprinted from *Journal of Multilingual and Multicultural Development* 19(2).]

2 I P

The underachievement of ethnic minorities has been the subject of much reflection and action by educators and researchers world-wide. This two-part study uses archival and empirical research to focus on the acquisition of English by another group, speakers of Jamaican Creole: a unique typology which can neither be categorized as foreign-language nor mother-tongue teaching. Both English and Creole share a common lexis, but Creole speakers need expert help in acquiring the phonology, morphology and syntax of English. In Part I, archival/historical data drawn primarily from the Annual Reports of 'Her Majesty's Inspectors' for a part of the colonial period, 1891-1921, highlight the systemic failure of pupils to acquire English in elementary schools. But in Part II, an investigation which the author conducted in the 1990s in secondary schools in postcolonial independent Jamaica finds a similar cycle of underachievement among Creole speakers. The inference to be drawn is that successive generations of these language learners have left schools, in the words of Skutnabb-Kangas and Cummins (1988 p. 1), as an 'undereducated underclass'. The paper analyses the issues that have bedeviled the education of Creole speakers in both centuries. Then, it outlines new political initiatives designed to effect change and redress the inequities of the past before the twenty-first century begins.

McCreight, Jennifer. 2011. The Importance of Being Heard: Responses of One First Grade Class to the Representation of AAVE in Picture Books. *Journal of Language and Literacy Education* 7.35–48.

1 L R S

A teacher's account of bringing attention to dialect differences in her first-grade classroom by comparing the language in Ezra Jack Keats' *Peter's Chair* and Eloise Greenfield's *She Come Bringing Me that Little Baby Girl*, two picture books featuring African American characters addressing the theme of sibling rivalry, but written with greater and lesser use of AAVE. The author concludes that even young children possess a keen interest in exploring dialect differences and observes that her African American students seemed to 'crave' stories that reflected their cultural and linguistic experiences.

McCrum, Robert, William Cran & Robert MacNeil. 1986. *The Story of English*. New York: Elizabeth Sifton Books/Viking.

1 2 6 F

This book is a companion to the Public Broadcasting Service (PBS) television series, *The Story of English*. Chapters 4 and 5 deal with Scots and Irish English respectively. Chapter 6, 'Black on White,' deals with Pidgin and Creole Englishes and African American Vernacular English. Chapter 9 deals with 'The New Englishes' in Asia, Africa and the Americas, including the Caribbean.

McDavid, Raven. 1962. Dialectology and the Classroom Teacher. *College English* 24.111–16.

F I S T

McDougal, Serie, III. 2009. 'Break It Down': One of the Cultural and Stylist Instructional Preferences of Black Males. *Journal of Negro Education* 78.432–40. [Reprinted with permission of the journal from *Journal of Negro Education* 78(4), 432.]

1 C

Interviews with students at an all-Black, all-male school in a major northeastern city revealed that a significant proportion of the participating students had a strong preference for practical, demonstrative explanations of new concepts and information that are directly related to their everyday experiential realities. These findings suggest that the participating students would benefit greatly from problem-based teaching strategies and culturally relevant instructional techniques.

McKay, Sandra Lee & Sau-Ling Cynthia Wong. 1996. Multiple Discourses, Multiple Identities: Investment and Agency in Second-Language Learning among Chinese Adolescent Immigrant Students. *Harvard Educational Review* 66.577–608.

3 I N T W

McKenry, Rosemary. 1996. *Deadly Eh, Cuz! Teaching Speakers of Koorie English*. Melbourne: Language Australia.

2 I S T

McLaughlin, Margaret A. 2010. Teacher Attitudes toward African American Language Patterns: A Close Look at Attrition Rates. In *Attending to the Margins: Writing, Researching, and Teaching on the Front Lines,* ed. by V. Balester & M. H. Kells, 114–30. Portsmouth, NH: Boynton/Cook.

1 I W

McMillan, James B. & Michael B. Montgomery. 1989. *Annotated Bibliography of Southern American English*. Tuscaloosa: The University of Alabama Press.

2 6 E F I

McRae, David. 1994. *Langwij Comes to School: Promoting Literacy among Speakers of Aboriginal English and Australian Creoles*. Canberra, Australia: DEET.

2 6 I R S

McWhorter, John. 1998. *The Word on the Street: Fact and Fable About American English*. New York: Plenum.

1 F I K P

McWhorter, John H. 1997. Wasting Energy on an Illusion. *The Black Scholar* 27.1.9–14.

1 B K S

McWhorter, John H. 1997. Wasting Energy on an Illusion: Six Months Later. *The Black Scholar* 27.2.2–5.

1 B I K S V X

After outlining the arguments of his article in the previous edition of *The Black Scholar* against teaching Black children Standard English as a foreign language, McWhorter now argues against the use of dialect readers, given what he sees as flaws in the studies that support them, and previously unconsidered studies indicating that they are not helpful. He then reemphasizes the effectiveness of language immersion and explains how attempts to teach Standard English as a foreign language alienate students from it, as it becomes a mere tool to be used in a "White" world. In concluding the paper, he offers three strategies to be used in conjunction with Standard English immersion: (1) train teachers in the systematicity of AAVE in order to dispel myths that it is degenerate; (2) allow younger Black children to speak AAVE in the classroom, under the expectation that through immersion they will gradually begin to express themselves in Standard English, and (3) establish Afrocentric curricula for predominantly African American classrooms, so that children will not feel alienated in the school context.

Meacham, Shuaib. 2000. Black Self-Love, Language, and the Teacher Education Dilemma: The Cultural Denial and Cultural Limbo of African American Preservice Teachers. *Urban Education* 34.571–96.

1 I T

Meacham explores the language-related personal dilemmas of two African American preservice teachers with strong cultural identities. Linda and Tanya each participated in four interviews concerning their family background, linguistic biographies, educational experiences, and philosophies. Linda grew up speaking AAVE without being conscious of its stigmatization in mainstream society; when her colleagues and teachers began to correct her, she experienced a devaluation of herself, her family and her culture until she gained a better understanding of the language ideologies governing society. Tanya, on the other hand, grew up pressured to speak Standard English despite her awareness of the legitimacy of AAVE. As a result of her speech, colleagues would mention to her that she did not 'act Black,' which made her feel culturally compromised. In light of the teacher education program's intolerance for nonstandard English, the author recommends that such programs begin to "integrate [minority groups] into the fabric of teacher education" (p. 594) in order to better support the development of culturally sensitive teachers.

Meacham, Shuaib. 2002. The Clash of 'Common Senses': Two African American Women Become Teachers. In *The Skin That We Speak,* ed. by L. Delpit & J. K. Dowdy, 179–201. New York: New Press.

1 I T

Meade, Rocky R. 2001. *Acquisition of Jamaica Phonology.* Delft: De Systeem Drukkers, University of Amsterdam. Based on the author's thesis.

2 Q

Meek, Barbara A. 2006. And the Injun Goes "How!": Representations of American Indian English in White Public Space. *Language in Society* 35.93–128.

5 F I

Meier, Terry. 1997. Using Flossie and the Fox. *Rethinking Schools* 12. 1 (Fall):21.

6 S V

Meier, Terry. 1999. The Case for Ebonics as a Part of Exemplary Teacher Preparation. In *Making the Connection,* ed. by C. Adger, D. Christian & O. Taylor, 97–114. Washington, D.C.: CAL/Delta.

1 I T

In this spirited essay, Meier argues that teachers of AAVE-speaking students need knowledge about their vernacular to teach them more effectively in several respects, e.g., to prevent misunderstandings in the classroom, and to prevent students being "underestimated or assessed inappropriately" (p. 102). The essay concludes with this memorable quote (p. 112): "As I tell my bright, eager, committed-to-making-a-difference students, they don't need to know anything about Ebonics to become teachers. They only need that knowledge if they want to become great teachers."

Meier, Terry. 2008. *Black Communications and Learning to Read: Building on Children's Linguistic and Cultural Strengths.* New York: Teachers College Press.

1 E F N Q R S W
A sophisticated synthesis of research and practice on literacy instruction for AAVE speaking children in grades K through 4. A central argument of the book is that in order to effectively teach AAVE speaking children to read, teachers must be aware not only of the core linguistic components of AAVE but also its stylistic and rhetorical components. The book is divided into four parts. The first part overviews the lexical, grammatical and phonological features of AAVE as well its stylistic and rhetorical features. The author places special emphasis on the intimate relationship between language, culture, and history, as illustrated through a brief look at kinship terms, proverbs, and cultural stories. The second part surveys research on language socialization among African American children, focusing on ritual spaces and communicative events such as Sunday school lessons, 'playing the dozens,' conflict talk, and storytelling. The author develops a list of twelve linguistic abilities that African American children likely develop as a consequence of language socialization—abilities that, the author argues, provide a solid foundation for literacy instruction. The third part focuses on reading comprehension skills, discussing the ways in which the linguistic abilities of African American children can be drawn upon to develop reading comprehension. Using examples from African American children's literature, the author details five comprehension strategies: connecting, visualizing, inferring, questioning, and summarizing/retelling. Finally, the fourth part focuses on decoding text, discussing strategies for teaching alphabet knowledge and phonological and phonemic awareness, and reviewing relevant research in these areas.

Melmed, Paul Jay. 1973. Black English Phonology: The Question of Reading Interference. In *Language Differences: Do They Interfere?*, ed. by J. Laffey & R. Shuy, 70–85.

1 R X

Mendoza-Denton, Norma. 1999. Sociolinguistics and Linguistic Anthropology of US Latinos. *Annual Review of Anthropology* 28.375–95.

4 F U

Mendoza-Denton, Norma. 2008. *Homegirls: Language and Cultural Practice among Latina Youth Gangs.* Malden, MA: Blackwell.

4 F U

Mendoza-Denton, Norma & Melissa Iwai. 1993. 'They Speak More Caucasian': Generational Differences in the Speech of Japanese Americans. In Salsa I: *Proceedings of the First Annual Symposium About Language and Society*, ed. by R. Queen & R. Barrett, 58–67. Austin: Department of Linguistics, University of Texas.

3 6 F I

Menken, Kate. 2009. No Child Left Behind and Its Effects on Language Policy. *Annual Review of Applied Linguistics* 29.103–17.

E P

Messner, Kyle. 1997. *Evaluative Summary of Appalachian Dialect Awareness Program.* Boone, NC: Appalachian State University.

6 L

Mesthrie, Rajend. 1992. *English in Language Shift: The History, Structure and Sociolinguistics of South African Indian English.* Cambridge: Cambridge University Press.

6 F

Mesthrie, Rajend. 2008. *Africa, South and Southeast Asia*. Berlin: Mouton de Gruyter.

6 F

Mesthrie, Rajend. 2010. *A Dictionary of South African Indian English*. Cape Town, South Africa: University of Cape Town Press.

6 F

Michaels, Sarah. 1981. "Sharing Time": Children's Narrative Styles and Differential Access to Literacy. *Language in Society* 10.423–42. 1

C N O

Michaels, Sarah & Courtney Cazden. 1986. Teacher/Child Collaboration as Oral Preparation for Literacy. In *The Acquisition of Literacy: Ethnographic Perspectives*, ed. by B. B. Schieffelin & P. Gilmore, 132-54.. Norwood, NJ: Ablex.

1 N S T

Michaels, Sarah & James Collins. 1984. Oral Discourse Styles: Classroom Interaction and the Acquisition of Literacy. In *Coherence in Spoken and Written Discourse*, ed. by D. Tannen, 219–44. Norwood, NJ: Ablex.

1 C N O

Mickan, Margaret. 1992. Kriol and Education in the Kimberley. In *Pidgins, Creoles and Nonstandard Dialects in Education, Applied Linguistics Association of Australia Occasional Paper No. 12*, ed. by J. Siegel, 42–52. Melbourne: Applied Linguistics Association of Australia.

2 S

Mickelson, Norma & Charles Galloway. 1973. Verbal Concepts of Indian and Non-Indian School Beginners. *The Journal of Educational Research* 67.55–56.

5

Migge, Bettina, Isabelle Leglise & Angela Bartens. 2010. Creoles in Education: A Discussion of Pertinent Issues. In *Creoles in Education: An Appraisal of Current Programs and Projects*, ed. by B. Migge, I. Leglise & A. Bartens, 1-30. Amsterdam: John Benjamins.

2 P V

Migge, Bettina, Isabelle Leglise & Angela Bartens. 2010. *Creoles in Education: An Appraisal of Current Programs and Projects*. Amsterdam: John Benjamins.

2 E P S V

Mihalic, F. 1971. *The Jacaranda Dictionary and Grammar of Melanesian Pidgin*. Milton, Queensland, Australia: The Jacaranda Press.

2 F

Miller, D. D. & Gail Johnson. 1974. What We've Learned About Teaching Reading to Navajo Indians. The Reading Teacher 27.550–54.

5 I R S

Miller, Mary Rita. 1967. Attestations of American Indian Pidgin English in Fiction and Nonfiction. *American Speech* 42.142–47.

2 5 F W

Miller, Mary Rita. 1977. *Children of the Salt River: First and Second Language Acquisition among Pima Children.* Bloomington: Indiana University Language Science Monographs.

5 Q

Mitchell, Arlene Harris & Darwin Henderson. 1990. Black Poetry: Versatility of Voice. *The English Journal* 79.4.23–28.

1 C N
This article examines the use of African American Vernacular English in the poetry of well-known Black writers—including analyses of works by Langston Hughes, Paul Lawrence Dunbar, Gewendolyn Bennett, Alice Dunbar Nelson, Claude McKay, Sterling A. Brown, Lucille Clifton, and Nikki Giovanni. The article ends (p. 28) on a particularly affirming note: "These black poets' versatility reminds students of their own various language registers and voices...Students bring it all with them."

Mitchell, Felicia. 2005. *Appalachian Dialects in the College Classroom: Linguistic Diversity and Sensitivity in the Classroom.* Paper presented to the National Conference on College Composition and Communication, San Francisco, 2005. [Abstract prepared by the author and reprinted with permission of the author from the Educational Resources Information Center at eric.ed.gov.]

6 F I T
The purpose of this presentation is to encourage college teachers of writing, inside and outside Appalachia, to look at dialect-based errors in a more expansive way even as they help students to make better choices about standard usage. The discussion, which is presented within the context of a socio-cultural perspective on bias in perceptions of error, is intended to invite teachers to be more tolerant of diversity as they guide students to use Standard American English. Errors illustrating the discussion have been adapted from the writing and oral speech of students from southern Appalachia and are analyzed within the context of linguistic roots and language evolution. Linguistic analysis of errors includes the common "had went" contrasted with a more archaic yet "correct" usage, as well as nonstandard verbs and participles. Related attention is given to how oral pronunciation can invite biased perceptions of error. The presentation concludes with advice on how to be sensitive to diversity issues in the classroom.

Kernan-Mitchell, Claudia. 1971. *Language behavior in a Black urban community.* Berkeley, CA: University of California, Berkeley.

Mitchell-Kernan, Claudia. 1972. On the Status of Black English for Native Speakers: An Assessment of Attitudes and Values. In *Functions of Language in the Classroom,* ed. by C. Cazden, V. John & D. Hymes, 195–210. New York: Teacher's College Press.

1 I U
Mitchell-Kernan draws on ethnographic observations of a Black urban community to discuss native speakers' attitudes toward AAVE. While many features of AAVE were stigmatized within the community and referred to as 'flat', 'country' or 'bad English', Standard English was in turn often derided as being overly 'proper'. Social context played a large role in determining the appropriate use for each variety, and therefore, there was much dialectal variation even within a single speaker. Some speakers reported feeling both embarrassed about their own nonstandard speech and reluctant to conform to the standard. The author concludes that the gap between Standard English and AAVE will likely diminish due to the devaluation of the latter, but that because of an ideological need for distinctness there will always be some differences.

Mix, Julie Ann. 2003. Evidencing Nonstandard Feature Dynamics: "Speak Aloud and Write" Protocols by African American Freshman Composition Students. *Written Communication* 20.307–32.

1 W X

Moats, Louisa. 1994. The Missing Foundation in Teacher Education: Knowledge of the Structure of Spoken and Written Language. *Annals of Dyslexia* 44.81–102.

F R T
Experienced teachers of reading, language arts, and special education were tested to see if they possessed sufficient awareness of the building blocks of language (phonemes, morphemes, and syllables) and sound-symbol correspondences. The results were, in the author's words, "surprisingly poor," and Moats goes on to provide a convincing, highly practical case for the necessity of linguistic training in teacher education.

Moats, Louisa, Barbara Foorman & Patrick Taylor. 2006. How Quality of Writing Instruction Impacts High-Risk Fourth-Grader's Writing. *Reading and Writing* 19.363–91.

1 T W

Mocombe, Paul. 2006. The Sociolinguistic Nature of Black Academic Failure in Capitalist Education: A Reevaluation of "Language in the Inner City" and Its Social Function, "Acting White". *Race, Ethnicity & Education* 9.395–407. [Reprinted from *Race, Ethnicity & Education* 9(4).]

1 A I N
Studies on the "acting White" hypothesis—the premise that Black students purposefully underachieve in school and on standardized tests because of racialized peer pressure—to explain the Black-White achievement gap have not been able to negate the fact that a "burden of acting White" exists for some Black students, even though it is not prevalent among the group. This article rethinks the conventional understanding of "acting White," as the basis for the Black-White achievement gap, within a world-system analysis that reconceptualizes the very premise of the construct in order to get at a better understanding of its social psychological manifestation. The author concludes that the construct has very little to do with anti-school norms, but everything to do with a mismatch of linguistic structures and functions.

Mohawk, John C. 1985. Seeking a Language of Understanding. *Social Education* 49.104–05. [Abstract prepared by ERIC.]

5 I
American Indian children are not succeeding in school. A major reason is language. American Indians speak their own indigenous language as well as an indigenous English. Linguistic pressures by teachers are viewed by an Indian child as an attack on his/her identity. Teacher education concerning the relationship between language and identity is needed.

Moll, Luis. 1988. Some Key Issues in Teaching Latino Students. *Language Arts* 65.465–72.

4 A C T

Monroy Ochoa, Alberto & Karen Cadiero-Kaplan. 2004. Towards Promoting Biliteracy and Academic Achievement: Educational Programs for High School Latino English Language Learners. *The High School Journal* 87.27–43.

4 P

Monteith, Mary. 1980. Implications of the Ann Arbor Decision: Black English and the Reading Teacher. *Journal of Reading* 23.556–59.

1 K R S

Montgomery, Michael B. & Joseph S. Hall. 2004. *Dictionary of Smoky Mountain English.* Knoxville: The University of Tennessee Press.

6 F

Moore, Alex. 1999. Working with Bidialectal Students. In *Teaching Multicultured Students,* ed. by A. Moore, 126–52. London: Falmer Press.

2 A B R

Morales, Erik. 2009. Powerful Words: Skillful and Sensitive Empowerment of Urban Undergraduate Pre-Service Teachers through Improvement of Standard English Usage. *Educational Action Research* 17.311–25.

1 B T W
This article details the efforts of a teacher education professor to increase vernacular-speaking teacher candidates' access to Standard English. Informed primarily by the literature on muliticultural education, which stresses respect for all ways of speaking but places less emphasis on additive methods of language teaching, the author's action research project begins with language awareness activities but concludes with traditional corrective methods of writing revision. Results of this action research study, which are limited to a single teacher education course, include positive feedback from participants and an observed increase in use of Standard English conventions such as subject-verb agreement.

Moran, Michael J. 1993. Final Consonant Deletion in African-American Children Speaking Black English: A Closer Look. *Language, Speech, and Hearing Services in Schools* 24.161–66.

1 F X

Mordaunt, Owen G. 2011. Bidialectalism in the Classroom: The Case of African-American English. *Language, Culture and Curriculum* 24.77–87. [Abstract prepared by ERIC.]

1 B I S
This article provides a brief description of the linguistic features of African American English (AAE) and reviews the positions that have been taken up about its role in American education, ranging from those in which AAE is seen as an obstacle to the education of Black children to those in which it becomes a language that is different from Standard American English to be taught as a second or foreign language. This article argues that a bidialectal paradigm is needed to describe the prevailing situation accurately and goes on to outline the steps that are necessary, within this paradigm, for the maintenance and development of AAE in the education of African American children.

Morgan, Hani. 2010. Teaching Native American Students: What Every Teacher Should Know. *Education Digest: Essential Readings Condensed for Quick Review* 75.44–47.

5 C N S T
The author surveys several issues related to effective Indigenous education, including cross-cultural communication.

Morgan, Marcyliena. 2002. *Language, Discourse and Power in African American Culture.* Cambridge: Cambridge University Press.

1 F I N P U

Morren, Diane & Ronald Morren. 2007. Are the Goals and Objectives of Jamaica's Bilingual Education Project Being Met? *SIL Electronic Working Papers* 2007–09.

2 B P

Morren, Ronald. 2002. Creole-Based Trilingual Education in the Caribbean Archipelago of San Andres, Providence and Santa Catalina. *Journal of Multilingual and Multicultural Development* 22.227–41.

2 V

Morris, Edward. 2007. "Ladies" or "Loudies"?: Perceptions and Experiences of Black Girls in Classrooms. *Youth & Society* 38.490–515. [Reprinted with permission of Sage Publications, the publisher, from *Youth & Society* 38(4), 490.]

1 N T

Although much scholarship has focused on the schooling experiences of African American boys, this article demonstrates that African American girls encounter unique educational perceptions and obstacles. Black girls in a predominately minority school performed well academically, but educators often questioned their manners and behavior. Some tried to mold many of these girls into "ladies," which entailed curbing behavior perceived as "loud" and assertive. This article advances theories of intersectionality by showing how race and class shape perceptions of femininity for Black girls, and how the encouragement of more traditionally feminine behavior could ultimately limit their academic potential.

Morrow, Lesley Mandel, Robert Rueda & Diane Lapp. 2009. *Handbook of Research on Literacy and Diversity.* New York: Guilford Press.

E M R

Moses, Rae, Harvey Daniels & Robert Gundlach. 1976. Teachers' Language Attitudes and Bidialectalism. *International Journal of the Sociology of Language* 8.77–91.

B I T

Moses et al. examine the history of teachers' language attitudes as a framework for better understanding the educational dilemma over language variation. They find that as far back as 1918, with NCTE's establishment of Better Speech Week, teachers have been largely unwilling to accept the legitimacy of nonstandard usage, even as the NCTE later repealed its absolutist stance in 1935.When the absolutist-relativist debate began to focus on the status of nonstandard dialects in the 1960's, teachers maintained their absolutist stance, clinging to language deficit theories despite linguists' affirmation that all varieties are fully developed languages. Although some teachers did abandon eradication of nonstandard dialects in favor of bidialectalism, this was generally not accompanied by an adoption of the egalitarian assumptions behind bidialectalism. The authors conclude that teachers' language attitudes play a large role in shaping classroom language policy, and that in light of the long tradition of absolutism, changes are extremely unlikely to occur in the near future (p. 89).

Mufwene, Salikoko, John R. Rickford, Guy Bailey & John Baugh (eds.) 1998. *African American English: Structure, History and Use.* London: Routledge.

1 E F N

Mufwene, Salikoko S. 2001. Ebonics and Standard English in the Classroom: Some Issues. In *Language in Our Time: Bilingual Education and Official English, Ebonics and Standard English, Immigration and the Unz Initiative (Georgetown University Round Table on Language and Linguistics 1999)*, ed. by J. E. Alatis & A.-H. Tan, 253-61. Washington, D.C.: Georgetown University Press.

1 B I S

Mühleisen, Susanne. 2002. *Creole discourse: Exploring prestige formation and change across Caribbean English-lexicon creoles.* Amsterdam: John Benjamins.

2 I N V

Murray, Denise. 1997. Tesol Speaks on Ebonics. *TESOL Matters* 7.1–22.

1 B K

Murray, Denise E. 2001. Whose "Standard"? What the Ebonics Debate Tells Us About Language, Power and Pedagogy. In *Language in Our Time: Bilingual Education and Official English, Ebonics and Standard English, Immigration and the Unz Initiative (Georgetown University Round Table on Language and Linguistics 1999)*, ed. by J. E. Alatis & A.-H. Tan, 281–91. Washington, D.C.: Georgetown University Press.

1 I T

Murrell, Peter C., Jr. 1997. Digging Again the Family Wells: A Freirian Literacy Framework as Emancipatory Pedagogy for African-American Children. In *Mentoring the Mentor: A Critical Dialogue with Paulo Freire*, ed. by P. Freire, 19–58. New York: Peter Lang.

1 I L P S

Murtagh, Edward. 1982. Creole and English Used as Languages of Instruction in Bilingual Education with Aboriginal Australians: Some Research Findings. *International Journal of the Sociology of Language* 36.15–33.

2 6 B I S

Musgrave, Marianne. 1962. Teaching English as a Foreign Language to Students with Sub-Standard Dialects. *College Language Association Journal* 1.84–91.

B R

Myers-Scotton, Carol. 2009. Code-Switching. In *The New Sociolinguistics Reader*, ed. by N. Coupland and A. Jaworski, 473–89. London: Palgrave Macmillan.

U

Narang, H. L. 1974. Improving Reading Ability of Indian Children. *Elementary English* 51.190–92.

5 R

National Research Council. 2010. *Language Diversity, School Learning, and Closing Achievement Gaps: A Workshop Summary.* Washington, D.C.: The National Academies Press.

1 4 A B Q

Ndolo, Ike S. 1989. The Case of Promoting the Nigerian Pidgin Language. *Journal of Modern African Studies* 27.679–84.

2 I

Neba, Ayu'nwi, Evelyn Fogwe Chibaka & Gratien Atindogb. 2006. Cameroon Pidgin English (Cpe) as a Tool for Empowerment and National Development. *African Study Monographs* 27.39–61.

2 I P

Nelson, Nickola & Robert McRoskey. 1978. Comprehension of Standard English at Varied Speaking Rates by Children Whose Major Dialect Is Black English. *Journal of Communication Disorders* 11.37–50.

1 A O X

Nelson, Nickola Wolf. 2010. Changes in Story Probes Written across Third Grade by African American and European American Students in a Writing Lab Approach. *Topics in Language Disorders* 30.223–52.

1 W

Nelson-Barber, Sharon. 1982. Phonologic Variations of Pima English. In *Language Renewal among American Indian Tribes: Issues, Problems, and Prospects,* ed. by R. St. Clair & W. Leap, 115–31. Rosslyn, VA: National Clearinghouse for Bilingual Education.

5 F

Nembhard, Judith. 1983. A Perspective on Teaching Black Dialect Speaking Students to Write Standard English. *Journal of Negro Education* 52.75–82.

1 B I S T W
Effective communication is becoming increasingly necessary for any individual to be a viable member of US society. This article highlights the dramatic movement in English departments across the nation towards providing the successful teaching of writing composition to its students. The article focuses on the recurring question of whether or not it is possible to retrain teachers with enough skill to teach Black students to be effective writers also. The article explains that many theorists, due to labels which stigmatize the assumed ability of Black students, often speculatively suggest that teaching Black students to become effective writers in Standard English is impossible. However, it argues that successes of bidialectalism and positive systematic teaching methods at universities such as Howard demonstrate the opposite. In fact, the article asserts that teaching Blacks Standard English is often similar in difficulty to teaching non-Black students with linguistic problems. The article also addresses the issue of possible social oppression; it affirms that the teaching of Standard English as another dialect, rather than the correct form, of English often ensures Black students' writing success without negative effects on their feelings of self and cultural worth.

Nero, Shondel. 1997. English Is My Native Language, or So I Believe. *TESOL Quarterly* 31.585–92.

2 B

Nero, Shondel. 1997. ESL or ESD? Teaching English to Caribbean English Speakers. *TESOL Journal* 7.6–10.

2 B I W
In order to achieve a better understanding of the implications of teaching Standard American English (SAE) to Caribbean English speakers, Nero examines the linguistic perceptions and behaviors of four college students who had immigrated to the United States from Guyana and Jamaica within the past ten years. Interviews showed that the four students, of diverse socioeconomic backgrounds, all considered themselves native speakers of English and avoided the term 'Creole', though three conceded that

in informal settings they used 'broken' English. Analysis of writing portfolios showed that the greatest divergent morpho-syntactic feature of their writing was zero inflection for verbs. Two showed zero inflection for plurals and possessives as well, and one relied heavily on phonetic spellings. For informal writing assignments, all four used Creole features with higher frequency. In terms of discourse features, students were very explicit in narrative writing, but often vague in expository writing. In conclusion, Nero recommends against using English as a Second Language (ESL) techniques given the students' high receptive knowledge of SAE and their perception that they already speak English. Instead, she recommends integrating into the lessons discussions of language attitude, analysis of the differences between SAE and Creole, and an understanding of Caribbean history and culture.

Nero, Shondel. 2000. The Changing Faces of English: A Caribbean Perspective. *TESOL Quarterly* 34.483–510.

2 B I S

Nero, Shondel. 2001. *Englishes in Contact: Anglophone Caribbean Students in an Urban College.* Cresskill, NJ: Hampton Press.

2 B W

Nero, Shondel (ed.) 2006. *Dialects, Englishes, Creoles, and Education.* (Esl & Applied Linguistics Professional Series. Mahwah, NJ: Lawrence Erlbaum Associates.

2 3 4 A B E I K P R U V W
This edited book contains various articles regarding the appearance, acceptance, and use of various English vernaculars such as African American Vernacular English, West African Pidgin English, and Hawaiian Pidgin in public school education systems across the United States. The book is broken down into the following seven categories: World Englishes, Creoles, and Education; African-American Vernacular English/Ebonics; Caribbean Creole English; Hawai'i Creole English/Pidgin; Hispanized English; West African Pidgin English; and Asian Englishes. For more information, see the annotations for the Siegel, Rickford, Delpit, Winer, Pratt-Johnson, Eades et al., Kells, Kleine, Govardhan, and Tayao 2005 articles cited in this bibliography.

Nero, Shondel. 2006. Language, Identity, and Education of Caribbean English Speakers. *World Englishes* 25.501–11. [Abstract graciously provided by Shondel Nero.]

2 F I
Over the last two decades, North American schools and colleges have witnessed a significant increase in students speaking Caribbean English (CE), especially in New York City and Toronto, due to rapidly increasing migration from the Anglophone Caribbean to the United States and Canada. Such students publicly self-identify as native speakers of English, but their variety of English is often misunderstood by North American teachers. This article discusses the extent to which CE speakers challenge their teachers' assumptions about the definition and ownership of English as well as linguistic identity. In addition to providing examples of CE features that are likely to be misunderstood in North American classrooms, the author calls for new paradigms for language placement, instruction, and assessment with respect to CE speakers. The author also proposes concrete suggestions for addressing the linguistic and broader educational needs of CE speakers.

Nero, Shondel. 2010. Language, Literacy, and Pedagogy of Caribbean Creole English Speakers. In *Ethnolinguistic Diversity and Education: Language, Literacy, and Culture,* ed. by M. Farr, L. Seloni & J. Song, 212–40. New York: Routledge.

2 C T W

Neufeld, Paul, Steven Amendum, Jill Fitzgerald & Karren Guthrie. 2006. First-Grade Latino Students' English-Reading Growth in All-English Classrooms. *Reading Research and Instruction* 46.23–52.

4 R

Neufeld, Paul & Jill Fitzgerald. 2001. Early English Reading Development: Latino English Learners in the "Low" Reading Group. *Research in the Teaching of English* 36.64–109.

4 R

Newman, Michael. 2010. Focusing, Implicational Scaling, and the Dialect Status of New York Latino English. *Journal of Sociolinguistics* 14.207–39.

4 F

Newman, Michael & Angela Wu. 2011. "Do You Sound Asian When You Speak English?": Racial Identification and Voice in Chinese and Korean Americans' English. *American Speech* 86.152–79.

3 F

Nichols, Patricia. 1977. A Sociolinguistic Perspective on Reading and Black Children. *Language Arts* 54.150–67.

1 A I R T

Nichols, Patricia. 1989. Storytelling in Carolina: Continuities and Contrasts. *Anthropology and Education Quarterly* 20.232–45.

1 C N

Nidue, Joseph. 1992. A Survey of Teachers' Attitudes toward the Use of Tok Pisin in Community Schools in Papua New Guinea. In *Pidgins, Creoles and Non-Standard Dialects in Education [Applied Linguistics Association of Australia Occasional Paper Number 12]* ed. by J. Siegel, 12–14. Clayton, Victoria, Australia: Applied Linguistics Association of Australia.

2 I T

This short summary outlines the results of a twenty-question survey administered to sixty-nine teachers in Papua New Guinea. Over 90% of the teachers were against introducing Tok Pisin into the classroom despite the communicative benefits it would provide. On the other hand, the survey confirms that the indigenous people's attitude toward the language is more favorable than it used to be given its increased use as a common language for thousands of speakers. A more rigorous study is planned for determining teacher attitude toward bilingual education.

Nolen, Patricia A. 1972. Reading Nonstandard Dialect Materials: A Study at Grades Two and Four. *Child Development* 43.1092–097.

1 R V X

Nolen investigates whether reading recall ability is influenced by the dialect of the reading passage. One hundred and fifty-six Caucasian and African American second- and fourth-grade students of low socioeconomic background were each given three reading passages appropriate to their grade levels: a standardized SAE passage, a standardized SAE passage rewritten in AAVE, and an original AAVE passage. Students filled out a recall test for each passage. It was hypothesized that students would perform better on texts that more closely approximated their own speech patterns, and that this effect would be more pronounced for second-grade African Americans than for their fourth-grade counterparts. Neither of these predictions was borne out; a test for significance indicated only that African American second-graders performed significantly better on the AAVE-rendered SAE passage than on the original AAVE passage, and that Caucasian fourth-graders performed significantly better on all three passages than the African American fourth-graders. The author suggests that perhaps the predictions would have been confirmed had the African American students been introduced to reading through dialect materials, and concludes that the use of introductory dialect materials may be inadvisable pending an increased understanding of the way reading skills interact with language.

Norment, Nathaniel. 1995. Discourse Features of African American Students' Writings. *Journal of Black Studies* 25.558–76.

1 N W

Norment, Nathaniel (ed.) 2005. *Readings in African American Language: Aspects, Features, and Perspectives, Vol. 2.* New York: Peter Lang.

1 E F N P S W
Of particular relevance to our readers are the following articles in this edited collection: Michele D. Foster, "Sociolinguistics and the African American community: Implications for pedagogy"; Daniel H. Morrow, "Dialect interference in writing: Another critical view"; Nathaniel Norment, Jr., "Quantitative and qualitative analyses of textual cohesion in African American students' writing in narrative, argumentative, and expository modes"; Nathaniel Norment, Jr., "Some effects of culture-referenced essay topics on the writing performance of African American students"; Geneva Smitherman, "Toward Educational Linguistics for the First World"; and Thomas Kochman, "Culture and communication: Implications for Black English in the classroom."

Ntiri, Daphne Williams. 1990. Review of *Dialect and Education* by Cheshire et al. (1989). *Journal of Reading* 34.78–80.

C E I P
Among other things, Ntiri observes (p. 79): "The patterns of linguistic variation in Britain are far more distinct than in the other countries. Though status is awarded for mainland European accents, the British show strong disfavor for nonstandard dialects. The British situation is complicated by the presence of foreign linguistic minority communities and the inroads their languages have made into Standard English. Since accent and dialect go together, it takes deviation in only one or the other to make speech "nonstandard." Standard English speakers with British English accents are therefore more favorably evaluated and credited with higher intelligence and more academic potential than speakers with regional dialects. The politicised attitude on this issue has led to a proliferation of language-awareness courses that highlight areas of risk and promote students' linguistic resourcefulness."

O'Neal, Debra & Marjorie Ringler. 2010. Broadening Our View of Linguistic Diversity. *Phi Delta Kappan* 91.48–52. [Reprinted with permission of Phi Delta Kappan from *Phi Delta Kappan* 91.]

B I S
The definition of English language learners needs to be broadened to include the marginalized dialects of English. Not all native speakers speak Standard English, and even those who do need to learn Academic English to succeed in school. By using strategies developed for ELLs, teachers can help all students become fluent in the language of school.

O'Neil, Wayne. 1972. The Politics of Bidialectalism. *College English* 33.433–39.

B I P

O'Neil, Wayne. 1990. Dealing with Bad Ideas: Twice Is Less. *English Journal* 79.142–55.

1 A X
A highly critical review of Orr 1987. O'Neil argues that dialect interference cannot account for all or even most of the Black-White achievement gap.

O'Neil, Wayne. 2010. Bringing Linguistics into the School Curriculum: Not One Less. In *Linguistics at School: Language Awareness in Primary and Secondary Education,* ed. by K. Denham & A. Lobeck, 24–34.

L

Odlin, Terrence. 1989. *Language Transfer: Cross-Linguistic Influence on Language Learning.* Cambridge: Cambridge University Press.

X

Oetting, Janna & April Garrity. 2006. Variation within Dialects: A Case of Cajun/Creole Influence within Child Saae and Swe. *Journal of Speech, Language, and Hearing Research* 49.16–26.

1 F I X

Oetting, Janna & Janet McDonald. 2001. Nonmainstream Dialect Use and Specific Language Impairment. *Journal of Speech, Language and Hearing Research* 44.207–23.

1 6 D

Oetting, Janna, Brandi Newkirk, Lekeitha Hartfield, Christy Wynn, Sonja Pruitt & April Garrity. 2010. Index of Productive Syntax for Children Who Speak African American English. *Language, Speech, and Hearing Services in Schools* 41.328–39.

1 D Q

Ogbu, John. 1991. Cultural Diversity and School Experience. In *Literacy as Praxis: Culture, Language, and Pedagogy,* ed. by C. Walsh, 25–50. New York: Ablex Publishing.

A C I

Ogbu, John. 1992. Understanding Cultural Diversity and Learning. *Educational Researcher* 21.5–14.

C I
Ogbu suggests that core curriculum education and multicultural education are inadequate methods for improving minority student achievement. Instead, he argues for the importance of distinguishing between 'voluntary' minorities and 'involuntary' minorities. Whereas those minority groups who freely immigrated to a new land generally learn to succeed without forsaking their cultural identity, those groups who were forced into an alien culture often develop a secondary set of values in opposition to those of the dominant culture, resulting in underachievement in school. The author proposes a number of strategies for involuntary minority communities to correct this problem, such as teaching that it is possible to succeed without losing ethnic identity, demonstrating that the community values academic success, and focusing on making children responsible for their adjustment within the school.

Ogbu, John. 1999. Beyond Language: Ebonics, Proper English, and Identity in a Black-American Speech Community. *American Education Research Journal* 36.147–84.

1 C I

Ogbu, John. 2003. *Black American Students in an Affluent Suburb: A Study of Academic Disengagement.* Mahwah, NJ: Lawrence Erlbaum Associates.

1 A B C I U

See editor's review by Dorinda J. Carter, in *Harvard Educational Review*, Winter 2004, available at http://www.hepg.org/her/abstract/38. Among other things, Carter reports on Ogbu's discussion of bidialectalism and code-switching among Black students in the affluent Shaker Heights, Ohio, suburb that is the focus of his book, and about what Ogbu sees as popular misinterpretations of Fordham and Ogbu's (1986) "acting White" hypothesis.

Oh, Sunyoung. 2002. Cross-Language Blending of /L/ Gestures by Bilingual Korean-English Children. In *Proceedings of the 26th Annual Boston University Conference on Language Development,* ed. by A. Do, S. Fish & B. Skarabela, 473–84. Somerville, MA: Cascadilla Press.

3 F

Ohama, Mary, Carolyn Gotay, Ian Pagano, Larry Boles & Dorothy Craven. 2000. Evaluations of Hawaii Creole English and Standard English. *Journal of Language and Social Psychology* 19.357–77.

2 I

In order to assess attitudes toward Hawaii Creole, Ohama et al played one of two forty-five-second audio recordings to 197 students at the University of Hawaii at Manoa. One recording featured a man talking about painting using Standard English; the other recording featured the same speaker and the same content, translated into Hawaii Creole. On a twenty-three-item Likert-type survey, students rated the speakers in terms of superiority, attractiveness, dynamism and language quality. Results indicated that students found the Standard English guise to be significantly higher in superiority and quality, and the Creole guise significantly higher in 'dynamism' (e.g., active, confident). Furthermore, Hawaiian students found the Creole guise significantly more attractive than did Japanese or Chinese students. Those students with the most knowledge of Creole rated the Creole guise more favorably over all than did students with less knowledge of it. The authors recommend increased instruction in language variation in order to counteract the negative attitudes exposed in this study.

Ohannessian, Sirarpi & William W. Gage (eds.) 1969. *Teaching English to Speakers of Choctaw, Navajo and Papago: A Contrastive Approach* (Indian Education Curriculum Bulletin). Washington, D.C.: Center for Applied Linguistics.

5 B E S

Oladejo, James. 1991. The National Language Question in Nigeria: Is There an Answer? *Language Problems and Language Planning* 15.256–67.

2 I

Oliver, Rhonda & Yvonne Haig. 2005. Teacher Perceptions of Student Speech: A Quantitative Study. *Australian Review of Applied Linguistics* 28.44–59. [Abstract prepared by ERIC.]

I T

This study reports on teachers' attitudes towards their students' speech varieties of English. A sample of 172 primary, district high and secondary teachers in Western Australian was surveyed on their attitudes towards language variation and towards their students' use of specific English variants. The teachers were found to have generally conservative attitudes, particularly with regard to their students' use of non-standard features. These features were also associated with falling language standards. The impact of the teacher background factors of gender, age, level of teaching qualification, teaching experience and professional development on attitudes was also considered. However, only teacher qualifications and length of experience were found to be significant and this influence was restricted to attitudes towards language varieties. Such findings have important implications for speakers of non-standard sociolects who would tend to use these features more often. It is of particular concern where teachers associate the use of non-standard varieties with lower academic ability as has been found in other research. The findings suggest that teachers need to understand the relationships between standard and non-standard varieties, written and spoken forms, formal and informal registers, and developmental and non-standard features.

Oliver, Rhonda, Judith Rochecouste, Samantha Vanderford & Ellen Grote. 2011. Teacher Awareness and Understandings About Aboriginal English in Western Australia. *Australian Review of Applied Linguistics* 34.60–74. [Abstract prepared by ERIC.]

2 6 B I T
Repeated assessments of literacy skills have shown that Aboriginal students do not achieve at the same level as their non-Aboriginal peers. Many Aboriginal students speak Aboriginal English, a dialect different from the Standard Australian English used in schools. Research shows that it is crucial for educators in bidialectal contexts to be aware of students' home language and to adopt appropriate educational responses. For over a decade, the ABC of "Two-Way Literacy and Learning Professional Development Program" has sought to improve outcomes for Aboriginal students in Western Australia. By promoting a two-way bidialectal approach to learning, Aboriginal English is valued, accommodated and used to bridge to learning in Standard Australian English. This paper draws on a large research project, which used qualitative and quantitative methods to evaluate the impact of the on-going professional development for teachers. It reports on the attitudes and understandings of teachers, with and without professional development and working in different contexts.

Oloruntoba, Christiana Iyetunde. 1992. *Sociocultural Dimensions of Nigerian Pidgin Usage (West Niger Delta of Nigeria)*. Ann Arbor: University of Michigan Press.

2 I

Orbe, Mark. 1994. 'Remember, It's Always White's Ball': Descriptions of African American Male Communication. *Communication Quarterly* 42.287–300. [Reprinted from *Communication Quarterly*, 42(3).]

1 I N
This paper represents a phenomenological approach to studying the communication of African American men. Through the use of critical incidents, in-depth interviews, and focus group discussions, descriptions of lived experiences were collected from over thirty-five co-researchers over a two-year period. Six essential themes are discussed as central to African American male communication: (1) the importance of other African Americans, (2) learning how to communicate with non-African Americans, (3) keeping a safe distance, (4) playing the part (snap!), (5) testing the sincerity of non-African Americans, and (6) an intense social responsibility. Implications for further research are discussed.

Orr, Eleanor. 1987. *Twice as Less: The Performance of Black Students in Mathematics and Science.* New York: Norton.

1 A X
See review by O'Neill (1990), cited in this volume.

Osborn, Terry (ed.) 2007. *Language and Cultural Diversity in US Schools: Democratic Principles in Action.* Blue Ridge Summit, PA: Rowman & Littlefield Education. [Abstract prepared by ERIC and reprinted with permission of the Department of Education from the Education Resources Information Center at eric.ed.gov.]

1 C E P
Intended for a general audience, this work explains how diversity is an essential element in classroom settings as well as in a vital democracy. This book contains nine chapters: 1—"Introduction: Participating in Democracy Means Participating in Schools" (Terry A. Osborn and Dina C. Osborn); 2—"Emergent Possibilities for Diversity in Reading and the Language Arts" (Cara Mulcahy); 3—"Bilingual Education: Good for U.S.?" (Mileidis Gort); 4—"Accent and Dialects: Ebonics and Beyond" (Timothy Reagan); 5—"A Case Study in Cultural and Linguistic Difference: The DEAF-WORLD" (Timothy Reagan); 6—"Foreign Language Education: It's Not Just For Conjugation Anymore" (Terry A. Osborn); 7—"Multicultural Education Is Good for the United States Beyond Sensitivity Training" (Wanda DeLeon and Xae Alicia Reyes); 8—"Policies for a Pluralistic Society" (Casey Cobb and Sharon F. Rallis); and 9—"What September 11 Also Teaches Us" (David Gerwin and Terry A. Osborn).

Österberg, Tore. 1961. *Bilingualism and the First School Language: An Educational Problem Illustrated by Results from a Swedish Dialect Area.* Umeå, Sweden: Västerbottens tryckeri.

B

Ovington, Gary. 1992. Teaching English to Kriol Speakers: The Kartiya Game. In *Pidgins, Creoles and Nonstandard Dialects in Education, Applied Linguistics Association of Australia Occasional Paper No. 12,* ed. by J. Siegel, 87–98. Melbourne: Applied Linguistics Association of Australia.

2 S

Pablo, Josephine Dicsen, Belen Ongteco & Stan Koki. 2001. *A Historical Perspective on Title Vii Bilingual Education Projects in Hawaii.* Honolulu, HI: Pacific Resources for Education and Learning.

2B

PACE. 1990. *Pidgins and Creoles in Education.*

2 F P
PACE (*Pidgins and Creoles in Education*), started out as an annual hard copy newsletter, edited by Jeff Siegel, in 1990. Publication in hard copy stopped in 2003 with issue 14. It has been replaced with a website with the same name (http://www.hawaii.edu/satocenter/pace/index.htm), which includes electronic versions of earlier versions of the PACE newsletter from 1990 to 2003, and is updated more regularly. In addition to providing information on new publications, PACE has sections on Conferences, Programs, and Resources. It's an invaluable resource for anyone interested in the educational aspects of pidgins and creoles lexically based on English (or other languages, for that matter).

Padak, Nancy. 1981. The Language and Educational Needs of Children Who Speak Black English. *Reading Teacher* 35.144–51.

1 B R S T

Paige, Rod, Elaine P. Witty & ebrary Inc. 2010. *The Black-White Achievement Gap Why Closing It Is the Greatest Civil Rights Issue of Our Time.* New York: AMACOM.

A R

Palacas, Arthur. 2001. Liberating American Ebonics from Euro-English. *College English* 63.326–52.

1 B I T W

Palacas advocates classifying Ebonics as a language fundamentally distinct from English by making the historical claim that it derives from African languages with overlaid English vocabulary, and by drawing on grammatical theory to show that what appear to be superficial grammatical disparities between Standard English and Ebonics are actually indicative of deep typological differences. Standard English, for example, indicates the perfective aspect according to tense by using different forms of the auxiliary verb 'have'. Ebonics, on the other hand, indicates the perfective aspect not according to tense, but by remoteness to the present, using 'done' for near past and 'bin' for remote past. The author explains that knowledge of these differences would not only help educators better appreciate the difficulty with which speakers of Ebonics learn Standard English, but also help students gain confidence as they learn that their speech is not just incorrect English but rather a language in its own right.

Palacas, Arthur. 2002. *Write About Ebonics: A Course in Composition, Culture, and Linguistic Awareness.* Akron, OH: University of Akron.

1 B F I M W

Pandey, Anita. 2000. Toefl to the Test: Are Monodialectal Aal-Speakers Similar to ESL Students? *World Englishes* 19.89–106.

1 A B

Pandey assesses the extent to which AAVE-speakers can be compared to English as a Second Language (ESL) students. Two classes of adult African American students were made aware of language variation and taught using an explicitly 'contrastive analytic' approach, and each student took the TOEFL test at the start of the semester, the midway point, and the end of the semester. For comparison, a 'control' group of twenty-two non-AAVE speakers and an ethnically 'mixed' group of twenty-one students also took the TOEFL test at the start and end of the semester. Results indicated that the AAVE-speakers scored on par with low-level ESL students on their first test, yet improved with each retake. Native SAE speakers of the 'control' and 'mixed' groups had higher scores, but on average these groups did not improve with either retake. The author concludes that AAVE-speakers learning SAE can be justifiably compared to ESL students, and that contrastive analysis is an effective method for improving SAE proficiency.

Paris, Django. 2009. "They're in My Culture, They Speak the Same Way": African American Language in Multiethnic High Schools. *Harvard Educational Review* 79.428–48. [Django Paris, Abstract, "They're in my culture, they speak the same way": African American language in multiethnic high schools." *Harvard Educational Review* 79:3 (Fall 2009), pp. 428–47. Copyright © by the President and Fellows of Harvard College. All rights reserved. For more information, please visit harvardeducationalreview.org.]

1 U

In this article, Paris explores the deep linguistic and cultural ways in which youth in a multiethnic urban high school employ linguistic features of African American Language (AAL) across ethnic lines. The author also discusses how knowledge about the use of AAL in multiethnic contexts might be applied to language and literacy education and how such linguistic and cultural sharing can help us forge interethnic understanding in our changing urban schools. The article not only fosters an understanding of how AAL works in such multiethnic urban schools, but also sheds light on opportunities for a pedagogy of pluralism—a stance toward teaching both within and across differences.

Paris, Django. 2011. *Language across Difference: Ethnicity, Communication, and Youth Identities in Changing Urban Schools.* Cambridge: Cambridge University Press. [Abstract for Paris, Django. 2011 graciously provided by Django Paris.]

1 C I N U

Once a predominantly African American city, South Vista in the San Francisco Bay Area opened the twenty-first century with a large Latino/a majority and a significant population of Pacific Islanders. Combining critical ethnography and social language methodologies, this book offers the voices and experiences of South Vista youth as a window into how today's young people challenge and reinforce ethnic and linguistic difference in demographically changing urban schools and communities. The ways African American Language (AAL), Spanish, and Samoan are used within and across ethnicity in social and academic interactions, text messages, and youth authored rap lyrics show urban young people enacting both new and old visions of pluralist cultural spaces. The book illustrates how understanding youth language, ethnicity, and identities in changing urban landscapes like South Vista offers crucial avenues for researchers and educators to push for more equitable schools and a more equitable society.

Parker, Henry & Marilyn Crist. 1995. *Teaching Minorities to Play the Corporate Language Game.* Columbia, SC: National Resource Center for the Freshman Year Experience and Students in Transition, University of South Carolina.

1 B I S

Parker and Crist present a guide aimed at helping freshmen studies teachers and advisors prepare their students for the linguistic demands of the professional world. The authors take a pragmatic approach, explaining that while 'Neighborhood English' (AAVE) and 'Corporate English' (SAE) are linguistically equal, stereotypes against AAVE make it beneficial for speakers to learn SAE. Twenty-two major phonologically and syntactically contrastive points between SAE and AAVE are outlined in an easily accessible way, along with examples for each point. Since "just 22 items could make the difference between what is interpreted as idiocy and as literacy" (p. 21), the authors advocate a contrastive analysis approach for helping students internalize SAE. To this end, a brief sample set of response drills is provided.

Parks, Stephen. 2000. *Class Politics: The Movement for the Students' Right to Their Own Language.* Urbana, IL: NCTE.

P W

Parmegiani, Andrea. 2006. On Race, Language, Power, and Identity: Understanding the Intricacies through Multicultural Communication, Language Policies, and the Ebonics Debate. *TESOL Quarterly* 40.641–48.

1 I K P

Patrick, Donna. 2006. English and the Construction of Aboriginal Identities in the Eastern Canadian Arctic. In *English and Ethnicity*, ed. by J. Brutt-Griffler & C. E. Davies, 167–90. New York: Palgrave Macmillan.

5 I

Patterson, Janet L. 1994. A Tutorial on Sociolinguistics for Speech-Language Pathologists: An Appreciation of Variation. *National Student Speech Language Hearing Association Journal* 21.14–30.

A C I N

Paulston, Christina Bratt & Susanne McLaughlin. 1994. Language-in-Education Policy and Planning. *Annual Review of Applied Linguistics* 14.53–81. [Abstract prepared by ERIC.]

2 6 E P

A descriptive review of research on language-in-education policy and planning is offered. It covers national languages (North America, Southern Africa, Central Asia); minority languages (New Zealand, North America); European minority languages and language policies in the European Community; testing and evaluation; teacher education; and literacy.

Pavlenko, Aneta. 2004. Review of "America's Second Tongue: American Indian Education and the Ownership of English, 1860–1900". *International Journal of Bilingual Education and Bilingualism* 7.475–79.

5 I P

Pearson, Barbara, Shelley Velleman, Timothy Bryant & Tiffany Charko. 2009. Phonological Milestones for African American English-Speaking Children Learning Mainstream American English as a Second Dialect. *Language, Speech, and Hearing Services in Schools* 40.229–44.

1 A D Q

Pena, Elizabeth & Ronald Gillam. 2000. Dynamic Assessments of Children Referred for Speech and Language Evaluations. In *Dynamic Assessment: Prevailing Models and Applications,* ed. by C. Lidz & J. Elliott, 543–75. New York: Elsevier Science.

A D

Penalosa, Fernando. 1980. *Chicano Sociolinguistics: A Brief Introduction.* Rowley, MA: Newbury House.

4 F I U

Pendarvis, Edwina. 2010. Review of Appalachian Children's Literature: An Annotated Bibliography, by Roberta Teague Herrin and Sheila Quinn Oliver, 2009. *Appalachian Heritage* 38.88–89.

6 E M

Penfield, Susan. 1975. A Grant Proposal: Suggestions for Dealing with Mohave English. In *Southwest Languages and Linguistics in Educational Perspective,* ed. by G. Cantoni-Harvey & M. F. Heiser, 335–64. San Antonio, TX: Trinity University Press.

5 P

Penfield-Jasper, Susan. 1982. Mohave English and Tribal Identity. In *Essays in Native American English,* ed. by H. G. Bartelt, 23–31. San Antonio, TX: Trinity University Press.

5 I

Penn Reading Initiative & William Labov. 2010. *The Reading Road.* Philadelphia: Linguistics Laboratory, University of Pennsylvania. http://www.upenn.edu/nwlabov/PRI

1 M R S

Perez, Samuel A. 2000. Using Ebonics or Black English as a Bridge to Teaching Standard English. *Contemporary Education* 71.34–37.

1 B S

Perez explains that in order to use AAVE as a 'bridge' to teaching SAE, teachers must integrate into their instruction a respect for AAVE as a language, and an understanding of its features. To this end, the author reviews several contrastive analysis techniques. First, word and sentence discrimination drills, home-school discrimination drills, and translation and response drills based on Feigenbaum (1970) are presented. In another technique based on Tompkins and McGee (1983), students encounter a new syntactic pattern in a children's book, and then practice using it in a variety of reinforcement exercises until they are comfortable producing it in their own writing. Lastly, the author outlines a method in which students write or dictate stories for the teacher to rewrite in SAE. Students then read aloud the new versions while comparing them to the originals, and then revise their original stories further by expanding sentences to include more complex patterns and vocabulary. A word of caution: references to the AAVE literature are old, and at least one of the putative patterns (we have —> us got) is incorrect.

Perry, Theresa & Lisa Delpit (eds.) 1997. *The Real Ebonics Debate: Power, Language, and the Education of African American Children.* Boston: Beacon Press.

1 A C E I K

Perry, Theresa, Claude Steele & Asa Hilliard. 2003. *Young, Gifted and Black: Promoting High Achievement among African-American Students.* Boston: Beacon Press.

1 A C I T

Perryman-Clark, Staci. 2009. Wra 125 — Writing: The Ethnic and Racial Experience — an Afrocentric Approach. *Composition Studies* 37.126–34.

M W

The author provides the syllabus for a college-level composition course that takes the racial experience of African Americans as a thematic starting point, and emphasizes the use of African American Language and African American Rhetoric as fully legitimate modes of written communication, on par with Standard English.

Pewewardy, C. 1998. Fluff and Feathers: Treatment of American Indians in the Literature and the Classroom. *Equity & Excellence* 31.69–76.

5 C I

Philips, Susan. 1972. Participant Structures and Communicative Competence: Warm Springs Children in Community and Classroom. In *The Function of Language in the Classroom,* ed. by C. Cazden, V. John & D. Hymes. New York: Teachers College Press.

5 C N

Piché, Gene, Michael Michlin, Donald L. Rubin & Allen Sullivan. 1977. Effects of Dialect-Ethnicity, Social Class and Quality of Written Compositions on Teachers' Subjective Evaluations of Children. *Communication Monographs* 44.60–72.

A T W

Piché, Gene, Donald L. Rubin, Lona Turner & Michael Michlin. 1978. Teachers' Subjective Evaluations of Standard and Black Nonstandard English Compositions: A Study of Written Language and Attitudes. *Research in the Teaching of English* 12.107–18.

1 I T W

Piestrup, Ann McCormick. 1973. *Black Dialect Interference and Accommodation of Reading Instruction in First Grade*. Monographs of the Language-Behavior Research Laboratory, No. 4. Berkeley, CA: University of California.

1 I S T X

Pietras, Thomas & Pose Lamb. 1978. Attitudes of Selected Elementary Teachers toward Non-Standard Black Dialects. *Journal of Educational Research* 71.292–97.

1 I T
Pietras and Lamb assess teacher permissiveness toward nonstandard English as a function of various biographical features. After analyzing results from an eighteen-item questionnaire completed by ninety teachers in a midwestern elementary school system, they find that there is no correlation between a respondent's permissiveness and his/her age, gender, race, academic background, or years of teaching experience. When separately analyzing the results of those thirty teachers who had completed a workshop on dialectology, however, it was found that younger teachers, male teachers, and teachers with more academic background all exhibited greater permissiveness, although race and years of teaching experience again played no role. Over all, the workshop group was significantly more permissive than the group as a whole. The authors conclude that the workshop format implemented here is likely an effective method for improving teachers' attitudes toward nonstandard dialects, which may correspond to a better education for their students.

Plank, Gary A. 1994. What Silence Means for Educators of American Indian Children. *Journal of American Indian Education* 34.3–19. [Abstract prepared by ERIC.]

5 N O T
Navajo children's silence in the classroom may be related to unwillingness to put themselves above peers and to the culturally defined role of pupil as silent observer. Interviews with sixteen Navajo and non-Navajo teachers of Navajo children examined their attitudes toward student silence, classroom strategies used to accommodate silence, and teacher preparation for working with Indian children.

Politzer, Robert. 1993. A Researcher's Reflections on Bridging Dialect and Second Language Learning: Discussion of Problems and Solutions. In *Language and Culture and Learning: Teaching Spanish to Native Speakers of Spanish,* ed. by B. Merino, H. Trueba & F. Samaniego, 45–57. London: The Falmer Press.

B

Politzer, Robert, Mary Rhodes Hoover & Dwight Brown. 1974. A Test of Proficiency in Black Standard and Nonstandard Speech. *TESOL Quarterly* 8.27–35.

1 A F

Politzer, Robert L. & Mary Hoover. 1974. On the Use of Attitude Variables in Research in the Teaching of a Second Dialect. *International Review of Applied Linguistics in Language Teaching* 12.43–51.

1 B I
Politzer and Hoover examine the interaction of language teaching method and student language attitudes. One class of Black elementary school children participated in a five-week program in which contrastive analysis was used to point out systematic differences between SE and AAVE. Another class participated in a similar program in which the same points of Standard English grammar were covered without reference to AAVE. Although the authors hypothesized that students participating in the contrastive analysis program would generate higher scores on a test of spoken Standard English, this was not found to be the case. It was found, rather, that children with positive attitudes toward AAVE benefited more from the contrastive analysis program, and children with more negative attitudes benefited more from the noncontrastive approach. As this suggests that the effectiveness of contrastive analysis will vary depending on the background attitudes of the students, the authors recommend further investigation into this phenomenon in the instruction of other foreign dialects and languages.

Pollard, Velma. 1978. Code-Switching in Jamaica Creole: Some Educational Implications. *Caribbean Journal of Education* 5.16–31.

2 U

Pollard, Velma. 1979. The Child and the Language Arts Classroom: An Interdisciplinary Approach. *CARSEA* 4.9–12.

2 S

Pollard, Velma. 1980. Word and Meaning in Jamaica Creole: Some Problems for Teachers of English. *TORCH* 27.25–34.

2 F T

Pollard, Velma. 1983. The Classroom Teacher and the Standard Language. *Caribbean Journal of Education* 10.33–44.

2 T

Pollard, Velma. 1993. *From Jamaican Creole to Standard English: A Handbook for Teachers.* New York: Caribbean Research Center, Medgar Evers College (CUNY). [Abstracts for *From Jamaican Creole to Standard English: A Handbook for Teachers* and *Dread Talk: The Language of Rastafari* by Velma Pollard graciously provided by Velma Pollard.]

2 F M S T
This book offers a simple description of Jamaica Creole with an emphasis on how it differs from Jamaican English. The stated intention is to help teachers of all subjects Wherever they are located, teachers of children who speak an Anglophone creole at home and are expected to produce English in school, should benefit from the clarification this book offers.

Pollard, Velma. 1995. Indirectness in Afro-American Speech Communities: Some Implications for Classroom Practice. *Caribbean Journal of Education* 17.71–78.

1 2 N

Pollard, Velma. 1996. Cultural Connections: The Verbalization of Recall in Some Creole-Speaking Communities. In *Caribbean Language Issues Old & New,* ed. by P. Christie, 86–100. Kingston, Jamaica: The Press University of the West Indies.

2 F N

Pollard, Velma. 1998. Code Switching and Code Mixing: Language in the Jamaican Classroom. *Caribbean Journal of Education* 20.9–20.

2 B S U

Pollard, Velma. 1999. Beyond Grammar: Teaching English in an Anglophone Creole Environment. In *Creole Genesis, Attitudes and Discourse,* ed. by J. R. Rickford & S. Romaine, 323–36. Philadelphia: John Benjamins.

2 B S W

Pollard, Velma. 2000. *Dread Talk: The Language of Rastafari.* Mona, Barbados: Canoe Press. [Abstracts for *From Jamaican Creole to Standard English: A Handbook for Teachers* and *Dread Talk: The Language of Rastafari* by Velma Pollard graciously provided by Velma Pollard.]

2 E F

This book describes 'Dread Talk' as predominantly an adjustment of the lexicon of Jamaica Creole and of Jamaican English to reflect the sociological position of its creators and user, the Rastafari, who are primarily from the lower socio-economic levels of society. Word-Meaning for them is required to be true to word-sound. So, for example, the man who is at the bottom of the society is not UPpressed (oppressed) but DOWNpressed. (In short, they don't believe in the arbitrariness of the linguistic sign.) The book illustrates the use of the language in a variety of situations in Jamaica and the Eastern Caribbean.

Pon, Gordon, Tara Goldstein & Sandra R. Schecter. 2003. Interrupted by Silences: The Contemporary Education of Hong Kong-Born Chinese Canadians. In *Language Socialization in Bilingual and Multilingual Societies,* ed. by R. Bayley & S. R. Schecter. Clevedon, UK: Multilingual Matters.

3 I N T

Postal, Paul. 1972. Language Differences and Prescriptivism. In *Language and Cultural Diversity in American Education,* ed. by R. Abrahams & R. Troike, 112–17. Upper Saddle River, NJ: Prentice-Hall Inc.

I T

In a way accessible to a general audience, Postal briefly discusses a few points of linguistic theory relevant to widespread misconceptions in education. In teaching grammar, schools tend to emphasize only the differences between Standard English and nonstandard dialects, which belies the vast number of properties in common to all of them. Although standardization is not necessarily undesirable, it is important to remember that the standard is not linguistically superior, but rather merely associated with social prestige. The author then explains that prescriptivism is fueled by the notion that language is deteriorating and must be preserved, and that children must be explicitly taught how to speak their own language, when in fact, change is the natural state of language, and children acquire language naturally. Finally, the author explains that speech is the natural manifestation of language and that writing is a mere invention overlaid upon it, despite the misconception that writing is the purest form of language.

Potter, Lance D. 1981. American Indian Children and Writing: An Introduction to Some Issues. In *The Writing Needs of Linguistically Different Students,* ed. by B. Cronnell, 129–60. Los Alamitos, CA: SWRL Educational Research and Development.

5 R

Pratt-Johnson, Yvonne. 1993. Curriculum for Jamaican Creole-Speaking Students in New York City. *World Englishes* 12.257–64.

2 C O S

Pratt-Johnson, Yvonne. 2006. Teaching Jamaican Creole-Speaking Students. In *Dialects, Englishes, Creoles, and Education,* ed. by S. Nero, 119–36. Mahwah, NJ: Lawrence Erlbaum Associates.

2 C F S

Preston, Dennis. 1991. Language Teaching and Learning: Folk Linguistic Perspectives. In *Linguistics and Language Pedagogy: The State of the Art,* ed. by J. Alatis, 583–602. Washington, D.C.: Georgetown University Press.

6 I

Pruitt, Sonja L., April W. Garrity & Janna B. Oetting. 2010. Family History of Speech and Language Impairment in African American Children: Implications for Assessment. *Topics in Language Disorders* 30.154–64.

1 A D

Purcell-Gates, Victoria. 1993. 'I Ain't Never Read My Own Words Before'. *Journal of Reading* 37.210–19.

6 R W

Purcell-Gates, Victoria. 1995. *Other People's Words: The Cycle of Low Literacy.* Cambridge, MA: Harvard University Press.

6 R T W

Purcell-Gates, Victoria. 1996. Stories, Coupons, and the 'Tv Guide:' Relationships between Home Literacy Experiences and Emergenct Literacy Knowledge. *Reading Research Quarterly* 31.406–28.

4 5 6 R W

Purcell-Gates, Victoria. 2002. 'As Soon as She Opened Her Mouth!': Issues of Language, Literacy, and Power. In *The Skin That We Speak,* ed. by L. Delpit & J. K. Dowdy, 121–44. New York: The New Press.

6 I T
Purcell-Gates argues that low literacy achievement rates among children of poverty are due to a lack of reading exposure in the preschool years. Importantly, however, this constitutes not a learning deficit, but a different cultural experience. When such children are written off as incapable of learning, they pass on without simply receiving the experiential knowledge they need. Among the author's evidence is a case study involving a lower-class Appalachian child with illiterate parents. Because he grew up unaware of the concept of reading, he did not understand the initial reading instruction he was given, and thus fell behind. The school, however, already having deemed Donny incapable, refused to entertain his mother's pleas to hold him back, until the author intervened. The author concludes that teachers must accept that children of poverty are fully capable of learning, that these children's home languages are the vehicle through which they will begin to learn, and that these children are capable of learning different registers for use in written communication.

Rahman, Jacquelyn. 2008. Middle-Class African Americans: Reactions and Attitudes toward African American English. *American Speech* 83.141–76.

1 I U

Ramirez, J. David, Terrence Wiley, Gerda de Klerk, Enid Lee & Wayne E. Wright (eds.) 2005. *Ebonics in the Urban Education Debate, 2nd Ed.* Clevedon, UK: Multilingual Matters.

1 B C E K P T V
Revised second edition of a collection first published in 1999 by the Center for Language Minority Education and Research, California State University, Long Beach. The first half of the book includes articles by Terrence G. Wiley ("Ebonics: Background to the current policy debate"), John R. Rickford ("Using the vernacular to teach the standard"), John Baugh ("Educational implications of Ebonics"), Geneva Smitherman ("Black language and the education of Black children: One mo Once"), Subira Kifano and Ernie A. Smith ("Ebonics and education in the context of culture: Meeting the language and cultural needs of LEP African American students"), and Carolyn Temple Adger ("Language varieties in the school curriculum: Where do they belong and how will they get there"). The second half of the book includes background materials to the Ebonics Debate (e.g., the original and amended Oakland School District resolution on Ebonics), Examples of legislate reaction, Legal background, Linguists' reactions (with papers by Charles Fillmore, "A linguist looks at the Ebonics debate"; Walter Wolfram, "Ebonics and linguistics science: Clarifying the issues"; John R. Rickford and Angela E. Rickford, "Dialect readers revisited"; and William Labov, "Congressional Testimony"), Organizational responses, and Recommended readings on Ebonics.

Rampton, Ben. 1995. *Crossing: Language and Identity among Adolescents.* New York: Longman.

2 6 I U

Ramsey, P. A. 1985. Teaching the Teachers to Teach Black Dialect Writers. In *Tapping Potential: English and Language Arts for the Black Learner,* ed. by C. Brooks, 176–81. Urbana: NCTE.

1 T W

Rankie Shelton, Nancy. 2009. Positionality: Using Self-Discovery to Enhance Pre-Service Teachers' Understanding of Language Differences. In *Affirming Students' Right to Their Own Language: Bridging Language Policies and Pedagogical Practices,* ed. by J. Cobb Scott, D. Straker & L. Katz, 117–31. New York: Routledge National Council of Teachers of English.

I T

Ray, Chelsey. 1996. Report: Papua New Guinea. *PACE Newsletter* 7.

2 P V

Ray, George B. 2009. Language and Interracial Communication in the United States: Speaking in Black and White. New York: Peter Lang.

1 F I O

Reaser, Jeff. 2010. Developing Sociolinguistic Curricula That Help Teachers Meet Standards. *In Linguistics at School: Language Awareness in Primary and Secondary Education,* ed. by K. Denham & A. Lobeck, 91–105. Cambridge: Cambridge University Press.

A L

Outlines in detail the process by which two dialect awareness curricula—teaching materials developed to accompany the 2005 PBS documentary *Do You Speak American?* and the *Voices of North Carolina* social studies curriculum—were developed with a keen awareness of the central role of national and state learning standards.

Reaser, Jeffrey. 2010. Using Media to Teach About Language. *Language and Linguistics Compass* 4.782–92.

L S

The author argues for the use of 'medialingual' products in the classroom as an effective means of encouraging language study and offers considerations in developing and using multimedia tools to promote language awareness.

Reaser, Jeffrey & Carolyn Adger. 2007. Developing Language Awareness Materials for Nonlinguists: Lessons Learned from the *Do You Speak American?* Curriculum Development Project. *Language and Linguistics Compass* 1.

1 L

Details the process used by linguists at Center for Applied Linguistics used to develop a language awareness curriculum for high school, college, and teacher education settings. Discusses challenges and decisions that must be made when developing linguistic materials for non-linguists, including using/avoiding specialized linguistic terminology, maintaining an accessible writing style, and incorporating best practices in instructional methods.

Reaser, Jeffrey, Carolyn Adger & Susan Hoyle. 2005. *Curriculum Accompanying the Public Broadcasting Service Series 'Do You Speak American?'*. Washington, D.C.: MacNeil-Lehrer Productions.

1 4 I L M

Includes video clips, readings, discussion questions, and interactive website features to lead users through five language awareness themes: perspectives on written and spoken English; major regional dialects; African American English; Spanish and Chicano English; and communicative choices and linguistic style.

Reaser, Jeffrey & Carolyn Temple Adger. 2008. Vernacular Language Varieties in Educational Settings: Research and Development. In *Handbook of Educational Linguistics*, ed. by B. Spolsky & F. Hult, 161–73.

1 A B L R

Reaser, Jeffrey & Walt Wolfram. 2007. *Voices of North Carolina: Language and Life from the Atlantic to the Appalachians*. Raleigh, NC: North Carolina Language and Life Project.

6 I L M U

Redd, Teresa & Karen Schuster Webb. 2005. *A Teacher's Introduction to African American English: What a Writing Teacher Should Know*. Urbana, IL: NCTE. [Abstract prepared by ERIC and reprinted with permission of the Department of Education from the Education Resources Information Center at eric.ed.gov.]

1 E F W X

In this book Teresa M. Redd and Karen Schuster Webb explain not only what African American English (AAE) is, but also what role it may play in students' mastery of Standard Written English. Designed especially for writing teachers, this volume is a concise, coherent, and current source that summarizes the major schools of thought about AAE—without polemics or unnecessary jargon—so that readers can draw their own conclusions about AAE and understand how it might influence teaching and learning.

Citing leading scholars in the field, the authors explain how AAE differs from other varieties of English, how it developed, how it might influence students' ability to write Standard English, and how AAE speakers can learn to write Standard English more effectively. This book is organized into two parts. Part I: The Nature of AAE, contains the following chapters: (1) What Is AAE?; and (2) What Are the Distinctive Features of AAE? Part II, AAE and the Teaching of Writing; (3) Does AAE Affect Students' Ability to Write SWE?; and (4) How Can AAE Speakers Become Effective SWE Writers? The following are appended: (1) Student Writing Samples and Analyses; (2) Sample Assignments; and (3) Selected Web Sites.

Renn, Jennifer & J. Michael Terry. 2009. Operationalizing Style: Quantifying the Use of Style Shift in the Speech of African American Adolescents. *American Speech* 84.367–90.

1 F

Rentel, Victor & John J. Kennedy. 1972. Effects of Pattern Drill on the Phonology, Syntax, and Reading Achievement of Rural Appalachian Children. *American Educational Research Journal* 9.87–100.

6 B R S

Rentel and Kennedy examine the effects of pattern drills on improving SAE proficiency among Appalachian children. The test group and control group each consisted of sixty students divided evenly among three first-grade classes. For fifteen minutes per day over a period of six weeks, the test group listened to taped utterances of sentences in SAE that contrasted syntactically and phonologically with Appalachian English, and repeated each one back. For post-testing, each student in both groups took a twenty-frame oral language test, as well as the Word Reading subtest of the Stanford Achievement Test. Three judges rated the responses on the oral language test for syntactic and phonological standardness. Results indicated that the test group approximated the syntax of SAE significantly more than the control group, although there was no significant difference between the two groups in phonological standardness or reading ability. The authors caution, however, that the oral test examined mere imitative ability as opposed to productive ability, and that it is not known which specific syntactic features of SAE improved among the test group; consequently, further research is warranted.

Reveron, Wilhelmina. 1984. Language Assessment of Black Children: The State of the Art. *Papers in the Social Sciences* 4.79–94.

1 A

Reyes, Angela. 2005. Appropriation of African American Slang by Asian American Youth. *Journal of Sociolinguistics* 9.509–32.

1 3 F I

Reyes, Angela. 2007. *Language, Identity, and Stereotype among Southeast Asian American Youth: The Other Asian*. Mahwah, NJ: Lawrence Erlbaum Associates.

3 I

Reyes, Angela & Adrienne Lo (eds.) 2009. *Beyond Yellow English: Toward a Linguistic Anthropology of Asian Pacific America*. New York: Oxford University Press.

3 E I U

Reyhner, Jon (ed.) 1994. *Teaching American Indian Students*. Norman: University of Oklahoma Press.

5 E F O R S
Of special relevance to readers of this book are sections III Language Development (with articles by T. L. McCarty and Rachel Schaffer, "Language and literacy development"; Edwina Hoffman, "Oral language development"; and William L. Leap, "American Indian English"), and IV Reading and Literature (especially the articles by Sandra Fox, "The whole language approach"; and Daniel L. Pearce, "Improving reading comprehension").

Reyhner, Jon & Denny S. Hurtado. 2008. Reading First, Literacy, and American Indian/ Alaska Native Students. *Journal of American Indian Education* 47.82–95.

5 C P R

Reynolds, Susan. 1999. Mutual Intelligibility? Comprehension Problems between American Standard English and Hawai'i Creole English in Hawai'i's Public Schools. In *Creole Genesis, Attitudes and Discourse,* ed. by J. R. Rickford & S. Romaine. Philadelphia: John Benjamins.

2 A O T

Richards, Cynthia & Yvonne Pratt-Johnson. 1995. The Use of Jamaican Creole in the Jamaican Classroom and Educational Implications for the NYC Public School and Cuny Systems. In *Caribbean Students in New York,* ed. by J. A. G. Irish, 59–71. New York: Caribbean Diaspora Press.

2 I O T W

Richardson, Elaine. 1998. The Anti-Ebonics Movement: "Standard" English Only. *Journal of English Linguistics* 26.156–69.

1 I K P

Richardson, Elaine. 2003. *African American Literacies.* New York: Routledge. [Abstract for Richardson, Elaine. 2003. *African American Literacies* graciously provided by Elaine Richardson.]

1 B N U W
In a move toward developing an African American-centered theory of composition, Richardson problematizes the traditional view of bidialectalism and advocates a shift to a more holistically Black style, or a trickster style, which employs deliberate Black patterns and discourse or standardized syntax and conventions depending on the language user's assessment of the rhetorical situation. The author advocates what she calls (Bl)academic Discourse.

Richardson, Elaine. 2003. Race, Class(Es), Gender, and Age: The Making of Knowledge About Language Diversity. In *Language Diversity in the Classroom: From Intention to Practice,* ed. by G. Smitherman & V. Villanueva, 40–66. Carbondale: Southern Illinois University Press.

I T
The author presents results from a 1997 NCTE-commissioned survey of teachers' language attitudes, knowledge, and beliefs.

Richardson, Elaine. 2008. African American Literacies. In *Encyclopedia of Language and Education,* ed. by B. Street & N. Hornberger, 738–49. New York: Springer Science.

1 C N W

Richardson, Elaine & Ronald L. Jackson (eds.) 2004. *African American Rhetoric(S): Interdisciplinary Perspectives*. Carbondale: Southern Illinois University Press.

1 E N S W

Rickford, Angela E. 1999. *I Can Fly: Teaching Reading Comprehension to African American and Other Ethnic Minority Students*. Lanham, MD: University Press of America.

1 A C N R S
Rickford reports on a study of twenty-five low-income twelve- and thirteen-year-old students (most African American, the rest Latina/o, Tongan and Fijian) in a failing school district in California. The author used story maps to reveal the structure of the narratives, and a variety of comprehension questions, ranging from simple recall to more challenging questions. The results challenge conventional wisdom: Students performed better on the higher order interpretive and creative questions than on the lower order recall questions. Additionally, while students all enjoyed the culturally relevant materials, were more stimulated by the longer, more complex stories than by shorter, simpler stories with low readability levels. Ethnically relevant texts, even including elements of AAVE, seemed to boost interest, as did more challenging materials and comprehension questions. The appendix includes copies of all the narratives and questions.

Rickford, Angela E. 2001. The Effect of Cultural Congruence and Higher Order Questioning on the Reading Enjoyment and Comprehension of Ethnic Minority Students. *Journal of Education for Students Placed at Risk* 6.357–88.

1 C R

Rickford, Angela E. 2002. The Effects of Teacher Education on Reading Improvement. *Journal of Reading Improvement* 38.147–69.

A R T

Rickford, Angela E. & John R. Rickford. 2007. Variation, Versatility, and Contrastive Analysis in the Classroom. In *Sociolinguistic Variation: Theories, Methods, and Applications*, ed. by R. Bayley & C. Lucas. Cambridge: Cambridge University Press.

1 B C S
The authors argue that linguistic versatility should be seen as the applied counterpart of the theoretical, sociolinguistic study of variation in language. The authors suggest that Contrastive Analysis (CA), which requires teachers and students alike to become students of linguistic variability themselves, is a good strategy for developing versatility in the standard and the vernacular. Numerous examples are given, both from the United States and the Caribbean. Variationists are urged to use their expertise to help design English and language arts curricula that "could improve the performance of vernacular speakers in the classroom and on the job front, without the damage to their identities and psyches that current vernacular-eschewing strategies often involve" (p. 296).

Rickford, Angela E. & John R. Rickford. 2010. From Outside Agitators to inside Implementers: Improving the Literacy Education of Vernacular and Creole Speakers. In *Ethnolinguistic Diversity and Education: Language, Literacy, and Culture*, ed. by M. Farr, L. Seloni & J. Song, 241–59. New York: Routledge.

1 2 B S T
As linguists move from the status of outside agitators or commentators to inside implementers, in response to increasing invitations to advise school districts or textbook publishers, what practical contributions can they make to the academic improvement

of literacy and language arts instruction for vernacular and Creole speaking students? Rickford & Rickford attempt to answer this question, drawing on their own professional experiences and the work of others. They draw insights from (a) examining, with a team of researchers, the University of California Subject A writing placement exams of African American students; (b) lecturing on AAVE and Education to California teachers and other personnel; (c) observing the implementation of the University of the West Indies' (UWI) experimental Creole education project; and (d) supervising the teaching of reading and language Arts in Northern California schools. With respect to (a), the authors conclude that the students' essays would not have been improved simply by correcting for AAVE features, because their writing was weak in terms of structure, organization, and ideas more generally, and these are therefore areas that teachers need to focus on. With respect to (b), they point to the fact that as practitioners, teachers tend to be less interested in theoretical constructs, and more excited by hands-on strategies and techniques that can be immediately implemented in their classrooms. With respect to (c), Rickford & Rickford explain that the potential benefits of the UWI experimental bilingual project were strong, but would be maximized if teachers combined it with excellent pedagogy. Finally, with respect to (d), they propose six deep teaching principles that distinguish effective teachers from ineffective ones, and offer specific examples from teachers in the field that reflect their expertise in teaching the basic elements of reading and language arts.

Rickford, John R. 1985. Standard and Non-Standard Language Attitudes in a Creole Continuum. In *Language of Equality,* ed. by N. Wolfson & J. Manes, 145–62. Berlin: Mouton de Gruyter.

2 I

Rickford, John R. 1987. *Dimensions of a Creole Continuum: History, Texts, Linguistic Analysis of Guyanese Creole.* Stanford, CA: Stanford University Press.

2 F

Rickford, John R. 1997. Suite for Ebony and Phonics. *Discover* 18.81–87

1 F I K R

Rickford, John R. 1997. Unequal Partnership: Sociolinguistics and the African American Community. *Language in Society* 26.161–97.

1 B V

Rickford, John R. 1999. *African American Vernacular English: Features, Evolution, Educational Implications.* Oxford: Blackwell.

1 B F I K R V W
Especially relevant is chapter 1, "Phonological and grammatical features of African American Vernacular English (AAVE)," which also examines variation in AAVE feature use by social class, age, gender and style, and discusses the distinctiveness of AAVE vis-a-vis other American Varieties, and the four chapters in part III, Educational Implications. These include: chapters 13—"Attitudes towards AAVE, and Classroom Implications and Strategies"; 14—Unequal partnership: Sociolinguistics and the African American community"; 15—"Suite for Ebony and Phonics"; and 16—"Using the vernacular to teach the standard."

Rickford, John R. 1999. Language Diversity and Academic Achievement in the Education of African American Students: An Overview of the Issues. In *Making the Connection,* ed. by C. Adger, D. Christian & O. Taylor, 1–29. Washington, D.C.: CAL/Delta.

1 A B K S V

This article, a response to the furor following the acknowledgement of Ebonics by the Oakland Unified School District (OUSD) in December 1996, argues that we should pay more attention to the obstacles that African American Vernacular English (AAVE) speakers face in the classroom. Rickford goes on to argue that we should improve the teaching of Standard English, especially via Contrastive Analysis and improve the teaching of reading. In connection with this last point, linguistically informed research on successful strategies for teaching reading, including Black Artful teaching and dialect readers, is cited. The conclusion of this overview stresses the need for linguists to use their expertise in tackling practical crises in American life, including the ones that children face in the classroom.

Rickford, John R. 1999. The Ebonics Controversy in My Backyard: A Sociolinguist's Experiences and Reflections. *Journal of Sociolinguistics* 3.267–75.

1 A K

Rickford, John R. 1999. Using the Vernacular to Teach the Standard. In *African American Vernacular English: Features, Evolution, Educational Implications*. Oxford: Blackwell.

1 B R V

After reviewing data on the Black-White achievement gap, Rickford argues that attending to dialect differences is one means of addressing disparities in educational outcomes. Rickford identifies three ways to take AAVE into account in classroom instruction: (1) the linguistically informed approach, in which teachers understand how AAVE operates use this knowledge to effectively instruct their students; (2) Contrastive Analysis, in which children study SAE through examining its systematic differences between SAE and AAVE, and (3) the use of initial reading materials written in AAVE (so-called Dialect Readers) before transitioning to materials in SAE. Quantitative evidence supporting the effectiveness of each technique is presented. These techniques have received little attention despite their "promise and success" (p. 345), and the author concludes that they should be more fully explored and implemented.

Rickford, John R. 2002. Linguistics, Education, and the Ebonics Firestorm. In *Round Table on Languages and Linguistics, 2000: Linguistics, Language and the Professions*, ed. by J. Alatis, H. Hamilton & A.-H. Tan, 25–45. Washington, D.C.: Georgetown University Press.

1 A B K R W

The author explores some of the historical connections between linguistics and education, and the linguistic underpinnings of the Oakland Unified School District's (OUSD) Ebonics controversy in 1996. After discussing data showing unacceptably low achievement rates for African American K-12 students, the author takes a detailed look at the revised 1997 resolution passed by the OUSD, focusing on the often misconstrued intention of the OUSD to take Ebonics or AAVE into account to facilitate classroom instruction in Standard English. He also observes that four years after the Oakland Ebonics resolution, much of the reformist vigor that inspired it seems to have gone, because of personnel changes at the level of teachers, the district Superintendent and School Board, and because the Standard English Proficiency program is no longer a favored pedagogical strategy in the OUSD.

Rickford, John R. 2006. Linguistics, Education, and the Ebonics Firestorm. In *Dialects, Englishes, Creoles, and Education,* ed. by S. Nero, 71–92. Mahwah, NJ: Lawrence Erlbaum Associates. [Reprint of J. R. Rickford, 2002].

1 B K

Rickford, John R. 2011. Le Page's theoretical and applied legacy in sociolinguistics and creole studies. In *Variation in the Caribbean*, eds. Lars Hinrichs and Joseph Farquharson, pp. 251–271. Amsterdam: John Benjamins.

2 V

Rickford, John R. & Barbara Greaves. 1978. Nonstandard Words and Expressions in the Writing of Guyanese School-Children. In *A Festival of Guyanese Words,* ed. by J. R. Rickford, 40–56. Georgetown: University of Guyana.

2 F W

Rickford, John R. & Angela E. Rickford. 1995. Dialect Readers Revisited. *Linguistics and Education* 7.107–28.

1 C I R V

Rickford, John R. & Russell J. Rickford. 2000. *Spoken Soul: The Story of Black English.* New York: John Wiley.

1 E F I K N
In this trade book written for a popular audience, the authors explore, in the introductory chapter, the contrast between the admiration for AAVE expressed by writers in the 1960s and 1980s, and the animosity and disdain directed at it by prominent figures and the general public after the Ebonics controversy of 1996/97. They attribute the negativity in part to misunderstandings of the Oakland School Board's proposals, and to misinformation about the vitality, systematicity and ubiquity of AAVE. In successive chapters, they show the vibrant use of AAVE by writers, preachers and prayers, comedians and actors, and singers. Using examples from every day speech by ordinary people, they then discuss the vocabulary, pronunciation, grammar and history of Spoken Soul (as author Claude Brown called it—see his 1968 article, cited in this bibliography). Part Four, The Ebonics Firestorm, contains chapters on education, the media, and Ebonics "Humor" (some of it viciously racist). Part Five, The Double Self, closes with a chapter on "The Crucible of identity." The authors close with suggestions for revaluing Spoken Soul, but precede this with a discussion of double consciousness in African American history and identity. Among other things, they quote from a school-office conversation in AAVE between a second-grade student, a school secretary and a parent, and comment that "These speakers, youth and adults alike, used Spoken Soul because it is the language in which comfortable informal conversation takes place daily for them—as is true of vast segments of the African American community. They drew on it … because it came naturally; because it was authentic; because it resonated for them,… because to have used Standard English might have marked the relationship between the participants as more formal or distant … For these individuals, not to have used Spoken Soul might have meant they were not who or what or where they were and wanted to be." (p. 222).

Rickford, John R., Julie Sweetland & Angela E. Rickford. 2004. African American English and Other Vernaculars in Education: A Topic-Coded Bibliography. *Journal of English Linguistics* 32.230–320.

1 E

Rickford, John R. & Elizabeth Closs Traugott. 1985. Symbol of Powerlessness and Degeneracy, or Symbol of Solidarity and Truth? Paradoxical Attitudes toward Pidgins and Creoles. In *The English Language Today,* ed. by S. Greenbaum, 252–61. Oxford: Pergamon.

2 I

Rickford, John R. & Walt Wolfram. 2009. *Explicit Formal Instruction in Oral Language (as a Second Dialect)*. Paper presented at the NRC Workshop on the role of language in school learning: Implications for closing the achievement gap, Menlo Park, CA. See www.nap.edu/catalog.php?record_id=12907

1 B I O P S

Rivers, Kenyatta, Linda Rosa-Lugo & Dona Hendrick. 2004. Performance of African American Adolescents on a Measure of Language Proficiency. *The Negro Educational Review* 55.117–27.

1 A Q

This article discusses a study in which the Woodcock-Johnson Language Proficiency Battery (WLPB) test was used in order to investigate a possible difference in language proficiency testing patterns of standard and non-standard English speaking students with culturally and linguistically diverse (CLD) backgrounds. Noting that previous studies had indicated that WLPB tests place CLD adolescents at a disadvantage, this study sought to determine if this standardized testing created a bias in the proficiency assessment of students. However, no significant correlation was found between adolescent African American English speakers and their performance on the seven clusters of WLPB testing. Finally, the article proposes that the unbiased WLPB assessments could potentially be used to properly identify language deficits in CLD adolescents.

Rizzo, B. & S. Villafane. 1975. Spanish Language Influences on Written English. *Journal of Basic Writing* 1.62–71.

4 W X

Robbins, Judy Floyd. 1989. 'Broadcast English' for Nonstandard Dialect Speakers. *Education Digest* 54.52–54.

1 B O

Roberts, Peter. 1983. Linguistics and Language Teaching. In *Studies in Caribbean Language,* ed. by L. Carrington, 230–44. St. Augustine, Trinidad: Society for Caribbean Linguistics.

B N X

Roberts, Peter. 1994. Integrating Creoles into Caribbean Classrooms. *Journal of Multilingual and Multicultural Development* 15.47–62.

2 S

Roberts, Peter. 2007. *West Indians and Their Language*. Cambridge: Cambridge University Press.

2 A B C E F P S

In addition to chapters describing features and sources of Creole English and other language varieties in the Caribbean, Roberts' book includes two chapters that deal explicitly with educational issues: Chapter 7, "Language in the Classroom," and Chapter 8, "Language Education Policy."

Roberts, Sarah. 2004. The Role of Style and Identity in the Development of Hawaiian Creole. In *Creoles, Contact, and Language Change: Linguistics and Social Implications,* ed. by G. à. Æ. Escure & A. Schwegler, 331–50. Amsterdam: John Benjamins.

2 F I K

Robertson, Ian. 1996. Language Education Policy (1): Towards a Rational Approach for Caribbean States. In *Caribbean Language Issues, Old and New: Papers in Honour of Professor Mervyn Alleyne on the Occasion of His Sixtieth Birthday,* ed. by P. Christie, 112–19. Kingston, Jamaica: The Press University of the West Indies.

2 P

Robinson-Zanartu, Carol. 1996. Serving Native American Children and Families: Considering Cultural Variables. *Language, Speech, and Hearing Services in Schools* 27.373.

5 A C N

Rodekohr, Rachel & William Haynes. 2001. Differentiating Dialect from Disorder: A Comparison of Two Processing Tasks and a Standardized Language Test. *Journal of Communication Disorders* 34.255–72.

1 A D

Rodriguez, Jose I., Aaron Castelan, Cargile & Marc D. Rich. 2004. Reactions to African-American Vernacular English: Do More Phonological Features Matter? *Western Journal of Black Studies* 28.407–14.

1 F I

Romaine, Suzanne. 1984. *The Language of Children and Adolescents: The Acquisition of Communicative Competence.* New York: Blackwell.

N Q
In a relatively early contribution to the sociolinguistic aspects of child language acquisition, Romaine focuses on how children develop the skills needed to be able to interpret and produce utterances appropriately within particular social contexts. While most of the data come from research conducted with schoolchildren in Edinburgh, a careful consideration of the role of class and culture is woven throughout the book, and the theoretical framework is valuable for researchers considering a wide range of vernacular varieties. "The measurement of communicative competence" takes up the issue of Standard English and standardized testing, and may be of particular interest to readers of this volume.

Romaine, Suzanne. 1988. *Pidgin and Creole Languages.* Burnt Mill, England: Longman. **2 F Q**

Romaine, Suzanne. 1992. *Language, Education and Development: Urban and Rural Tok Pisin in Papua New Guinea.* Oxford: Oxford University Press.

2 I P Q

Romaine, Suzanne. 1999. Changing Attitudes to Hawai'i Creole English: Fo' Find One Good Job, You Gotta Know How Fo' Talk Like One Haole. In *Creole Genesis, Attitudes and Discourse,* ed. by J. R. Rickford & S. Romaine, 287–303. Philadelphia: John Benjamins.

2 I

Rosa, Marc. 1994. Relationships between Cognitive Styles and Reading Comprehension of Expository Text of African American Male Students. *Journal of Negro Education* 63.546–55.

1 A R S
Rosa examines whether reading comprehension rate is correlated with cognitive style. Past research has made a distinction between two cognitive styles: field-independent

(analytical, object-oriented) and field-dependent (relational, inferential). The former was purported to correlate with high academic achievement and the latter with low academic achievement. Forty-three fourth-grade African American males each took the Group Embedded Figures Test, designed to determine the extent to which a subject's cognitive style is field-independent. When scores were correlated with raw scores from a comprehension test of expository text, it was found that high field-independent subjects scored significantly higher on the comprehension test than did low field-independent subjects. The authors therefore suggest that in teaching a diverse group of students, teachers would benefit from taking into account these different learning styles. Low field-independent learners may require a more explicit instructional style that helps guide them along the necessary cognitive processes involved in text interpretation.

Rosenthal, Marilyn. 1974. The Magic Boxes: Pre-School Children's Attitudes toward Black and Standard English. *The Florida FL Reporter.*55–62; 92–93.

I

Rosenthal, Robert & Lenore Jacobson. 1968. *Pygmalion in the Classroom: Teacher Expectations and Pupils' Intellectual Achievement.* New York: Holt, Rinehart and Winston.

A I T

Round Table, The. 1993. Mini-Lessons on Language. *English Journal* 82.75–77.

L M S

Several lessons on language structure and language variation are described, including language change, onomatopoeia, slang, word origin, dialect, and language functions.

Roy, Alice Myers. 1984. Alliance for Literacy: Teaching Non-Native Speakers and Speakers of Nonstandard English Together. *College Composition and Communication* 35.439–48. [Abstract prepared by ERIC.]

B S

The author discusses evidence in support of combining nonnative speakers and native speakers of nonstandard English for instructional purposes. Discusses the goals and strategies for language learning these two groups have in common, arguing that the two produce many of the same linguistic forms and can interact profitably toward language acquisition.

Rubin, Donald L. 1992. Nonlanguage Factors Affecting Undergraduates' Judgments of Nonnative English-Speaking Teaching Assistants. *Research in Higher Education* 33.511–31.

3 I

Rubinstein-Avila, Elaine. 2006. Connecting with Latino Learners. *Helping Struggling Students* 63.38–43.

4 A

Ruddell, Robert. 1965. The Effect of Oral and Written Patterns of Language Structure on Reading Comprehension. *Reading Teacher* 18.270–75.

R X

Rupley, William, Willliam Dee Nichols & Timothy Blair. 2008. Language and Culture in Literacy Instruction: Where Have They Gone? *The Teacher Educator* 43.238–48. [Abstract courtesy of journal.]

C T

An important, yet either often missing or under-emphasized realization in both federal and state standards for literacy is that literacy is primarily a language process and culture is a reflection of language. As such, language and culture must be retained as essential components upon which reading instruction is based. Our nation and our states truly want individuals who can use literacy to learn and to enhance their quality of life as well as the quality of life of those around them. This article looks at essential considerations that must be given to the role of language and culture in literacy instruction.

Rynkofs, J. Timothy. 2008. Culturally Responsive Talk between a Second Grade Teacher and Native Hawaiian Children During "Writing Workshop". *Educational Perspectives* 41.44–54. [Abstract prepared by ERIC and reprinted with permission of the Department of Education from the Education Resources Information Center at eric.ed.gov.]

2 C T U

In this article, the author describes a three-month study he conducted in Ellen Hino's classroom during writing workshop. The major purpose of the study was to look at the ways this native-born teacher responds orally to students who share her own bidialectical background. Most of these students are Native Hawaiian and speak a nonprestigious dialect called Hawai'i Creole (HC) as their primary language and Standard English (SE) as their secondary language. Not only do these students speak a dialect particular to the Hawaiian Islands, but their classroom interactions can be strikingly different from those of mainstream American culture. This study addresses issues of linguistic and cultural differences in the context of what is called "writing workshop."

Rystrom, Richard. 1970. Dialect Training and Reading: A Further Look. *Reading Research Quarterly* 5.581–99.

1 R X

Rystrom, Richard. 1973. Perceptions of Vowel Letter-Sound Relationships by First Grade Children. *Reading Research Quarterly* 9.170–85.

1 R X

Sailaja, P. 2009. *Indian English*. Edinburgh, Scotland: Edinburgh University Press.

6 F

Sakoda, Kent & Jeff Siegel. 2003. *Pidgin Grammar: An Introduction to the Creole Language of Hawai'i*. Honolulu, HI: Bess Press.

2 F

Sakoda, Kent & Eileen Tamura. 2008. Kent Sakoda Discusses Pidgin Grammar. *Educational Perspectives* 41.40–43.

2 F

This is the text of Eileen Tamura's brief interview with Kent Sakoda, a native of Kuai, Hawaii, a lecturer at the University of Hawaii at Manoa, and co-author of Pidgin Grammar: An Introduction to the Creole Language of Hawaii (Sakoda & Siegel 2003). Sakoda explains that the grammar of Hawaiian Creole English (known locally as "Pidgin") is systematic, and different from that of Standard English. He describes some of its features and points out their possible influences from Hawaiian, Chinese, and other heritage languages.

Sala, Bonaventure. 2009. Writing in Cameroon Pidgin English: Begging the Question. *English Today* 25.11–17.

2 P W
This article explores the question of an appropriate writing system for Cameroon Pidgin English, in connection with the author's work on *A Dictionary of Contemporary Cameroonian Pidgin*. After reviewing earlier proposals and practices, and taking the plusses and minuses of alternatives into account, the author recommends following the English orthography as far as possible.

Salaberry, M. Rafael (ed.) 2009. *Language Allegiances and Bilingualism in the U.S.* Buffalo, NY: Multilingual Matters.

4 E I

Salomone, Rosemary. 2010. *True American: Language, Identity, and the Education of Immigrant Children*. Cambridge, MA: Harvard University Press.

4 I P

Samant, Sai. 2010. Arab Americans and Sound Change in Southeastern Michigan. *English Today* 26.27–34.

6 F Q

Sandoval, Jonathan, Craig Frisby, Kurt Geisinger, Julia Ramos-Grenier & Janice Dowd Scheuneman (eds.) 1998. *Test Interpretation and Diversity: Achieving Equity in Assessment*. Washington, D.C.: American Psychological Association.

A E

Sandred, Karl Inge. 1996. A West African Creole Language in an Atlantic Perspective: The Origins and Present State of Krio. In *Language Contact across the North Atlantic,* ed. by P. S. Ureland & I. Clarkson, 528–42. Tübingen, Germany: Niemeyer.

2

Santa Ana, Otto. 1993. Chicano English and the Nature of the Chicano Language Setting. *Hispanic Journal of Behavioral Sciences* 15.3–35.

4 F

Santa Ana, Otto. 2002. *Brown Tide Rising: Metaphors of Latinos in Contemporary Public Discourse*. Austin: University of Texas Press.

4 P

Santa Ana, Otto (ed.) 2004. *Tongue Tied: The Lives of Multilingual Children in Public Education*. Oxford: Rowman & Littlefield. [Abstract graciously provided by the editor, Otto Santa Ana.]

1 4 5 6 A E I T
This anthology seeks to give voice to millions of people who, on a daily basis, are denied the opportunity to speak in their own words. Surprisingly, many Americans believe that some people should be silenced, for their own good. Among the tongue-tied are school children who do not speak English, and those who do not speak Standard English. Modern educational theories say to silence students is to deny them an equal opportunity to learn. Yet, it is commonplace to insist that they shut up, rather than speak with their own voices. Another voiceless segment of the US population is the parents of these children. Schoolteachers are the very important third group

who are also constrained by the prevailing hegemony of monolingualism. Tongue-Tied creates a forum for these people to speak up in their own defense. Tongue-Tied is designed to open the hearts of its readers to these children, by way of literature, and through accessible scientific essays. First-person accounts by Amy Tan, Sherman Alexie, bell hooks, Richard Rodriguez, and less familiar authors open windows onto the lives of linguistic minority students, initiating a much-needed dialogue which includes these silenced citizens. With such an inclusive conversation, the current linguistic bigotry of the United States, which most easily perpetuates itself through their silence, can finally be cross-examined.

Santa Ana, Otto & Robert Bayley. 2008. Chicano English: Phonology. In *Varieties of English Vol. 2: The Americas and the Caribbean,* ed. by E. Schneider, 219–38.

4 F

Sato, Charlene. 1985. Linguistic Inequality in Hawaii: The Post-Creole Dilemma. In *Language of Equality,* ed. by N. Wolfson & J. Manes, 255–72. Berlin: Mouton de Gruyter.

2 I P

Sato, Charlene. 1989. A Nonstandard Approach to Standard English. *TESOL Quarterly* 23.259–82.

1 2 B C K P

The author makes the case that minority varieties of English are legitimate communication systems whose maintenance is both inevitable and desirable, and hence that the teaching of Standard English as a second dialect should be viewed as 'additive bidialectalism' rather than 'remediation'. 'Assimilationist ideology' is rejected in favor of sociolinguistic diversity. After providing neutral (nonprescriptive) characterizations of the terms 'dialect', 'creole', and 'standard', the author reviews two relevant areas of research. First, research on Black English Vernacular and Hawaiian Creole English shows that, contrary to common belief, these varieties differ from Standard English in their core features to a degree that can impede mutual intelligibility between standard and nonstandard varieties. Second, ethnographic research on minority varieties in the classroom reveals similar findings: differences in interactional styles and discourse organization across speakers of different varieties of English can also be great in a way that hinders understanding between teachers and linguistic minority students. As a solution, the author recommends that teacher education programs train teachers to observe and analyze sociolinguistic variation and its effects on teacher-student interactions. Teachers should "begin where students are," employing material from minority varieties where appropriate for the purpose of teaching via contrastive analysis.

Saville, Muriel. 1978. Bilingual Education and the Native American. In *International Dimensions of Bilingual Education,* ed. by J. E. Alatis, 125–32. Washington, D.C.: Georgetown University Press.

5 P

Scanlon, Michael & Alicia Beckford Wassink. 2010. African American English in Urban Seattle: Accommodation and Intraspeaker Variation in the Pacific Northwest. *American Speech* 85.205–24.

1 F

Scarborough, Hollis, Dawn Hannah, Anne Charity & Jane Shore. 2003. Distinguishing Dialect Differences from Reading Errors in Oral Text Reading by Speakers of African-American Vernacular English (AAVE). In *Tips from the Experts: A Compendium of Advice on Literacy Instruction from Educators and Researchers,* ed. by A. Pincus. Long Valley, NJ: International Dyslexia Association, New Jersey Branch.

1 R S

Schecter, Sandra & Robert Bayley. 1997. Language Socialization Practices and Cultural Identity: Case Studies of Mexican-Descent Families in California and Texas. *TESOL Quarterly* 31.513–41.

4 I U

Schecter, Sandra & Robert Bayley. 2002. *Language as Cultural Practice: Mexicanos En El Norte.* Mahwah, NJ: Lawrence Erlbaum Associates.

4 I N

Schierloh, Jane McCabe. 1991. Teaching Standard English Usage: A Dialect-Based Approach. *Adult Learning* 2.20–22.

1 4 6 B S T W

Schneider, Edgar (ed.) 2008. *Varieties of English, Vol. 2: The Americas and the Caribbean.* Berlin: Mouton de Gruyter.

1 2 4 6 E F

Schneider, Edgar W. 2007. *Postcolonial English: Varieties around the World.* Cambridge: Cambridge University Press.

E F

Schneider, Edgar W. 2010. *English around the World: An Introduction.* Cambridge: Cambridge University Press.

E F

Schneider, Edgar W. & Bernd Kortmann (eds.) 2004. *A Handbook of Varieties of English: A Multimedia Reference Tool.* Berlin: Mouton de Gruyter.

E F

Schotta, S. G. 1970. Toward Standard English through Writing: An Experiment in Prince Edward County, Virginia. *TESOL Quarterly* 4.261–76.

1 B S W

Schreier, Daniel, Peter Trudgill, Edgar Schneider & Jeffrey Williams (eds.) 2010. *The Lesser-Known Varieties of English: An Introduction.* Cambridge: Cambridge University Press.

2 3 6 E F
Following an introduction by the editors, the book is divided into five parts, with contributions from leading sociolinguistic scholars: Part I The British Isles (chapters on Orkney and Shetland, and Channel Island English); Part II The Americas and the Caribbean (chapters on Canadian Maritime English, Newfoundland and Labrador English, Honduras/Bay Islands English, Euro-Caribbean English varieties, Bahamian English, Dominican Kokoy, and Anglo-Argentine English; Part III The South Atlantic Ocean (chapters on Falkland Islands English, St. Helenian English, and Tristan da Cunha English); Part IV Africa (chapters on LI Rhodesian English, and White Kenyan English); Part V Australasia and the Pacific (Eurasian Singapore English; Peranakan English in Singapore, and Norfolk Island and Pitcairn varieties).

Schröder, Anne. 2003. *Status, Functions, and Prospects of Pidgin English: An Empirical Approach to Language Dynamics in Cameroon.* Tübingen, Germany: Narr.

2 I

Schwartz, Judith (ed.) 1980. *Teaching the Linguistically Diverse.* Rochester: New York State English Council.

E S T

Schwartz, Judith. 1982. Dialect Interference in the Attainment of Literacy. *Journal of Reading* 26.440–46.

1 I R W X

Sclafani, Jennifer. 2008. The Intertextual Origins of Public Opinion: Constructing Ebonics in the New York Times. *Discourse & Society* 19.507.

1 I K

Scollon, Ronald & Suzanne Scollon. 1979. *Literacy as Interethnic Communication: An Athabaskan Case.* Austin, TX: Southwest Educational Development Laboratory.

5 N

Scollon, Ronald & Suzanne B. K. Scollon. 1981. *Narrative, Literacy, and Face in Interethnic Communication.* Norwood, NJ: Ablex Publishing.

5 N

Scoon, Annabelle R. 1971. Affective Influences on English Language Learning among Indian Students. *TESOL Quarterly* 5.285–91.

5 I

Scott, Chris & Kathleen Brown. 2008. Rising above My Raisin'?: Using Heuristic Inquiry to Explore the Effects of the Lumbee Dialect on Ethnic Identity Development. *American Indian Quarterly* 32.485–521.

5 I

Scott, Cheryl & Lisa Rogers. 1996. Written Language Abilities of African American Children and Youth. In *Communication Development and Disorders in African American Children: Research, Assessment and Intervention*, ed. by A. Kamhi, K. Pollock & J. Harris, 307–32. Baltimore: Paul H. Brookes Publishing.

1 E W

Scott, Joyce. 1997. Official Language, Unofficial Reality: Acquiring Bilingual/Bicultural Fluency in a Segregated Southern Community. *Rethinking Schools* 12.30–31.

1 B

Scott, Jerrie Cobb. 1990. The Silent Sounds of Language Variation in the Classroom. In *Perspectives on Talk and Learning*, ed. by S. Hynds & D. L. Rubin, 285–97. Urbana, IL: NCTE.

1 B C N O S

The author describes an oral dialogue project with African American middle school students. Students were videotaped planning for, implementing, and critiquing student-to-student dialogues on self-selected issues. Scott's project represents an indirect critique of the bidialectal model, which she claims "failed ... to adequately address the bidialectal ideal and focused on the teaching of one, instead of several, English-lects" (p. 286).

Scott, Jerrie Cobb. 1993. Literacies and Deficits Revisited. *Journal of Basic Writing* 12.46–56.

A I W
Reprinted in *Landmark Essays on Basic Writing*, 2001, ed. by Kay Halasek and Nels P. Highberg, 205–212. Mahwah, NJ: Lawrence Erlbaum Associates.

Scott, Jerrie Cobb & Geneva Smitherman. 1985. Language Attitudes and Self-Fulfilling Prophecies in the Elementary School. In *The English Language Today,* ed. by S. Greenbaum, 302–14. Oxford: Pergamon.

I T

Scott, Jerrie Cobb, Dolores Straker & Laurie Katz (eds.) 2009. *Affirming Students' Right to Their Own Language: Bridging Language Policies and Pedagogical Practices*. New York: NCTE and Routledge. [Abstract graciously provided by Jerrie Cobb Scott.]

1 3 4 6 C E I P
This book explores the many faces of language policies and pedagogical practices that have surfaced over the last three decades in support of the rights of students to use their primary language and culture as resources for learning. But some of the same conditions that were addressed over three decades ago by the Conference on College Composition and Communication's Students' Right to Their Own Language Resolution have re-emerged today with intensity. The book Part I, "Setting the Context," chronicles the development of litigation, legislation, and related resolutions. Part II, "Educational Policies, Attitdues, and Unfulfilled Promises," focuses on language policies and attitudinal impediments to fulfilling the promises for equal educational opportunities for ALL students. Part III, "Toward A Pedagogy of Success in Classrooms," presents hands-on, research-based instructional strategies for giving students access to their primary language and cultural orientations to foster more meaningful, effective learning.

Scott, Jerrie Cobb, Dolores Straker & Laurie Katz. 2009. Cross-Currents in Language Policies and Pedagogical Practices. In *Affirming Students' Right to Their Own Language: Bridging Language Policies and Pedagogical Practices,* ed. by J. Cobb Scott, D. Straker & L. Katz, 3–17. New York: Routledge and National Council of Teachers of English.

1 C I P S

Screen, Robert M. & Henry L. Taylor, Jr. 1972. Relevancy of Speech and Hearing Facilities to the Black Community. *Language, Speech and Hearing Services in Schools* 3.56–61.

D

Sealey-Ruiz, Yolanda. 2005. Spoken Soul: The Language of Black Imagination and Reality. *The Educational Forum* 70.37–46.

1 F N

Sealey-Ruiz, Yolanda. 2007. Wrapping the Curriculum around Their Lives: Using a Culturally Relevant Curriculum with African American Adult Women. *Adult Education Quarterly: A Journal of Research and Theory* 58.44–60. [Reprinted with permission of Sage Publications, publisher of *Adult Education Quarterly: A Journal of Research and Theory* 58(1), 44.]

1 C I

This study examines how African American adult female students respond to a culturally relevant curriculum. Research confirms that adults enter college classrooms with a variety of experiences that they value and experiences to which they wish to connect. Black female students in particular possess knowledge unique to their positionality in American society, and they want to apply this knowledge to what they are learning. A curriculum that speaks to their personal experiences and ways of knowing can be a bridge to connect what they want and need to learn. Three themes emerged from this study involving Black women and culturally relevant curriculum: language validation, the fostering of positive self and group identity, and self-affirmation or affirmation of goals. The study's findings reveal that the approach of integrating students' experiences as an explicit part of the learning agenda encourages them to participate to the fullest extent in their own education.

Searider Productions. 2009. *Ha Kam Wi Tawk Pidgin Yet?* Searider Productions and the Charlene J. Sato Center for Pidgin, Creole, and Dialect Studies, University of Hawai'i at Manoa.

2 L Z
"A video ethnography created by Searider Productions of Waianae High School in conjunction with the Charlene J. Sato Center for idgin, Creole and Dialect Studies, and Da Pidgin Coup." [From YouTube site with an excerpt from the video: http://www.youtube.com/watch?v=NesfQ2oNBcA]

Sebba, Mark. 1997. *Contact Languages: Pidgins and Creoles.* London: Macmillan Press.

1 2 F

Sebba, Mark. 2000. Writing Switching in British Creole. In *Multilingual Literacies,* ed. by M. Martin-Jones & K. Jones, 171–88. Amsterdam: John Benjamins.

2 U W

Secret, Carrie. 1997. Embracing Ebonics and Teaching Standard English. *Rethinking Schools* 12.18, 34.

1 B C K S
Carrie Secret, a fifth-grade teacher in the Oakland Unified School District, is interviewed regarding her teaching methods. At Prescott Elementary School, where she began teaching in 1966, most teachers have voluntarily adopted the (California) Standard English Proficiency (SEP) program. Under SEP, Secret incorporates a respect for African American language and culture into teaching Standard English, and emphasizes literacy skills and proficiency in the content language associated with each curriculum area rather than mere grammar drilling. While students are encouraged to use Standard English in the classroom, they are not barred from using the language they bring from home, and students are exposed to great literature written in AAVE. Each day begins with inspirational poetry and songs followed by journal writing, and daily lessons draw connections with African culture where possible.

Sedlatschek, Andreas. 2009. *Contemporary Indian English: Variation and Change.* Amsterdam: John Benjamins.

6 F

Seitz, Victoria. 1975. Integrated Versus Segregated School Attendance and Immediate Recall for Standard and Nonstandard English. *Developmental Psychology* 11.217–33.

1 A O X

Seligman, C. R., G. Richard Tucker & Wallace E. Lambert. 1972. The Effects of Speech Style and Other Attributes on Teachers' Attitudes toward Pupils. *Language in Society* 1.131–42.

6 A I T
Thirty-six Grade 3 English-speaking boys at two elementary schools in Montreal each wrote a composition, drew a picture, and submitted a personal photograph and speech sample. After a separate group of judges rated each set of items, four 'good' drawings were matched with four 'good' compositions, and four 'poor' drawings were matched with four 'poor' compositions. Every combination of poor/good photograph, poor/good voice and poor/good drawing-composition then formed eight hypothetical students. Nineteen female pre-service teachers were asked to use these materials to judge each 'student' along a number of characteristics using a 7-point scale. Students with 'good' voices were rated significantly higher than those with 'poor' voices, and similarly students with 'good' photographs were rated higher than those with 'poor' photographs. Moreover, when a student's drawing-composition was 'good,' his photograph made little difference in the judge's evaluation, but the ratings of those with poor drawing-compositions fluctuated considerably on the basis of their photographs.

Serwer, Blanche. 1969. Linguistic Support for a Method of Teaching Beginning Reading to Black Children. *Reading Research Quarterly* 4.449–67.

1 R S

Setter, Jane, Cathy S. P. Wong & Brian Hok-Shing Chan. 2010. *Hong Kong English.* Edinburgh, Scotland: Edinburgh University Press.

6 F

Severson, Roger & Kristin Guest. 1970. Toward the Standardized Assessment of the Language of Disadvantaged Children. In *Language and Poverty: Perspectives on a Theme,* ed. by F. Williams, 309–44. Chicago, IL: Markham Publishing Company.

1 A

Seymour, Harry. 1986. Clinical Intervention for Language Disorders among Nonstandard Speakers of English. In *Nature of Communication Disorders in Linguistically Diverse Populations,* ed. by O. Taylor, 135-52; San Diego, CA: College-Hill Press.

D

Seymour, Harry, Lamya Abdulkarim & Valerie Johnson. 1999. The Ebonics Controversy: An Educational and Clinical Dilemma. *Topics in Language Disorders* 19.66–77.

1 A D K

Seymour, Harry & Linda Bland. 1991. A Minority Perspective in Diagnosis of Child Language Disorders. *Clinical Communication Disorders* 1.39–50.

1 A D

Seymour, Harry, Linda Bland-Stewart & Lisa Green. 1998. Difference Versus Deficit in Child African American English. *Language, Speech, and Hearing Services in Schools* 29.96–108.

1 A D

Seymour, Harry, Tempii Champion & Janice Jackson. 1995. The Language of African-American Learners: Effective Assessment and Instructional Programming for Special

Needs Children. In *Effective Education of African-American Exceptional Learners: New Perspectives,* ed. by B. Ford, F. Obiakor & J. Patton. Austin, TX: Pro Ed.

1 A D S

Seymour, Harry & Dalton Jones. 1981. Language and Cognitive Assessment of Black Children. *Speech and Language: Advances in Basic Research and Practice* 6.204–63.

1 A D

Seymour, Harry & Patricia Ralabate. 1985. The Acquisition of a Phonologic Feature of Black English. *Journal of Communication Disorders* 18.139–48.

1 Q

Seymour, Harry & Thomas Roeper. 1999. Grammatical Acquisition of African American English. In *Language Acquisition across North America: Cross-Cultural and Cross-Linguistic Perspectives,* ed. by O. Taylor & L. Leonard. San Diego, CA: Singular Press.

1 Q

Seymour, Harry, Thomas Roeper & Jill de Villiers. 2003. *Diagnostic Evaluation of Language Variation—Criterion Referenced Test (DELV-CR).* San Antonio, TX: The Psychological Corporation.

1 6 A D M

The DELV Screening Test and Criterion Referenced Test were both made commercially available in 2003. The Criterion Referenced (CR) Test which was a follow-up diagnostic assessment to the screener was eventually faded out and replaced with the Norm Referenced (NR) Test in 2005. (See Seymour et al. 2005.) The NR test contains the majority of the same items as the CR with some slight modification and with norm-referenced scores added, which clinicians prefer. (Abstract note courtesy of Toya Wyatt.)

Seymour, Harry, Thomas Roeper & Jill de Villiers. 2003. *Diagnostic Evaluation of Language Variety—Screening Test.* San Antonio, TX: The Psychological Corporation.

1 6 A D M

Seymour, Harry, Thomas Roeper, Jill de Villiers with contributions by Peter A. de Villiers. 2005. *Diagnostic Evaluation of Language Variation—Norm-Referenced Test (DELV-NR).* San Antonio, TX: The Psychological Corporation.

A D M

Seymour, Harry & Charlena Seymour. 1979. The Symbolism of Ebonics: I'd Rather Switch Than Fight. *Journal of Black Studies* 9.397–410.

1 B I

Seymour and Seymour argue that whereas in the civil rights movement of the 1960s African Americans embraced AAVE and other symbols of cultural identity such as the Afro hairstyle, the decline of the movement saw a rejection of such symbols in favor of assimilation with mainstream culture. Unfortunately the rejection of AAVE was linguistically uninformed; teachers' negative attitudes toward AAVE negatively affect student performance, and students' use of distinctively AAVE features was often misdiagnosed as an indication of speech disorders. Ultimately, the authors argue that a program in bidialectalism would be an effective way to foster an ability to style-switch between dialects, so that African Americans could both maintain their cultural identity through AAVE, and have SAE (Standard American English) available in order to avoid discrimination in mainstream settings.

Seymour, Harry & Charlena M. Seymour. 1981. Black English and Standard American English Contrasts in Consonantal Development of Four- and Five-Year Old Children. *Journal of Speech and Hearing Disorders* 46.274–80.

1 F Q

Seymour, Harry & Luciano Valles. 1998. Language Intervention for Linguistically Different Learners. In *Introduction to Communication Disorders: A Multicultural Approach,* ed. by C. M. Seymour & E. H. Nober. Boston: Butterworth-Heineman.

D

Shafer, Gregory. 2009. Crossing over into Language Exploration. *Teaching English in the Two-Year College* 37.58–65. [Abstract prepared by ERIC and reprinted with permission of the Department of Education from the Education Resources Information Center at eric.ed.gov.]

1 I

Although many linguists seek to demonstrate the validity and profundity of African American Vernacular English (AAVE), much of the pop culture world seems to use it as a way to sell products and to rebel against parents. Each time that the dialect is pulled into the sphere of pop culture—and each time that it is reduced to a stereotype—its relevance as a unique form of communication is enervated. This essay explores the diverse uses, misperceptions, and passionate convictions about African American Vernacular among college students, revealing its complicated relevance to human culture.

Shankar, Shalini. 2008. Speaking Like a Model Minority: 'FOB' Styles, Gender, and Racial Meanings among Desi Teens in Silicon Valley. *Journal of Linguistic Anthropology* 18.268–89.

3 6 F I

Shankar, Shalini. 2011. Asian American Youth Language Use: Perspectives across Schools and Communities. *Review of Research in Education* 35.1–28.

3 E I

Shapiro, Mary. 2010. Using "Bad" Undergraduate Research to Foster "Good" Attitudes. *College Teaching* 58.47–51. [Reprinted from *College Teaching* 58(2).]

1 I L

This paper postulates that having students engage in albeit limited and flawed research is a more effective way of changing attitudes than lecture or discussion. A common goal of the introductory linguistics course is to instill healthy language attitudes, but there is little extant research on the pedagogy of linguistics indicating how this may be accomplished. This case study presents an experimental design that allows students to develop empathy for speakers of stigmatized dialects and serves simultaneously to introduce students to the scientific method and to reinforce the idea of linguistics as a science. It offers ideas that instructors in any discipline dealing with multiculturalism may be able to adapt.

Sharifian, Farzad. 2001. Schema-Based Processing in Australian Speakers of Aboriginal English. *Language and International Communication* 1.120–33.

6 N

Sharifian, Farzad. 2005. Cultural Conceptualisations in English Words: A Study of Aboriginal Children in Perth. *Language and Education* 19.203–28.

6 F N

Sharifian, Farzad. 2008. Aboriginal English in the Classroom: An Asset or a Liability? *Language Awareness* 17.131–38.

6 C P

Sharifian, Farzad, Judith Rochecouste & Ian Malcolm. 2004. 'But It Was All a Bit Confusing...' Comprehending Aboriginal English Texts. *Language, Culture and Curriculum* 17.203–28. [Reprinted with permission of the authors from *Language, Culture and Curriculum* 17(3).]

6 N O
The study reported in this paper explored the schemas that Aboriginal and non-Aboriginal educators bring to the task of comprehending oral narratives produced by Aboriginal children. During each data collection session, a participant listened to a series of eight passages and tried to recall each passage immediately after listening. The participants had a chance to listen to each narrative twice and produce two recalls of each passage. The participants were also given a chance to read a transcript of each passage and to make comments on their experience after the recall process. The data were then analyzed in three stages. The first stage involved the analysis of recall protocols for the idea units out of which they were composed. This was carried out to explore the content schemas that were employed by the participants in comprehending the original narratives. The second stage was a comparison of formal schemas that appeared to inform the original narratives and the recall protocols. Finally, the recalls by Aboriginal participants were examined for any general patterns or strategies recruited during the recall. The results overall showed a continuum of familiarity on the part of participants with the schemas that appeared to underlie the narratives.

Sharma, Devyani. 2005. Dialect Stabilization and Speaker Awareness in Non-Native Varieties of English. *Journal of Sociolinguistics* 9. 194-224.

1 6 A F Q

Sharma, Devyani. 2005. Language Transfer and Discourse Universals in Indian English Article Use. *Studies in Second Language Acquisition* 27.535–66.

B F Q

Sharma, Devyani. 2010. Review of Rajend Mesthrie and Rakesh M. Bhatt, *World Englishes: The Study of New Linguistic Varieties.* Cambridge: Cambridge University Press. *Language in Society* 39.3:413-17.

E F

Sharma, Devyani. 2011. Style Repertoire and Social Change in British Asian English. *Journal of Sociolinguistics* 15.464–92.

3 Q

Sharma, Devyani & John R. Rickford. 2009. AAVE/Creole Copula Absence: A Critique of the Imperfect Learning Hypothesis. *Journal of Pidgin and Creole Languages* 24.53–90.

1 2 F K Q

Sharpe, Margaret. 1979. Alice Springs Aboriginal Children's English. In *Australian Linguistic Studies,* ed. by S. Wurm, 733–47.

6 F

Shaughnessy, Mina. 1977. *Errors and Expectations: A Guide for the Teacher of Basic Writing.* New York: Oxford University Press.

W X

Shepherd, Michael. 2011. Effects of Ethnicity and Gender on Teachers' Evaluation of Students' Spoken Responses. *Urban Education.* [Reprinted with permission of Sage Publications, the publisher, from *Urban Education.* Original article available at uex. sagepub.com/content/46/5/1011.]

1 A I T

To update and extend research on teachers' expectations of students of different socio-cultural groups, fifty-seven Black, White, Asian, and Hispanic teachers were asked to evaluate responses spoken by Black, White, and Hispanic second- and third-grade boys and girls. The results show that responses perceived as spoken by minority boys, minority girls, and White boys were evaluated less favorably than identically worded responses perceived as spoken by White girls. This suggests that teachers hold relatively low expectations of minority students and of boys. Teachers of all sociocultural groups evidenced such expectations, but Black and Hispanic teachers more strongly.

Shields, Portia. 1979. The Language of Poor Black Children and Reading Performance. *Journal of Negro Education* 48.196–208.

1 F R V X

Shields investigates whether dialect features elicited in spontaneous speech in a school setting affect oral reading, silent reading, and listening comprehension levels. One hundred and thirty African American third graders each provided a speech sample prompted by a short silent science-oriented film. Samples were coded for instances of copula deletion and zero inflection, along with their Standard American English (SAE) counterparts, and then correlated with scores on oral, silent, and listening tasks. Results indicated that use of zero copula was significantly negatively correlated with performance on all three tasks, and use of copula was significantly positively correlated with such tasks. Furthermore, use of past tense inflection was significantly positively correlated with performance on the oral reading task. No other significant correlations were found. The author concludes that the few minimal associations exposed in this study were not sufficient to support use of special Dialect Readers, repetition programs, or any of the special curricula used in many schools attended by poor and Black children (p. 207). However, the author states that in order to be effective, teachers will need quality training and resources, in addition to increased understanding and acceptance of AAVE.

Shin, Hyunjung & Ryuko Kubota. 2008. Post-Colonialism and Globalization in Language Education. In *Handbook of Educational Linguistics,* ed. by B. Spolsky & F. Hult, 206–19. Malden, MA: Blackwell.

6 I P

Shin, Sarah J. & Lesley Milroy. 1999. Bilingual Language Acquisition by Korean School-children in New York City. *Bilingualism* 2.147–67.

3 A O Q

Shin, Sarah J. & Lesley Milroy. 2000. Conversational Code Switching among Korean-English Bilingual Children. *International Journal of Bilingualism* 4.351–83.

3 U

Shnukal, Anna. 1992. The Case against a Transfer Bilingual Program of Torres Strait Creole to English in Torres Strait Schools. In *Pidgins, Creoles and Nonstandard Dialects in Education, Applied Linguistics Association of Australia Occasional Paper No. 12*, ed. by J. Siegel, 1–11. Melbourne: Applied Linguistics Association of Australia.

2 P

Shnukal, Anna. 2002. Some Language-Related Observations for Teachers in Torres Strait and Cape York Peninsula Schools. *Australian Journal of Indigenous Education* 30.8–24.

2 F W X

Shuy, Roger. 1969. A Linguistic Background for Developing Beginning Reading Materials for Black Children. In *Teaching Black Children to Read*, ed. by J. Baratz & R. Shuy, 117–37. Washington, D.C.: Center for Applied Linguistics.

1 R V X

Shuy, Roger. 1969. Teacher Training and Urban Language Problems. In *Teaching Standard English in the Inner City*, ed. by R. Fasold & R. Shuy, 120–41. Washington, D.C.: Center for Applied Linguistics.

1 I T

Shuy, Roger. 1970. Subjective Judgments in Sociolinguistic Analysis. In *Report of the Twentieth Annual Round Table Meeting on Linguistics and Language Studies*, ed. by J. Alatis, 174–88. Washington, D.C.: Georgetown University Press. [Abstract courtesy of journal.]

1 F I

Subjective judgments are useful in linguistic studies to supplement information from objective language data, enlarge our knowledge of public conceptions of social speech communities (such as Negro speech), provide techniques for discussion of social markedness of standard and nonstandard varieties of English, and provide techniques for observations of laymen's evaluations and attitudes toward speech samples. In the Detroit Language Study, analysis of subjective judgments of taped speech supported the objective data that multiple negation, cluster reduction, and pronominal apposition correlate closely with socioeconomic status of the speaker. The characterization of Negro speech as a distinct variety of speech is confirmed by correct identification, from taped samples, of the race of the speaker over 80% of the time. The fact that the lower the socioeconomic status of the speaker, the more accurately it was identified indicates that the speech of the working class is socially marked and the speech of the middle class socially unmarked.

Shuy, Roger. 1973. Nonstandard Dialect Problems: An Overview. In *Language Differences: Do They Interfere?*, ed. by J. Laffey & R. Shuy, 3–16. Newark, DE: International Reading Association.

1 I X

Shuy, Roger. 1973. The Study of Vernacular Black English as a Factor in Educational Change. *Research in the Teaching of English* 7.297–311.

1 A E O R T W

The author reviews the history of research on Vernacular Black English and summarizes the lines of inquiry current in 1973: the teaching of oral language; the teaching of reading; the teaching of writing; the development of teacher training; and evaluation of bias in assessments; and reports briefly on a teacher seminar series offered in Norfolk, Virginia.

Shuy, Roger & Ralph Fasold. 1973. *Language Attitudes: Current Trends and Prospects*. Washington, D.C.: Georgetown University Press.

1 I

Siegel, Jeff (ed.) 1992. *Pidgins, Creoles, and Nonstandard Dialects in Education, Applied Linguistics Association of Australia Occasional Paper No. 12*. Melbourne: Applied Linguistics Association of Australia.

2 B C E I O P S V X

This volume includes papers drawn primarily from a workshop held at the 16th Annual Congress of the Applied Linguistics Association of Australia in 1991 on "Pidgins, Creoles and Non-Standard Dialects in Education: Issues and Answers." Varieties covered include Aboriginal English in Australia, Tok Pisin in Papua New Guinea, Torres Strait Creole, and Caribbean English Creoles (as spoken in Carriacou, Grenada, and by Caribbean immigrants in Illinois). Contributors include Katherine Fischer, Joyce Hudson, Ronald Kephart, Margaret Mickan, Ian G. Malcolm, Joseph Alfred Nidue, Gary Ovington, Anna Shnukal, and Jeff Siegel. Their papers are listed separately in this bibliography (e.g., as Ovington 1992).

Siegel, Jeff. 1992. Teaching Initial Literacy in a Pidgin Language: A Preliminary Evaluation. In *Pidgins, Creoles and Nonstandard Dialects in Education, Applied Linguistics Association of Australia Occasional Paper No. 12*, ed. by J. Siegel. Melbourne: Applied Linguistics Association of Australia.

2 V

Siegel, Jeff. 1993. Pidgins and Creoles in Education in Australia and the Southwest Pacific. In *Atlantic Meets Pacific: A Global View of Pidginization and Creolization*, ed. by F. Byrne & J. Holm, 299–308. Amsterdam: John Benjamins.

2 V

Siegel, Jeff. 1996. The Use of Melanesian Pidgin in Education. In *Pacific Languages in Education*, ed. by F. Mugler & J. Lynch, 155–74. Suva, Fiji and Vila, Vanuatu: Institute of Pacific Studies, University of the South Pacific.

2 P

Siegel, Jeff. 1997. Using a Pidgin Language in Formal Education: Help or Hindrance? *Applied Linguistics* 18.86–100. [Abstract graciously provided by Jeff Siegel.]

2 K S V X

One of the arguments against using pidgin and creole languages in formal education is that they would interfere with students' acquisition of the standard form of the lexifier language. This article presents the results of research examining the validity of this argument. The research was part of an evaluation of a preschool program in Papua New Guinea which used Tok Pisin (Melanesian Pidgin English) as the language of instruction and initial literacy for students who then went on to an English-medium community school. The results show that rather than exacerbating interference as predicted by some educators, initial instruction in Tok Pisin actually was advantageous for students in their learning of English and other subjects.

Siegel, Jeff. 1999. Creole and Minority Dialects in Education: An Overview. *Journal of Multilingual and Multicultural Development* 20.508–31.

2 B P

Siegel, Jeff. 1999. Stigmatized and Standardized Varieties in the Classroom: Interference or Separation? *TESOL Quarterly* 33.701–28.

1 2 V X

Siegel, Jeff. 2001. Pidgins, Creoles and Minority Dialects in Education. In *Concise Encyclopedia of Sociolinguistics,* ed. by R. Mesthrie, 747–49. Oxford: Elsevier.

1 2 B

Siegel, Jeff. 2002. Applied Creolistics in the 21st Century. In *Pidgin and Creole Linguistics in the Twenty-First Century,* ed. by G. Gilbert, 7–48. New York: Peter Lang.

2 P

Siegel, Jeff. 2005. Applied Creolistics Revisited. *Journal of Pidgin and Creole Languages* 20.293–323.

2 I P T

Siegel, Jeff. 2005. Literacy in Pidgin and Creole Languages. *Current Issues in Language Planning* 6.143–63. [Reprinted with permission of the author from *Current Issues in Language Planning* 6(2).]

2 P V

Pidgin and creole languages are spoken by more than 75 million people, but the vast majority of their speakers acquire literacy in another language—usually the language of a former colonial power. This paper looks at the origins of pidgins and creoles and explores some of the reasons for their lack of use in formal education. Then, it describes some language planning efforts that have occurred with regard to instrumentalisation and graphisation of these languages, and the few cases where they are actually used to teach initial literacy. The paper goes on to discuss how speakers of pidgins and creoles more commonly acquire literacy in the standard European language officially used in formal education. It concludes with a short section on the role of pidgins and creoles in newspapers, literature and other writing.

Siegel, Jeff. 2006. Keeping Creoles and Dialects out of the Classroom: Is It Justified? In *Dialects, Englishes, Creoles, and Education,* ed. by S. Nero, 39–67. Mahwah, NJ: Lawrence Erlbaum Associates.

1 B I P V

Siegel seeks to answer questions related to discriminatory linguistic practices in the classroom. He acknowledges the nature of teachers to completely avoid vernaculars and gives reasons for the absence of vernaculars in education. These reasons fall into the following categories: (1) beliefs about the nature of vernaculars as lacking grammatical rules; (2) misconceptions about the educational programs that use vernaculars; (3) ideas that the use of vernaculars will prove detrimental because it will waste time, create interference, and possibly force students to remain in the ghetto; and finally, (4) skepticism about the practicality of vernaculars in the classroom. Within the second category, Siegel discusses instrumental, accommodation, and awareness programs, all of which utilize a vernacular either as a medium of instruction, a tool of expression for students, or as an additional resource for acquiring proficiency in Standard English. The skepticism argument encompasses four main points against the use of vernaculars including: the immersion, similarity, no positive effects, and 'too hard' arguments.

All of these considerations lead Siegel to argue that the absence of vernaculars in the education system is not justified. He proceeds to discuss the benefits of using vernaculars including: easier acquisition of literacy, greater cognitive development, positive attitudes by teachers, increased motivation, and improved awareness of differences.

Siegel, Jeff. 2006. Language Ideologies and the Education of Speakers of Marginalized Language Varieties: Adopting a Critical Awareness Approach. *Linguistics and Education: An International Research Journal* 17.157–74. [Reprinted with permission of Elsevier, the publisher, from *Linguistics and Education* 17(2).]

1 2 I L P
For over forty years, sociolinguists have been demonstrating that all varieties of language are equal in linguistic terms. Yet vernacular varieties such as African American English and Hawai'i Creole are still generally marginalized and excluded from the educational process, with the result that speakers of these varieties are disadvantaged in education as well as other areas. This article discusses four interrelated language ideologies that contribute to this state of affairs. Then it describes the "awareness" teaching approach, which in opposition to these ideologies includes marginalized varieties in the curriculum. This is followed by an examination of the extent to which the awareness approach deals with the inequalities perpetuated by the prevailing language ideologies. The article goes on to argue that a critical version of the awareness approach is a more effective alternative.

Siegel, Jeff. 2007. Creoles and Minority Dialects in Education: An Update. *Language and Education* 21.66–86. [Reprinted with permission of the author from *Language and Education* 21(1).]

1 K P
This paper renews the call for greater interest in applied work to deal with the obstacles faced in formal education by speakers of creoles (such as Hawaii Creole and Jamaican Creole) and minority dialects (such as African American English). It starts off with an update on developments in the use of these vernacular languages in educational contexts since 1998, focusing on educational programs, publications and research by linguists and educators. It goes on to discuss some of the research and public awareness efforts needed to help the speakers of these vernacular varieties, with examples given from Hawaii.

Siegel, Jeff. 2008. Pidgin in the Classroom. *Educational Perspectives* 41.55–65.

2 B I P

Siegel, Jeff. 2009. Linguistic and Educational Aspects of Tok Pisin. In *The New Sociolinguistics Reader,* ed. by N. Coupland & A. Jaworski, 512–25. Basingstoke, UK: Palgrave Macmillan.

2 F I P

Siegel, Jeff. 2010. Bilingual Literacy in Creole Contexts. *Journal of Multilingual and Multicultural Development* 31.383–402. [Reprinted from *Journal of Multilingual and Multicultural Development* 31(4).]

2 B V
This article examines whether the conventional notion of bilingual literacy is applicable to speakers of creole languages in terms of autonomy, codification, instrumentalisation, education and literacy practices. It then goes on to describe alternative conceptions of both literacy and bilingualism that appear to be more relevant to creole contexts—namely, the sociocultural literacy approach and truncated bilingualism.

The article concludes with a discussion of the educational benefits to creole speakers of adopting either conventional or alternative bilingual literacy practices in the classroom.

Siegel, Jeff. 2010. Pidgins and Creoles. In *Sociolinguistics and Language Education,* ed. by N. Hornberger & S. McKay, 232–62. Bristol: Multilingual Matters.

1 2 F Q

Siegel, Jeff. 2010. *Second Dialect Acquisition.* Cambridge: Cambridge University Press.

1 2 B E I Q
This book synthesizes research about the process, methods, and difficulties of second dialect acquisition (SDA). The scope includes dialect coaching for actors, accent modification, and learning standard dialects in academic settings. The book discusses studies involving many languages all over the world, especially English. Chapters 7 and 8 address SDA in schools. Chapter 7, "SDA in classroom contexts," describes various kinds of situations where students' native dialect (D1) differs from the standard variety expected in school. It discusses the challenges to acquiring a standard variety in these situations and reports on four studies on patterns of SDA in the classroom. It concludes by criticizing arguments against having special programs for SDA. Chapter 8, "Education approaches for SDA," describes methods of teaching standard academic dialects to children, where the goal is primarily the acquisition of lexical and grammatical features. Siegel first reviews the history of techniques for teaching Standard English as a second dialect, and then introduces three common contemporary approaches: the instrumental approach, where the D1 is the main medium of instruction in early grades and students learn to read in that variety; the accommodation approach, where the D1 is validated in the classroom but is not the primary medium of instruction; and the awareness approach, where students and teachers learn about the relationships and differences between vernaculars and standardized varieties. For each of these approaches, the chapter details several programs and evaluative studies in the United States, Africa, Australia, the Caribbean, and other places. For example, Siegel reviews the current policy in Papua New Guinea, where local communities choose the language of initial literacy in early grades, switching to English later. Many communities have chosen Tok Pisin as that language, which is an instance of the instrumental approach. Siegel concludes that all of these approaches are more or less successful. In the final chapter, Siegel questions the societal structures that require the acquisition of a standard dialect and commends a new trend in pedagogy, critical language study, for encouraging students to deconstruct how language ideologies perpetuate systems of power and privilege. He ends by calling for more research in a new, independent field of SDA.

Silliman, Elaine, Ruth Bahr, Louise Wilkinson & Candida Turner. 2002. Language Variation and Struggling Readers: Finding Patterns in Diversity. In *Speaking, Reading, and Writing in Students with Language Learning Disabilities: New Paradigms in Research and Practice,* ed. by K. Butler & E. Silliman, 109–48. Mahwah, NJ: Lawrence Erlbaum Associates.

1 D Q R

Silliman, Elaine & Tempii Champion. 2002. Three Dilemmas in Cross-Cultural Narrative Analysis: Introduction to the Special Issue. *Linguistics and Education* 13.143–50.

N

Silverstein, Michael. 1996. Monoglot 'Standard' in America: Standardization and Met-aphors of Linguistic Hegemony. In *The Matrix of Language: Contemporary Linguistic Anthropology,* ed. by D. Brenneis & R. Macaulay, 284-306. Boulder, CO: Westview.

I

Simmons, Eileen. 1991. Ain't We Never Gonna Study No Grammar? *English Journal* 80.48–51.

B I S

Simmons, John & Lawrence Baines. 1998. *Language Study in Middle School, High School, and Beyond: Views on Enhancing the Study of Language.* Newark, DE: International Reading Association.

I S

Simmons-McDonald, Hazel. 1994. Comparative Patterns in the Acquisition of English Negation by Native Speakers of French Creole and Creole English. *Language Learning* 44.29–74.

2 Q

Simmons-McDonald, Hazel. 1996. Language Education Policy (2): The Case for Creole in Formal Education in St. Lucia. In *Caribbean Language Issues, Old and New: Papers in Honour of Professor Mervyn Alleyne on the Occasion of His Sixtieth Birthday,* ed. by P. Christie, 120–42. Cave Hill, Barbados: The Press, University of the West Indies.

2 P

Simmons-McDonald, Hazel. 1998. Developmental Patterns in the Acquisition of English Negation by Speakers of St. Lucian French Creole. In *Studies in Caribbean Language II,* ed. by P. Christie, B. Lalla, V. Pollard & L. Carrington, 75–99. St. Augustine, Trini-dad: Society for Caribbean Linguistics.

2 Q

Simmons-McDonald, Hazel. 2001. Competence, Proficiency and Language Acquisition in Caribbean Contexts. In *Due Respect: Papers on English and English-Related Creoles in the Caribbean in Honor of Professor Robert Le Page,* ed. by P. Christie, 37–60. Kings-ton, Jamaica: University of West Indies Press. [Abstract graciously provided by Hazel Simmons-McDonald.]

F Q

This paper discusses issues related to second language acquisition and the development of competency in English by speakers in the Caribbean with more particular reference to learners in St. Lucia. The discussion begins by making a distinction between the terms proficiency and competence and it interrogates Carrington's typology for first language acquisition in a Caribbean setting. The paper also presents data from lessons in English to illustrate how a particular teaching style may constrain the learning of English (as the school language) and the development of proficiency / literacy related skills. Data from speech and writing samples of students at primary and secondary levels are analyzed and discussed. The latter, in conjunction with the presentation of classroom process data are used to explain why non-native speakers of English have difficulty in developing proficiency in the English variety that is required for use in school. The paper recommends the introduction of a bilingual program for speakers of Creole French in the education system in St. Lucia.

Simmons-McDonald, Hazel. 2004. Trends in Teaching Standard Varieties to Creole and Vernacular Speakers. *Annual Review of Applied Linguistics* 24.187–208. [Abstract graciously provided by Hazel Simmons-McDonald.]

2 P V

This article reviews the policy and pedagogical literature regarding approaches used to teach a standard variety to creole and vernacular speakers, focusing attention especially on the development of literacy in a second language in the Caribbean region. Research has shown that literacy development, academic skills, and learning strategies transfer from the first language to the second and that literacy in the first language is a crucial base for literacy development in the second language. Issues of vernacular literacy situations where creole has the same lexical base as the second (standard) language—as opposed to situations in which the creole has a different lexical base than the second language—are explored. Outcomes resulting from the implementation of specific policies and approaches in the contexts presented, to the extent that such outcomes have been documented, are also summarized.

Simmons-McDonald, Hazel. 2006. Vernacular Instruction and Bi-Literacy Development: French Creole Speakers. In *Exploring the Boundaries of Caribbean Creole Languages,* ed. by H. Simmons-McDonald & I. Robertson, 118–46. Kingston, Jamaica: University of the West Indies Press. [Abstract graciously provided by Hazel Simmons-McDonald.]

2 R V

This chapter reports on a project which use of Creole French (Kwéyòl) was used as a language of instruction in St. Lucia. Based on the proposition that children who speak Kwéyòl as their native language should be helped to develop literacy in their vernacular while they are exposed to a program that fosters the learning of English for school purposes, the model establishes the following goals for learners: (1) development of proficiency in the second language; (2) proficiency in the learner's native language; (3) promotion of the use of the native language for a wider range of purposes, including academic; and (4) development of academic language proficiency in both the native language (Kwéyòl) and English to promote bilingualism and bi-literacy in these languages. The study used a single subject research design to track the development of proficiency of three students selected from a larger group identified as having reading problems. Based on evaluation of reading accuracy, self-correction rates, and other measures of reading performance, the study concludes that instruction in the learner's native language did not hinder the literacy development of the learners in the L2 – and moreover, seemed to help the development of their reading in English.

Simmons-McDonald, Hazel & Rod Ellis. 2002. *Let's Work with English.* Oxford: Heinemann Educational Publishers.

2 M S

Simmons-McDonald, Hazel, Linda Fields & Peter Roberts. 1997. *Writing in English: A Course Book for Caribbean Students.* Kingston, Jamaica: Ian Randle Publishers.

2 B M W

Simmons-McDonald, Hazel & Ian Robertson. 2006. *Exploring the Boundaries of Caribbean Creole Languages.* Kingston, Jamaica: University of the West Indies Press.

2 A E N O S V

Section 2 of this festschrift for Pauline Christie focuses on "Language and Education," with papers by Dennis Craig ("The Use of the Vernacular in West Indian Education"), Hazel Simmons-McDonald ("Vernacular Instruction and Bi-Literacy Development:

French Creole Speakers"), and Valerie Youssef ("Issues of Face-Saving in the Pre-School Classroom").

Simons, Herbert. 1974. Black Dialect Phonology and Work [Word] Recognition. *Journal of Educational Research* 68.67–70.

1 R X

Simons describes a study in which he tests whether Black children can read more easily those words whose Standard English pronunciation closely correspond to their AAVE pronunciation. After gathering seventy-six students in second to fourth grades at an all Black Title 1 school, experimenters tested each one individually by having them read aloud the words printed on index cards. The words consisted of pairs that were homophones in AAVE, such as "death" and "deaf," "cold" and "coal," and nonsense words such as "hust" and "hus." Although it was hypothesized that the word in each pair whose AAVE pronunciation matched its Standard English pronunciation would have a higher rate of correct readings, univariate and multivariate analyses of the results indicated no such correlation, and the author concludes that the difficulty with which some Black children learn to read probably stems from poor instruction methods rather than dialect differences.

Simons, Herbert. 1979. Black Dialect, Reading Interference, and Classroom Interaction. In *Theory and Practice of Early Reading,* ed. by L. Resnick & P. Weaver, 111–29. Mahwah, NJ: Lawrence Erlbaum & Associates.

1 R T X

Simons, Herbert & Kenneth Johnson. 1974. Black English Syntax and Reading Interference. *Research in the Teaching of English* 8.339–58.

1 R X

Simons and Johnson assess whether the syntactic mismatch between AAVE and Standard English will cause AAVE-speaking children to be more adept at reading and understanding texts written in their dialect rather than in Standard English. Sixty-seven second and third grade Black children who exhibited AAVE in their speech were recorded reading a short story in either standard English or its AAVE translation, and then given comprehension tests. Results indicate that there was no significant comprehension difference between the two texts, nor was there any greater use of context clues or graphophonic information in reading the AAVE version. It was shown, however, that fewer dialect-related errors occurred during the AAVE reading, although there was more of a tendency for the children to switch from AAVE to Standard English while reading rather than vice versa. While more rigorously designed studies would be needed to confirm these results, the authors conclude that future work in determining the causes of poor performance may have to look beyond mere dialect interference and consider student-teacher interaction.

Simpkins, Gary. 2002. *The Throwaway Kids.* Newton Upper Falls, MA: Brookline Books.

1 C R S V

In this monograph, Simpkins proposes a cross-cultural approach to reading instruction that takes into account the linguistic and cultural differences of 'Black non-mainstream' students and utilizes the language skills they bring to the classroom. After considering different proposed explanations for the great reading failure rate among such students, Simpkins zeroes in on the linguistic-cultural difference explanation, and provides guidelines for the development of material sensitive to this difference. The content of the Bridge Reading Program, first developed in the 1970s, is described in detail, along with information about its history and suggested implementation.

Divided into five sections, the program begins with stories written in AAVE before moving to a transition stage in which AAVE and SAE are mixed together; finally, it presents stories written exclusively in SAE. Study books and recordings accompany the reading booklets for each section. Preliminary evidence for the program's efficacy is provided through studies conducted in Los Angeles and Boston, and through Houghton Mifflin's national field test.

Simpkins, Gary & Charlesetta Simpkins. 1981. Cross Cultural Approach to Curriculum Development. In *Black English and the Education of Black Children and Youth: Proceedings of the National Invitational Symposium on the King Decision,* ed. by G. Smitherman, 221–40. Detroit, MI: Center for Black Studies, Wayne State University.

1 C R S V
Simpkins and Simpkins report an extensive test of the effectiveness of dialect readers. Their quasi-experimental study investigated whether it was possible to "improve students' reading ability by first teaching them in their dialect and then extending that learning via a series of steps to Standard Mainstream English Dialect" (p. 228). The authors term this strategy "Associative Bridging" and developed a set of five booklets (the *Bridge* series, see Simpkins, Holt and Simpkins 1971) that gradually moved from presenting text in "Black Vernacular," to "Transition Dialect," to "Standard English." The five booklets consisted of stories accompanied by comprehension questions and exercises focusing on reading subskills. The authors note that the fact that Black Vernacular passages preceded the Standard English versions served to actively demonstrate the validity of AAVE, and to allow students to initially learn skills in a more familiar context. The Bridge reading series was piloted in five predominantly African American school districts nationwide, with 417 students in 21 classes grades 7-12. The progress of these students was compared with a control group of six classes (123 students). At the end of four months, the experimental group had made significantly larger gains than the comparison group.

Simpkins, Gary, Charlesetta Simpkins & Grace Holt. 1977. *Bridge: A Cross-Cultural Reading Program.* Boston: Houghton Mifflin.

1 M R S V

Simpkins, Gary & Frank Simpkins. 2009. *Between the Rhetoric and Reality.* Pittsburgh, PA: Lauriat Press.

1 A B C P S V
After broadly introducing issues related to what the authors perceive as a crisis in Black education, this book describes two methods of reading instruction rooted in an understanding of AAVE: the peer control method, and the cross-cultural method. The latter method was the basis for the experimental dialect reader series *Bridge: A Cross-Cultural Reading Series.* This invaluable book makes ample use of excerpts from audio-recorded small group conversations among African American students using the Bridge dialect readers or other special materials—but as the transcripts date to the late 1970s, the peer language would need to be updated for use in today's classrooms.

Simpson, Lee, Geoff Munns & Sue Clancy. 1999. Language Tracks: Aboriginal English and the Classroom. *Primary English Notes* 120.1–6.

6 T

Sims, Rudine. 1975. Black Children and the Language Arts: A Call for Reform. In *Ebonics: The True Language of Black Folks,* ed. by R. L. Williams, 22–27. St. Louis, MO: Robert L. Williams and Associates, Inc.

1 S V

Singham, Mano. 1998. The Canary in the Mine: the Achievement Gap between Black and White Students. *Phi Delta Kappan* 80.8–15.

A I R

Singham, Mano. 2005. *The Achievement Gap in U.S. Education: Canaries in the Mine*. Lanham, MD: Rowman & Littlefield Education.

A R

Skutnabb-Kangas, Tove, Robert Phillipson & Mart Rannut. 1994. *Linguistic Human Rights: Overcoming Linguistic Discrimination*. Berlin: Mouton de Gruyter.

1 I P

Sledd, James. 1969. Bi-Dialectalism: The Linguistics of White Supremacy. *English Journal* 58.1307–15, 29.

1 B I P

Sledd argues that bidialectalism merely serves to reinforce social prejudice and to allow White linguists to earn money maintaining the status quo under the guise of compassion. He quotes bidialectalists to demonstrate their assumption that the prejudices of middle-class Whites cannot be changed, and notes the hypocrisy in proclaiming all linguistic varieties equal while at the same imposing Standard English, regardless of any psychological damage incurred on the part of the student. Even if bidialectalism were advisable, he argues, programs rely on incomplete lists of contrastive features taught through artificial drills. Adequate descriptions of AAVE and SAE are not as yet available, and mere classroom practice does not suffice to teach students who are proud of their language and do not want to speak SAE in the first place. Sledd concludes that in place of bidialectalism, students should be taught basic sociolinguistics so that they understand the nature of linguistic prejudice, and that effort should be taken to educate the public at large about the plight of the linguistic minority.

Sledd, James. 1972. Doublespeak: Dialectology in the Service of Big Brother. *College English* 33.439–56.

1 B P

Sledd, James. 1982. Review Article: The Ann Arbor Black English Case. *English World Wide* 3.239–48.

1 K P

Sledd, James. 1996. Grammar for Social Awareness in Time of Class Warfare. *The English Journal* 85.59–63.

I T

A fiery position piece which outlines the core arguments for a critical perspective on language variation, which Sledd summarizes as: "Students should never be set to study usage and grammar without conscious understanding of the nature and social functions of the dialect whose structure and use they are invited to learn. If students are ready for abstractions like predicates and subjects, they are ready for the abstractions of race and class."

Sligh, Allison & Frances Conners. 2003. Relation of Dialect to Phonological Processing: African American Vernacular English Vs. Standard American English. *Contemporary Educational Psychology* 28.205–28.

1 A R X

This article describes experiments, using phoneme deletion tasks, to measure the phonological processing abilities of Standard American English (SAE) and African

American Vernacular English (AAVE) speaking children. It explores the possible impact of dialect on children's performance in phonological processing; specifically it investigates if AAVE and SAE speakers differ in their phonological processing performance. Because the most effective reading-instruction varies for students with differing phonological processing abilities, a difference in AAVE and SAE phonological processing has potentially significant implications for classroom pedagogy. In the main study, in which children's actual dialect use was assessed, it was found that AAVE speakers outperformed SAE speakers on phonological processing, but not reading performance; one possible explanation is that standard psychometric tests may underestimate the reading abilities of AAVE speakers. A second finding was that SAE speakers had more phonological processing troubles with word-initial phoneme deletion, while AAVE speakers had more processing troubles with word-final deletions. Pedagogical implications of these and other findings are discussed.

Slomanson, Peter & Michael Newman. 2004. Peer Group Identification and Variation in New York Latino English Laterals. *English World-Wide* 25.199–216.

4 F

Smith, Brenda. 1979. It Ain't What You Say, It's the Way You Say It: Exercises for Teaching Mainstream American English to Ebonics-Speaking Children. *Journal of Black Studies* 9.489–93.

1 B M S

In this short paper, Smith outlines a series of contrastive analysis exercises for use with students in sixth grade and beyond. The first group of activities fosters an awareness of the ethnic significance of different speech varieties by, for example, having students guess the ethnicity of a speaker based solely on a recording of their speech. In the next group of activities, students study the specific points of contrast between AAVE and SAE by examining differences in verb paradigms and pronunciation, or by identifying AAVE and SAE in different sentences based on such features as subject-verb agreement. Finally, students practice producing MAE in their own speech through translation exercises and skits. The author asserts, however, that before using these exercises, teachers should identify specific points of interference in their students' speech so that the exercises can be tailored for maximum effectiveness.

Smith, Ernie. 1975. Ebonics: A Case History. In *Ebonics: The Language of Black Folks,* ed. by R. L. Williams, 77–85. St. Louis, MO: Robert L. Williams and Associates, Inc.

1 P U

Smith, Ernie. 1995. Bilingualism and the African American Child. In *Reading: The Blending of Theory and Practice, Vol 3,* ed. by M. Aice & M. Asaunders-Lucas. Bakersfield: California State University.

1 B T

Smith, Tina, Evan Lee & Hiram McDade. 2001. An Investigation of T-Units in African American English-Speaking and Standard American English-Speaking Fourth-Grade Children. *Communication Disorders Quarterly* 22.148–57.

1 A D

Smith, William. 1979. Toward a Philosophy of Education for the Culturally and Linguistically Distinct. In *Black Students, Multicultural Setting,* ed. by V. L. M. Van Brunt, 32–37. San Diego, CA: Institute for Cultural Pluralism.

1 C I T

Smitherman, Geneva. 1973. "Grammar and Goodness". *English Journal* 62.774–78.

1 I T

Smitherman, Geneva. 1973. White English in Blackface, or Who Do I Be? *Black Scholar* 4.32–39.

1 A I

Smitherman, Geneva. 1974. Soul'n Style. *The English Journal* 63.14–15.

1 B I
One in a series of six columns in *The English Journal* between February 1974 and February 1976 in which the inimitable Geneva Smitherman, writing in the vernacular, shared her opinion on various aspects of AAVE, often having to do with education. In this particular issue (63.3), she identifies and discusses three primary approaches to dealing with 'the Black Idiom' in schools: Eradicationist, Bidialectist, and Legitimizer (the approach she favors). Other 'Soul'n Style' columns appeared in the following issues of *The English Journal*: 63.2 (February 1974), 63.4 (April 1974), 63.5 (May 1974), 64.6 (September 1975), and 65.2 (February 1976).

Smitherman, Geneva. 1975. Linguistic Diversity in the Classroom. In *The Cultural Revolution in Foreign Language Teaching,* ed. by R. Lafayette, 32–48. Skokie, IL: National Textbook Company.

1 S T

Smitherman, Geneva. 1977. *Talkin and Testifyin: The Language of Black America*. Boston: Houghton Mifflin.

1 A B E F I K N P
For years the classic introduction to: 'The Language of Black America,' this book, written in Smitherman's vernacular style, was reissued by Wayne State University Press in 1986 with a brief "Afterword". The chapters shared by both editions are: 1—From Africa to the New World and into the Space Age (Introduction and History of Black English Structure); 2—"It Bees Dat Way Sometime" (Sounds and Structure of Present-Day Black English); 3—Black Semantics (Words and Concepts in Black English, Past and Present); 4—"How I Got Ovuh" (African World View and Afro-American Oral Tradition); 5—"The Forms of Things Unknown" (Black Modes of Discourse); 6—"Where It's At (Black-White Language Attitudes); 7—"Where Do We Go from Here? T.C.B!" (Social Policy and Educational Practice); Appendix A: Some Well-Known Black Proverbs and Sayings; Appendix B: Get Down Exercises on Black English Sounds and Structure; Appendix C: Black Semantics—A Selected Glossary.

Smitherman, Geneva. 1981. "What Go Round Come Round": King in Perspective. *Harvard Educational Review* 51.40–56.

1 K P

Smitherman, Geneva (ed.) 1981. *Black English and the Education of Black Children and Youth: Proceedings of the National Invitational Symposium on the King Decision*. Detroit, MI: Center for Black Studies, Wayne State University.

1 E I K P R W

Smitherman, Geneva. 1992. Black English, Diverging or Converging? The View from the National Assessment of Educational Progress. *Language and Education* 6.47–61.

1 A K W

Smitherman, Geneva. 1994. 'The Blacker the Berry, the Sweeter the Juice': African American Student Writers in the National Assessment of Educational Progress. In *The Need for Story: Cultural Diversity in Classroom and Community,* ed. by A. H. Dyson & C. Genishi, 80–101. Urbana, IL: NCTE.

1 A N W

Smitherman, Geneva. 1995. Students' Right to Their Own Language: A Retrospective. *English Journal* 84.21–27.

1 I P

Smitherman, Geneva. 1997. Black Language and the Education of Black Children—One Mo Once. *The Black Scholar* 27.28–35.

1 F I P

Smitherman, Geneva. 1998. 'Dat Teacher Be Hollin at Us'-What Is Ebonics? *TESOL Quarterly* 32.139–43.

1 F K

Smitherman, Geneva. 1998. Ebonics, King, and Oakland: Some Folk Don't Believe Fat Meat Is Greasy. *Journal of English Linguistics* 26.97–107.

1 F K

Smitherman, Geneva. 1998. Word from the Hood: The Lexicon of African American Vernacular English. In *African American English: Structure, History and Usage,* ed. by S. Mufwene, J. R. Rickford, G. Bailey & J. Baugh, 292-300. London: Routledge.

1 F

Smitherman, Geneva. 1999. CCCC's Role in the Struggle for Language Rights. *College Composition and Communication* 50.349–76.

1 P W

Smitherman, Geneva. 1999. Language Policy and Classroom Practices. In *Making the Connection,* ed. by C. Adger, D. Christian & O. Taylor, 115–24.

1 P S T
Smitherman argues that a school's failure to consider a student's dialect in teaching reading will result in failure, and that there needs to be a national policy affirming the breadth of languages and dialects spoken in the United States. The national multilingual policy, Smitherman suggests, should be written into law, with resources designated to ensure the program's implementation throughout the United States. Another point argued in the chapter is that the institution of the school is the main agent of social change with respect to language diversity and language attitudes. Smitherman insists that "better speech" pledges and linguistic exorcising are futile, as it does not work for any student. Smitherman states that classroom practices that are successful for African American students are those that build on students' existing language resources and that teach from a linguistic philosophy of bi- or multiculturalism. A national language policy that requires multilingualism, according to Smitherman, would advance the education of African American students along with students belonging to other ethnic and racial groups.

Smitherman, Geneva. 2000. *Black Talk: Words and Phrases from the Hood to the Amen Corner.* Boston: Houghton Mifflin.

1 E F N P

Smitherman, Geneva. 2000. *Talkin That Talk: Language, Culture and Education in African America*. London: Routledge.

1 B F I P S T W

Smitherman, Geneva. 2001. A Commentary on Ebonics: From a Ghetto Lady Turned Critical Linguist. In *Ebonics and Language Education of African Ancestry Students*, ed. by C. Crawford, 214–34. New York: Sankofa World Publishers.

1 I K P

Smitherman relates her own experiences regarding prejudice and misinformation about AAVE (e.g., being placed in a speech therapy class in college) and transitions into a discussion on language and power, the history of AAVE research, and the King and Oakland controversies. Among the points made is that in order to effect social change and improve education for African Americans, a change in language attitude is important. The author states that AAVE is not only legitimate as its own language, but is also influential on American English, which has borrowed such AAVE terms as *jazz* and the use of the word *bad* to mean 'good.' Furthermore, the author notes the irony that in the wake of the *Oakland* decision, Reverend Jesse Jackson and Sister Maya Angelou, both competent speakers of AAVE, were among the first to speak out against Ebonics. Smitherman closes with four propositions for language in education: that there be a multi-lingual policy to ensure that students maintain their home language while also learning SAE and a foreign language; that education seek social change; that students learn about the social and cultural context of language; and that schools capitalize on the oral-tradition language skills students bring into the classroom.

Smitherman, Geneva. 2002. Toward a National Public Policy on Language. In *The Skin That We Speak*, ed. by L. Delpit & J. K. Dowdy.

1 P

Smitherman, Geneva. 2004. Language and African Americans: Movin on up a Lil Higher. *Journal of English Linguistics* 32.186–96.

1 I P

Smitherman, Geneva. 2004. Meditations on Language, Pedagogy, and a Life of Struggle. In *Rhetoric and Language*, ed. by K. Gilyard & V. Nunley, 3–12. Portsmouth, NH: Heinemann.

1 I N S T

Smitherman, Geneva. 2006. *Word from the Mother: Language and African Americans*. New York: Routledge.

1 E F N P

Smitherman, Geneva & John Baugh. 2002. The Shot Heard from Ann Arbor: Language Research and Public Policy in African America. *Howard Journal of Communications* 13.5–24.

1 E K N P

Smitherman, Geneva & Sylvia Cunningham. 1997. Moving Beyond Resistance: Ebonics and African American Youth. *Journal of Black Psychology* 23.227–32.

1 C I

Smitherman, Geneva & Minnie Quartey-Annan. 2011. African American Language and Education: How Far Have We Come? In *Contours of English and English Language Studies,* ed. by A. Curzan & M. Adams, 274–77. Ann Arbor: University of Michigan Press.

1 C I K P

Smitherman, Geneva & Jerrie Cobb Scott. 1984. Language Attitudes and Self-Fulfilling Prophecies in the Elementary School. In *The English Language Today,* ed. by S. Greenbaum, 302–14. Oxford: Pergamon Press.

1 I T
Smitherman and Scott review research on language attitude and its effects in a classroom setting, and then discuss possible recourses. Studies involving attitude surveys administered to subjects exposed to recorded speech samples indicate that people often unwittingly use speakers' speech patterns to assess their class, ethnicity, and personal qualities. Additional research shows how this phenomenon correlates to self-fulfilling prophecies in an educational setting: teachers size up a student's potential based on, among other things, the extent to which his/her use of English is perceived as standard, and the student in turn responds in accordance with these expectations. In the last section, the authors discuss several reasons why changing teacher attitude is difficult, and recommend a three-step approach toward correcting the problem: establishing programs to inform teachers about language and variation; monitoring teacher behavior in the classroom in order to ensure more positive interaction with students; and finally monitoring teachers' evaluations of students to ensure that they build on the students' strengths rather than merely exposing their weaknesses. In this way, the authors maintain, school will start to become "the societal leader that it should be, rather than the follower that it has been" (p. 313).

Smitherman, Geneva & Victor Villanueva (eds.) 2003. *Language Diversity in the Classroom: From Intention to Practice.* Carbondale: Southern Illinois University Press.

1 A E P T W

Snow, Catherine, M. Susan Burns & Peg Griffin (eds.) 1998. *Preventing Reading Difficulties in Young Children.* Washington, D.C.: National Academy Press.

1 E R

Snow, Catherine E., Peg Griffin & M. Susan Burns. 2005. *Knowledge to Support the Teaching of Reading: Preparing Teachers for a Changing World.* San Francisco, CA: Jossey-Bass.

R

Somervill, Mary. 1975. Dialect and Reading: A Review of Alternative Solutions. *Review of Educational Research* 45.247–62.

1 E R X
Somervill reviews literature concerning five proposed language-related approaches to teaching Black children to read (teaching SAE first, allowing dialect rendering of traditional texts, neutralizing features in texts, reading texts that incorporate AAVE features, and using the language experience approach). First, the few studies that involved giving children explicit instruction in the structure of SAE have shown that such techniques are largely ineffective in improving reading ability. Two ideas lacking any research at the time of the writing were allowing children to render texts in their own dialect during oral reading, and using basal texts that employ only dialect-neutral features. While the latter technique would be impractical, there is also the possibility of devising texts that avoid only those features of SAE that would be most unfamiliar to children. Finally, both the use of basal texts that incorporate AAVE features and

the language experience approach have met with some initial success. Somervill ultimately concludes that each area still requires extensive investigation.

Soukup, Barbara. 2000. *'Y'all Come Back Now, Y'hear!?': Language Attitudes in the United States Towards Southern American English.* Vienna, Austria: University of Vienna.

1 6 I
Available online at http://othes.univie.ac.at/15934/

Southard, Bruce & Al Muller. 1993. Blame It on Twain: Reading American Dialects in "the Adventures of Huckleberry Finn.". *Journal of Reading* 36.630–34. [Abstract prepared by ERIC.]

L R S
The article offers a language-centered approach to the teaching of Mark Twain's *The Adventures of Huckleberry Finn,* which can help students read the dialects in the novel and develop an appreciation for the varieties of language.

Souto-Manning, Mariana. 2009. Acting out and Talking Back: Negotiating Discourses in American Early Educational Settings. *Early Child Development and Care* 179.1083–94. [Reprinted from *Early Child Development and Care* 179(8).]

1 I N T
As a first-grade teacher preparing for the upcoming year, I was shocked to learn that George was on my new roll. His previous teacher wrote that George was a "behaviour problem", was defiant, talked back to adults, didn't speak properly, was behind academically and spent over half of kindergarten in detention. George initially gave me negative impressions, using non-Standard English and more direct speech than I expected. Yet, by listening closely and employing classroom discourse analysis, I came to recognizse George's contributions, consequently working to dispel the myth that African American Vernacular English (AAVE) is wrong. I started analyzing my own talk, instead of blaming George for misunderstandings. We openly talked about the use of direct and indirect statements. Through this study, I suggest that kidwatching, looking closely at interactions and contexts, and seeing AAVE as a resource in class, can positively affect young children and their teachers.

Spack, Ruth. 2002. *America's Second Tongue: American Indian Education and the Ownership of English, 1860–1900.* Lincoln: University of Nebraska Press.

5 P

Spack, Ruth. 2006. English Lessons. *TESOL Quarterly* 40.595–604.

1 5 C I

Spanjer, R. Allan & B. H. Layne. 1983. Teacher Attitudes toward Language: Effects of Training in a Process Approach to Writing. *Journal of Educational Research* 77.60–62.

I T W
Seventy-eight writing teachers from elementary school through college were given a language attitude survey before and after participating in a summer workshop on teaching writing as a process approach. On the 100-question survey, one point was awarded for each answer that was in harmony with the judgments of at least seven out ten linguists from American universities and colleges. The mean pretest score was 43.72 while the mean posttest score was 52.50. As this difference achieves statistical significance, the authors conclude that the workshop on teaching writing reduced prescriptivism and brought teachers' attitudes toward language somewhat closer to

those of professional linguists. Because such attitudes may translate into more effective writing instruction, the authors recommend further research on language attitudes and teacher effectiveness in order to refine workshop techniques.

Speidel, Gisela. 1987. Conversation and Language Learning in the Classroom. In *Children's Language,* ed. by K. Nelson & A. van Kleek, 99–135. Hillsdale, NJ: Lawrence Erlbaum Associates.

2 C N

Spence, Lucy K. 2008. Generous Reading: Discovering Dialogic Voices in Writing. *English in Education* 42.253–68.

4 W

Spence, Lucy K. 2010. Generous Reading: Seeing Students through Their Writing. *The Reading Teacher* 63.634–42.

4 W

Spencer, Margaret Beale, Elizabeth Noll, Jill Stolzfus & Vinay Harpalani. 2001. Identity and School Adjustment: Revisiting the 'Acting White' Assumption. *Educational Psychologist* 36.21–30.

A

The authors challenge the 'acting White' explanation for Black student underachievement presented in Fordham & Ogbu 1986, and advocate a more complex analysis. Five hundred and sixty-two Black middle school students were measured in terms of school expulsion or suspension rate, self-esteem, racial identity, academic achievement, and physical changes brought about by puberty. Results indicate, among other things, a positive correlation between high achievement, high self-esteem, and the extent to which each student has become secure in his or her own racial identity. Also found was a general consensus among the students that receiving poor grades is 'very bad' and receiving academic honors is 'pretty/very good'. In conclusion the authors emphasize the importance of considering the many nuanced cultural and contextual factors that contribute to each student's outlook rather than labeling all defiant behavior as an aversion to 'acting White'.

Spencer, Robert. 1950. Japanese American Language Behavior. *American Speech* 25.241–52.

3 F

Sperling, Melanie. 1996. Revisiting the Writing-Speaking Connection: Challenges for Research on Writing and Writing Instruction. *Review of Educational Research* 66.53–86.

E O W X

Spolsky, Bernard & Francis Hult (eds.) 2008. *Handbook of Educational Linguistics.* Malden, MA: Blackwell.

1 2 C E I P

Starks, Judith. 1983. The Black English Controversy and Its Implications for Addressing the Educational Needs of Black Children: The Cultural Linguistic Approach. In *Black English: Educational Equity and the Law,* ed. by J. Chambers, 97–132. Ann Arbor, MI: Karoma.

1 C K P

Steele, Claude. 1992. Race and the Schooling of Black Americans. *The Atlantic Monthly* 269(4).68–78.

1 A I

Steele, Claude. 2010. *Whistling Vivaldi: And Other Clues to How Stereotypes Affect Us*. New York: W.W. Norton & Co.

1 A I

Steffensen, Margaret, Ralph Reynolds, Erica McClure & Larry Guthrie. 1982. Black English Vernacular and Reading Comprehension: A Cloze Study of Third, Sixth, and Ninth Graders. *Journal of Reading Behavior* 14.285–98.

1 R X

Sternglass, Marilyn. 1974. Dialect Features in the Composition of Black and White College Students: The Same or Different? *College Composition and Communication* 25.259–63.

1 W X

Stewart, Michele M. 2010. The Expression of Number in Jamaican Creole. *Journal of Pidgin and Creole Languages* 26.363–85.

6 F

Stewart, William (ed.) 1964. *Non-Standard Speech and the Teaching of English*. Washington D.C.: Center for Applied Linguistics.

1 B E S

Stewart, William. 1969. Language Teaching Problems in Appalachia. *The Florida FL Reporter* 7.58–59; 111.

1 6 B S

Stewart, William. 1969. On the Use of Negro Dialect in the Teaching of Reading. In *Teaching Black Children to Read*, ed. by J. Baratz & R. Shuy, 156–219. Washington, D.C.: Center for Applied Linguistics.

1 R V

Stewart, William. 1970. Foreign Language Teaching Methods in Quasi-Foreign Language Situations. In *Teaching Standard English in the Inner City*, ed. by R. Fasold & R. Shuy, 1–19. Washington, D.C.: Center for Applied Linguistics.

1 B S

Stewart makes a distinction between "first" language teaching (e.g., development of literacy, vocabulary, and stylistic control) and "second" language teaching (acquisition of features of new language via contrasts with native language). The author draws on examples of grammatical features of Jamaican Creole English, Liberian Pidgin English, Mexican-American English and AAVE to illustrate that nonstandard varieties are in many ways different enough from Standard English to warrant "second" language teaching techniques for speakers learning the standard. For example, absence of third-person singular inflectional morpheme -s in AAVE is indicative of a large-scale difference between SAE and AAVE which will require explicit contrastive-analytic instruction rather than mere "patchwork correction" (p. 14). The author concludes that accurate linguistic descriptions of nonstandard varieties will be necessary for educators to use as a basis for teaching the standard.

Stewart, William. 1978. The Laissez-Faire Movement in English Teaching: Advance to the Rear? In *A Pluralistic Nation,* ed. by M. Lourie & N. F. Conklin, 333-56. Rowley, MA: Newbury House.

1 I T X

Stockman, Ida. 1986. Language Acquisition in Culturally Diverse Populations: The Black Child as a Case Study. In *Nature of Communication Disorders in Culturally and Linguistically Diverse Populations,* ed. by O. Taylor, 117–55. San Diego, CA: College Press.

1 D Q

Stockman, Ida. 1989. Addressing New Questions About Black Children's Language. In *Current Issues in Linguistic Theory: Language Change and Variation,* ed. by R. Fasold & D. Schiffrin, 275–300. Amsterdam: John Benjamins.

1 Q

Stockman, Ida. 1996. Phonological Development and Disorders in African American Children. In *Communication Development Disorders in African American Children: Research, Assessment and Intervention,* ed. by A. Kamhi, K. Pollack & J. Harris, 117–54. Baltimore: Paul H. Brookes Publishing.

1 D Q

Stockman, Ida. 2000. The New Peabody Picture Vocabulary Test-III: An Illusion of Unbiased Assessment? *Language, Speech, and Hearing Services in Schools* 31.340–53.

A D

Stockman, Ida. 2007. Social-Political Influences on Research Practices: Examining Language Acquisition by African American Children. In *Sociolinguistic Variation: Theories, Methods, and Applications,* ed. by R. Bayley & C. Lucas, 297–317. Cambridge: Cambridge University Press.

1 P Q
Stockman argues that science is necessarily affected by social and cultural context. She then discusses the specific effects of the socio-political environment on research regarding language acquisition of African American children, especially the research she conducted in partnership with Fay Vaugn-Cooke. She concludes that the research community had seen middle-class White populations as the only population worth studying. It had seen all other groups as deviations which should only be studied in contrast with the "normal" group. This chapter is a levelheaded critique of research bias and the scientific enterprise.

Stockman, Ida. 2010. A Review of Developmental and Applied Language Research on African American Children: From a Deficit to Difference Perspective on Dialect Differences. *Language, Speech, and Hearing Services in Schools* 41.23–38.

1 A D E Q

Stockman, Ida & Fay Vaughn-Cooke. 1992. Lexical Elaboration in Children's Locative Action Expression. *Child Development* 63.1104–25.

F Q

Stoller, Paul (ed.) 1975. *Black American English: Its Background and Its Usage in Schools and in Literature.* New York: Delta.

1 A B E I R S V W

Stoller, Paul. 1975. The Case against Black English in the Schools: A Brief Review. In *Black American English: Its Background and Its Usage in Schools and in Literature,* ed. by P. Stoller, 186–89. New York: Delta.

1 I P V

Stout, Steven & Carol Erting. 1977. Uninflected Be in Isletan English. In *Studies in Southwestern Indian English,* ed. by W. Leap, 101–19. San Antonio, TX: Trinity University Press.

5 F

Straker, Dolores. 1985. Reading Materials. In *Tapping Potential: English and Language Arts for the Black Learner,* ed. by C. Brooks, 139–46. Urbana, IL: NCTE.

1 C R V

Strickland, Dorothy & Donna Alvermann (eds.) 2004. *Bridging the Literacy Achievement Gap: Grades 4–12.* New York: Teachers College Press.

1 A E P R W

Strickland, Dorothy & William Stewart. 1974. The Use of Dialect Readers: A Dialogue. In *Black Dialects and Reading,* ed. by B. Cullinan, 146–51. Urbana, IL: NCTE.

1 R V

Stuart, Amy. 2006. Equal Treatment as Exclusion: Language, Race and US Education Policy. *International Journal of Inclusive Education* 10.235–50. [Reprinted from *International Journal of Inclusive Education* 10(2).]

1 P

This paper examines the political meanings of language in the United States, from the perspectives of both majority- and minority-language groups, and focuses especially on Mainstream US English, African American Vernacular English, and Spanish. It briefly traces the history of language policy in US education and argues that because language serves as a proxy for race, power and identity, language policy alone is not sufficient to address exclusionary practices. As long as the issues underlying language are not addressed, the rhetoric of equal treatment and language policies based on such rhetoric will continue to be manipulated to serve an exclusionary agenda that reinforces traditional social hierarchies.

Sullivan, Richard. 1971. *A Comparison of Certain Relationships among Selected Phonological Differences and Spelling Deviations for a Group of Negro and a Group of White Second Grade Children.* Final Report. Project No. 1F038, Bureau of Research, Office of Education, US Department of Health, Education and Welfare, Washington, DC. Available for download (record ED057021) from Education Resources Information Center (ERIC) at: http://eric.ed.gov/ERICWebPortal/search/detailmini.jsp?_nfpb=true&_&ERICExtSearch_SearchValue_0=ED057021&ERICExtSearch_SearchType_0=no&accno=ED057021.

1 O W X

Sutcliffe, David. 1982. *British Black English.* Oxford: Blackwell.

6 F

Sutcliffe, David & Ansell Wong (eds.) 1986. *The Language of Black Experience: Cultural Expression through Word and Sound in the Caribbean and Black Britain.* Oxford: Blackwell.

2 6 E F I N P

Sweetland, Julie. 2006. *Teaching Writing in the African American Classroom: A Sociolinguistic Approach.* Ph.D. dissertation. Stanford University Department of Linguistics, Stanford, CA.

1 B C I T S W X
This study evaluates the outcomes of a ten-week elementary language arts curriculum designed to improve the writing achievement and experiences of children who speak AAVE. The curriculum integrated sociolinguistic research with contemporary language arts pedagogy, using multicultural children's literature to teach about regional and social language variation, and incorporating dialect-based grammar instruction (contrastive analysis) into the writing process. Based on an analysis of language attitude surveys, interviews with teachers and students, and an analysis of pre- and post-intervention writing samples, the study concludes that participation in the intervention was associated with several positive outcomes, including positive changes in teacher attitudes toward language variation; an increase in students' writing self-efficacy; an increase in students' facility with Standard English in writing; and growth in several traits of effective writing, including content quality, organization, author's voice, sentence fluency, and conventions. Moreover, children who were encouraged to use AAVE in creative writing used a variety of vernacular varieties to create effective texts.

Sweetland, Julie. 2010. Fostering Teacher Change: Effective Professional Development for Sociolinguistic Diversity. In *Linguistics at School: Language Awareness in Primary and Secondary Education,* ed. by K. Denham & A. Loebeck, 161–74. Cambridge: Cambridge University Press.

1 I L T
The author reports on a study in which elementary classroom teachers piloted a language awareness curriculum with African American elementary students. Pre- and post-intervention language surveys and interviews indicated that teachers who implemented dialect awareness and contrastive analysis learning activities with students developed more pluralist attitudes toward language variation and AAVE in particular. The author identifies three strategies for fostering change: linking desired innovations to teachers' existing concerns and practices; treating negative language attitudes as a baseline, not a barrier; and capitalizing on the influence of classroom practice.

Swisher, Karen Cayton & John W. Tippeconnic (eds.) 1999. *Next Steps: Research and Practice to Advance Indian Education.* Charleston, WV: ERIC Clearinghouse on Rural Education and Small Schools.

5 E

Syrquin, Anna. 2006. Registers in the Academic Writing of African American College Students. *Written Communication* 23.63–90. [Reprinted with permission of Sage Publications, the publisher, from *Written Communication* 23(1), 63.]

1 F N W
The study examines the development of the registers of academic writing by African American college-level students through style and grammar: indirection inherent in the oral culture of the African American community and the paratactic functions of "because." Discourse analysis of seventy-four samples of academic writing by twenty African American undergraduate students and of sixty-one samples by a control group showed that first, only African American subjects used indirection; second, paratactic functions of "because" were significantly more prevalent among African American students than in the control group; and third, among African American students, those from low-income families showed statistically significant higher frequencies of the use

of both indirection and paratactic "because." A relationship of hierarchy in the uses of indirection and paratactic "because" was also evident in the data.

Taavitsainen, Irma, Gunnel Melchers & Pa ivi Pahta (eds.) 1999. *Writing in Nonstandard English*. Philadelphia: John Benjamins.

1 E V W

Tabouret-Keller, Andree, Robert Le Page, Penelope Gardner-Chloros & Gabrielle Varro (eds.) 1997. *Vernacular Literacy: A Re-Evaluation*. Oxford: Clarendon Press.

E V

Talmy, Steven. 2004. Forever Fob: The Cultural Production of Esl in a High School. *Pragmatics* 14.149–72.

3 I O T

Talmy, Steven. 2009. A Very Important Lesson: Respect and the Socialization of Order(S) in High School Esl. *Linguistics and Education* 20.235–53.

2 3 I T

Talmy, Steven. 2010. Becoming "Local" in Esl: Racism as Resource in a Hawai'i Public High School. *Journal of Language, Identity and Education* 9.36–57.

2 3 I T

Tamura, Eileen. 1996. Power, Status, and Hawai'i Creole English: An Example of Linguistic Intolerance in American History. *Pacific Historical Review* 65.431–54.

2 I P

Tamura, Eileen. 2002. African American Vernacular English and Hawaii Creole English: A Comparison of Two School Board Controversies. *Journal of Negro Education* 71.17–30.

1 2 I K P

Tamura compares the controversy over the Oakland school board decision to a similar controversy that occurred regarding the Hawaii school board decision about Hawaii Creole English (HCE). In both cases, the purpose was to teach SAE to speakers of nonstandard English. While the proposed methods were different (Oakland advocated using AAVE as a bridge to SAE, and Hawaii initially advocated a ban on the use of HCE in the classroom), both decisions resulted in public indications of a lack of understanding about the nature of language variation, and in both cases this was spurred on by the media. In light of the comparison, the author draws two sets of implications for educational policymakers. First, although nonstandard dialect use does not necessarily in and of itself impede academic achievement, schools are responsible for teaching their students SAE for its professional and social benefits. To this end, the author lists four points of agreement in the literature regarding the best way to teach a second dialect. Second, the public sentiment stirred by each decision suggests that scholars need to work to dispel myths among the public about nonstandard varieties.

Tamura, Eileen ed. 2008. Special Issue: Hawaii Creole (Pidgin), Local Identity, and Schooling. *Educational Perspectives: Journal of the University of Hawai'i at Manoa* 41.

2 B E F I K P S

Tapia, Elena. 1999. "I Wouldn't Think Nothin' of It": Teacher Candidates Survey Public on Nonstandard Usage. *English Education* 31.295–309.

I L

Tarone, Elaine. 1973. Aspects of Intonation in Black English. *American Speech* 48.29–39.

1 F O

Tatham, Susan Masland. 1970. Reading Comprehension of Materials Written with Select Oral Language Patterns: A Study at Grades Two and Four. *Reading Research Quarterly* 5.402–26.

R X

Tauber, Robert. 1997. *Self-Fulfilling Prophecy: A Practical Guide to Its Use in Education.* Westport, CT: Praeger.

A I T

Taylor, Denny & Catherine Dorsey-Gaines. 1988. *Growing up Literate: Learning from Inner-City Families.* Portsmouth, NH: Heimann.

1 C R

Taylor, Gail Singleton. 1994. Multicultural Literature Preferences of Low Ability African American and Hispanic American Fifth Graders. *Reading Improvement* 34.37–48.

M R
A study involving two dozen fifth grade students compared their interest in children's books that took a 'melting pot' approach to race versus those that took a 'culturally conscious' approach, which involved the use of the vernacular by characters. African American children strongly preferred the culturally conscious books; the author concludes that the use of such books can increase Black children's interest and proficiency in reading.

Taylor, Hanni. 1989. *Standard English, Black English, and Bidialectalism: A Controversy.* New York: Peter Lang Publishing.

1 B W
As an English professor at a predominantly White private college, Hanni Taylor was disturbed by the fact that many of her promising Black students struggled with written self-expression and the academic and cultural demands of the university. She responded by initiating "Project Bidialectalism," a series of eleven weekly meetings with a group of ten Black students from inner-city Chicago. Taylor (1989) describes her work with these students as an "informal experiment" drawing on "eclectic methods" with twin goals: (1) to increase student awareness of language attitudes and (2) to increase the expression of Standard English features while decreasing interfering Black English features in writing. To these ends, the students engaged in activities that Taylor developed by adopting and adapting methods from second-language acquisition theory. These included pattern-practice drills on recognition, discrimination, and production of target features such as possessive marking and verb forms. However, these drills were only a limited part of the intervention, taking no more than fifteen minutes of each class period. Other, more contextualized exercises supplemented the drills, including translation tasks, written "imitations" of published work written in a variety of styles, and discussion of AAVE features found in literature. In all of these exercises, Taylor led the students to use the technique of "contrastive analysis," in which a language learner discerns small but crucial differences between her native variety and the target variety as a step toward L2 mastery. Finally, and in Taylor's view, crucially, these exercises did not stand alone, but were supported by "counseling-learning" intended to develop and communicate "heightened ethnosensitivity." Often this consisted simply of engaging students in dialogue about their experiences in a racialized society. Another technique involved discussion of contrasting pieces of

literature written by White and Black authors that "centered on Black culture or the mainstream" (p. 136). In these discussions, linguistic forms were subject to analysis but weren't the main focus; instead, students uncovered and analyzed the values and beliefs implicit in texts such as Lorraine Hansberry's Raisin in the Sun or Geneva Smitherman's "White English in Blackface." In incorporating critical discussions of the larger social issues connected with linguistic variation, Taylor explicitly "joined linguistic and philosophical goals, as equivalents" (p. 104). At the end of eleven weeks, Taylor compared the writing of "Project Bidialectalism" students with the writing of a control group of ten students who had also responded to the initial letter of invitation and were similar to the experimental group in terms of background and academic achievement as measured by ACT scores and university GPA. The control group participated in eleven weekly sessions with the researcher, but Taylor reports that this group "did not experiment with contrastive mechanical features—the focus was on Standard English" and otherwise "followed closely traditional English Department techniques" (p. 148). While this cursory description of the comparison group's curriculum renders the comparative data less powerful than it might be ideally, Taylor's results are impressive nonetheless. Occurrences of AAVE features in the writing of "Project Bidialectalism" students were reduced by 59.3% overall, with some features showing even more drastic reduction (for example, a 91.7% reduction in unmarked third-person singular verbs) (p. 149). By contrast, the control group, showed an 8.9% increase in use of AAVE features in their writing over the same time period.

Taylor, Janet. 1983. Influence of Speech Variety on Teachers' Evaluation of Reading Comprehension. *Journal of Educational Psychology* 75.662–67. [Abstract reprinted from journal.]

1 I R T
This study investigated how two speech varieties, Standard English and Black English, used during an oral reading and recall task, influenced sixty-four White and eight Black teachers' (mean age thirty-six years) evaluations of reading comprehension and how teachers' attitudes toward Black English related to those evaluations. Measures included the Oral Reading and Recall Evaluation, the Reading Miscue Inventory, and the Language Attitude Scale. Although the proportion of variance accounted for by the overall model was not great (11%), significant contrasts between the evaluations of two readers, one a Black English speaker and one a Standard English speaker, were found with teachers who held negative attitudes toward Black English. No significant contrasts were found with teachers who held positive attitudes toward Black English. Results indicate that Black English readers were rated lower in reading comprehension than equivalent Standard English readers when teachers held a negative attitude toward their language.

Taylor, JoAnn. 1987. Teaching Children Who Speak a Non-Standard Dialect to Read. *Reading Improvement* 24.160–62.

I R

Taylor, Marsha & Andrew Ortony. 1980. Rhetorical Devices in Black English: Some Psycholinguistic and Educational Observations. *Quarterly Newsletter of the Laboratory of Comparative Human Cognition* 2.21–26.

1 N

Taylor, Orlando L. 1972. An introduction to the historical development of Black English: Some implications for American education. *Language, Speech and Hearing Services in Schools* 3 (4): 5–15.

1 D

Taylor, Orlando. 1973. Teachers' Attitudes toward Black and Nonstandard English as Measured by the Language Attitude Scale. In *Language Attitudes: Current Trends and Prospects*, ed. by R. Shuy & R. Fasold, 174–201. Washington, D.C.: Georgetown University Press.

1 I T
Four hundred and twenty-two teachers from across the United States were given a 25-question Likert-type survey in order to assess their opinions on Black and nonstandard English. Among the more important findings, was the fact that most teachers had positive or neutral attitudes concerning the use of nonstandard language, although there was an even split between negative and positive attitude concerning its inherent structural legitimacy. Although the gender of the teacher played no significant role in determining attitude, teachers at predominantly black schools had more positive attitudes than those at predominantly White schools. Furthermore, teachers with three to five years of teaching experience exhibited more positive attitudes than those with less or more experience. The implication is that teachers may be more receptive than was previously believed toward implementing new methods of instruction that remain sensitive to language variation, and that teachers with three to five years of experience may be the optimal starting point for introducing such methods.

Taylor, Orlando. 1975. Black Language and What to Do About It: Some Black Community Perspectives. In *Ebonics: The True Language of Black Folks*, ed. by R. L. Williams, 29–39. St. Louis. MO: Institute of Black Studies.

1 B I P

Taylor, Orlando. 1983. Black English: An Agenda for the 1980s. In *Black English, Educational Equity and the Law*, ed. by J. Chambers Jr, 133–43. Ann Arbor, MI: Karoma Publishers.

1 B

Taylor, Orlando. 1986. A Cultural and Communicative Approach to Teaching Standard English as a Second Dialect. In *Treatment of Communication Disorders in Culturally and Linguistically Diverse Populations*, ed. by O. Taylor, 153–78. San Diego, CA: College Hill Press.

1 B C

Taylor, Orlando (ed.) 1986. *Nature of Communication Disorders in Culturally and Linguistically Diverse Populations*. San Diego, CA: College Hill Press.

1 A D E

Taylor, Orlando. 1998. Ebonics and Educational Policy: Some Issues for the Next Millenium. *Journal of Negro Education* 67.35–42.

1 K P
Taylor gives a synopsis of the evolution of African American English legitimacy. Taylor demonstrates that early European explorers in Africa already made unflattering references to the languages spoken by the African people they encountered. Not until the 1930s did a scholarship emerge which suggested that African American English had a legitimate linguistic basis. The article focuses on the ramifications of the Oakland California schools board's Ebonics proposal and the major challenge that educators currently face. Lessons learned from the Oakland Ebonics proposal mainly include ways teachers and administrators can improve their teaching methods. Taylor mentions that non-standard English dialects are not solely spoken by African Americans, which goes against the media-portrayed stereotype. In addition, Taylor rebuffs

another media stereotype, pointing out that the schools are not teaching in slang but rather in a dialect. It is in the nation's best interest to produce children who can speak, read, and write Standard English. The system should facilitate cohesion among the nation's diverse groups, teaching the literacy necessary for academic and economic achievement, and at the same time preserve the cultural heritages of all people.

Taylor, Orlando. 1999. Testimony of Orlando L. Taylor on the Subject of "Ebonics". In *Making the Connection: Language and Academic Achievement among African American Students,* ed. by C. T. Adger, D. Christian & O. Taylor, 169–75. Washington, D.C., and McHenry, IL: Center for Applied Linguistics, and Delta Systems, Co., Inc.

1 K P S
Reprint of Taylor's testimony before the "Ebonics" panel/hearing of the United States Senate Committee on Appropriations Subcommittee on Labor, Health and Human Services and Education, chaired by the Honorable Arlen Specter, January 23, 1997.

Taylor, Orlando & Laurence Leonard (eds.) 1998. *Language Acquisition across North America: Cross-Cultural and Cross-Linguistic Perspectives.* San Diego, CA: Singular Publishing Group.

E F Q U

Taylor, Orlando & Maryon Matsuda. 1988. Storytelling and Classroom Discrimination. In *Discourse and Discrimination,* ed. by G. Smitherman & T. A. van Dijk, 206–20. Detroit. MI: Wayne State University Press.

1 N T

Taylor, Orlando, Kay Payne & Patricia Cole. 1983. A Survey of Bidialectal Language Arts Programs in the United States. *Journal of Negro Education* 52.35–45.

1 B I
A 35-item questionnaire was distributed to 40 administrators and directors of bidialectal programs across the United States regarding the characteristics of their program, and its personnel, participants, and evaluation methods. The fourteen surveys returned indicated that almost all of the programs tended to be developed internally, but relied on external funding. The majority of the program administrators had a 'mixed' or 'negative' attitude about the program whereas the majority of students and parents had a 'positive' or 'very positive' attitude. Finally, most respondents considered their program 'successful' or 'very successful'. In light of the limited number of programs uncovered in the search, the authors advocate increased program implementation, and conclude that programs would benefit from increased communication with each other, and from standardized guidelines for program development and evaluation.

Terrell, Sandra L. & Francis Terrell. 1983. Effects of Speaking Black English Upon Employment Opportunities. *ASHA* 25.27–29.

1 I

Terry, J. Michael, Sandra Jackson, Evangelos Evangelou & Richard L. Smith. 2010. Expressive and Receptive Language Effects of African American English on a Sentence Imitation Task. *Topics in Language Disorders* 30.119–34.

1 A F X

Terry, Nicole Patton. 2006. Relations between Dialect Variation, Grammar, and Early Spelling Skills. *Reading and Writing: An Interdisciplinary Journal* 19.907–31. [Reprinted with permission of Springer, the publisher, from *Reading and Writing* 19(9).]

1 X

Relationships among African American English (AAE), linguistic knowledge, and spelling skills were examined in a sample of 92 children in grades one through three whose speech varied in the frequency of morphosyntactic AAE features. Children were separated into groups of high (AAE speakers) and low (standard American English, SAE, speakers) use of AAE features in speech, and asked to produce, recognize, and spell four inflected grammatical morphemes because variable omission of these endings in speech is a morphosyntactic characteristic of AAE. The groups differed in their spelling and elicited spoken production of inflections, but not recognition of these forms. AAE speakers omitted the inflections more often at each grade. Density of morphosyntactic AAE features in speech was related directly to spelling inflections, but this effect was mediated by children's understanding of standard grammatical forms.

Terry, Nicole Patton. 2008. Addressing African American English in Early Literacy Assessment and Instruction. *Perspectives on Communication Disorders and Sciences in Culturally and Linguistically Diverse Populations* 15.54–61.

1 A R X

Terry, Nicole Patton, Carol McDonald Connor, Shurita Thomas-Tate & Michael Love. 2010. Examining Relationships among Dialect Variation, Literacy Skills, and School Context in First Grade. *Journal of Speech, Language, and Hearing Research* 53.126–45.

1 6 F R X
Terry et al. study 617 first graders (48% African American, 52% White) to examine the relationships between the use of nonstandard American English dialects, literacy skills, and school environment. The authors look at the relationship between the students' dialect variation (DVAR) and their vocabulary, phonological awareness, and word reading skills, taking into account schoolwide socioeconomic status (SES). The results showed the relationship between DVAR and literacy outcomes varied by the outcome measured and race generally did not affect the trajectory or the strength of the relationship between DVAR and outcomes. The authors suggest a relationship between dialect variation and literacy achievement that may be sensitive to school environment but not to race. They ultimately conclude that their results demonstrate a complex relationship between nonstandard American English dialect use, school context, race, and early reading achievement.

Tett, Lyn & Jim Crowther. 1998. Families at a Disadvantage: Class Culture and Literacies. *British Educational Research Journal* 24.449–60.

2 A C

Thiede, Ralf. 1983. A Black English/Standard English Interim Grammar in College Composition: A Case Study. *Transactions (Missouri Academy of Science)* 17.

1 W X

Thomas, Erik R. 2007. Phonological and Phonetic Characteristics of African American Vernacular English. *Language and Linguistics Compass* 1.450–75.

·1 F

Thomas, Erik R. & Alicia Beckford Wassink. 2010. Variation and Identity in African-American English. In *Language and Identities*, ed. by C. Llamas & D. Watt, 157–65. Edinburgh, Scotland: Edinburgh University Press. [Abstracts for "Variation and Identity in African-American English" by Erik Thomas and Alicia Wassink, "Historically Low Prestige and Seeds of Change: Attitudes toward Jamaican Creole" and ""My Teacher Says...," Mastery of English and the Creole Learner" by Alicia Wassink, and

"Addressing Ideologies around African American English" by Alicia Wassink and Anne Curzan graciously provided by Alicia Wassink.]

1 F I

African American English (AAE) can be said to have norms that cut across region and social class, although individual speakers may not use all the variants that comprise these norms. However, despite the existence of such norms, African American English does exhibit regional variation, and knowledge of such differences is necessary for a fuller understanding of AAE as a variety. Furthermore, a nuanced appreciation of the construction of identity is necessary when examining variation in AAE. We need an understanding of the language/identity nexus that goes beyond monolithic assumptions regarding the AAE ethnicity and use of AAE. This chapter presents a description of AAE and some of the regional variation observed in the variety to date, then turns to a consideration of the identity-making and -marking functions of the variety.

Thomas, Gail. 1983. The Deficit, Difference, and Bicultural Theories of Black Dialect and Nonstandard English. *The Urban Review* 15.107–18.

1 C E I

Thomas, Linda. 1999. The Standard English Debate. In *Language, Society and Power: An Introduction,* ed. by L. Thomas & S. Wareing, 151–71. London: Routledge.

F I

Thomas-Tate, Shurita, Julie A. Washington, Holly K. Craig & Mary Packard. 2006. Performance of African American Preschool and Kindergarten Students on the Expressive Vocabulary Test. *Language, Speech and Hearing Services in Schools* 37:143-49.

1 A Q

Thompson, Connie, Holly K. Craig & Julie A. Washington. 2004. Variable Production of African American English across Oracy and Literacy Contexts. *Language, Speech and Hearing Services in Schools* 35.269–82.

1 O R U W

Thompson, Nicole L., Dwight Hare, Tracie T. Sempier & Cathy Grace. 2008. The Development of a Curriculum Toolkit with American Indian and Alaska Native Communities. *Early Childhood Education Journal* 35.397–404.

5 C M S

The article outlines the development of the "Growing and Learning with Young Native Children" curriculum toolkit, which includes strategies that teachers can use to support Native people in preserving and maintaining their culture and language.

Thomson, Jack. 1977. Social Class Labeling in the Application of Bernstein's Theory of the Codes to the Identification of Linguistic Advantage and Disadvantage in Five-Year-Old Children. *Educational Review* 29.273–83.

A

Todd, Loreto. 1984. *Modern Englishes: Pidgins and Creoles.* Oxford: Blackwell in association with A. Deutsch.

2 6 F

Tolerance, Teaching. 1996. A Mountain Legacy: Children of Appalachia Gain Pride in Their Heritage and History. *Teaching Tolerance* 5.52–59.

6 L S

The article profiles efforts of Appalachian educators to connect area children with their heritage, and argues that teaching students the history behind their own dialect and customs can improve both social-emotional and academic outcomes.

Tompkins, Gail & Lea McGee. 1983. Launching Nonstandard Speakers into Standard English. *Language Arts* 60.463–69.

B S

Torbert, Benjamin. 2002. *Hyde Talk: The Language and Land of Hyde County, North Carolina* [video] Raleigh, NC: North Carolina Language and Life Project, North Carolina State University.

1 6 F I

Toribio, Almeida Jacqueline. 2003. The Social Significance of Language Loyalty among Black and White Dominicans in New York. *The Bilingual Review/La Revista Bilingue* 27.3–11.

1 4 I P

Toribio, Almeida Jacqueline. 2006. Linguistic Displays of Identity among Dominicans in National and Diasporic Settings. In *English and Ethnicity*, ed. by J. Brutt-Griffler & C. E. Davies, 131–58. New York: Palgrave Macmillan.

4 I

Torres, Lourdes. 2010. Puerto Ricans in the United States and Language Shift to English. *English Today* 26.49–54.

4 Q

Torrey, Jane. 1970. Illiteracy in the Ghetto. *Harvard Educational Review* 40.253–59.

1 A R X

Torrey, Jane. 1971. Teaching Standard English to Speakers of Other Dialects. In *Applications of Linguistics: Selected Papers of the Second International Congress of Applied Linguistics, Cambridge 1969*, ed. by G. Perren & J. Trim. Cambridge: Cambridge University Press.

B

Treiman, Rebecca. 2004. Spelling and Dialect: Comparisons between Speakers of African American Vernacular English and White Speakers. *Psychonomic Bulletin & Review* 11.338–42.

1 O X

Troike, Rudolph. 1972. Receptive Bidialectalism: Implications for Second-Dialect Teaching. In *Language and Cultural Diversity in American Education,* ed. by R. Abrahams & R. Troike, 305–10. Upper Saddle River, NJ: Prentice-Hall.

1 B Q X

Troike combats prevailing assumptions in language instruction that underestimate young children's linguistic competence and awareness. Previous research indicated that children who were asked to repeat back SAE utterances did so in their native dialect (e.g., the prompt "Mother helps Gloria" was rendered back as "Mother help Gloria" by an African American child.) Since translation requires comprehension, it was apparent that children already had receptive competence in much of SAE. By the same token, when met with an utterance containing an unfamiliar pattern, children had difficulty repeating it back. Thus, in second-dialect instruction, teachers can first use this repeating technique to assess which patterns of SAE students already understand, and use them as a starting point from which to build productive competence. The author then relates three anecdotes indicating that even at the age of five or six, children possess some awareness of dialectal differences, and argues that second-dialect instruction should begin between the ages of five and eight when a child's language learning ability is still optimum.

Troutman, Denise. 1997. Whose Voice Is It Anyway? Marked Features in the Writing of Black English Speakers. In *Writing in Multicultural Settings,* ed. by C. Severino, J. Guerra & J. Butler, 27–39. New York: Modern Language Association of America.

1 C F W

Troutman, Denise. 1998. The Power of Dialect: Ebonics Personified. In *Lessons to Share on Teaching Grammar in Context,* ed. by C. Weaver, 209–27. Portsmouth, NH: Boynton/Cook.

1 F I K N S

Troutman, Denise & Julia Falk. 1982. Speaking Black English and Reading: Is There a Problem of Interference? *Journal of Negro Education* 51.123–33.

1 R X

Troutman and Falk review literature concerning linguistic interference in the task of reading for AAVE-speakers. The seven studies reviewed present largely negative evidence for such interference. According to the authors, limitations of the studies included the erroneous assumption that Black students would be better at reading AAVE texts than SAE texts despite never having been introduced to the former, the lack of longitudinal testing, the elimination of non-reading subjects who might have otherwise exhibited the most interference, the use of non-representative grade samples, and the possible lack of generalizability. Given the continued low reading performance rate of many AAVE-speakers despite years of studies, the authors ask whether researchers are isolating the correct variables. Since studies have shown that such children are able to read in SAE by third grade yet national norms indicate that their performance drops with time, perhaps children in Grade 6 and higher should be studied. Additionally, they ask whether prolonged studies are really necessary; perhaps AAVE-speakers should just be given more time to learn to read. Nevertheless, they consider the question of linguistic interference unanswered, and await additional, more sophisticated research.

Troyka, Lynn Quitman. 2000. How We Have Failed the Basic-Writing Enterprise. *Journal of Basic Writing* 19.113–23.

I K W

Trudgill, Peter & Jean Hannah. 2008. *International English: A Guide to Varieties of Standard English*. London: Hodder Education.

E F

Tucker, G. Richard & Wallace E. Lambert. 1969. White and Negro Listeners' Reactions to Various American English Dialects. *Social Forces* 47.463–68.

1 I

Tyndall, Belle. 1991. What Influences Raters' Judgment of Student Writing. *Linguistics and Education* 3.191–202. [Reprinted with permission of Elsevier, the publisher, from *Linguistics and Education* 3(3).]

T W

This article compares the results of a linguistic analysis of thirty students' compositions with the holistic ratings of nine independent judges. The compositions were the examination scripts of seventeen-year-old high school students drawn from the two levels of the Caribbean Examinations Council English Language examinations: General Proficiency and Basic Proficiency. The General Proficiency compositions, according to the examination syllabus, were expected to display a greater "maturity of expression" than compositions at the Basic Proficiency level. The linguistic analysis was based on four potential indicators of maturity: morphological (past tense morpheme only), syntactic, semantic, and discourse. The judges' holistic ratings, the method used to divide the compositions into two groups, "more mature" and "less mature," were based on the judges' definition of the criterion "maturity of expression." A comparison of the two sets of results on an implicational scale revealed that the factor that weighed most heavily with the judges was correct past tense usage.

Underwood, Gary. 1974. Bidialectal Freshman Handbooks—the Next Flim Flam. *The Florida FL Reporter* 12.45–48.

1 B
Underwood offers several theoretical flaws associated with bidialectalism. First, programs do not take into account whether students already have receptive competence in the standard. Furthermore, the nature of language variation is not yet well enough understood to be able to teach exactly how one dialect differs from another. Turning to composition specifically, Underwood argues that educators are under the misconception that students must be taught to speak SAE before being taught to write in SAE, when, in fact, English orthography is largely morphophonemic and does not require knowledge of a specific system of pronunciation. The author accuses texts of using the term 'nonstandard' when really only the nonstandard dialect of African Americans is meant. Although texts may claim to be based on English as a Foreign Language [EFL] methods, many are modifications of traditional methods, with, for example, the term *vernacular dialect* or *VD* used in place of *ungrammatical*. Finally, texts assume that SAE and VD are two categorical varieties, which belies the continuum of variation between them to the confusion and discouragement of the student.

Urciuoli, Bonnie. 1985. Bilingualism as Code and Bilingualism as Practice. *Anthropological Linguistics* 27.363–86.

4 6 N U

Urciuoli, Bonnie. 1996. *Exposing Prejudice: Puerto Rican Experiences of Language, Race, and Class*. Boulder, CO: Westview.

4 I P

Ure, Jean. 1981. Mother Tongue Education and Minority Languages: A Question of Values and Costs. *Journal of Multilingual and Multicultural Development* 2.303–08.

V
After making three arguments in favor of initial instruction to children in their mother tongue (since it is the language of traditional values, the vehicle of creative thought, and the link to the children's home community), Ure proposes a method involving the use of language-neutral textbooks filled with exercises involving illustrations, diagrams, numerals and symbols that can be used in conjunction with any language. Teachers can use such a book to foster confidence and oral articulateness in their students before transitioning into a foreign, written language.

Valdes, Guadalupe. 2001. *Learning and Not Learning English: Latino Students in American Schools*. New York: Teachers College Press.

4 A C Q

Valdes, Guadalupe, Jeff MacSwan & Laura Alvarez. 2009. *Perspectives on Language and Education*. Paper presented at the Workshop on the role of language in school learning: Implications for closing the achievement gap, Menlo Park, CA.

1 B I Q

Van Duinen, Deborah Vriend & Marilyn Wilson. 2008. Holding the Words in Our Mouths: Responses to Dialect Variations in Oral Reading. *English Journal* 97.31–37. [Reprinted from English Journal 97(3).]

1 I L
Deborah Vriend Van Duinen and Marilyn J. Wilson confront normalized notions of "correct" English. They offer suggestions for teaching about marginalized voices and introducing students to the complexities of English dialect variations.

Van Hofwegen, Janneke & Walt Wolfram. 2010. Coming of Age in African American English: A Longitudinal Study. *Journal of Sociolinguistics* 14.427–55.

1 F Q

Van Keulen, Jean, Gloria Weddington & Charles DeBose. 1998. *Speech, Language, Learning, and the African American Child*. Boston: Allyn and Bacon.

1 A B D I Q T

Van Sickle, Meta, Olaiya Aina & Mary Blake. 2002. A Case Study of the Sociopolitical Dilemmas of Gullah-Speaking Students: Educational Policies and Practices. *Language, Culture and Curriculum* 15.75–88. [Abridged from original abstract in *Language, Culture and Curriculum* 15(1).]

1 2 O X
Most of the languages spoken along the West African coastline are different from European languages but similar to Black English. Gullah, a West African and English Creole language, still spoken today on the sea islands of South Carolina and Georgia, is the predecessor of American Black English which is most similar to the languages of West Africa. Early research in reading comprehension and science language development has supported the belief that divergent language usage, such as Gullah, has a negative impact on the visible demonstration of academic reading achievement (Goodman, 1965; Hunt, 1975). Unfortunately, the educational system has been insensitive and ineffective in addressing the issue of the language differences between Black English and White English. Qualitative case study (Bogdan & Biklen, 1998) was chosen because we needed students with extreme examples of non-traditional English to illustrate easily the patterns that emerged. For all the students, description through language was a very complex issue. Often they omitted words or did not know the specific content words to complete a description. While their indigenous language patterns created holistic pictures, they did not use the exact or precise word to communicate the appropriate meaning to those unfamiliar with their language.

Vasquez, Olga, Lucinda Pease-Alvarez & Sheila Shannon. 2008. *Pushing Boundaries: Language and Culture in a Mexicano Community*. Cambridge: Cambridge University Press.

4 U

Vaughn-Cooke, Fay. 1983. Improving Language Assessment in Minority Children. *ASHA* 25.29–34.

1 A D
Because of the systematic ways in which various dialects of English differ from Standard English, traditional standardized tests for assessing linguistic ability are not

suitable for speakers of nonstandard dialects. In this paper, Vaughn-Cooke discusses seven proposed alternatives aimed at providing sufficient assessment of speakers of such dialects, and explains why each one is inadequate in its current state. These alternatives include standardizing or modifying existing tests for non-mainstream English speakers, using a language sample of a non-mainstream speaker in order to make assessments, and developing a new test aimed at more accurate assessment of nonstandard dialects. Vaughn-Cooke concludes that "a crisis exists in the area of assessment for non-mainstream speakers," and that diagnosticians need "valid, reliable assessment tools" (p. 33) in order to correct the problem.

Vaughn-Cooke, Fay. 1999. Lessons Learned from the Ebonics Controversy: Implications for Language Assessment. In *Making the Connection,* ed. by C. Adger, D. Christian & O. Taylor, 137–68. Washington, D.C.: CAL/Delta.

1 A I K P

Velleman, Shelley L. & Barbara Zurer Pearson. 2010. Differentiating Speech Sound Disorders from Phonological Dialect Differences: Implications for Assessment and Intervention. *Topics in Language Disorders* 30.176–88.

1 A D

Venezky, Richard. 1981. Non-Standard Language and Reading—Ten Years Later. In *The Social Psychology of Reading,* ed. by J. Edwards, 193–206. Silver Spring, MD: Institute of Modern Languages Inc.

1 E I P R S X
Venezky reviews the major developments of the 1970s in literacy instruction for nonstandard dialect speakers and non-English speakers. He explains that despite the inconclusiveness of research in characterizing AAVE and its relation to reading, the decade saw important attitudinal changes, including the increased awareness of language stereotypes, and the acceptance that SAE would supplement rather than replace the language a child uses at home. The important Ann Arbor decision declaring AAVE a language in its own right met with much public dissent, although its primary aim was to help educators better teach their students SAE. Major policy developments in instruction for non-English speakers involved the narrowing of the scope of the Bilingual Education Act of 1968, which allowed a broad range of instructional programs, including both transitional approaches and the immersion approaches. At the time of the writing, however, no adequate program evaluation was available to test the efficacy of such programs. The author emphasizes that the goal toward which such programs strive is nothing more than equal education opportunity for non-English speakers, and concludes that it still remains to be determined which approach best achieves this goal.

Vernon-Feagans, Lynne. 1996. *Children's talk in communities and classrooms.* Cambridge, MA: Blackwell.

1 C N

Victorian Curriculum & Assessment Authority. 2011. *Victorian Certificate of Education: English Language.* http://www.vcaa.vic.edu.au: State Government of Victoria (Australia).

L M
Victoria, Australia has offered secondary students a course of study specializing in 'English Language' since 2006. The study (akin to a concentration) is made up of four units, which deal directly with sociolinguistic themes: language and communication; language change; language variation and social purpose; and language variation and identity. The curricular materials available online include learning objectives, assessments, and sample learning activities, all suitable for high school students.

Viereck, Wolfgang, Edgar W. Schneider & Manfred Görlach. 1984. *A Bibliography of Writings on Varieties of English, 1965–1983*. Amsterdam: John Benjamins.

E

Villegas, Ana Maria & Tamara Lucas. 2002. Preparing Culturally Responsive Teachers: Rethinking the Curriculum. *Journal of Teacher Education* 53.20–32.

1 C T

Virginia English Bulletin. 1987. *Special Issue: Language, the Forgotten Content. 37.*

B L R S T W
This focused journal issue includes over a dozen highly practical essays discussing methods of heightening dialect awareness. Full-text is available on ERIC.

Waitt, Alden. 2006. 'A Good Story Takes Awhile': Appalachian Literature in the High School Classroom. *Journal of Appalachian Studies* 12.79–101.

6 C R

Walker, Emilie V. Siddle. 1992. Falling Asleep and Failure among African-American Students: Rethinking Assumptions About Process Teaching. *Theory Into Practice* 31.321–27.

1 C T W

Walker-Moffat, Wendy. 1995. *The Other Side of the Asian American Success Story*. San Francisco, CA: Jossey-Bass.

3 U

Washington, Julie A. 1996. Issues in Assessing the Language Abilities of African American Children. In *Communication Development and Disorders in African American Children: Research, Assessment and Intervention,* ed. by A. Kamhi, K. Pollock & J. Harris. Baltimore: Paul H. Brookes Publishing.

1 A D

Washington, Julie A. 1998. African American English Research: A Review and Future Directions. *African American Research Perspectives* 4.1–3.

1 E F P

Washington, Julie A. 1998. Socioeconomic Status and Gender Influences on Children's Dialectal Variations. *Journal of Speech, Language and Hearing Research* 41.618–26.

1 F Q

Washington, Julie A. 2001. Early Literacy Skills in African-American Children: Research Considerations. *Learning Disabilities Research & Practice* 16.213–21.

1 A I R

Washington, Julie A. 2003. Literacy Skills in African American Students: The Legacy of the Achievement Gap? *African American Research Perspectives* 9.1–9.

1 A C R S T
Washington reviews three kinds of explanations (child-based, home-based, and instruction-based) for the long-standing Black-White achievement gap in literacy skills. Child-based explanations focus on the cultural and linguistic mismatch between the children and their school environment. In some studies, African American

children show limited 'world knowledge', evident in their decreased vocabulary. The linguistic distinctness of AAVE from SAE also appears relevant, but the extent to which it interferes with learning to read is unclear. Home-based explanations involve factors like low socioeconomic status (43% of Blacks, vs. 16% of Whites grow up 'poor'), low parental education, and limited reading to children by caregivers. Finally, instruction-based explanations involve issues like teacher-centered instruction versus child-centered instruction, low teacher expectation, and teachers' cultural bias. Studies suggest that low-achieving students might benefit from teacher-centered instruction. Washington concludes that all these variables and more likely contribute to low achievement, and that "we face increased pressure at a national level to teach every child to read at appropriate grade levels" (pp. 5-6).

Washington, Julie A. & Holly K. Craig. 1992. Articulation Test Performances of Low-Income, African-American Preschoolers with Communication Impairments. *Language, Speech, and Hearing Services in Schools* 23.203–07.

1 A D

Washington, Julie A. & Holly K. Craig. 1992. Performances of Low-Income, African American Preschool and Kindergarten Children on the Peabody Picture Vocabulary Test-Revised. *Language, Speech, and Hearing Services in Schools* 23.329–33.

1 A Q

Washington, Julie A. & Holly K. Craig. 1994. Dialectal Forms During Discourse of Poor, Urban, African American Preschoolers. *Journal of Speech and Hearing Research* 37.816–23.

1 O Q

Washington, Julie A. & Holly K. Craig. 1999. Performances of at-Risk, African American Preschoolers on the Peabody Picture Vocabulary Test-Iii. *Language, Speech and Hearing Services in Schools* 30.75–82.

1 A Q

Washington, Julie A. & Holly K. Craig. 2001. Reading Performance and Dialectal Variation. In *Literacy in African American Communities,* ed. by J. Harris, A. Kamhi & K. Pollock, 147–68. Mahwah, NJ: Lawrence Erlbaum Associates.

1 R

Washington, Julie A. & Holly K. Craig. 2002. Morphosyntactic Forms of African American English Used by Young Children and Their Caregivers. *Applied Psycholinguistics* 23.209–31.

1 F Q

Washington, Julie A. & Holly K. Craig. 2004. A Language Screening Protocol for Use with Young African American Children in Urban Settings. *American Journal of Speech-Language Pathology* 13.329–40.

1 A D

Washington, Julie A., Holly K. Craig & Amy J. Kushmaul. 1998. Variable Use of African American English across Two Language Sampling Contexts. *Journal of Speech, Language and Hearing Research* 41.1115–124.

1 F Q

Washington, Valerie Moss & Dalton Miller-Jones. 1989. Teacher Interaction with Non-standard English Speakers During Reading Instruction. *Contemporary Educational Psychology* 14.280–312. [Reprinted with permission of Elsevier, the publisher, from *Contemporary Educational Psychology* 14(3).]

1 S T
This study examined classroom interactions between two second grade teachers, who differed in their knowledge of Black English, in order to determine whether these teachers also differed in their responses to students who showed Strong (high) versus Weak (low) Black and Nonstandard English (NSE) usage. Teachers' knowledge of the phonological, syntactical, and stylistic features of Black English and NSE was found to be significantly related to the way teachers respond to the reading miscues of children with various amounts of NSE in their speech. In response to Strong speakers of Black English and NSE, the teacher who was more knowledgeable of Black English evidenced more behaviors considered to be supportive of reading development, i.e., behaviors that encourage greater student self-regulation and control over the reading process and greater 'depth of processing' by providing more decoding and contextual strategies. The hypothesis that the teacher who is less knowledgeable about Black English would be less constructive and more negative in response to miscues produced by Strong Black English and NSE speakers was partially confirmed. This teacher's responses seemed to be more influenced by the student's level of reading achievement than by their use of NSE. However, students who were both low in reading ability and Strong NSE speakers received more nonsupportive responses from that teacher.

Wassink, Alicia Beckford. 1999. Historically Low Prestige and Seeds of Change: Attitudes toward Jamaican Creole. *Language in Society* 28.57–92. [Abstracts for "Variation and Identity in African-American English" by Erik Thomas and Alicia Wassink, "Historically Low Prestige and Seeds of Change: Attitudes toward Jamaican Creole" and ""My Teacher Says...," Mastery of English and the Creole Learner" by Alicia Wassink, and "Addressing Ideologies around African American English" by Alicia Wassink and Anne Curzan graciously provided by Alicia Wassink.]

2 I
Speakers from a semi-rural community within the Jamaican Creole continuum were asked what kind of linguistic entity they believe the Creole to be, where it is in use, who they understand to be its users, and which domains they deem appropriate and inappropriate for its use. A language-attitude interview schedule yielding an Attitude Indicator Score (AIS) was developed for use in this community. This schedule contained two sets of questions, Attitude and Description questions, which were designed to capture information concerning overt and covert language attitudes. Results show respondents' attitude systems to be multi-valued: They were generally ambivalent in their attitudes toward Jamaican Creole, but they judged it appropriate or inappropriate for use in different contexts according to their social distance from or solidarity with an interlocutor. Gender grading and an age by gender effect were found.

Wassink, Alicia Beckford. 2005. "My Teacher Says...," Mastery of English and the Creole Learner. In *Language in the Schools: Integrating Linguistic Knowledge into K-12 Teaching*, ed. by K. Denham & A. Lobeck, 55–70. Mahwah, NJ: Lawrence Erlbaum Associates. [Abstracts for "Variation and Identity in African-American English" by Erik Thomas and Alicia Wassink, "Historically Low Prestige and Seeds of Change: Attitudes toward Jamaican Creole" and ""My Teacher Says...," Mastery of English and the Creole Learner" by Alicia Wassink, and "Addressing Ideologies around African American English" by Alicia Wassink and Anne Curzan graciously provided by Alicia Wassink.]

1 2 B F I S

In this chapter, we see that not only do individual's attitudes toward language reflect social factors, but individuals' understandings of what constitutes a language, and of how their own language works, change along with these language attitudes. Key linguistic facts about Creole languages are presented, as well as some general facts about the socio-historical settings in which creole languages develop and are subsequently used, and the ways that students' understandings about their language impact the extent to which they are able to synthesize new material presented in the language arts classroom. The discussion is based upon the outcomes of linguistic and educational research conducted in one particular country, Jamaica, from the early 1980s to the present. Teachers will find in this chapter a number of suggestions for building a bridge in the student's linguistic understanding—between the knowledge of their Creole they bring to the classroom (but are unlikely able to articulate), to the new base of knowledge the teacher desires to build in standard (North American) English.

Wassink, Alicia Beckford & Anne Curzan. 2004. Addressing Ideologies around African American English. *Journal of English Linguistics* 32.171–85. [Abstracts for "Variation and Identity in African-American English" by Erik Thomas and Alicia Wassink, "Historically Low Prestige and Seeds of Change: Attitudes toward Jamaican Creole" and ""My Teacher Says...," Mastery of English and the Creole Learner" by Alicia Wassink, and "Addressing Ideologies around African American English" by Alicia Wassink and Anne Curzan graciously provided by Alicia Wassink.]

1 I

This paper is the introductory essay of a special issue of the *Journal of English Linguistics* commemorating the fiftieth anniversary of *Brown vs. the Board of Education*, the 1954 Supreme Court Decision that removed legal segregation in education. This special issue attempts to take stock of where studies of African American English stand, and envision the next steps. One of the issues that appears to be critical lies at the intersection between linguistics and education: it is the issue of language ideology. Here, linguists can make connections between research and practice, between linguistic knowledge and public knowledge. We argue that aspects of the standard language ideology dominating American discourse present a barrier that has, and potentially could continue to, prohibit linguistic knowledge from informing pubic understandings about AAE. In order to inform the public debate about AAE and related educational questions, we must confront both scholars' and laypeople's ideologies. We argue that the power of language ideology to foster and hinder the uptake of scholarly research is nowhere as evident as it is in the controversy surrounding the naming of AAE.

Watson-Gegeo, Karen. 1994. Language and Education in Hawaii: Sociopolitical and Economic Considerations of Hawaii Creole English. In *Language and the Social Construction of Identity in Creole Situations,* ed. by M. Morgan, 101–20. Los Angeles, CA: UCLA Center for African American Studies.

2 P

Watson-Gegeo, Karen Ann & Stephen T. Boggs. 1977. From Verbal Play to Talk-Story: The Role of Routine in Speech Events among Hawaiian Children. In *Child Discourse,* ed. by S. Ervin-Tripp & C. Mitchell-Kernan, 67–90. New York: Academic Press.

2 C N

Webber, Kikanza. 1985. Teaching About Black English: An Annotated Syllabus. *Western Journal of Black Studies* 9.23–29.

1 S

Weber, Rose-Marie. 1973. Dialect Differences in Oral Reading: An Analysis of Errors. In *Language Differences: Do They Interfere?*, ed. by J. Laffey & R. Shuy, 47–61. Newark, DE: International Reading Association.

1 R X

Weber, Rose-Marie. 1983. Reading: United States. *Annual Review of Applied Linguistics* 4.111–23. [Abstract prepared by ERIC.]

1 6 E R

An exploration of the increasingly important role of linguistics in literacy research and instruction, the article reviews literature on reading comprehension, written language, orthography, metalinguistics, classroom language use, reading disabilities, native tongues, nonstandard dialects, bilingual education, adult literacy, and second-language reading.

Webster, Anthony. 2010. "Still, She Didn't See What I Was Trying to Say": Towards a History of Framing Navajo English in Navajo Written Poetry. *World Englishes* 29.75–96.

5 I N

Weddington, Gloria. 2010. It's Not the Language: Alternative Explanations of the Education Gap for African American Children. *Topics in Language Disorders* 30.48–56.

1 A

Weinstein-Shr, Gail. 1994. From Mountaintops to City Streets: Literacy in Philadelphia's Hmong Community. In *Literacy across Communities,* ed. by B. J. Moss, 49–83. Cresskill, NJ: Hampton.

3 R W

Weiss, Bernard. 1963. *Language, Linguistics, and School Programs*. Paper presented to the National Conference of Teachers of English Spring Institutes, Louisville, KY and Atlantic City, NJ.

I W

Weldon, Tracey. 2000. Reflections on the Ebonics Controversy. *American Speech* 75.275–77.

1 I K

Western Australian Department of Education. 2002. *Ways of Being, Ways of Talk*. Perth: Western Australia Department of Education.

2 B M S Z

The discussion is on Aboriginal English in Australia and its differences from Australian English in four fifteen- to twenty-minute videos. Professor Ian Malcolm was a key consultant on this video. A *Users Guide* is available on the web. The "ABC" element in the name of the television production company is associated with a larger "ABC of Two-Way Literacy and Learning" project funded jointly by the Department of Education and Training, Western Australia, and the Commonwealth Department of Education, Science and Training. The "ABC" name is explained in the *Users Guide* (p. 6) as deriving "from the following foundation principles: A—accept Aboriginal English (AE); B—bridge to Standard Australian English (SAE); and C—cultivate Aboriginal ways of approaching experience and knowledge."

Wheeler, Rebecca. 2003. Vignette: Flossie and the Fox: Codeswitching between the Languages of Home and School. In *Grammar Alive! A Guide for Teachers,* ed. by B. Haussamen, A. Benjamin, M. Kolln & R. Wheeler, 12–14. Urbana, IL: NCTE.

1 B O S

Wheeler, Rebecca. 2005. Contrastive Analysis and Codeswitching: How and Why to Use the Vernacular to Teach Standard English. In *Language in the Schools: Integrating Linguistic Knowledge into K-12 Teaching,* ed. by K. Denham & A. Lobeck. Mahwah, NJ: Lawrence Erlbaum Associates.

1 B U

Wheeler, Rebecca. 2006. "What Do We Do About Student Grammar—All Those Missing -'Ed's' and -'S's'?" Using Comparison and Contrast to Teach Standard English in Dialectally Diverse Classrooms. *English Teaching: Practice and Critique* 5.16–33. [Reprinted with permission of the journal from *English Teaching: Practice and Critique* 5(1), 16.]

1 B P

This paper explores the long and winding road to integrating linguistic approaches to vernacular dialects in the classroom. After exploring past roadblocks, the author shares vignettes and classroom practices of her collaborator, Rachel Swords, who has succeeded in bringing Contrastive Analysis and Code-switching to her second and third grade students (children seven and eight years old) in urban Virginia. The author then shares principles that have allowed her to successfully defuse social and political concerns of principals, central school office administrators, teachers, students, parents, politicians and reporters, as she shows how to use tools of language and culture to teach Standard English in urban areas.

Wheeler, Rebecca. 2008. Becoming Adept at Code-Switching. *Educational Leadership* 65.54–58. [Reprinted with Permission of the Publisher. Source: "Becoming Adept at Code-Switching" ASCD Abstract, Retrieved Nov. 5, 2011 from http://www.ascd.org/ publications/educationalleadership/apr08/vol65/num07/abstract.aspx#Becoming_ Adept_at_Code_Switching. © 2008 by ASCD. Reprinted with permission. Learn more about ASCD at www.ascd.org.]

1 B S

Many teachers lack the linguistic training required to build on the language skills that African American students from dialectally diverse backgrounds bring to school. When students correctly use the language patterns of their communities, such teachers may diagnose language deficits and attempt to teach them the "right" grammar. Research has shown that such traditional correction methods fail to teach students the speaking and writing skills they need. The author and her colleague, an elementary educator, have developed a structured approach to engage students in critical thinking about language. Students analyze Informal English patterns, compare and contrast them with Standard English patterns, and use metacognition to learn code-switching so that they can intentionally choose the appropriate language style for a particular setting.

Wheeler, Rebecca. 2009. "Taylor Cat Is Black": Code-Switch to Add Standard English to Students' Linguistic Repertoires. In *Affirming Students' Right to Their Own Language: Bridging Language Policies and Pedagogical Practices,* ed. by J. Cobb Scott, D. Straker & L. Katz, 176–91. New York: Routledge/National Council of Teachers of English.

1 B S T

Wheeler, Rebecca. 2010. Fostering Linguistic Habits of Mind: Engaging Teachers' Knowledge and Attitudes toward African American Vernacular English. *Language and Linguistics Compass* 4.954–71.

1 I T

Wheeler, Rebecca. 2010. From Cold Shoulder to Funded Welcome: Lessons from the Trenches of Dialectally Diverse Classrooms. In *Linguistics at School: Language Awareness in Primary and Secondary Education,* ed. by K. Denham & A. Loebeck, 129-48. Cambridge: Cambridge University Press.

1 B I P
The author argues that in order to maintain a presence in schools, linguists need to connect lessons and materials to teachers' immediate needs (such as teaching students to write in Standard English) rather than to their own goals of raising awareness and tolerance of dialect diversity. Wheeler offers several practical principles for operating in school contexts that are not hospitable to themes of language variation.

Wheeler, Rebecca, Kelly Cartwright & Rachel Swords. 2012. Factoring AAVE into Elementary Reading Assessment and Instruction. *Reading Teacher* 65.5:416–425.

1 A B R

Wheeler, Rebecca & Rachel Swords. 2004. Codeswitching: Tools of Language and Culture Transform the Dialectally Diverse Classroom. *Language Arts* 81.470–80.

1 B O S
Wheeler and Swords briefly review literature on the achievement gap and describe how Swords, after two years of vainly trying to "correct" the speech of her third grade students, successfully applied a contrastive analysis approach. Swords used a class discussion on the appropriateness of formal versus informal clothing in different social contexts to segue into a similar discussion on formal versus informal language so that children would begin to see that different varieties are legitimate in their own right. She then engaged students in analysis of the systematic ways in which AAVE and SAE differ from each other by writing contrastive sentences side-by-side on the board and asking students to determine how each variety conveys different grammatical features, e.g., plurality and possession. Discussion of variation and codeswitching was supplemented by literature in which different characters used different varieties of English, an idea which students were then allowed to implement in their own writing. Swords noted a "tremendous growth in [her] students' command of language," (p. x) and after one year of implementation, her "Black and White children performed equally well on year-end benchmarks" (p. y).

Wheeler, Rebecca & Rachel Swords. 2006. *Code-Switching: Teaching Standard English in the Urban Classroom.* Urbana, IL: NCTE.

1 B I M S

Wheeler, Rebecca & Rachel Swords. 2010. *Code-Switching Lessons: Grammar Strategies for Linguistically Diverse Writers. A Firsthand Curriculum.* Portsmouth, NH: FirstHand Heinemann.

1 B M S
This book details lesson plans for teaching Standard English grammar to linguistically diverse students in grades 3 through 6. The goal of the lessons is to get students to recognize linguistic variation not as error but rather as reflecting a distinction in relative formality, as in, for example, possessive marking in I play on Derrick team (informal) vs. I play on Derrick's team (formal).Students learn first to recognize the distinction (contrastive analysis) and then to control it (code-switching). Topics include units on possession, pluralization, past tense, subject-verb agreement, and use of be. The core units contain four lessons each. In the first, students learn to define the formal and informal variants. In the second, students practice classifying variants as formal or informal. In the third, students practice using the formal variant. Finally, in the fourth lesson, students practice editing writing for the formal variant. These core units are

flanked by an introductory unit on the formal vs. informal distinction in everyday life and a concluding unit on the use of different language varieties in literature.

Wheldall, Kevin & Ruth Joseph. 1985. Young Black Children's Sentence Comprehension Skills: A Comparison of Performance in Standard English and Jamaican Creole. *First Language* 6.149–54.

1 2 O X

Whiteman, Marcia Farr (ed.) 1980. *Reactions to Ann Arbor: Vernacular Black English and Education.* Arlington, VA: Center for Applied Linguistics.

1 E I K P

Whiteman, Marcia Farr. 1981. Dialect Influence in Writing. In *Variation in Writing: Functional and Linguistic-Cultural Differences,* ed. by M. F. Whiteman, 153–66. Hillsdale, NJ: Lawrence Erlbaum Associates.

W X

Whitney, Jessica. 2005. Five Easy Pieces: Steps toward Integrating AAVE into the Classroom. *English Journal* 94.64–69.

1 B C O S W
An English teacher herself, Whitney argues that teachers should value students' home language and use it to help them become more effective rhetoricians. She offers five steps that an educator should take to help the students: (1) Learn more about AAVE (African American Vernacular English); (2) Incorporate multiculturalism into the classroom; (3) Create a learning environment rich in oral language; (4) Encourage and demonstrate code-switching in the classroom; (5) Allow students to write like real writers.

Whyte, Kenneth J. 1986. Strategies for Teaching Indian and Metis Students. *Canadian Journal of Native Education* 13.1–20. [Abstract prepared by ERIC.]

5 C S
The author reviews research on effective teaching methods for teachers of American Indian and Metis students and outlines factors inhibiting school success while discussing learning style theories and language and cultural barriers. Whyte summarizes effective methods, processes, context, structures, resources in four categories: classroom organization, instruction/instructional resources, verbal activities, and community relations.

Wible, Scott. 2006. Pedagogies of the "Students' Right" Era: The Language Curriculum Research Group's Project for Linguistic Diversity. *College Composition and Communication* 57.442–78. [Reprinted from *College Composition and Communication* 57(3).]

1 B L P W
This essay examines a Brooklyn College-based research collective that placed African American languages and cultures at the center of the composition curriculum. Recovering such pedagogies challenges the perception of the CCCC's 1974 "Students' Right to Their Own Language" resolution as a progressive theory divorced from the everyday practices and politics of the composition classroom.

Wilcox, Lydia & Raquel Anderson. 1998. Distinguishing between Phonological Difference and Disorder in Children Who Speak African-American Vernacular English: An Experimental Testing Instrument. *Journal of Communication Disorders* 31.315–35.

1 D

Wiley, Terrence & Marguerite Lukes. 1996. English-Only and Standard English Ideologies in the United States. *TESOL Quarterly* 30.511–35.

I P
Wiley and Lukes discuss the hegemonic nature of monolingualism and standard language ideology in the United States. Under monolingualism, various questionable assumptions underlie the arguments that immigrants should be required to learn the language of the land, and indigenous minorities are often lumped into the same category despite their different background. Under standard language ideology, the privileged class has the unfair advantage of speaking the language most closely related to the standard, while speakers of minority dialects are thought to be less intelligent.

Williams, Frederick. 1970. *Language and Poverty: Perspectives on a Theme.* Chicago, IL: Markham.

1 6 A E I R S W
Chapters include some classic references in the study of vernacular varieties of English and education, including both sides of the early deficit (Englemann)/difference (Labov) debate. Especially relevant to this book are: Joan C. Baratz, "Teaching reading in an urban Negro school system"; Basil Bernstein, "A sociolinguistic approach to socialization: with some reference to educability"; Siegfried Engelmann, "How to construct effective language programs for the poverty child"; William Labov, "The logic of Nonstandard English"; Lynn R. Osborn, "Language, poverty, and the North American Indian"; Roger A. Severson and Kristin E. Guest, "Toward the standardized assessment of the language of disadvantaged children"; Roger W. Shuy, "The sociolinguists and urban language problems"; William A. Stewart, "Toward a history of American Negro dialects"; Frederick Williams, "Language, attitude and social change"; David E. Yoder, "Some viewpoints of the Speech, Hearing and Language clinician"; and Frederick Williams and Rita Naremore, "An annotated bibliography of journal articles."

Williams, Frederick. 1970. Language, Attitude, and Social Change. In *Language and Poverty: Perspectives on a Theme,* ed. by F. Williams, 380–99. Chicago, IL: Markham.

1 I

Williams, Frederick. 1972. Training and Retraining of Speech, Hearing and Language School Specialists. *Language, Speech and Hearing Services in Schools* 3.50–55.

D

Williams, Frederick. 1973. Some Research Notes on Dialect Attitudes and Stereotypes. In *Language Attitudes: Current Trends and Prospects,* ed. by R. Shuy & R. Fasold, 113–28. Washington, D.C.: Georgetown University Press.

1 A I
Williams reports on several studies in Chicago, Memphis and Central Texas conducted by himself and his colleagues that use semantic differential scales (e.g., fluent-nonfluent) to quantify teachers' attitudes towards students' speech samples on two broad dimensions: 'confidence-eagerness' and 'ethnicity-nonstandardness'. For instance, samples of Black middle-status students in Chicago were rated as sounding more 'confident-eager' and 'nonethnic-standard' than samples of Black low-status students, and samples of corresponding White students were rated similarly. Additionally, even without a speech sample, stereotypical attitudes could be elicited to ethnic or status descriptions and labels; e.g., a child labeled 'Black' or 'Mexican American' was rated as likely to sound less 'confident-eager' and more 'ethnic-nonstandard' than a child labeled 'Anglo'. Teachers' stereotypes appear to "define an anchor point" (p. 124)

around which actual audio or video samples are evaluated. In one telling study, teachers rated the same Standard English audio track as sounding much more 'nonethnic-standard' and somewhat more 'confident-eager' when associated with a video image of a White child than with a video image of either a Black or Mexican American child.

Williams, Frederick. 1976. *Explorations of the Linguistic Attitudes of Teachers.* Rowley, MA: Newbury House.

1 I T

Williams, Frederick & Jack Whitehead. 1973. Language in the Classroom: Studies of the Pygmalion Effect. In *Language, Society, and Education: A Profile of Black English,* ed. by J. DeStefano, 169–76. Worthington, OH: Jones Publishing.

1 I T

Previous research suggested that some teachers relied more on racial stereotypes than individual qualities when judging children based on recorded speech samples. Williams and Whitehead investigate this idea further, first by replicating a previous study with videotapes rather than mere audio recordings; results are generally the same. Second, they assess the relation between a teacher's stereotypes and her judgments of individual children. This is achieved by presenting teachers with descriptions of six children, each of which falls into a different stereotype, and comparing their judgments of these descriptions to their judgments of children in videotaped samples. Results indicate that although teachers may use stereotypes to condition their judgments of individual children, they are also sensitive to the idiosyncrasies of each child. The authors conclude that teachers should be trained to increase this sensitivity to individual differences, and should be taught the validity of nonstandard speech in order to mitigate the effects of language-related stereotypes.

Williams, Frederick, Jack Whitehead & Leslie Miller. 1971. Ethnic Stereotyping and Judgments of Children's Speech. *Speech Monographs* 38.166–70.

1 I

Williams, Frederick, Jack Whitehead & Leslie Miller. 1972. Relations between Language Attitudes and Teacher Expectancy. *American Education Research Journal* 9.263–77.

I T

Williams, Ronald. 1975. The Struggle to Know, the Struggle to Survive. In *Ebonics: The True Language of Black Folks,* ed. by R. L. Williams, 55–63. St. Louis, MO: Robert L. Williams and Associates, Inc. [Abstract prepared by ERIC.]

1 P

The factors of race, politics, economics, and the social sciences provide a unique dilemma for Black communication scholars. Such scholars must respond to forces which seek to suppress their work and must also seek better ways of understanding the unique characteristics of communication among Blacks. Investigations in Black English should seek an understanding of the Black's linguistic past and present, as well as the Black's language usage as it affects the quality of his children's education and his efforts to succeed in his occupation. However, much research by Whites in Black communication mistakenly concentrates on "street talk" and is adversely affected by two racial assumptions: first, that Blacks are basically happy, sensuous people, and second, that extensive use of profanity is a distinctive characteristic of all Black communication. Therefore, although communication studies by Whites can help Blacks gain a better understanding of themselves, they do little to contribute to their struggle for liberation. Black scholars' research offers greater promise.

Williams, Robert L. 1975. Developing Cultural Specific Assessment Devices: An Empirical Rationale. In *Ebonics: The Language of Black Folks,* ed. by R. L. Williams, 110–32. St. Louis, MO: Robert L. Williams and Associates, Inc.

1 A C

Williams, Robert L. (ed.) 1975. *Ebonics: The True Language of Black Folks.* St. Louis, MO: Robert L. Williams and Associates, Inc.

1 B C E F I N P V

Williams, Robert L. 1997. The Ebonics Controversy. *Journal of Black Psychology* 3.208–14.

1 K

Williams, Robert L. & L. Wendell Rivers. 1975. The Effects of Language on the Test Performance of Black Children. In *Ebonics: The Language of Black Folks,* ed. by R. L. Williams, 96–109. St. Louis, MO: Robert L. Williams and Associates, Inc.

1 A

Williamson, Juanita. 1971. A Look at Black English. *Crisis* 78.169–73.

1 F

Williamson contends that most of the features said to be characteristic of "Black English," like the lack of contrast between pin and pen, r-lessness, simplification of final consonant clusters, and zero copula and auxiliary, also occur in White or Southern speech more generally, and should simply be regarded as "American." This article was reprinted in Robert L. Williams (1975) *Ebonics: The True Language of Black Folks,* 11–21.

Willinsky, John. 1988. *The Well-Tempered Tongue: The Politics of Standard English in the High School.* New York: Teachers College Press.

I P

Wilson, Marilyn. 2001. The Changing Discourse of Language Study. *The English Journal* 90.31–36. [Abstract prepared by ERIC and reprinted with permission of the Department of Education from the Educational Resources Information Center at eric.ed.gov.]

I T

The author argues that a study of dialects, language attitudes and biases, and issues of power related to language policies should be part of courses for preservice English teachers. Wilson describes class activities that deal with investigating language attitudes, validating linguistic variation, validating all dialects, understanding the politics of language, and learning the complexities of language and the major principles of language learning.

Wiltse, Lynne. 2011. "But My Students All Speak English": Ethical Research Issues of Aboriginal English. *TESL Canada Journal.*

2 I P

Wiltse explores three ethical issues in teaching Aboriginal students who speak a dialect of English: the relationship between the dialect spoken by Aboriginal students and the heritage language they no longer speak; the educational implications of Aboriginal English-speakers in the classroom; and positionality of a non-Aboriginal English-speaking researcher working in the areas of Aboriginal education and language.

Winch, Christopher & John Gingell. 1994. Dialect Interference and Difficulties with Writing: An Investigation in St. Lucian Primary Schools. *Language and Education* 8.157–82.

2 W X
The authors report on the writing performance of Saint Lucian schoolchildren with particular reference to possible dialect interference in written speech. The study focuses on characteristic errors in the writing as well as the causes and significance of these errors and explores the available remedies. [Abstract courtesy of ERIC.]

Winer, Lise. 1986. An Analysis of Errors in Written Compositions of Trinidadian Secondary Students. *Caribbean Journal of Education* 13.1–2.

2 W X

Winer, Lise. 1993. Teaching Speakers of Caribbean English Creoles in North American Classrooms. In *Language Variation in North American English: Research and Teaching,* ed. by W. Glowka & D. Lance, 191–98. New York: Modern Language Association of America.

2 I T

Winer, Lise. 1999. Comprehension and Resonance: English Readers and English Creole Texts. In *Creole Genesis, Attitudes, and Discourse,* ed. by J. R. Rickford & S. Romaine, 391–406. Philadelphia: John Benjamins.

2 R

Winer, Lise. 2006. Teaching English to Caribbean English Creole-Speaking Students in the Caribbean and North America. In *Dialects, Englishes, Creoles, and Education,* ed. by S. Nero, 105–18. Mahwah, NJ: Lawrence Erlbaum Associates.

2 I P T
In this chapter, Winer examines historical and current issues in the teaching of English to speakers of Caribbean English Creole [CEC]. Within the Caribbean, bidialectalism in the local Creole and Standard English [SE] is largely accepted as a goal, with language awareness and contrastive analysis (see Siegel 1999) increasingly being used to achieve it. But competence in SE still varies significantly, depending on location and socioeconomic background. Within North America, the teachers of CEC speakers, unfamiliar with their vernacular, are more likely to misunderstand them, teach them by sink-or-swim methods, or place them inappropriately in Special Education and English as a Second Language classes. Some innovative language awareness and SE as a Second Dialect programs were developed in Canada and the United States between the 1970s and 1990s, but most of these have been terminated due to funding cuts. Nonetheless, Winer suggests that teachers of CEC students everywhere should value the students and their linguistic diversity, and she continues to advocate language awareness approaches and other principles (e.g., #7 "Respect the Logic of a Student's Language") to help them do so.

Winer, Lise. 2009. *Dictionary of the English/Creole of Trinidad and Tobago, on Historical Principles.* Montreal, Canada: McGill-Queen's University Press.

2 F
As the most recent and longest [1039 pages] dictionary of a Caribbean creole English variety, this dictionary should be useful to scholars and to teachers of Caribbean English creole or vernacular students from Trinidad and Tobago, the Caribbean, and elsewhere. [Abstract]

Winford, Donald. 1976. Teacher Attitudes toward Language Varieties in a Creole Community. *International Journal of the Sociology of Language* 8.45–75.

2 I T

One hundred and twelve preservice teachers at two teacher colleges in Trinidad were given a detailed free-response questionnaire to assess their opinions regarding both the speech of the average Trinidadian and their own speech. Results were analyzed as a function of the respondents' ethnicity (Black or Indian) and geographical background (town or country). Results include the finding that a high degree of awareness of language variation existed among the respondents, and that they generally considered language used in town areas to be 'more correct' than that of country areas. On the other hand, there was much discrepancy concerning the appropriate domains of usage for Standard English and Creole; one extreme found the latter completely unacceptable, while the other extreme found it appropriate in certain contexts. Still, the author considers this study to be only the first step in understanding the complex role of language in a creole community.

Winford, Donald. 2003. Ideologies of Language and Socially Realistic Linguistics. In *Black Linguistics: Language, Society and Politics in Africa and the Americas,* ed. by S. Makoni, G. Smitherman, A. F. Ball & A. K. Spears, 21–39. London: Routledge.

1 I

Wiruk, Edward. 2000. Report: Papua New Guinea. *PACE Newsletter* 11.

2 P V

Wolf, Hans-Georg. 2001. *English in Cameroon.* Berlin: Mouton de Gruyter.

2 F I

Wolf, Hans-Georg & Herbert Igboanusi. 2006. Empowerment through English — a Realistic View of the Educational promotion of English in Post-Colonial Contexts: The Example of Nigeria. In *'Along the Routes to Power': Explorations of Empowerment through Language,* ed. by M. Pütz, J. Fishman & J. Neff, 333–56. Berlin: Mouton de Gruyter.

2 I

Wolff, Ekkehard H. 2006. The Language Factor in Discourse on Development and Education in Africa. In *Language Planning for Development in Africa,* ed. by S. Kembo, S. Mwangi & N. O. Ogechi, 1–22. Eldoret, Kenya: Moi University Press.

2 I

Wolford, Tonya. 2006. Variation in the Expression of Possession by Latino Children. *Language Variation and Change* 18.1–13.

4 F O

Wolford, Tonya & Phillip M. Carter. 2010. The "Spanish-as-Threat" Ideology and Cultural Aspects of Spanish Attrition. In *Spanish in the U.S. Southwest: A Language in Transition,* ed. by S. Rivera-Mills & D. Villa, 111–31. Madrid, Spain: Iberoamericana /Vervuert.

4 I P

Wolfram, Walt. 1969. *A Sociolinguistic Description of Detroit Negro Speech.* Washington D.C.: Center for Applied Linguistics.

1 F

Wolfram, Walt. 1970. Sociolinguistic Alternatives for Teaching Reading to Speakers of Non-Standard English. *Reading Research Quarterly* 6.9–33.

B R S V X

Wolfram, Walt. 1970. Sociolinguistic Implications for Educational Sequencing. In *Teaching Standard English in the Inner City,* ed. by R. Fasold & R. Shuy, 105–19. Washington, D.C.: Center for Applied Linguistics.

1 B S

Wolfram, Walt. 1974. *Sociolinguistic Aspects of Assimilation: Puerto Rican English in New York City.* Arlington, VA: Center for Applied Linguistics.

4 F

Wolfram, Walt. 1976. Levels of Sociolinguistic Bias in Testing. In *Black English: A Seminar,* ed. by D. Harrison & T. Trabasso, 263–87. Hillsdale, NJ: Lawrence Erlbaum Associates.

1 A

Wolfram, Walt. 1979. *Speech Pathology and Dialect Differences.* Arlington, VA: Center for Applied Linguistics.

1 6 D

Wolfram, Walt. 1980. Dynamic Dimensions of Language Influence: The Case of American Indian English. In *Language: Social Psychological Perspectives,* ed. by H. Giles, W. Robinson & P. Smith, 377–88. Oxford: Pergamon Press.

5 F

Wolfram, Walt. 1983. Test Interpretation and Sociolinguistic Differences. *Topics in Language Disorders.*21–34.

1 A
In this paper Wolfram discusses some of the problems facing the development of appropriate standardized tests for assessing language ability, particularly among speakers of non-mainstream dialects of English. He begins by assessing basic linguistic problems (e.g., "knowing a word" involves syntactic, semantic, stylistic, morphological and phonological information, yet in practice, tests only assess a small subset of this range.) He then treats sociolinguistic topics: sociolinguistic variation of form, "task orientation" (the ways in which different social groups will interpret language instructions differently), and finally, the ways in which different social groups will react to testing, given the inherently non-neutral context in which it occurs. He concludes that "there is no unidimensional axis along which sociological information can be applied to the results of standardized assessment instructions" (p. 31) and provides a number of questions to be entertained in evaluating the appropriateness of a given test.

Wolfram, Walt. 1984. Unmarked Tense in American Indian English. *American Speech* 59.31–50.

5 F X

Wolfram, Walt. 1986. Black-White Dimensions in Sociolinguistic Test Bias. In *Language Variety in the South: Perspectives in Black and White,* ed. by M. B. Montgomery & G. Bailey, 373–85. Tuscaloosa: University of Alabama Press.

1 A

This essay aims to address possible areas of sociolinguistic bias faced by Black and White non-mainstream speakers of English. The essay states the three levels on which sociolinguistic bias may occur: differences in language forms; differences in how language is used to tap information, or task orientation; and differences in the social occasions that relate to language use in testing. The essay then proceeds to discuss how each aforementioned dimension of sociolinguistics can create a bias on a non-mainstream English speakers' sociolinguistic test scores respectively. Differences in linguistic form are said to construct the direct bias of incorrect response due to inability. Task characteristics develop a bias in information transfer; the incompatibility of semantic, syntactic, stylistics, morphological, and pragmatic linguistic features of the English spoken by the test-giver and the test-taker result in incorrect question analysis and response. Finally, the essay finds that even test-takers themselves can engender a sociolinguistic bias in the manner in which they choose to answer questions due to the difference in social language of their own non-mainstream English, and the Standard English expected for them to use.

Wolfram, Walt. 1991. *Dialects and American English*. Englewood Cliffs, NJ: Prentice Hall, and Center for Applied Linguistics.

F I

Wolfram, Walt. 1993. Ethical Considerations in Language Awareness Programs. *Issues in Applied Linguistics* 4.225–55.

I L

Wolfram discusses some of the ethical issues requiring consideration in the implementation of experimental language awareness programs, and highlights the 'principle of linguistic gratuity'—the responsibility of sociolinguists who benefit from data collected in speech communities to give back to those communities.

Wolfram, Walt. 1994. Bidialectal Literacy in the United States. In *Adult Biliteracy in the United States,* ed. by D. Spener, 71–88. McHenry, IL: Center for Applied Linguistics and Delta Systems Co, Inc.

B R V

Wolfram, Walt. 1994. The Phonology of a Sociocultural Variety: The Case of African American Vernacular English. In *Child Phonology: Characteristics, Assessment, and Intervention with Special Populations,* ed. by J. Bernthal & N. Bankson. New York: Thieme Medical Publishers.

1 D F

Wolfram, Walt. 1998. Language Ideology and Dialect: Understanding the Ebonics Controversy. *Journal of English Linguistics* 26.108–21.

1 I K

Wolfram, Walt. 1998. The Myth of the Verbally Deprived Black Child. In *Language Myths,* ed. by L. Bauer & P. Trudgill, 103–12. London: Penguin Books.

1 A I

This often-cited article refutes the myth of the 'verbally deprived Black child.' Through highlighting the rich oral culture of African Americans and the inconsistencies in racially, anatomically, and syntactical based arguments for the inferiority of African American Vernacular English, the article disproves the notion that AAVE spoken by African Americans is an intellectually inferior language to Standard English. The article challenges its readers to recognize the horizontal syntactical parallels between AAVE and other accepted intellectual languages such as French and Spanish and discusses the misguided normalized principles of standardized testing and the cultural factors which may contribute to the seemingly less grammatical knowledge and verbose nature of African American children to their White counterparts. Finally, the article forces its readers to recognize the conversational richness that dialects such as AAVE bring into the English language.

Wolfram, Walt. 1999. Repercussions from the Oakland Ebonics Controversy: The Critical Role of Dialect Awareness. In *Making the Connection,* ed. by C. Adger, D. Christian & O. Taylor, 53–60. Washington, D.C.: Center for Applied Linguistics.

1 I K L

Wolfram, Walt. 2001. From Definition to Policy: The Ideological Struggle of African American Vernacular English. In *Georgetown University Roundtable on Language and Linguistics,* ed. by J. Alatis & A.-H. Tan, 292–313. Washington, D.C.: Georgetown University Press.

1 I P

Wolfram, Walt. 2001. Reconsidering the Sociolinguistic Agenda for African American English: The Next Generation of Research and Application. In *Sociocultural and Historical Contexts of African American English,* ed. by S. Lanehart, 331–62. Philadelphia: John Benjamins.

1 A B I S V

Wolfram, Walt. 2004. Social Varieties of American English. In *Language in the USA,* ed. by E. Finegan & J. R. Rickford, 58–75. Cambridge: Cambridge University Press.

1 F I

Wolfram, Walt. 2010. Dialect Awareness, Cultural Literacy, and the Public Interest. In *Ethnolinguistic Diversity and Education: Language, Literacy, and Culture,* ed. by M. Farr, L. Seloni & J. Song, 129–49. New York: Routledge.

1 I L

In seeking to change negative language attitudes, Wolfram argues, linguists must be patient, prepared, and proactive. Patience is called for because beliefs about core cultural constructs such as religion, politics, and language are slow to change. Preparation is essential because teachable moments arise unexpectedly in the form of language controversies and current events. A proactive approach, such as the model provided by the North Carolina Language and Life Project's, can foster greater dialect awareness through a variety of means, including film documentaries, museum exhibits, and curricula for students and teachers. Each of these elements of NCLLP is described in some detail.

Wolfram, Walt, Carolyn Temple Adger & Donna Christian. 2007. *Dialects in Schools and Communities.* Mahwah, NJ: Lawrence Erlbaum Associates.

1 A E I R S V W

Wolfram et al. reconsider and expand upon the discussion of dialects in educational settings as discussed in the first edition (1999) of this book. As the authors intend for this book to educate educators about the role of dialect in teaching reading, writing, and speaking in schools and communities, they explain sources of variation as natural and critique the attitude that dialect differences represent deficits. They dispel other misconceptions about dialect and cultural differences and then describe dialect variations in vocabulary, syntax, and pronunciation, along with examples and dialect samples. In five in-depth chapters, Wolfram et al. then explore language and teaching rituals in the classroom and instruction methods for reading, writing and speaking as well as cultural style. They conclude with a chapter of exposition, exercises and examples designed to develop dialect awareness on the part of the students, and an appendix listing an inventory of vernacular structures that teachers should find helpful.

Wolfram, Walt, Phillip Carter & Rebecca Moriello. 2004. Emerging Hispanic English: New Dialect Formation in the American South. *Journal of Sociolinguistics* 8.339–58.

4 F

Wolfram, Walt & Donna Christian. 1976. *Appalachian Speech*. Arlington, VA: Center for Applied Linguistics.

6 F
Wolfram and Christian provide a comprehensive description of Appalachian English. In six chapters they introduce the history of the Appalachian dialect, describe the social and linguistic aspects of variation for dialects, identify phonological and grammatical features of the Appalachian dialect, and examine the educational implications of dialect diversity. They strive to make their work meaningful for educators, reading specialists, English teachers, language arts specialists, and speech pathologists. In doing so, they describe at length language attitudes and dialect diversity with respect to testing. Wolfram and Christian provide guidelines they intend to serve as a basis for developing adequate strategies for teaching Standard English. In addition, they discuss strategies for teaching written English and integrating dialect diversity into Language Arts and reading.

Wolfram, Walt & Donna Christian. 1976. Educational Implications of Dialect Diversity. In *A Pluralistic Nation,* ed. by M. Lourie & N. F. Conklin, 357–81. Rowley, MA: Newbury House.

A I L R

Wolfram, Walt & Donna Christian. 1989. *Dialects and Education: Issues and Answers*. Englewood Cliffs, NJ: Prentice Hall.

F I S T

Wolfram, Walt, Donna Christian, William Leap & Lance Potter. 1979. *Variability in the English of Two Indian Communities and Its Effect on Reading and Writing*. Arlington, VA: Center for Applied Linguistics.

5 F R W
This study describes the varieties of English in the two American Indian communities of San Juan and Laguna, New Mexico, and examines the effect of language diversity on certain educational skills. Wolfram et al. outline the educational importance of looking at the American Indian communities, and then explain the history of the two communities, the development of English within them, and the ancestral language community of Native Americans. Chapter Three describes grammatical and phonological features of San Juan English and Chapter Four provides an inter-community comparison of San Juan and Laguna English with respect to grammar and pronunciation. The authors then examine the effect of linguistic diversity on the reading and writing process generally, and then specifically in San Juan and Laguna. Wolfram et al. conclude by looking at the educational implications of varieties of English in the Pueblos and explore appropriate and inappropriate "remedies" for education.

Wolfram, Walt, Clare Dannenberg, Stanley Knick & Linda Oxendine. 2002. *Fine in the World: Lumbee Language in Time and Place*. Raleigh: North Carolina State University.

5 F

Wolfram et al. highlight the significance of the Lumbee Language (an English vernacular) to the heritage and culture of Lumbee Indians of Robeson County, North Carolina. The authors examine the present Lumbee community of Robeson, and discuss language attitudes there and the importance of ethnic identification through language. They continue this discussion with a history of Native American Languages in North Carolina and posit that the combination of political and economic factors during the settlement of North Carolina aided a shift to English in an otherwise Native American territory. Wolfram et al. then look at the roots of Lumbee English (LE) stemming from the Highlanders and Ulster Scots and African Americans. In their assessment of the development of LE, the authors conduct a cross-dialectal comparison of sentence structure, lexical items, and pronunciation, and outline possible links to the languages spoken by residents of the Outer Banks. They conclude by reiterating the importance of Lumbee English in relation to identification with the Lumbee community.

Wolfram, Walt & Ralph Fasold. 1969. Toward Reading Materials for Speakers of Black English: Three Linguistically Appropriate Passages. In *Teaching Black Children to Read,* ed. by J. Baratz & R. Shuy, 138–55.

1 R V

Wolfram, Walt & Ralph W. Fasold. 1974. *The Study of Social Dialects in American English.* Englewood Cliffs, N.J., Prentice-Hall.

1 6 F

Wolfram, Walt & Deborah Hatfield. 1986. The English of Adolescent and Young Adult Vietnamese Refugees in the United States. *World Englishes* 5.47–60.

3 F

Wolfram, Walt, Mary Kohn Kohn & Erin Callahan-Price. 2011. Southern-Bred Hispanic English: An Emerging Variety. In *Cascadilla: Selected Proceedings of the 5th Workshop on Spanish Sociolinguistics,* ed. by J. Michnowicz & R. Dodsworth, 1–13. Somerville, MA: Cascadilla Proceedings Project.

4 F

Wolfram, Walt & Jeffrey Reaser. 2005. *Dialects and the Ocracoke Brogue.* Ocracoke, NC: Ocracoke School.

6 F L M

Wolfram, Walt, Jeffrey Reaser & Charlotte Vaughn. 2008. Operationalizing Linguistic Gratuity: From Principle to Practice. *Language and Linguistics Compass* 2.1109–34.

I L

Wolfram, Walt & Natalie Schilling-Estes. 1997. *Hoi Toide on the Outer Banks: The Story of the Ocracoke Brogue.* Durham: The University of North Carolina Press.

6 F

Wolfram, Walt & Natalie Schilling-Estes. 2006. *American English: Dialects and Variation.* Malden, MA: Blackwell Publishing.

1 6 F I

Wolfram, Walt & Ben Ward (eds.) 2006. *American Voices: How Dialects Differ from Coast to Coast*: Blackwell Publishing.

1 4 5 6 E F

After an introduction that assesses the State of American Dialects, the book consists of thirty-nine short, accessible chapters by various contributors, including some of the leading sociolinguists and students of American dialects. Chapters are grouped into six sections: Part I The South (chapters on Appalachian, Smoky Mountains, South Carolina, Texas, New Orleans, LA, and Memphis, TN); Part II The North (chapters on New England, Boston, MA, Maine, Pittsburgh, PA, New York City, NY, Philadelphia, PA, and Canada); Part III The Midwest (chapters on Midwest English, Chicago, IL, Ohio, St. Louis, MO, and Michigan's Upper Peninsula; Part IV The West (chapters on California, Utah, Portland, OR, and Arizona); Part V Islands (chapters on Hawai'i, West Indies, Sea Islands, SC and GA, Bahamas, Outer Banks, NC, Smith Island, MD, Newfoundland, Canada, and Tristan da Cunha); Part VI Sociocultural Dialects (chapters on African American English, Chicano English, Cajun English, Lumbee Vernacular English, Jewish English, and Pennsylvania German).

Wolfram, Walt & Marcia Farr Whiteman. 1971. The Role of Dialect Interference in Composition. *Florida FL Reporter* 9.34–38.

1 W X

Wong, Amy. 2007. Two Vernacular Features in the English of Four American-Born Chinese. In *Selected Papers from Nwav 35,* ed. by T. Cook & K. Evanini, 217–30. Philadelphia: Department of Linguistics, University of Pennsylvania.

3 F

Wong, Amy Wing-mei. 2007. New York City English and Second Generation Chinese Americans. *English Today* 26.3–11.

3 F

Woodworth, William & Richard Salzer. 1971. Black Children's Speech and Teachers' Evaluations. *Urban Education* 6.167–73.

1 A I T

One hundred and nineteen elementary teachers enrolled in graduate-level education courses listened to and evaluated what were presented as sixth-graders social studies reports. Identical reports were read alternately by Black and White male sixth-grade students, and teachers were exposed to both versions at sessions separated by an interval of three weeks. Teachers evaluated the reports on fifteen factors, including logical sequence, unity, clarity, and critical thinking. The results revealed a consistent statistical difference between teachers' evaluations of material presented orally by Black and White children, with the mean scores invariably higher for the White children than the Black. The authors note (p. 171) that the Black reader did not alter syntax or lexicon in his reading, and "neither did he appear to deviate substantially from conventional pronunciation of words." Thus, the judgments were made solely on the basis of paralinguistic cues that the teachers associated with race. The authors conclude (p. 172) that "perhaps the most useful outcome of this study is the evidence that even experienced teachers sometimes do not distinguish between language forms and content."

Wright, Richard. 1998. Sociolinguistic and Ideological Dynamics of the Ebonics Controversy. *Journal of Negro Education* 67.5–15.

1 I K

Wroge, Diane. 1998. The Testing of Reading Proficiency in Vernacular Languages. *Notes on Literacy* 24.9–33.

A R V

Wyatt, Toya. 1995. Language Development in African American English Child Speech. *Linguistics and Education* 7.7–22.

1 F Q

Wyatt, Toya. 1999. An Afro-Centered View of Communicative Experience. In *Constructing (in)Competence: Disabling Evaluations in Clinical and Social Interactions,* ed. by D. Kovarsky, J. Duchan & M. Maxwell, 197–221. Mahwah, NJ: Lawrence Erlbaum Associates.

1 A D N

Wyatt, Toya. 2001. The Role of Family, Community and School in Children's Acquisition and Maintenance of African American English. In *Sociocultural and Historical Contexts of African American English,* ed. by S. Lanehart, 261–80. Philadelphia: John Benjamins.

1 A Q

Wyatt, Toya & Harry Seymour. 1999. Assessing the Speech and Language Skills in Preschool Children. In *Assessing and Screening Preschoolers: Psychological and Educational Dimensions,* ed. by E. V. Nuttall, I. Romero & J. Kalesnik, 218–39. Boston: Allyn and Bacon.

A Q

Wynne, Joan. 2002. 'We Don't Talk Right. You Ask Him.'. In *The Skin That We Speak,* ed. by L. Delpit & J. K. Dowdy. New York: The New Press.

1 I T

Yaeger-Dror, Malcah & Erik Thomas. 2010. *African American English Speakers and Their Participation in Local Sound Changes: A Comparative Study.* Durham, NC: Duke University Press for the American Dialect Society.

1 F

Yamamoto, Akira Y. 1994. Teaching American Indian Students. *Language Culture and Curriculum* 7.183–87.

5
This is a review article on Reyhner 1994.

Yancy, George. 2011. The Scholar Who Coined the Term Ebonics: A Conversation with Dr. Robert L. Williams. *Journal of Language, Identity and Education* 10.41–51.

1 A I K P

Yang, KaYing. 2004. Southeast Asian American Children: Not the "Model Minority". *The Future of Children* 14.127–33.

3 A C

Yokota, Thomas. 2008. The "Pidgin Problem": Attitudes About Hawai'i Creole. *Educational Perspectives* 41.22–29. [Abstract prepared by ERIC and reprinted with permission of the Department of Education from the Educational Resources Information Center at eric.ed.gov.]

2 I

In this essay, the author examines the attitudes that people in Hawai'i have about Hawai'i Creole. The author first describes the background of the language and explores educators' views from the 1920s to 1940s about Hawai'i Creole (HC), which was first viewed as the "Pidgin problem" in Hawai'i. The frustrations expressed by educators might help to reveal why people believe that the "Pidgin problem" is still present today. In this essay, the author focuses on the connections people have made with HC and their own identity. To understand why the HC issue continues today, the author decided to interview residents of Hawai'i. The author sought to understand the different values people hold toward this language. The people being interviewed considered themselves to be middle class, and that had a strong influence on their attitudes toward Hawai'i Creole. The persistence of this language issue reveals an interesting conflict that lies beneath the surface of Hawai'i's local culture. It reveals that people in Hawai'i are still divided on issues of material success and local identity. The interviews reveal that many HC speakers are affected unconsciously by numerous factors that challenge their identities. Ironically, HC serves as a means of identifying local culture that translates variously into a source of pride and shame.

Young, Clara, James Wright & Joseph Laster. 2005. Instructing African American Students. *Education* 125.516–24.

1 C S T

Young, Robert W. 1968. *English as a Second Language for Navajos: An Overview of Certain Cultural and Linguistic Factors.* Albuquerque, NM: Albuquerque Area Office, Bureau of Indian Affairs.

5 S

Young, Vershawn Ashanti. 2004. Your Average Nigga. *College Composition and Communication* 55.693–715.

1 B C I

To illustrate this struggle of African American males in educational settings, Young describes his own experiences as a Black man, and presents excerpts from the essay of one of his male students at Columbia College. Through these lenses, Young attempts to analyze the divide between Black culture and literacy. He comments on the decision of many young boys, regardless of race, to resist education and White English Vernacular [WEV] since it is viewed as effeminate. Moreover, he argues that Black boys not only feel coerced to give up their masculinity if they do well in school, but they also feel forced to abandon their race, the ultimate impossibility (p. 700). Young presents existing alternatives to the resistance of education, mentioning Campbell's call to privilege AAVE such that native speakers of the dialect can maintain their Blackness in the classroom and their neighborhoods; Delpit's embrace of code switching; and Gilyard's idea of pluralism where students can adopt multiple identities in different settings. Young disagrees with all three stances, and instead, he argues that to achieve equal social prestige and acceptance of both dialects, society must get rid of the notion that Black and White varieties are substantially different.

Young, Vershawn Ashanti. 2009. "Nah, We Straight": An Argument against Code-Switching. *JAC: A Journal of Composition Theory* 29.49–76.

1 B P

Youssef, Valerie. 2006. Issues of Face-Saving in the Pre-School Classroom. In *Exploring the Boundaries of Caribbean Creole Languages,* ed. by H. Simmons-McDonald & I. Robertson, 147–69. Kingston, Jamaica: University of the West Indies Press.

N Q U

Zeni, Jane & Joan Krater Thomas. 1990. Suburban African-American Basic Writing: A Text Analysis. *Journal of Basic Writing* 9.15–39. [Abstract prepared by ERIC and reprinted with permission of the Department of Education from the Educational Resources Information Center at eric.ed.gov.]

1 A W
The authors compare White and African American basic writers' texts produced during districtwide holistic writing assessments. Results show that White basic writers differ little from African American basic writers, although African Americans tend to use a stronger personal voice and drop standard word ending. The authors conclude that dialect is not the key issue.

Zentella, Ana Celia. 1981. *Ta Bien* You Could Answer Me *En Cualquier Idioma*: Puerto Rican Code Switching in Bilingual Classrooms. In *Latino Language and Communicative Behavior,* ed. by R. Duran, 109–12. Norwood, NJ: Ablex.

4 U

Zentella, Ana Celia. 1997. *Growing up Bilingual: Puerto Rican Children in New York.* London: Blackwell.

1 4 F N U
Zentella provides an in-depth analysis of the bilingualism of the New York Puerto Rican community, while addressing the attitudes, culture, and features of "Spanglish." Her ethnographic study of the residents of El bloque discusses its five varieties of Spanish and English: Standard Puerto Rican Spanish, Non-standard Puerto Rican Spanish, Puerto Rican English, African American Vernacular English, and Hispanized English. She describes language networks in the community, domains for Spanish-English overlap, and the social and cultural consequences of limited Spanish. She also profiles the five children who were the focus of her study, focusing on their home experiences with bilingualism. Zentella outlines the "hows and whys" of bilingualism, describing the grammar, strategies, and choices of speaking "Spanglish." In the seventh chapter, Zentella describes how changes in el bloque and the socioeconomic politics of the 1990s had a profound impact on the linguistic development and cultural attitudes of the five children. She profiles the children again and describes how their changing networks have affected their respective uses of their bilingualism. She assesses the Spanish competence of the subjects at young-adulthood and then offers observations and recommendations for raising the next generation of New York Puerto Ricans to have expanded repertoires of bilingualism.

Zentella, Ana Celia. 1997. Latino Youth at Home, in Their Communities, and in School: The Language Link. *Education and Urban Society* 30.122–30.

4 U

Zentella, Ana Celia (ed.) 2006. *Building on Strength: Language and Literacy in Latino Families and Communities.* New York: Teachers College Press.

4 E I N P U

Zephir, Flore. 1999. Challenges for Multicultural Education: Sociolinguistic Parallels between African American English and Haitian Creole. *Journal of Multilingual and Multicultural Development* 20.134–54.

1 2 C I

Zuidema, Leah. 2005. Myth Education: Rationale and Strategies for Teaching against Linguistic Prejudice. *Journal of Adolescent and Adult Literacy* 48.666–75. [Abstract courtesy of journal. This material is reproduced by permission of John Wiley & Sons, Inc.]

I S

People frequently make assumptions about others because of their spoken or written use of a particular dialect or language. The varieties of English that people use are often regarded as indicators of corresponding intelligence, competence, motives, and morality. Such assumptions—frequently based on myths and misconceptions about the nature of language—can lead to discriminatory practices. Literacy educators should work to combat prejudice by dispelling linguistic myths and working with students to expose and critique the processes and institutions that perpetuate such misconceptions. This article outlines and critiques common myths that contribute to language-based discrimination. These myths include misunderstandings about grammar and usage rules, misinformed beliefs about particular language varieties as "random" rather than rule governed, and misconceptions about how to judge the relative value or quality of specific language varieties. In addition, the author suggests activities that encourage learners to investigate the actual nature of linguistic diversity and to question the ways that linguistic prejudice is propagated institutionally.

ABOUT THE AUTHORS

John R. Rickford is the J.E. Wallace Sterling Professor of Linguistics and the Humanities at Stanford University. He is also professor by courtesy in Education, and Pritzker University Fellow in Undergraduate Education. His research is especially focused on the relation between language and ethnicity, social class and style, language variation and change, pidgin and creole languages, African American Vernacular English, and the application of linguistics to educational problems. He is the author of numerous scholarly articles, and author or editor of many books.

Julie Sweetland is Director of Learning at the FrameWorks Institute, where she leads the translation of communications research findings into learning tools for nonprofit leaders. Julie has worked to improve teaching and learning for over a decade, first as a classroom teacher, and then as a researcher, teacher educator and education reform advocate. Prior to joining FrameWorks, she was Director of Teaching and Learning at the Center for Inspired Teaching and launched a graduate teacher preparation program for the University of the District of Columbia. A linguist by training (B.A., Georgetown University, Ph.D., Stanford University), she is an adjunct lecturer in Linguistics at Georgetown.

Angela E. Rickford is Professor of Education at San Jose State University. Her research and teaching focus on the teaching of reading and language arts to low-income African American, ethnic minority, and other students. She has extensive experience in teacher supervision and training, and has served as a consultant and literacy coach to several school districts. She is the recipient of the 1999 Dean's Award for Excellence and Equity in Education. She is the author of many scholarly articles and a multiply reprinted book, *I Can Fly*.

Thomas Grano completed his B.A. in Linguistics (Hons.) at Stanford University and his Ph.D. in Linguistics at The University of Chicago, specializing in syntax, semantics, and their interface. His dissertation investigated control and restructuring from the perspective of the syntax-semantics interface. Thomas has also investigated topics in gradability and comparison in Mandarin Chinese and Japanese. He is currently a Postdoctoral Research Associate in Linguistics at the University of Maryland.